KU-487-786

a brit's guide
TO
NEW YORK

TALL
ANNAHATTA !

KAREN MARCHBANK
with AMANDA STATHAM

foulsham
LONDON • NEW YORK • TORONTO • SYDNEY

foulsham
The Publishing House, Bennetts Close, Cippenham,
Slough, Berkshire, SL1 5AP, England

Dedication

For Jennifer, who thoroughly enjoyed biting off a chunk of the Big Apple on our recent visit, and Dale Rondaburg, a New York-based journalist who was a tremendous help with all of the tricky research.

ISBN 0-572-03033-9

Maps by PC Graphics (UK) Limited

A CIP record for this book is available from the British Library

Other books in this series:
A Brit's Guide to Las Vegas and the West 2004–2005, Karen Marchbank, 0-572-02926-8
A Brit's Guide to Orlando and Walt Disney World 2005, Simon Veness, 0-572-03037-1
A Brit's Guide to Disneyland Resort Paris 2004–2005, Simon Veness, 0-572-02949-7
A Brit's Guide to Choosing A Cruise 6th edition, Simon Veness, 0-572-02946-2

Printed in Malaysia

Contents

Acknowledgements

With grateful thanks for all their help to Clive Burrow, Audrey Bretillot and Rebecca Pisani at the New York Travel Advisory Bureau, Sarah Handy, Helen Povall and Christos Louvieris at NYC & Company Convention and Visitors Bureau, Tom Darro, Stan Rydelek and John Percy at Niagara Falls Convention and Visitors Bureau, and Markly Wilson and Deirdre Cumberbatch at the New York State Department of Economic Development.

My thanks also to the Lower East Side Tenement Museum, the Metropolitan Museum of Art, Ellis Island Immigration Museum, the Museum of Modern Art, the Museum of Jewish Heritage, the Whitney Museum of American Art, *Intrepid* Sea-Air-Space Museum, the Frick Collection, the Skyscraper Museum, the National Museum of the American Indian, the Children's Museum of Manhattan, the Empire State Building, the American Museum of Natural History, the New York Stock Exchange, the Brooklyn Museum of Art, NY Waterways, the Sex And The City Tour, Harlem Spirituals, the Big Apple Greeters, David Watkins and Ponycabs, the Queens Jazz Trail, Gangland Tours, Big Onion walking tours, Rabbi Beryl Epstein and the Hassidic Discovery Center, former NYPD cop Gary Gorman, Gray Line, Food Tours of Greenwich, Ryan Hawkins (known as jazz aficionado Ed Lockjaw), The Ritz-Carlton at Battery Park, The Warwick, The Mark, Waldorf Astoria, Le Parker Meridien, The Marriott Marquis, The Wellington, The Doral, Le Cirque, The Bull & Bear, The View at the Marriot Marquis, American Park at the Battery, Serafina Fabulous Grill, The Boathouse, Picholine, Sylvia's Restaurant, The River Café, The Water Club, World Yacht Dining Cruise, Europa Grill, The 21 Club, Tavern on the Green, Zoe's Restaurant and ONE c.p.s.

My thanks also to the following individuals who were a fount of great knowledge: Loraine Heller, Neal Smith, Russell Brightwell, Maria Pieri, the divine Kirsty Hislop, Annie Davies, Colin Macrae and Neil Wadey.

Introduction

Welcome to the 2005 edition of this guide book, which I hope will inspire you to want to visit the Big Apple again and again.

For this is a city which really does capture the heart. Very few people visit once and don't return, simply because they're always left with the feeling that there's so much more to see and do. Once you've ticked the major sights off your list, such as the Empire State Building, Statue of Liberty and Central Park, you can start investigating the cosmopolitan neighbourhoods of the likes of SoHo, Greenwich Village and Chelsea and in each new place you venture into you'll be delighted to discover a veritable treasure of shops, cafés, hotels and bars and to watch the 'zoo' of residents all going about their daily business.

Not even the terrorist attack of September 11, 2001, which destroyed the twin towers of World Trade Center and killed nearly 3,000 people, has managed to put this frenetic, exciting city on hold. New hotels such as the prestigious Mandarin Oriental and Ritz-Carlton at Battery Park have risen from the dust since that tragic event, with foreign visitors from all over the world continuing to pour into the Big Apple and experience its breathtaking pace and love of life.

A New York street

THE NEW YORK STATE OF MIND

I once saw a great sign on 5th Avenue around 58th Street, but I was on a bus at the time so I couldn't get a photo (believe me, I wanted to). It said: 'Don't even think about parking here.' Now that's the kind of thing you would think, possibly even say to yourself if you were in your car, but to make an official sign saying it? That, it seems, is the difference between us and the native New Yorker!

By this I don't mean the Algonquin Indians, but the modern-day residents, who are genuine born-and-bred New Yorkers rather than immigrants from around the globe or even other parts of America. They really are a breed unto themselves and I've learnt how you can spot them. In the first place they have a sort of totally cheesed-off-with-the-world don't-mess-with-me look. Secondly, they often speak incredibly quickly as if they were eating their own words as they went along, so it really is hard to understand them. Scratch the surface though, and you just have your ordinary, everyday kind of person with the same kind of worries, fears and doubts as the rest of us. I've discovered two things that work a treat. Firstly, smiling like mad and being genuinely polite. Secondly, the British accent. You can see them looking at you askance when you smile (I mean, smile? Who on earth does that in New York?), but then deciding that you must be one of those British eccentrics they've heard about. It does the trick, though, because they'll more often than not respond in a helpful way.

And don't go thinking that all New Yorkers will tell you to f*** off if you ask for directions. Some will, but many are happy to help and I've even had people stop to help me work out where I'm going without any request on my part. This heady mix of rudeness and helpfulness is no better demonstrated than in the following anecdote from New York author Douglas Kennedy.

'On a crosstown bus I noticed two visitors from Japan having difficulty with the exact change for the fare,' he recounts. 'The driver, an overweight guy with a scowl, started giving them a hard time. "Like can't you read English or what?" he said loudly. "It says a buck-fifty. Surely they teach you how to count in Japan."

'The Japanese looked as if they wanted to commit hara-kiri on the spot until an elegantly dressed woman in her late sixties seated opposite the door came to their defence. Out of nowhere she turned to the driver and said: "Hey asshole, be polite."'

The Ritz-Carlton is home, too, to one of the city's most appropriate cultural venues – the Skyscraper Museum – which recounts the making of the world's most famous skyline. One of its first exhibitions in the aftermath of the tragedy was the story of how the Twin Towers had come into being. That was not only a fitting tribute to the World Trade Center's 30-year history, but also a timely reminder of one very important aspect of New York. The city has always been about regeneration, about removal of the old to make way for the new and, hopefully, the bigger and the better. In fact, in the 1960s, that is exactly what the Twin Towers themselves were all about.

And in the finest New York tradition, a new scheme for use of the 6.5-hectare (16-acre) Ground Zero site was approved – following extensive consultations with members of the public – in 2003.

Called the Memorial Foundations at World Trade Center, the plan originally allowed for a remembrance garden, a museum and five new buildings – three to be mixed-use skyscrapers, plus a 541-m (1,776-ft) glass edifice that would reach for the sky. However, amid much wrangling behind the scenes between the bastions of art, commerce and politics, the plans are being modified. And set against this background of controversy, the building work officially started on Independence Day 2004 with the unveiling of the cornerstone of the Freedom Tower.

If you do want to pay your respects at Ground Zero, remember that this is also an ideal place from which to visit Wall Street and the Statue of Liberty, so give yourself time to explore lower Manhattan.

In the meantime, the city has continued its constant process of renewal, regeneration and regrowth. The AOL Time Warner Center at Columbus Circle, with its shops, flats, hotel and cultural space has proved to be a tremendous success. And all over the city new museums, shops, hotels, clubs and restaurants have been opening, while others have been expanding or undergoing refurbishment.

New York has not only managed to remember and honour its dead, but has also got on with life to keep the city one of the most vibrant, exciting and interesting in the world. Now it's very much business as usual, so enjoy!

PLANNING YOUR HOLIDAY

One of New York's greatest charms is its cosmopolitan nature, its hugely diverse ethnic mix. In this city you will find any type of cuisine, often available at any time of the day or night. Where music's concerned, everything from jazz and R&B to techno and rap is out there on any night of the week and the many nightclubs are among the hippest and most happening of any in the world.

The drawback is that it may seem a bit overwhelming and it doesn't help that everyone gives the impression of being in the biggest hurry ever and far too busy to help. But beneath the ice-cool veneer of most New Yorkers you'll find people who will be willing to answer any question or plea for help.

In this book, I hope not only to provide all the information you need about the sights, sounds and attractions, but also to give an insight into what makes the city tick and how to really get the most out of it. The book is filled with tips and insider information, but I'm always open to hearing other people's views and am happy to receive suggestions by email at: **amanda@mrhoppy.freeserve.co.uk**

Once you have decided to go to New York, the next step is to work out what you want to do there, otherwise you could end up wasting a lot of valuable time. The city is so big and diverse and everyone's tastes are so different that each visit to New York is a unique experience. Are you a museum buff? Do you like to get off the beaten track? Want to see a great Broadway show and some of the outstanding sights of the city? Your priorities will reflect not only your tastes but also whether it is your first, second or even third visit to the Big Apple, as well as the time you have available. Whatever the case, the key to making the most of your time is in the planning.

The thing I really try to stress is the importance of location, location, location. When you fly into New York, seeing all the skyscrapers from your lofty perch makes Manhattan look pretty small, but do not be fooled by this. It is a narrow island, but it's longer than it looks from high in the sky – 21km (13 miles) in fact – so don't be duped into believing it is easy to walk from Downtown to the Upper East Side. Nothing could be further from the truth.

If you really want to get an insight into how a New Yorker thinks, read the Metropolitan Diary in Monday's edition of the *New York Times*. It's full of stories of New York life supplied by the locals.

It's also the case that the city's subway is nowhere near as fast as our much-maligned tube system in London, nor is it that good for getting from east to west or vice versa. That means using buses is often necessary and they, of course, like taxis, can get stuck in heavy traffic. So, when planning your activities for the day, it is best to stick to one particular area so that walking everywhere – which really is the best way to see the city – won't be so tiring.

Most people tend to go for between two and seven days. For the former it's like dipping your toes in the water, for the latter it's a great big commitment to getting to know the city. Regardless of how many days you have, though, you can't fit everything in so you have to be selective.

Make the most of your time by planning each day carefully – but don't try to do too much, and give yourself enough breaks each day to recharge your batteries.

HOW TO USE YOUR GUIDEBOOK

I've tried to help you with your choices in as many ways as possible. For instance, I've put the top sights and museums in an order of importance so you can go straight to the ones you will most likely want to see, and in each case I've specified the area they are in – again to help you plan your day. Most of the main Broadway shows are easy enough to plan for because they tend to be in the Theater District and the restaurant chapter gives an area-by-area guide that makes light work of planning for lunch and dinner.

I've also provided a complete outline of all the different transport systems in New York and how to use them, plus a description of all the different neighbourhoods with itineraries so that you will be able to get the most out of them.

In each case I've arranged the different areas geographically from south to north rather than by an A-Z system because it just seems to make more sense. For instance, if you're looking for a restaurant, shop or hotel in one area, it's good to be able to see some alternatives in a nearby location without having to flick through too many pages.

That means the Financial District – which takes in Battery Park, Battery Park City, Wall Street, the South Street Seaport and the Civic Center area – always comes first. It's followed by TriBeCa, Chinatown/Little Italy, SoHo, NoLiTa, the Lower East Side, Greenwich Village, West Village, East Village, Chelsea, Union Square, Gramercy Park, Madison Square, 34th Street, Murray Hill, Midtown, Midtown East, Midtown West, the Theater District, the Upper East Side, Upper West Side, Morningside Heights and Harlem.

I've put the accommodation chapter towards the back of the book because I think choosing a hotel should be one of your final decisions. If the sights, sounds, shops and museums you want to see are all in a particular area, then you should try to find a hotel or accommodation as close to it as possible. That way you can reduce the time and money you spend on travelling. Unless of course the hotel is the reason you're travelling to the city; for some people the experience of staying in exclusive accommodation such as The Plaza or Waldorf are worth a visit to NYC before they've even thought about sightseeing.

I've tried to include everything I believe the average Brit will be interested in seeing while they are in New York, but if you come across a sight, museum, shop, gallery, coffee shop, club, hotel or restaurant not in this book, which you think is worth including, please feel free to contact me at the email address given on page 9.

Finally, I'd just like to wish you a wonderful trip to what is still one of the greatest cities in the world!

An aerial view of the city

CHAPTER 1

Understanding the City

So what is New York all about? Due to the vast number of movies set in different periods of the city, many of the key people in its history, sights and areas are familiar to us Brits, though I suspect that, like me, you're a little hazy as to their whereabouts or true influence.

Understanding a little of its history is a good way of understanding its modern-day psyche and to familiarise yourself with the different areas of New York and the buildings named after its great movers and shakers. Many of them were men and women of great vision and courage and their contributions to New York's rich and diverse culture, business and entertainment are all part of what makes the city so remarkable today.

A SHORT HISTORY OF NEW YORK

The great story that is New York's started in 1524 when Florentine Giovanni da Verrazano arrived on the island now known as Manhattan. It was a mixture of marshes, woodland, rivers and meadows and was home to the Algonquin and Iroquois tribes of Native Americans.

No one settled on the island, though, until British explorer Henry Hudson arrived in 1609. Working for the Dutch West India Company, he discovered Indians who were happy to trade in furs, skins, birds and fruit. In 1613, a trading post was set up at Fort Nassau and by 1624 the Dutch West India Company was given the right to govern the area by the Dutch government.

Dutch settlers soon began to arrive; Manhattan was named New Amsterdam and governor Peter Minuit bought the island for $24-worth of trinkets and blankets. The Dutch, of course, thought they had a bargain. The irony is that they were trading with a tribe of Indians who were simply passing through the area! Peaceful relations between the Europeans and Native Americans were disturbed, however, by the settlers' insistence on taking over the land and a costly and bloody war ensued, lasting two and a half years. Finally Peter Stuyvesant was hired by the Dutch West India Company to restore peace.

Stuyvesant was an experienced colonialist and went about establishing a strong community with a proper infrastructure. One of the first things he did

Ice-skating in Central Park

was to order the building of a defensive wall and ditch along what we know today as Wall Street. The new settlement prospered and even doubled in size, but Governor Stuyvesant was not well liked. He introduced new taxes, persecuted Jews and Quakers and even limited the amount of alcohol people could drink. Trouble followed, and the locals became less and less inclined to obey him. By the time four British warships sailed into the harbour in late 1664, he had no alternative but to surrender to Colonel Richard Nichols without a shot being fired. The colony was immediately renamed New York in honour of the Duke of York, brother to the English king, and thereafter remained mostly in the hands of the British until the end of the American Revolution.

A NEW VOICE

By 1700, the population had reached 20,000, made up of immigrants from England, Holland, Germany, Ireland and Sweden. It was already the rich melting-pot of cultures and religions that it remains today. Over the next 74 years, the colony gradually began to establish itself and there was a growing belief among well-educated and powerful Americans – including Thomas Jefferson and Benjamin Franklin – that the government should be fair and democratic.

In 1764, following the Seven Years War between the British and French, the Brits passed a number of laws, including the Stamp Act, allowing them to raise taxes in the colony. In response, Americans from all over the country banded together and rescinded Britain's right to collect taxes from them. The Stamp Act was repealed but it seemed that the Brits hadn't learned their lesson. They introduced the Townshend Act, which imposed taxes on various imports and led to a bloody confrontation in 1770. In 1774, the Americans set up the Continental Congress, made up of representatives from each of the colonies. Later that year, those representatives urged all Americans to stop paying their taxes and just two years later the Declaration of Independence was drawn up, largely by Jefferson. During the War of Independence that inevitably followed, New York was considered strategically vital as it stood between the New England colonies and those in the south. In 1776, British commander Lord Howe sailed 500 ships into the harbour and occupied the city. George Washington's army was defeated and forced to leave. The peace process began in 1779 and led to a treaty in 1783. The Brits, who had remained in New York since the end of the war, left just before George Washington returned to claim victory.

New York then became the country's first capital and George Washington its first president, taking his oath of office in 1789. The city was capital for just one year, but business boomed. The New York Stock Exchange, established under a tree on Wall Street by Alexander Hamilton in 1792, positively buzzed with activity as new companies were set up, bought and sold.

WHAT'S IN A NAME?

The Big Apple has become synonymous with New York City, but came into being during the 1920s when horse-racing writer John Fitzgerald popularised the term. On assignment in New Orleans for *The Morning Telegraph*, he overheard stablehands refer to New York City racing tracks as The Big Apple and decided to call his column on New York's racing scene 'Around the Big Apple'.

A decade later, jazz musicians adopted the term to refer to New York City. The favourite story of Big Onion tour guides is related to Small's Big Apple jazz club in Harlem. The story goes that when the musicians from the club went on tour around America they'd say to each other 'I'll see you in the Big Apple'.

But the term was still relatively unknown until it was adopted by the New York Convention and Visitors' Bureau in 1971, when they launched The Big Apple campaign.

So there you have it – it's a marketing device invented by the city to lure in visitors and it certainly seems to work as more than 34 million business people and tourists arrive each year.

Many New Yorkers like to call the city Gotham – taken from the Batman stories that are based in Gotham City and believed by many to be a thinly veiled reference to New York. The name Manhattan is derived from Mannahatta, the name given to the island by its first inhabitants, the Algonquin Indians.

USEFUL WEBSITES

www.citysearchnyc.com Calendar of events happening in New York.
www.cityguideny.com The online site of the weekly *City Guide* that is provided to hotels.
www.clubnyc.com Complete list of what's cool, where and why.
www.downtownny.com Directory of places to visit in Downtown.
www.halloween-nyc.com The official Halloween Parade site with history, how to get involved and information about the forthcoming event.
www.nycvisit.com The New York Convention and Visitors' Bureau's comprehensive listing includes suggested itineraries for where to stay and shop and what to do.
www.nytab.com The New York Travel Advisory Bureau's site is helpful for trip planning and gives information on major savings.
www.nytimes.com The online site for the *New York Times.*
www.nyctourist.com An official tourism site for the city.
www.villagevoice.com The online site of *The Village Voice.*

As the city grew, it became clear that a proper infrastructure and sanitation system was needed, so the governors introduced a grid system throughout the entire island. North of 14th Street, it abandoned all the existing roads except for Broadway, which followed an old Indian trail, and set up wide avenues that ran south to north and streets that ran between the rivers. Everything, it seemed, was pushing the city north, from illness to prosperity: while the grid system was being put on paper, a series of epidemics drove residents from the old Downtown into what is now known as Greenwich Village.

THE RICH GET RICHER...

By 1818, reliable shipping services between New York and other American cities and Europe were well established and trade was booming. It was boosted further by the opening of the Erie Canal in 1825, which, together with the new railroads, opened trade routes to the Midwest. With so much spare cash to play with, businessmen started to build large summer estates and mansions along 5th Avenue up to Madison Square. At the same time, many charities and philanthropic institutions were set up and great libraries were built, as education was seen as being very important.

But the divide between rich and poor was getting wider. While water supplies, indoor plumbing and central heating were being installed in the 5th Avenue mansions, thousands of immigrant families – particularly from Ireland – had no choice but to live in the appalling tenement buildings that were being erected on the Lower East Side of Manhattan.

These people were forced to eke out a wretched existence in the old sweatshops by day and contend with the punitive living conditions of the tenements by night. Entire families were crammed into one or two rooms that had no windows, no hot water, no heat and, of course, no bathroom. Toilet facilities had to be shared with neighbours.

The impending Civil War over the question of slavery became a major issue for the poor of New York, who couldn't afford to buy their way out of conscription. Uppermost in their minds was the concern that freed slaves would be going after their jobs. The fear reached fever pitch and led to America's worst-ever riot, a four-day-long affair in which over 100 people died and thousands, mostly blacks, were injured. By 1865, however, the abolitionists won the war, finally freeing four million black people from the plight of slavery.

BOOM TIME FOR IMMIGRATION

At the same time, New York and Boston were being hit by great tidal waves of immigrants. In the 1840s and 1850s it was the Irish fleeing famine; in the 1860s it was the Germans fleeing persecution; and in the 1870s it was the Chinese, brought into America specifically to build the railroads. In the 1880s it was the turn of the Russians, along with 1.5 million Eastern European Jews. Over eight million immigrants went through Castle Clinton in Battery Park between 1855 and 1890. Then the Ellis Island centre was built in 1892 and handled double that number. Between 1880 and 1910, 17 million immigrants passed through the city and, by 1900, the population had reached 3.4 million.

Most of the new arrivals who chose to stay in New York ended up in the crowded tenements of the Lower East Side. Finally in 1879, after the terrible conditions were brought to light, the city passed new housing laws requiring landlords to increase water supplies and toilets, install fire escapes and build air shafts between buildings to let in air and light. The introduction of streetcars and elevated railways also helped to alleviate the transport problem.

THE GILDED AGE

Meanwhile, the wealthy were enjoying the Gilded Age, as Mark Twain dubbed it. Central Park opened in 1858 and more and more mansions were built on 5th Avenue for the likes of the Whitneys, Vanderbilts and Astors. Row houses were also being built on the Upper West Side for wealthy European immigrants.

Henry Frick, who made his fortune in steel and the railroads, built a mansion (now a museum) on the east side of the park at 70th Street, just 10 blocks from the new Metropolitan Museum of Art. Luxury hotels such as the original Waldorf Astoria and the Plaza opened, as did the original Metropolitan Opera House. The Statue of Liberty, St Patrick's Cathedral, the Brooklyn Bridge and Carnegie Hall were all built at this time.

Those were the days of the people whose names we associate with New York but don't necessarily know why – like Cornelius Vanderbilt, a shipping and railroad magnate; Andrew Carnegie, a steel and railroad baron; and John D Rockefeller, who made his millions in oil. The names of many of these millionaires live on in the gifts they gave back to the city: they provided concert halls, libraries and art museums, and donated entire collections to put in them. Carnegie built and donated Carnegie Hall to the city, Rockefeller was one of three major backers behind the opening of the Museum of Modern Art, and the Whitneys created a museum containing their own collection of modern American works of art.

At the same time, the structure of the city itself was undergoing a transformation. In 1904, the IRT subway opened 135km (84 miles) of track, which meant that people could move away from the polluted downtown areas, and by 1918 the New York City Transit System was complete.

The turn of the century also saw the birth of another phenomenon, which was to become one of the city's most famous facets – the skyscraper. First to be built, in 1902, was the Flatiron Building, which was constructed using the new technology for the mass production of cast iron. Frank Woolworth's Gothic structure followed in 1913. The beautiful Chrysler Building went up in 1929 and the Empire State Building was completed in 1931.

PROHIBITION ARRIVES

In the meantime, the Volstead Act of 1919 banned the sale of alcohol at the start of the Roaring Twenties. Fuelled by lively speakeasies, illegal booze, gangsters, the Charleston and jazz, this was the real heyday of famous venues like Harlem's Cotton Club and the Apollo Theater. After several glittering years, the fun and frolics

The United Nations building and city skyscrapers

BEAT IT

The Beat Movement was a partly social, partly literary phenomenon with three centres – Greenwich Village in New York, the North Beach district of San Francisco and Venice West in Los Angeles. Socially, the movement was all about rejecting middle-class values and commercialism and embracing poverty, individualism and release through jazz, sexual experience and drugs. The term 'beat' conveys both the American connotations of being worn-out and exhausted, but also suggests 'beatitude' or 'blessedness'. The chief spokesmen were Allen Ginsberg, Jack Kerouac, whose most famous novel is *On The Road,* Gregory Corso, William S Burroughs, Lawrence Ferlinghetti and Gary Snyder.

came to an abrupt end with the collapse of the Wall Street stock market on October 29, 1929. It destroyed most small investors and led to huge unemployment and poverty right across the whole of America. Things only started to turn for the better after President Franklin D Roosevelt introduced the New Deal, employing people to build new roads, houses and parks.

In New York, Fiorello La Guardia was elected mayor and set up his austerity programme to enable the city to claw its way back to financial security. During his 12 years in office, La Guardia worked hard at fighting corruption and organised crime in the city, and introduced a massive public housing project.

These were also the days of a great literary and artistic scene in the city. Giants of the spoken and written word, including Dorothy Parker and George Kaufman, would meet at the famous Round Table of the Algonquin Hotel, where they were joined by stage and screen legends Tallulah Bankhead, Douglas Fairbanks and the Marx Brothers.

The Second World War was another watershed for New York, as people fled war-ravaged Europe and headed for the metropolis. Both during and after the war, huge new waves of immigrants arrived, fleeing first the Nazis and then the Communists. New York was as affected by McCarthy's hunt for 'reds' among the cultural and intellectual elite as the rest of the country, but it bounced back when a new building boom followed the election of President Harry S Truman, whose policies were aimed specifically at helping the poor.

The Port Authority Bus Terminal was finished in 1950, the mammoth United Nations Building was completed in 1953, and in 1959 work started on the huge Lincoln Center complex – built on the slums of the San Juan district that were the setting for *West Side Story.*

FROM BOOM TO BUST

By the 1950s, a new period of affluence had started for the middle classes of New York. The descendants of the earlier Irish, Italian and Jewish immigrants moved out to the new towns that were springing up outside Manhattan, leaving space for a whole new wave of immigrants from Puerto Rico and the southern states of America. It was also the decade of the Beat generation, epitomised by Jack Kerouac and Allen Ginsberg, which evolved into the hippy culture of the 1960s. This was when Greenwich Village became the centre of a new wave of artists extolling the virtues of equality for all.

By the 1970s, however, this *laissez-faire* attitude, coupled with New York's position as a major gateway for illegal drug importation and the general demoralisation of the working classes and ethnic groups, led to an escalation in crime. Muggings and murder were rampant, and the city was brought to the brink of bankruptcy.

Chaos was only averted by the introduction of austerity measures, which unfortunately mostly affected the poor. But good news was just around the corner, as new mayor Ed Koch implemented major tax

The Empire State and Chrysler buildings

CLIMATE

Month	Temp	Rainfall
Jan	-3-3°C (27-38°F)	8cm (3in)
Feb	-3-5°C (27-40°F)	8cm (3in)
Mar	1-9°C (34-49°F)	11cm (4¼in)
Apr	7-16°C (44-61°F)	10cm (4in)
May	12-22°C (53-72°F)	10cm (4in)
June	17-27°C (63-80°F)	8cm (3in)
July	20-29°C (68-85°F)	10cm (4in)
Aug	19-29°C (67-85°F)	10cm (4in)
Sep	16-25°C (60-77°F)	9cm (3½in)
Oct	10-19°C (50-66°F)	9cm (3½in)
Nov	5-12°C (41-54°F)	11cm (4¼in)
Dec	-1-6°C (31-42°F)	10cm (4in)

incentives to rejuvenate New York's business community. A boom followed, reflected in the erection of a series of mammoth new skyscrapers, including the World Trade Center and Trump Tower. The transformation was completed in the 1990s with Mayor Giuliani's clean-up operation. This was unpopular with the more liberal New Yorkers but there are many who believe it was his policies that turned New York into a city fit for the new millennium.

From the time of the earliest immigrants, New York has represented a gateway to a new life, a place of hope: the American dream offered a future filled with happiness and success. And nowadays New York still draws in people in their thousands. After all, as the song goes, 'If you can make it there, you'll make it anywhere.'

THE BEST TIMES TO GO

January to March and July and August are best for accommodation and good for flights. Just bear in mind that July and August are the hottest months, though it is not as bad as you might expect because all the shops and cabs have air-conditioning and you get blasts of lovely cool air from the shops as you pass.

In the run-up to Christmas it is very difficult to find accommodation in Manhattan, as it is in September and October when there are a lot of conventions. Surprisingly, the times around Thanksgiving and between Christmas and New Year are good times to go because people tend to be already at home with their families. April to June should be pleasantly cool (though it can be surprisingly warm) and is a popular time to go.

Check Chapter 13, Festivals and Parades (page 223) to find out when the major events are happening in the city, as it tends to be more crowded at these times.

WHAT TO WEAR

Layers are the key to comfortable clothes in New York, no matter what time of year you go. In summer the air-con in buildings can get pretty cold, while outside it is stiflingly hot. If you take a lightweight, rainproof jacket, you'll be covered for all eventualities, including the odd shower. In winter it is the other way round – warm buildings and cold streets – so it's best to have an overcoat of some sort, but nothing too heavy unless you're planning to be out of doors a lot. At any time of the year, the skyscrapers of the city act as a kind of wind tunnel and unless you're in the sun it can get nippy pretty quickly – another reason to make sure you have a cardigan or lightweight jacket in the summer. And in the winter, make sure you have a hat, scarf and gloves in your bag for times of emergency.

Don't worry if you spill wine all over your favourite outfit – most hotels have a valet service that can clean it for you overnight or there are plenty of dry cleaners throughout the city. Ask at the hotel reception desk.

DISABLED TRAVELLERS

According to the disabled people I've spoken to, New York is one of the easier destinations to tackle – and certainly puts Britain to shame. Most of the road corners, for instance, have kerbs that dip to the ground, making it a lot easier to wheel yourself about the city. Again, for the wheelchair-bound, the buses can be lowered to the same level as the pavement to allow easy access and, where possible, some of the subway stations have had elevators installed. To find out which stations are accessible to wheelchair passengers, phone 718-596 8585 6am–9pm. For up-to-date information on the accessibility status of lifts and escalators, call 1-800 734-6772 around the clock.

One of my favourite New York tales comes from Colin Macrae, a disabled person who regularly travels all over the world with his wife Joan. They were in New York one cold Christmas and Colin was sitting in his wheelchair all by himself, huddled up against the biting wind, while his wife went off to sort out tickets for the Circle Line cruise. As he waited, Colin was approached by a tramp, who pressed a quarter into his hand saying: 'I don't have much, but you can have what I've got.' Then he rushed off before Colin could reply or give him his money back. Just goes to show, the most unexpected and heartwarming things can happen in this amazing city.

Anyway, to make your life as easy as possible, here are the main organisations that deal with different aspects of travel for the disabled.

RESOURCES FOR THE DISABLED

Note: TTY = Telecommunication devices for the deaf.

Hospital Audiences Inc (HAI): 220 West 42nd Street, 13th floor, New York, NY 10036. Tel 212-575 7660 (voice) or 212-575 7673 (TTY). Publishes a book, *Access for All* ($5), which gives comprehensive information on venue access, toilet facilities and water fountains at a whole range of cultural centres from theatres to museums and major sights.

In addition, it has audio description services for people who are blind or visually impaired. Called **DESCRIBE**, this contains **Program Notes**, which describe all aspects of a show and staging in an audio cassette you can listen to before the performance. It also transmits a live **Audio Description**, during a pause in the dialogue, to audience members who have a small receiver. Reservations for both the tickets, which have to be bought either through HAI or the theatre, and receivers, which are provided free of charge, must be made through HAI. For more information call DESCRIBE on 212-575 7663.

New York Society for the Deaf: 817 Broadway at 12th Street. Tel 212-777 3900. Provides advice and information on facilities for the deaf.

Big Apple Greeter Access Coordinator: 1 Center Street, Room 2035, New York, NY 10007. Tel 212-669 2896 (voice) or 212-669 8273 (TTY). Will provide a free tour guide for anyone with a disability.

SIGN LANGUAGE INTERPRETED PERFORMANCES

The Theater Access Program: TAP is specifically for Broadway shows and is run by the Theater Development Fund. For more information phone 212-221 1103 (voice) or 212-719 4537 (TTY). Reservations for infrared headsets or neckloops for Broadway shows can be made by calling Sound Associates. Tel 212-582 7678.

Hands On: Provides sign language for Off-Broadway shows. For both voice and TTY phone 212-627 4898. Hands On also publishes a monthly calendar of events for the deaf community.

Lighthouse Incorporated: 111 East 59th Street. Tel 212-821 9200. Provides help and advice for blind people living in or visiting the city.

COMMUNICATIONS

PHONES

If you make any calls at all from your hotel you will pay a tremendous premium. To avoid this, you can either get a whole bucket of quarters to use in a public payphone or buy an international phone card before you leave home. A local call costs a minimum of 25c.

To call New York from abroad: Dial 001 and the prefix – for instance, the main prefix for Manhattan is 212 and the new one is 646 – then dial the seven-digit number.

To call abroad from New York: Dial 011 + country code + area code (dropping the first 0) + local number. The code for Britain is 44.

To call any number in New York from New York: Always dial 1 + the area code + the number.

Useful numbers:

Operator: 0

Directory enquiries: 411 (free from payphones)

Long distance directory enquiries: 1 + area code + 555 1212

Free numbers directory: 1 + 800 + 555 1212 (no charge)

The American ringing tone is long and the engaged tone is very short and high-pitched, almost like a beep.

MOBILE PHONES

It is now possible to get a mobile phone for use in New York. The Telephone Company supplies mobiles (or cell phones in American-speak) to international business travellers to the city with no rental fee, no minimum charge and free delivery and return. Tel 212-679 3800.

POST

To send a postcard costs 70c, to send a letter costs 80c for the first 25g (1oz). You can buy stamps in shops – the Duane Reade chain of chemists has machines – but there is a mark-up. If you don't want to pay over the odds for the convenience of these stamps, then go to one of the many post offices dotted around the city. The main post office on 34th Street at 8th Avenue is a beautiful Beaux Arts building and incredibly large. If the queues are long, you can buy stamps from the vending machines.

Post boxes are square dark blue metal boxes about 1.2m (4ft) tall with a rounded top that has a pull-down handle. They have a sign saying US Mail and a striking big American eagle logo on the side and can be found on street corners.

THE INTERNET

easyEverything: 234 West 42nd Street between 7th and 8th Avenues. Tel 212-398 0724. Subway A, C, E, 1, 2, 3, 7, 9, S, B, D, F, Q to 42nd Street/Times Square. Open 24 hours, it has over 800 computers, plus scanners, and prices start at just $1.

'Meet me between the lions' – one of the lion statues at New York Public Library

NEW YORK TALK

Of course, in addition to the differences between American and Brit-speak, the locals have a dialect and phraseology all of their own, influenced mainly by the Brooklyn accent, Mafia-speak and the fact that people often talk so quickly that words run into each other. Here are just a few that you may well come across:

All right already: Stop it, that's enough!
Big one: A $1,000 bill
Bloomies: Bloomingdale's
Capeesh: Pronunciation of *capisce*, Italian for 'understand'
Cattle call: A casting call at a Broadway theatre
Dead soldier: Empty beer can or bottle
Do me a solid: Do me a favour
Don't jerk my chain: Don't fool with me
DPh: Damned fool, based on transposing PhD
Eighth Wonder of the World: Brooklyn Bridge
Finger: Pickpocket (also mechanic, dip, cannon, goniff or moll buzzer)
Fuggedaboduid: No way
Guppies: Gay yuppies
JAPs: Jewish American princesses
Jocks: Sporty types, after their straps
Mazuma: Slang for money
Meet me between the lions: A favourite meeting place – the lion statues at the New York Public Library
Met: The Metropolitan Opera House or the Metropolitan Museum
No problem: You're welcome
Nudnik or nudge: A persistently dull and boring person
On account: Because
On line: Stand in a queue
Out in left field: Weird, unorthodox
Ozone: Very fresh, pure air
Shoot the works: Gamble or risk everything
Straphanger: Subway commuter
Suit: Businessman
Yard: Back garden

Cybercafé: 273 Lafayette Street at Prince Street. Tel 212-334 5140. Subway 6 to Bleecker Street, 4, 5, 6 to Spring Street and N, R to Prince Street. Area: NoLiTa. It's open 9am–10pm and costs around $6 for half an hour on the internet.

AMERICAN-SPEAK

It has often been said that the Brits and Americans are two races divided by a common language and when you make an unexpected faux pas you'll certainly learn how true this is. For instance, never, ever ask for a packet of fags as this is the American slang word for gays! There are plenty of other differences, too, which may not necessarily cause offence, but which will cause confusion, so to help you on your way, here is a guide to American-speak:

General:

English	American
Air hostess	Flight attendant
Anti-clockwise	Counterclockwise
At weekends	On weekends
Autumn	Fall
Behind	In back of
Camp bed	Cot
Cinema	Movie theater
City/town centre	Downtown (not Lower Manhattan!)
Coach	Bus
Cot	Crib
Diary (appointments)	Calendar
Diary (records)	Journal
From... to...	Through
Lift	Elevator
Nappy	Diaper
Ordinary	Regular, normal
Paddling pool	Wading pool
Post, postbox	Mail, mailbox
Pram, pushchair	Stroller
Tap	Faucet
Toilet	Restroom (public) or bathroom (private)
Trunk call	Long-distance call

There are no ground floors in America: what we call the ground floor, they call the first floor. It may seem a silly point, but it does cause confusion!

Money:

English	American
Bill	Check or tab
Banknote	Bill
Cashpoint	ATM
Cheque	Check
1 dollar	Single
25 cents	Quarter
10 cents	Dime
5 cents	Nickel
1 cent	Penny

Ellis Island Immigration Museum

Eating and stuff:

One of the biggest disappointments I had on my first trip to America was to order my breakfast eggs 'sunny-side up', only to end up with what seemed like a half-cooked egg! The Americans don't flick fat over the top of the egg when frying it, but turn it over to cook on both sides. So for eggs cooked on both sides but soft, I have to order eggs 'over easy' and if you like yours well done, then ask for eggs 'over hard'.

There are plenty of other anomalies. Many standard American dishes come with a biscuit – which is a corn scone to us. Breakfast may also include grits, a porridge-like dish of ground, boiled corn, and hash browns – grated, fried potatoes. Foods and food terms that are specific to New York have been put in Chapter 8, Restaurants (page 151). Here are some other differences:

English	American
Aubergine	Eggplant
Biscuit (savoury)	Cracker
Biscuit (sweet)	Cookie
Chick pea	Garbanzo bean
Chips	(French) fries
Choux bun	Cream puff
Clingfilm	Plastic wrap
Cornflour	Cornstarch
Courgette	Zucchini
Crayfish	Crawfish
Crisps	Chips
Crystallised	Candied
Cutlery	Silverware or place-setting
Demerara sugar	Light-brown sugar
Desiccated coconut	Shredded coconut
Digestive biscuit	Graham cracker
Double cream	Heavy cream
Essence (eg vanilla)	Extract or flavouring
Filled baguette	Sub or hero
Fillet (of meat/fish)	Filet
Fizzy drink	Soda
Golden syrup	Corn syrup
Grated, fried potatoes	Hash browns
Grilled	Broiled
Icing sugar	Powdered/confectioners' sugar
Jam	Jelly/conserve
Jelly	Jello
Ketchup	Catsup
King prawn	Shrimp
Main course	Entrée
Measure	Shot
Mince	Ground meat
Off-licence	Liquor store
Pastry case	Pie shell
Pips	Seeds (in fruit)
Plain/dark chocolate	Semi-sweet or unsweetened chocolate
Pumpkin	Squash
Scone	Biscuit
Shortcrust pastry	Pie dough
Single cream	Light cream
Soda water	Seltzer
Sorbet	Sherbet
Soya	Soy
Spirits	Liquor
Sponge finger biscuits	Lady fingers
Spring onion	Scallion
Starter	Appetiser
Stoned (cherries etc)	Pitted
Sultanas	Golden raisins
Sweet shop	Candy store
Take-away	To go
Tomato purée	Tomato paste
Water biscuit	Cracker

Shopping:

English	American
Brace	Suspenders
Bumbag	Fanny pack
Chemist	Drug store
Ground floor	First floor
Handbag	Purse
High street	Main street
Jumper	Sweater
Knickers	Panties
Muslin	Cheesecloth
Queue	Line, line up
Suspenders	Garters
Till	Check-out
Tights	Pantyhose
Trainers	Sneakers
Trousers	Pants
Underpants	Shorts, underwear
Vest	Undershirt
Waistcoat	Vest
Zip	Zipper

Travelling around:

English	American
Aerial	Antenna
Articulated truck	Semi
Bonnet	Hood
Boot	Trunk
Caravan	House trailer
Car park	Parking lot
Car silencer	Muffler
Crossroads/junction	Intersection
Demister	Defogger

Dipswitch	Dimmer
Dual carriageway	Four-lane (or divided) highway
Flyover	Overpass
Give way	Yield
Jump lead	Jumper cables
Lorry	Truck
Manual transmission	Stickshift
Motorway	Highway, freeway, expressway
Pavement	Sidewalk
Request stop	Flag stop
Ring road	Beltway
Slip road	Ramp
Subway	Pedestrian underpass
Turning	Turnoff
Underground	Subway
Walk	Hike
Wheel clamp	Denver boot
Windscreen	Windshield
Wing	Fender

New Yorkers may consider themselves broad-minded but, like any American, will be genuinely shocked if you ask where the toilet is. Ask for the restroom in a public place and the bathroom if you're in someone's house.

TOURIST INFORMATION

NYC & COMPANY CONVENTION & VISITORS BUREAU

www.nycvisit.com

London: Tel 020 7202 6368 – line open 9.30am–5.30pm Monday to Friday.
New York City's official tourism agency – call to discuss any queries you have with the information officers or ask them to send you a Visitors' Guide.
New York: 810 7th Avenue at 53rd Street. Tel 212-484 1200. Fax 212-245 5943. Subway N, R to 49th Street, B, D, F, Q to 47th–50th Streets/Rockefeller Center.
Area: Midtown.
A recently opened state-of-the-art visitors' information centre with touch-screen kiosks that provide up-to-date information on the city's attractions and events accompanied by a detailed map. There is also a cashpoint and a souvenir shop, plus an incredible range of brochures covering hotels, shops, museums, sights, tours and Broadway shows.

While you're at the NYC visitor centre in New York, pick up a copy of the *City Guide* magazine. It not only has up-to-date listings on Broadway shows, but also various money-off coupons.

NEW YORK TRAVEL ADVISORY BUREAU

www.nytab.com

An independently run tourism agency, which is most famous for its own pocket guide to New York, the NYPages, and the NYCard, which gives discounts to hotel, museums and attractions – check the website for the latest update on all their available discounts.

BRITISH INFORMATION SERVICES

www.britainusa.com

845 3rd Avenue, NY, NY 10022. Tel 212-745 0277. Fax 212-745 0359. This is the information service of the British Embassy in Washington and acts as the political, press and public affairs office of the New York Consulate-General, which covers the states of New York, New Jersey, Connecticut and Pennsylvania.

CURRENCY

Exchange rate for the US dollar at the time of writing is around $1.80/£1.
UK banks' and travel agencies' rates vary, so shop around to find the best. Also check the commission – some will charge for both selling and buying back, but many will only charge once so you can return unused dollars you bought from them free of charge. Best of all is the Post Office, who do not charge any commission at all.

You must have plenty of change and singles ($1 notes) as you'll be tipping everyone for everything and you'll also need change for the buses.

TIPS ON TIPPING

You won't get a lunch, drink, ride or even taxi door being opened for you without a tip being involved in America and it can add quite a lot to your overall expenses when you're on holiday. It's something that doesn't come naturally to us Brits, but you need to get used to it quickly.

Waiters: General rule of thumb is 15 to 20 per cent. The best way to work it out is to double the sales tax, which will come to 17 per cent, and add a little more if you are very impressed. Just remember, at a posh restaurant the tip alone can come to more than the price of a decent meal!

Taxi drivers: 15 per cent, and if you travel by private car or limousine they'll automatically add 20 per cent to the bill.

Hotel doormen: $1 for hailing a cab.

Porters: $1 per bag.

Maid service: $2 per day when you leave.

Bartender: $1 a round.

A lot of people use travellers' cheques, but it is often a real palaver to cash them, especially at banks in New York. Many banks simply won't take them, and if they do they'll need photo ID so you'll have to carry your passport around with you. Chase Manhattan Bank has more than 400 branches and doesn't charge a fee for exchanging currencies. Phone 212-935 9935 for details of where to find a branch.

The alternative is to do as I do, exchange a reasonable amount of cash in one hit to use for tips, buses and in cafés, then use your credit card as much as possible (the exchange rate is generally reasonable). If you need extra cash, make sure you know your PIN number for your credit card and you'll be able to use any of the many cashpoints (ATMs) around the city, for which there is usually a fee.

DISCOUNT DIVAS

NYC & Co: This company runs various money-off campaigns in association with the American Express Card that cover restaurants, hotels, theatres and sightseeing tours. The main one is **Paint the Town Red,** which runs from early January until the end of March.

Each year the popular **Summer Restaurant Week** takes place during the last week in June when you can get three-course meals at more than 150 of the city's top restaurants for around $20 (excluding tip, tax and drinks). Many restaurants also continue serving their prix fixe lunches to the end of August. Establishments include Nobu, Gramercy Tavern, Union Square Café, La Caravelle and Montrachet. For further information visit **www.nycvisit.com** or phone either 1-800 NYC VISIT (toll-free within America) or 212-397 8222.

South Street Seaport Fulton Market

CHAPTER 2

Getting Around New York

When most people talk about New York, they actually mean Manhattan, which is the long, thin sliver of an island in the middle of the four outer boroughs of Staten Island, Queens, the Bronx and Brooklyn.

You'll find diagrammatic maps, such as the one on page 28, dotted through the book to help you focus on the basic geography of the area. Once you get the hang of roughly where everything is, you'll find it easier to use the subway and bus maps on the inside front and back covers, and the street maps in the centre pages.

ORIENTATION

Manhattan is 21km (13 miles) long and 3.2km (2 miles) wide for the most part and almost all of it above 14th Street is on the grid system that was introduced quite early on in New York's history. The main exception is Greenwich Village, which, like Downtown (page 31), had already established its eccentric random arrangement of streets (like ours in the UK) and refused to get on the grid system. The other exception is Broadway, which follows an old Indian trail that runs largely north to south on the west side of the island, then cuts across to the East Side as it runs down towards Downtown.

Here are a few basic rules about the geography of Manhattan; it is useful to acquaint yourself with them as soon as possible, then you'll be able to walk around with confidence!

➡ All the roads going across Manhattan east to west are streets and all the roads going north to south are avenues.

➡ The city is divided between east and west by 5th Avenue and all the street numbers begin there. This means that 2 West 57th Street is just a few steps to the west of 5th Avenue while 2 East 57th Street is just a few steps to the east of 5th Avenue.

➡ Most streets in Manhattan are one-way. With a few exceptions, traffic on even-numbered streets travels east and traffic on odd-numbered streets travels west. Traffic on major 'cross-town' streets – so-called because they are horizontal on the street maps of Manhattan – travels in both directions. From south to north, these include Canal, Houston (pronounced Howston), 14th, 23rd, 34th, 42nd, 57th, 72nd, 79th, 86th and 96th Streets.

➡ When travelling north to south or vice versa, remember that traffic on York Avenue goes both ways, 1st Avenue goes south to north, 2nd Avenue goes south and 3rd goes north mostly, though there is a small two-way section. Lexington goes south, Park

Grand Central Station

goes in both directions, Madison goes north and 5th Avenue goes south. Central Park West goes both ways, Columbus Avenue goes south, Amsterdam Avenue north, Broadway goes in both directions until Columbus Circle, after which it continues southbound only to the tip of Manhattan. West End Avenue and Riverside Drive go in both directions.

➡ Numbered avenue addresses increase from south to north.

➡ To New Yorkers, 'downtown' does not mean the city centre, but means south, while 'uptown' means north. You will need to get used to these terms if you are planning to use the subway – which is simpler to use than it looks at first!

To calculate the distance from one place to another, 20 north-south blocks or 10 east-west blocks approximately equal 1.6km (1 mile). This rule does not apply to the Financial District or Greenwich Village.

ON ARRIVAL

JOHN F KENNEDY INTERNATIONAL AIRPORT

Tel: 718-244 4444
www.panynj.gov

JFK is in the borough of Queens and is the best place to enter or leave New York by air. It is 24km (15 miles) from Midtown Manhattan, a journey that will take you between 50 and 60 minutes. The cost of a yellow medallion taxi into town is a fixed rate of $35 (per taxi) as set by the New York Taxi and Limousine Commission. Bridge and tunnel tolls are extra (you can pay at the end of the journey) as is the 15 per cent tip. So think around $40.

There are various other ways to get into New York. An MTA bus and subway ride will each cost you $1.50 per person, private bus companies charge between $13 and $16 and the shuttle service costs $16. Private car services vary in price so you need to ask for specific quotes for your journey.

Subway train service: Take a free Port Authority bus from any JFK terminal to the newly opened Howard Beach-JFK Airport subway stop at the edge of the airport. You will then be on the A line, which will take you directly into Manhattan. It operates 24 hours a day, seven days a week and is every 10 to 15 minutes in rush hour – and all for the flat rate of $2!

Make sure that you get a city cab from a designated area outside the airport terminal and avoid hustlers offering taxi services, even if they proclaim to offer a cheaper price.

SuperShuttle: Tel 212-2315 3006 or 800-451 0455. A door-to-door shared limo-bus from the airport to your hotel operates 24 hours a day, 365 days a year. Go to the Ground Transportation desk at JFK, LaGuardia or Newark airports and dial SuperShuttle from the courtesy phone in the baggage claim area. Fares cost from $13 to $22.

New York Airport Service: Tel 718-875 8200. Runs every 15–30 minutes to Manhattan and also operates a minivan service from drop-off points in Manhattan to many hotels.

NEWARK LIBERTY INTERNATIONAL AIRPORT

Tel: 973-961 6000
www.panynj.gov

Getting into Manhattan from this airport has become quicker and cheaper thanks to AirTrain, a $415-million link from Newark International Airport that opened in 2003. Follow the signs for the New Jersey Transit Train, which will take you to Penn Station in just 20 minutes for a fee of $11.55 one way. Alternatively, if you prefer the comfort and ease of a taxi, the journey will take a good 60 minutes. In fact, if you have a lot of luggage and are not staying particularly close to Penn Station, it may work out more time and cost effective simply to jump in a taxi.

Set taxi fares start at $34 to West Manhattan and $38 to East Manhattan (as divided by 5th Avenue) plus bridge or tunnel toll, plus $1 per bag and tip, so think around $50. Private bus companies charge between $11 and $15 and the shuttle service costs between $13.50 and $18.

SuperShuttle: As From John F Kennedy International Airport (see page 24).

The PATH: Tel 800-234 PATH. Rapid transit from Newark to Penn Station (but you must take a taxi there from the airport) to stops in Downtown and Midtown Manhattan. Operates 24 hours, fare $1.50.

Olympia Trails Airport Express Bus: Tel 212-964 6233. Operates between Newark and three Manhattan locations – Penn Station (34th Street and 8th Avenue), Port Authority Bus Terminal (42nd Street and 8th Avenue) and Grand Central (41st Street between Lexington and Park Avenues). Also operates a hotel shuttle to all Midtown points between 30th and 65th Streets. Departs every 20 minutes, fare $11 (hotel shuttle $15).

LAGUARDIA AIRPORT (LGA)

Tel: 718-533 3400
www.panynj.gov

This is the airport you'll probably arrive at if you've taken an internal domestic flight from another state. TWIA, United Airlines and Continental Airlines all operate here. It's around 13km (8 miles) from the centre of Manhattan, between Queens and the Bronx and a taxi ride into the city takes around 20 to 35 minutes. You'll find a clearly marked taxi rank outside the main terminals. Unlike JFK you pay by the meter rather than a flat rate, and you will also be charged tolls. A cheaper option into town is by bus, which takes around 40 to 50 minutes. It's only $2 and they run daily (4am–1am), leaving every 30 minutes. To catch your ride into town, follow the Ground Transportation signs out of the terminal and wait at the M60 bus stop sign by the curb.

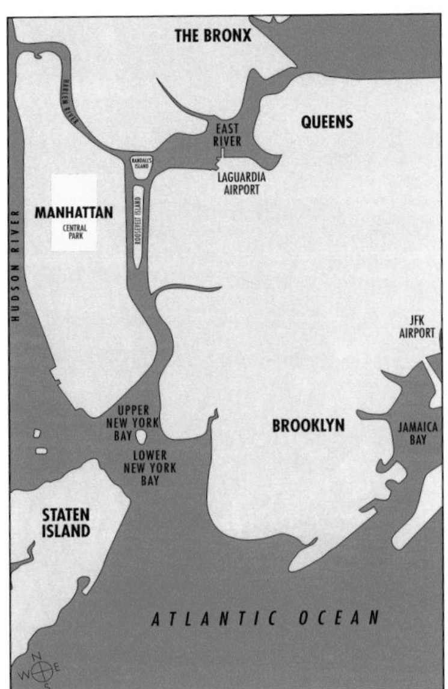

Areas of New York

AIRPORT SECURITY

Since September 11 the relaxed security systems which operated in most American airports have been seriously tightened up. Expect longer queues and subsequent waiting times getting through immigration and baggage checks. Remember that you can no longer carry any sharp items in your hand luggage, so make sure you put scissors, tweezers and nail files in your main check-in luggage. You should also be prepared to be asked to open your bags for inspection and to be frisked by a security guard with a hand-held scanner.

GETTING AROUND BY TAXI

No trip to Manhattan would be complete without a ride in a yellow cab. It's the preferred means of transport for many visitors to the city largely because there are so many about and the fares are reasonable. However, be warned. Even though the fares are much cheaper than in London, the cost still mounts up pretty quickly. Fares start at $2 and increase 30c every 0.32km (1/5 mile), or 20c per minute in stopped or slow traffic, with a 50c surcharge at night (8pm–6am). It's not just the cost of the ride that you have to take into consideration, but the $1 tip to the hotel doorman and the 15 per cent tip to the driver. In the end it works out to be an expensive option if used too often.

In any case, you will need to have a good idea of where you are going and how to get there, as most of the cab drivers in New York are the latest immigrants to have

Never get into an unofficial taxi. The official ones are licensed by the Taxi Limousine Commission and are instantly recognisable by their yellow colour and rates on the door.

arrived and have very little clue about how to get around the city. The best way to ensure you don't get into any difficulties is to always carry the full address of where you're going to, preferably with a map reference too. Fortunately, thanks to the grid system, it is relatively easy to educate yourself about where you are going and so you can give them directions!

➡ First off, never expect the driver to be the kind of chirpy, chatty Cockney character that you're used to in London. Most speak very little English and are not interested in making polite conversation, and many can be downright rude.

➡ Secondly, make sure you get into a taxi heading in the direction that you want to be going. If you are travelling uptown, but you're on a road heading downtown, walk a block east or west so you'll be pointing in the right direction. It saves time and money, and if you don't, the taxi driver will know immediately that you're a tourist.

➡ Hailing a taxi is not necessarily as easy as it looks – you have to be aware of the lighting system on the top of the yellow medallion taxis. If the central light is on, it means the taxi driver is working and available. If all the lights are out, it means the driver is working but already has a fare. If the outer two lights or all three lights are on, it means that the taxi driver is off-duty – look carefully and you'll see the words. The best method for actually hailing a cab is to hold out your arm while standing at the curb.

➡ When you get to a toll, expect the taxi driver to turn around and demand the cash to pay for it, but you are quite within your rights to ask him to add it to your final fare.

➡ Beware of trying to get a cab at around 4pm. Not only is it the approach of rush hour, it's also when most drivers change shifts so getting a taxi is well nigh impossible as they don't want to go anywhere but home! If you really need a taxi at this time be sure to call a car service company.

➡ Do not expect a taxi driver to change any bill larger than $20.

➡ In addition to the medallion on the roof, a legitimate taxi will have an automatic receipt machine mounted on the dashboard so that you can be given an immediate record of your trip.

➡ If you find yourself below Canal Street after business hours or at the weekend, you may have difficulty finding a yellow cab. Your best bet is to phone one of the many companies listed under Taxicab Service in the Yellow Pages. Fares are slightly higher than for the metered cabs, but they are a safer option.

➡ There is no extra charge per person or for luggage, but a licensed taxi won't be able to take more than four people.

➡ Fasten your seatbelt once in the cab. All taxis are now required by law to provide them and passengers in the front seat have to wear them.

CAR SERVICE COMPANIES

When you need to be certain you've got a taxi ride to the airport or some other destination, there are three main companies you can phone, all of which provide a 24-hour service:

All City Taxis: Tel 1-718 402 2323

Tristate: Tel 212-777 7171

Tel-Aviv: Tel 212-777 7777

A Gray Line double-decker bus

GETTING AROUND ON THE SUBWAY

The first time you take a look at a subway map of New York, you can be forgiven for thinking you need a degree in the whole system to get anywhere. The confusion is made worse by the fact that the signposts – both outside and inside the stations – are easily missed.

In addition, the Metropolitan Transportation Authority (MTA) is undergoing a billion-dollar rejuvenation programme of many subway stops and has introduced new, clean trains on to the network, though as a New Yorker told me: 'We'll soon fix that. People just graffiti them up. It's disgusting but New York is a dirty city. If you don't have the dirt, it doesn't feel right!' On the old subway trains, the conductor would always announce stops and interchanges. These, for the large part, were unintelligible, but the new trains have prerecorded announcements in a non-New York accent that can be understood.

METROCARD

A flat fare to travel on the subway is $2. However, you can no longer buy single fares; the cheapest ticket you can now get is the $10 MetroCard. This magnetically encoded card debits the fare when you swipe it through the turnstile in the subway or the farebox on a bus. You can purchase the cards from subway ticket offices (cash only), vending machines in most subways, from drugstores such as Rite Aid and Hudson News or from the Times Square Visitors Center at 1560 Broadway between 46th and 47th streets. Some hotels also sell them at the reception desk.

A $10 card gives you six rides for the price of five. The $20 MetroCard gives you 12 rides for the price of 10. Both of these tickets can be used by up to four people though, so, if there are two of you, you only need buy one MetroCard.

Unlimited Ride MetroCards include the 1-day Fun Pass for $7 (which lasts until 3am the following day), the 7-Day card for $21, the 30-Day card for $70 and the 7-Day Express Bus Plus for $33. For more details, phone 212-638 7622 or visit **www.mta.nyc.us/metrocard**.

THE SUBWAY MAP

There are subway maps on the inside back cover of this book for the city and on the inside front cover for Manhattan. You can also get hold of free MTA maps in most subways stations, hotel lobbies and information centres. The map looks impossible to interpret, so here's how to make sense of it:

➡ The subway lines are all indicated on the map by a colour, but unlike the London Underground, the colours are not used in the stations and on the trains. The important bit is the number or letter. Below the name of every stop you will find the letters and numbers of lines that stop there, such as 7, S Grand Central–42nd Street.

➡ When examining a subway map, a number or letter in a diamond means rush-hour service, in a circle it denotes normal service and a square indicates the end of a line. Black and white lines connecting white and black circles indicate a free subway transfer. White circles on coloured lines indicate express stops (express trains skip about three stops for every one that they make).

➡ If the numbers against your destination on the subway map are written in a lighter tone, they are peak-time only.

HOW TO SURVIVE THE SUBWAY

➡ Don't look for obvious signs indicating a subway; instead look for either the very discreet 'M' signs in blue or the signature red and green glass globes – red means the entrance is not always open and green means it's staffed 24 hours a day.

Generally, if you're going downtown, use subway entrances on the west side of the road and if you're going uptown, use subway entrances on the east side. This way you should be heading in the right direction, but do always check before entering.

➡ Before going down a subway entrance, check it is going in the right direction for you – many entrances take you to either 'downtown' or 'uptown' destinations, not both. It means that if you make the mistake of going in and swiping your ticket before you realise you're going in the wrong direction, you will have to swipe your card again to get in on the right side – so you'll

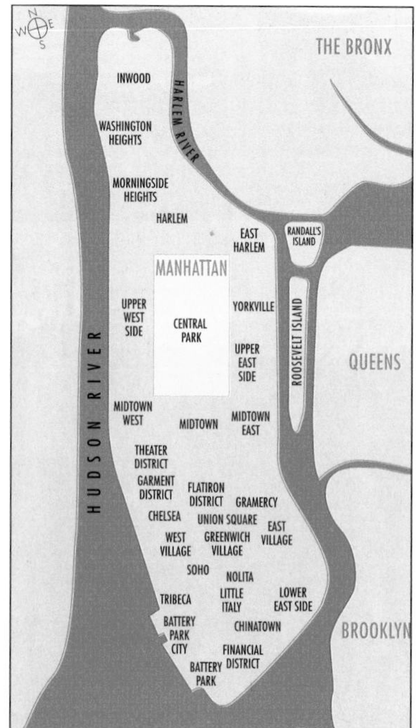

Areas of Manhattan

end up paying double. The alternative is to travel in the wrong direction until you get to one of the larger subway stations (such as 42nd Street) and then change.

➡ If you're in one of the outer boroughs the same rules apply, but instead of looking for a 'Downtown' or 'Uptown' sign, look for one that says 'Manhattan'.

➡ Some trains are express – they stop only at selected stations. At some stations you have to go down two flights to get to the platforms for express trains, while at others you don't, and it is easy to get on an express train by mistake.

➡ There are conflicting opinions (hotly debated by the locals) as to whether it is worth waiting for an express. On the plus side, they move quickly, but on the down side you could end up waiting 10 minutes for one, so you won't have saved any time in the end.

➡ There are many different lines going to the same destinations, but they don't all exit at the same place. For example, if you arrive at Fulton Street on the New York subway and head for the exit you can come out at four completely different locations. The Red Line exits at Fulton and William Streets, the Brown Line exits at John and Nassau Streets, the Blue Line exits at Fulton and Nassau Streets, and the Green Line exits at Broadway and John Street – all of which are quite a long way from each other.

➡ The locals consider that the subway is safe to travel on until around 11pm. After that opinions vary, but when making up your mind to travel do be aware that the subway service after 11pm is generally incredibly slow.

➡ The subway does have one very good point: because the island of Manhattan is largely made up of granite, they did not have to dig as deep as we have to in London to find the really strong foundation level. This means you generally only have to go down one flight of steps to find the line.

If you're taking the subway to or from Times Square, look out for the fabulous Roy Lichtenstein mural, which is part of the MTA's ongoing programme to introduce art into the subway

➡ If you've been to New York before, it's worth bearing in mind there have been a few changes to the subway network – and all for the better – thanks to a $17-billion expansion and renovation programme. These are the new lines:

➡ The L line runs almost the full width of Manhattan along 14th Street from 8th Avenue in the west to 1st Avenue in the east on its way to Queens. Other stops in Manhattan include 6th Avenue, Union Square and 3rd Avenue.

➡ The new S line should not be confused with the shuttle between Times Square and Grand Central Station. It is another good east–west train linking West and East Villages in Greenwich and runs from West 4th Street to Grand Street.

➡ In Manhattan, the new peak-time V line largely runs in conjunction with the F line and includes new stops at 5th Avenue and 53rd Street as well as Lexington Avenue and 53rd Street.

GETTING AROUND ON THE BUSES

Travelling by bus is always a little more nerve-wracking because you can never be sure whether you've arrived at your destination, but most people are pretty helpful if asked a direct question. I thought that taking to the buses would be more difficult than travelling by subway, but two of my friends put paid to that notion by going everywhere by bus on their first visit.

FINDING A BUS

Our Manhattan bus map inside the front cover will come in handy as often there are no route maps at the bus stops. However, as a general rule buses run north to south, south to north, east to west or west to east.

➡ You can recognise bus stops by a yellow-painted curb by a blue and white sign. Look at the Guide-a-Ride information which should show the route and service schedule.

RIDING THE BUSES

➡ Get on the bus at the front and click in your MetroCard or feed in $2. Exact change is essential – and it must be all in coins as no dollar bills are accepted.

➡ Although there are bus exits at the back, you can also get off at the front.

➡ Requesting a stop may be a little confusing – there are no clearly marked red buttons to press; instead there are black strips that run the full length of the bus between the windows or at the back along the tops of the handles. Simply press one of these to request the next stop.

➡ If the bus says 'Limited Stopping' it means it only stops at major stops, such as the cross-town streets of 14, 23, 34, 42, 50, 57, 68, 72, 79 and 86.

➡ The main bus routes used by tourists are M1, which travels from 5th Avenue and Central Park to Madison Avenue, M7, which runs from Union Square to Broadway and M6, which takes in Carnegie Hall to SoHo.

My favourite MetroCard is the $20 pass. Up to four people can use it at one time and if you transfer to a bus you only have to swipe the ticket once and it will register for everyone. You can also top it up in amounts as small as $5.

WATER TAXI

For a completely different way of getting around, you can go by water taxi, which runs around the lower part of Manhattan. The three bright yellow catamarans with black and white check are easy to spot and there are six stops, all easily accessible from subway and bus stops at Fulton Ferry Landing; Pier 11 Wall Street–South Street Seaport; Pier A Battery Park; North Cove–World Financial Center; Pier 62 West 22nd Street–Chelsea Piers; and Pier 84 West 44th Street–Circle Line–Intrepid.

A commuter service runs Monday to Friday 6.30–9.30am and 4–7pm for $3 one-way or buy a 10-trip booklet for $20. The Midday Service runs Monday to Friday 9.15am–4.30pm, Saturday and Sunday 11am–8pm. An All-Day Pass costs $15 adults, $12 seniors and under 12s and allows you to hop on and off the water taxi any time during one 24-hour period. The Fun Pass costs $19 adults, $16 seniors and under 12s. It gives the same water taxi access as the All-Day Pass, plus access to the subway and buses throughout the city. A One-Stop/One-Way Ticket costs $4 for all ages. A One-Way Ticket for more than one stop costs $8 adults, $6 seniors and under 12s. All under 2s travel free.

For more information, phone 212-742 1969 or visit **www.nywatertaxi.com**.

DRIVING IN NEW YORK

A word of advice: don't even think about it. Most of the streets will be jam-packed, while parking is extremely scarce and astronomically expensive at $8–10 an hour. You can park on the street, but watch out for what is known as alternate-side-of-the-street parking. This means you have to know which day of the week the cleaning truck comes by so you move the car over at the right time. Double parking is common, so it is easy to get boxed in, and frustrated drivers simply get in their cars and honk the horn until the guilty owner moves their car. As one New Yorker told me: 'People do not know how to park here. New Yorkers are not good drivers and are the wildest parkers.'

If you plan to take a trip upstate, though, and wish to do so by car, then there are some dos and don'ts about car hire. Firstly never hire a car in Manhattan – unless you want to pay through the nose to the tune of around $90–120 a day. Take a ferry to

FINDING A WC

I think it's worth raising this subject early as you'll probably be spending quite a lot of time walking around and you could easily get caught out. It is wise to know that public lavatories are thin on the ground in New York. In addition, subway loos – if they are actually open – are dangerous and unhygienic. I should also point out that it is considered impolite to use the word 'toilet' (*très* common, I'm afraid) – in America it is always referred to as the 'restroom'.

Okay, so you're in the middle of Greenwich Village, you're desperate, you don't want to pay through the nose for a beer so you can use the bar's facilities, so what do you do? I have it on good authority from those New Yorkers in the know that you can go to the following establishments:

Barnes & Noble: This is a newish chain of bookstores that offers restrooms because the company wants people to treat the stores as public meeting places.

Department stores: The restrooms are hidden away, however, and you have to ask where they are (this is to deter street people from using them).

Government buildings: Try places like the United Nations, though you'll have to go through a security check.

Lincoln Center: There are ten 'stalls' open to the public, close to the entrance.

Hotels: The restrooms are usually on the ground floor or you can ask and will be told.

McDonald's and Burger King: Unisex toilets that are usually clean and modern because they are built to the McDonald's spec rather than the typical New York building spec.

Public libraries: They all have public loos.

Restaurants: Some have signs saying 'For customers only', but if you ask authoritatively enough and look okay, they'll probably let you use them.

Statue of Liberty: In the gift shop.

the state of New Jersey and hire a car from there for $55–65 for a medium-sized car with unlimited mileage.

Secondly, don't consider hiring a car in the summer or at weekends, because that's what most New Yorkers will be doing and you'll find hire cars thin on the ground. Cars are also snapped up in the autumn when New Yorkers like to go to the country to see the autumn foliage.

Speed limits: Around town 30mph, on highways and freeways 55mph.

Private parking: There are many private parking facilities in the city, but they cost $25–40 per day.

A New York carriage ride

Tow away: Illegally parked cars will be towed away and there's a $150 fine plus $15 per day to be paid. Collect your car from Pier 76, West 38th Street at 12th Avenue (Midtown West). Tel 212-971 0772. It's open 24 hours a day from Monday to Saturday.

CAR HIRE

If you do decide to take the plunge and drive around the city, there are a number of car hire companies to choose from. Most are based at the major international airports, so you can simply pick them up on the day that you arrive. Prices vary enormously, from one-day rental from $90 to a week rate of between $225 and $300. Remember that to rent a car you'll need to be over 25, have a valid driver's licence, have your own insurance and have some photo ID.

CAR HIRE COMPANIES

Alamo: Tel 800-462 5266, **www.alamo.com**

Avis: Tel 800-331 1212, **www.avis.com**

Hertz: Tel: 800-654 3131, **www.hertz.com**

CHAPTER 3

The New York Neighbourhoods

It's worth getting to know the neighbourhoods of Manhattan as each one has a distinct flavour and is filled with its own unique sights and sounds. From the historic Downtown area of the Financial District to the charming cobbled streets of Greenwich Village and the vibrancy of Times Square, each is well worth visiting in its own right.

Here's an outline of what you'll find in each neighbourhood, what makes them so special and how to make the most of your time there. In Chapter 4, Seeing the Sights, there are also some suggestions for tours to take, including walking tours that will help you further to discover the streets of New York (pages 71–81).

DOWNTOWN

This is where the history of New York started and where some of the most important financial sites in the world were founded. The Downtown area covers the whole of the Financial District and the Civic Center, stretching from river to river and reaching as far north as the Brooklyn Bridge/Chambers Street (Map 1).

Look out for people wearing red jackets with red, white and black carts. Employed by the Downtown Alliance, they clean the streets and public areas, are an added level of security and answer queries on the area.

Today, the winding, narrow streets of the true Downtown – a square mile area south of Chambers Street that stretches from City Hall to the Battery – are a dizzying juxtaposition of colonial-era buildings and towering temples of capitalism. In the beginning, they were the location of some of the most important events in American history. This is where the Bill of Rights was signed, where George Washington was inaugurated as the first president and where millions arrived to begin their search for the American Dream.

Visit **www.downtownny.com** for more information on free events and services.

THE WALL STREET SHUFFLE

The Dutch were the first to arrive and it was Peter Stuyvesant, New York's first governor, who ordered the building of a wooden wall at the northern edge of what was then New Amsterdam, to protect the colonialists from possible attacks from Indians and the British. The name stuck and today it is known as **Wall Street**. This aspect of New York's history is presented in an exhibition in the Ionic-looking **Federal Hall National Memorial** (26 Wall Street, tel 212-825 6888), built on the site of New York's original City Hall. Cross the road into Broad Street and you're at the neo-classical entrance to the **New York Stock Exchange** (page 69).

Other fascinating landmarks include the **Federal Reserve Bank** in Liberty Street at Maiden Lane, which stores one quarter of the world's gold bullion, and the neo-Gothic **Trinity Church**, where Alexander Hamilton, the country's first secretary of the treasury, was buried after losing a duel. There has been a church on this site since the end of the 17th century and for the first 50 years after Trinity was built, it was actually the tallest structure in New York!

Just off Wall Street at 25 Broadway is probably one of the poshest post office buildings in the world. Known as the old **Cunard Building**, it was once home to the booking offices of the steamship company

View across New York City

in the days before aeroplanes took over the transportation needs of the masses from large liners, and the interior walls of the building are still lined with marble. There are other signs of its former use, too, with murals of ships and nautical mythology around the ceiling.

And it seems only fitting that the former headquarters of John D Rockefeller's Standard Oil Company at 28 Broadway should now be the home of one of New York's newest museums, the **Museum of American Financial History** (page 120).

The best subway lines are the 2, 3, 4, 5 to Wall Street.

The Bowling Green end of Broadway is lined with coffee shops, cafés and pizza parlours. A freshly cooked slice eaten in or taken to go makes a perfect pit stop.

BOWLING GREEN

Blink and you'll miss this oval of greenery at the end of Broadway. You know you're there by the presence of the Greek revival-style US Customs House, which is now the Smithsonian **National Museum of the American Indian** (page 121) and has the world's largest collection devoted to North, Central and South American Indian cultures. Bowling Green was the sight of the infamous business deal between the Dutch colony of New Amsterdam and the Indians, who were conned into selling Manhattan for a bucket of trinkets.

In the 18th century, the tiny turfed area was used for the game of bowls by colonial Brits on a lease of 'one peppercorn per year'. The iron fence that encloses it now is the original and was built in 1771, though, ironically, the once-proud statue of King George III was melted into musket balls for use in the American Revolution.

Here you'll also find the 3,175kg (7,000lb) life-sized bronze bull. A symbol of the Financial District's stock market, it appeared overnight outside the New York Stock Exchange in 1989. Now it is a tradition to rub him!

The nearest subways to take you to Bowling Green are the 4, 5 line to Bowling Green or R, W to Whitehall.

BATTERY PARK AND CASTLE CLINTON

Thanks to hundreds of years of landfill, the whole Downtown area is quite different to how it once was. Years ago, State Street houses looked over Upper New York Bay, and Water and Pearl Streets were named because they were at or near the water's edge. The excavation works required to build the deep foundations for the World Trade Center in the 1960s, destroyed by terrorists on September 11, 2001, created enough granite blocks of earth to form 9ha (23 acres) of new land, which then became home to Battery Park City and the World Financial Center.

In the Battery Park area, **Castle Clinton** originally stood on an island. Built in 1811 as one of several forts that defended New York harbour, it is now part of Manhattan. It has been an opera house, an aquarium and the original immigration sorting office, dealing with eight million immigrants before the opening of Ellis Island. It is now used as the ferry ticket office.

A plethora of new shops and cafés opening up and the remodelling of the Battery Park public spaces has given the area a whole new lease of life. The best subways to take here are the 1, 9 to South Ferry or 4, 5 to Bowling Green.

Battery Park is a beautiful spot for a picnic, or you can enjoy the fantastic views of the harbour and the Statue of Liberty by dining al fresco at the American Park at the Battery (page 155).

BATTERY PARK CITY

North-west of Battery Park, you'll find a relatively new area of land known as **Battery Park City**, which is actually the area created by landfill. It's still pretty much a quiet district, though there has been plenty of development. This is home to two of New York's newer museums. **The Museum of Jewish Heritage** (page 120) has been so successful, it is already being extended.

At 39 Battery Place is the **Skyscraper Museum** (page 115), which tells the fascinating story of the creation of all those famous buildings. On the southern tip of the 'City' is the recently landscaped **Robert Wagner Junior Park** with a café, some WCs and street vendors selling food and drink – it is a wonderful place to sit and gaze out at the harbour.

To the north is the **World Financial Center**, which has four tower blocks and a full calendar of fairs and festivals. It's worth coming here for the **Winter Garden** (page 70), a huge, glass-ceilinged public plaza decorated by massive palm trees. From here you can see the fancy private boats docked in **North Cove**.

The nearest subways are the A, C, 1, 2, 3, 9 to Chambers Street (for the World Financial Center) or the 1, 9 to South Ferry for the museums and park.

For fantastic views of Dame Liberty and the harbour, treat yourself to a drink in the hip new bar, Rise, on the 14th floor of the Ritz-Carlton Hotel in West Street (page 187).

EAST OF BATTERY PARK

To see what life was like in 18th-century Manhattan, head for the **Fraunces Tavern Block Historic District**, which has 11 early 19th-century buildings that escaped the fire of 1835. The three-storey Georgian brick house that is home to the **Fraunces Tavern Museum**, (page 118), on the corner of Pearl and Broad Streets was built in 1904 and houses an exhibition on the site's history.

A little further north-east along Water Street to the Old Slip, you'll see the tiny **First Precinct Police Station**, which was modelled on an Italian mansion and which has been used for exterior shots for both *Kojak* and *The French Connection*. Fittingly, this is now the permanent home of the **New York City Police Museum** (page 122). Down on the water's edge of South Street is to be the new home of the Guggenheim's Downtown museum project, a Frank Gehry design that will include a water garden, an ice rink and a public plaza. It is expected that the new museum will attract more than three million visitors a year.

Just off Water Street at 70 Pine Street is the incredibly beautiful Art Deco wedding-cake-shaped American International Building. It has one of the most beautiful Art Deco-designed lobbies in New York and visitors are welcome to come inside to have a look.

Don't miss the free outdoor concerts at the South Street Seaport Museum (page 124), held almost nightly throughout the summer.

A little further north at piers 16, 17 and 18, you find yourself in the heart of the **South Street Seaport** (page 66), which has a museum, a shopping and restaurant complex and the 150-year-old **Fulton Fish Market**, open midnight–8am daily.

Best subways to the area are the R, W to Whitehall Street, J, M, Z to Broad Street or the 2, 3 to Wall Street.

CITY HALL PARK AND THE CIVIC CENTER

City Hall Park is right opposite the entrance to Brooklyn Bridge and also the dividing point between the Financial District and Chinatown. From here you can stroll across the **Brooklyn Bridge** or visit the neo-Gothic **Woolworth Building** (page 69) on Broadway at Barclay Street, which is likely to be your main reason for swinging by. Check out the lobby's vaulted ceilings with its magnificent mosaics and mail boxes. When it was first built it was the tallest structure in New York and Mr Woolworth paid cash for it!

There is a farmers' market each Tuesday and Friday (April to December, 8am–6pm) in the City Hall Park where you can buy fresh fruits, vegetables and bread – a great way to create a picnic.

Back in the 1930s, when Prosecutor Dewey decided to target organised crime, he made the Woolworth Building his base and during that time he locked up 15 prostitutes in the building for four months. In the end, he worked out that the prostitutes were controlled by Lucky Luciano and successfully prosecuted him for white slavery. 'Lucky' got 32 years in prison, but

City Hall

lived up to his name by serving just ten before he was pardoned for his efforts on behalf of the American government during the Second World War. Just north of City Hall Park are the **Police Plaza, US Courthouse, New York County Courthouse** and **Criminal Court Building**.

It's useful to note that there is a Lower Manhattan information kiosk in City Hall Park where you can find information on attractions and upcoming events plus maps and directions.

The best subways to take are the R, W to City Hall or the 4, 5, 6 to Brooklyn Bridge-City Hall.

TRIBECA

This is where we start getting into the territory of New York acronyms. **TriBeCa** (Map 1) like other acronyms such as SoHo, is a shortening of the area's location. In this case it means the triangle below Canal Street. It is bounded by Canal to the north, Murray to the south, West Broadway to the east and the Hudson River. To get here on the subway, use the 1 and 9 to Canal or Franklin Streets or the 1, 2, 3 and 9 to Chambers Street.

TriBeCa provides a good idea of what SoHo looked like 20 years ago. With the increasing pressure to find affordable housing, the empty warehouses of TriBeCa were ripe for the 'gentrification' process that has been happening all over New York including SoHo, the East Village and even the Lower East Side to a certain extent. And the area certainly has its fair share of pretty cast-iron buildings and quaint cobbled streets. Along **Harrison Street** is a row of well-preserved Federal-style townhouses and the area around **White Street** is particularly picturesque.

In the late 1970s, the former industrial buildings were targeted by estate agents for residential dwellings, but it was not really until the late 1980s that the area became a favourite with artists priced out of SoHo. Now TriBeCa is home to a variety of media and artistic businesses such as galleries, recording studios and graphic companies.

Its most famous film company, the **TriBeCa Film Center** at 375 Greenwich Street, which is part owned by Robert De Niro, has production offices and screening rooms and is used by visiting film-makers. They, of course, frequent De Niro's extremely expensive **TriBeCa Grill** on the ground floor of the building. Visiting film-makers have also been given a boost by the opening of the triangular-shaped **TriBeCa Grand Hotel**, which has its own private screening room.

Now the area is deemed quite hip – being home to Harvey Keitel and Naomi Campbell among others – it has attracted a lot of upper middle-class families, while restaurants and nightclubs are frequented by residents from the nearby Battery Park City. It is also home to the **TriBeCa Film Festival**, which showcases independent movies during the second week of May.

CHINATOWN AND FIVE POINTS

The sprawling mass that is **Chinatown** (Map 1) has spread its wings north into the remnants of Little Italy, east into the Lower East Side and south in the Civic Center area. It is also home to the infamous **Five Points** area, once the most dangerous part of New York city.

Chinatown

Until recently only history books and tour guides referred to Five Points. The name is derived from the five streets that intersect next to Colombus Park. Originally called Orange, Mulberry, Anthony, Little Water and Cross Streets, they are now known as Bayard, Park, Worth, Mulberry and Baxter.

In the 1820s, a pond graced a lovely area where the rich had their country homes, but they started sub-letting to tanners, who polluted the lake. Attempts to get rid of the dreadful smells from the lake by building a canal down Canal Street failed, and in the end only the poorest came to live in the area, which included freed slaves and immigrant blacks.

Have a game plan when visiting Chinatown – it's so crowded that it's easy to feel daunted by all the hustle and bustle.

Irish immigrants arrived in the 1850s, then Italians and Eastern Europeans in the 1880s. Poverty was rife, and gangs flourished to such an extent that the streets were too unsafe for the police to patrol, and at least one person was killed each night. For almost 100 years, Five Points was considered the worst slum in the world and even shocked Charles Dickens. During that time the gangs were schools for criminals and politicians such as Johnny Torrio, Charles 'Lucky' Luciano, Al Capone and Frankie Yale. Paul Kelly set up boxing gyms to teach them how to be gangsters, use guns and extort money. Amazingly, the gangs even produced flyers with their 'services': $100 for the big job (murder), $50 for a slash on the face or $15 for an ear chewed off.

The appalling violence, corruption and history of this era has been brought to life by Martin Scorsese's movie *Gangs of New York*, which starred Leonardo DiCaprio and Daniel Day-Lewis. It genuinely gives a true insight into the psyche of the early American immigrants.

Take advantage of Big Onion's Gangs of New York walking tour (page 80).

Fortunately, now it's a very different place. Many of the overcrowded tenements were pulled down at the turn of the 20th century to build a park. Since then, they've also built the **Criminal Court Building** nearby, retaining a contact with the area's violent past!

The original Chinese immigrants to New York in the 1850s huddled around Pell Street. Sadly, it was not long before the Tongs with their extortion rackets, illegal gambling and opium dens gave the area a new reputation for violence.

As a result, the US Government passed the Exclusion Act in 1882, which banned

SoHo

Chinese from entering America. That all changed in 1965 with the new Immigration Act and a new wave of Chinese immigrants arrived. Very quickly the women in particular were snapped up for poorly paid work in the garment industry, which gradually moved from its old Garment District above 34th Street into Chinatown. In more recent years, there have been more changes as a new wave of immigrants from the Fujian province of China has once again changed the face of the area. Now many of the well-off Cantonese have moved to Queens and the Mandarin-speaking Fujinese have the upper hand.

The best way to get to Chinatown by subway is to take the A, C, E, J, M, N, Q, R, W, Z, 6 to Canal Street.

At 277 Canal Street at Broadway and up some rickety old stairs you will find **Pearl River Mart**, Chinatown's idea of a department store, stocking everything from crockery to Buddhas, pretty lacquered paper umbrellas, clothes, shoes and slippers.

Back on the street again, you could be forgiven for feeling a little overwhelmed by the licensed and unlicensed street traders of Chinatown, who sell anything from fake watches to jewellery and handbags. It's often impossible to walk on the pavements, but dangerous to step too far into the incredibly busy Canal Street, either.

You'll have a hard time getting a taxi on Canal Street – they just don't make it into Chinatown that often. Head toward The Bowery and try to hail a taxi as it comes off the Manhattan Bridge, or use the subway stations at Canal and Broadway.

Further down the road, you can get another real insight into the local lifestyle by visiting the **Kam Man** grocery store at 200 Canal Street. They offer a wide range from plucked ducks to squid. Not on your shopping list? Then here's something you can buy and eat while you walk around – a bag of Konja, which is filled with deliciously refreshing bite-sized pots of lychee jelly.

Mott Street is the main thoroughfare of Chinatown. Here, along with Canal, Pell, Bayard, Doyers and The Bowery, is a host of restaurants to suit any appetite along with tea and rice shops. South towards Doyers Street you'll find the **Church of the Transfiguration** – one of two so named in New York – which perfectly portrays the changing nature of the immigrant population here.

The oldest Catholic church building in New York, it was built in the early 19th century and Padre Felix Varela Morales, a Cuban priest who helped form the Ancient Hibernian Order, preached here. But between 1881 and 1943, no Chinese were allowed into it, apart from some wealthy merchants. It was first used by the Irish immigrants, then the Italians, but is now, finally, used by the Chinese and has services in Chinese.

It's pointless arriving at Chinatown before 10am as only the local McDonald's will be open.

May May restaurant at 35 Pell Street serves up fabulous dim sum. My favourite is the chicken and shrimp combo. *Dim sum,* incidentally, means the 'little delicacy that will lighten up your heart' – and it certainly does when it's good! Next door is the **Chinese Gourmet Bakery and Vegetarian Food Center**, from where you can buy enough ingredients to make your own picnic to eat sitting in the nearby **Confucious Plaza**.

Whether or not you choose to picnic, you should try to visit the beautiful **Bowery Savings Bank** on Bowery Street at Grand. When it was built in the 1890s, people liked to save locally and so the bankers tried to create the feeling that their building was a safe place for people to leave their money by making their banks stunningly beautiful inside. The neo-classical exterior is an incongruous sight here in Chinatown, but it's worth having a peek at.

SOHO

SoHo means south of Houston, pronounced 'Howston'. It is bounded by Lafayette Street at its eastern border, 6th Avenue to the west and Canal Street to the south (Map 2). The best subways are 6, C, E to Spring Street and N, R to Prince Street.

The main drag is on **West Broadway** though Spring and Prince Streets are major shopping havens too, and the whole area is reminiscent of Hampstead Village in London. Okay, so there are no hills and the roads are wider, but it has the same boutiquey, picturesque, design-conscious element.

If you're looking for a delicious latte and snack in SoHo, try the aptly named Space Untitled in Green Street between Houston and Prince Streets.

It's hard to imagine the totally trendy and oh-so-expensive SoHo as a slum, yet just over 30 years ago this was the case. Despite the arrival of cutting-edge artists in the 1940s, who'd spotted the great potential of the massive loft spaces once used by manufacturers and wholesalers, the whole area was run-down and shabby.

Then, in the 1960s, those same artists were forced to fight for their very homes when the city decided to pull down all the buildings because they were only supposed to be used for light industry and definitely NOT for living in. The artists successfully argued that the architecture of the cast-iron buildings was too valuable to be destroyed and the whole of SoHo was declared a historic district.

TASTES GOOD TO ME

SoHo is home to a complete first in New York City – a shop that can sell both wine and food. **Vintage New York** at 482 Broome Street at Wooster Street (212-226 9463) is owned by a vineyard from New York State, which means it can open on Sundays and sell proper alcoholic wine and food together – both of which are otherwise illegal in New York. The true secret to this little gem is that you can get five 1oz tastes of different wines for just $5, which actually works out to be one of the cheapest glasses of wine going in Manhattan! All the wines, incidentally, are from vineyards in the state of New York. Best time to visit Vintage is during the week when there are stools to sit on at the tasting bar.

In the 1970s, art galleries first started moving into the area and the art boom of the 1980s truly transformed it. In 1992 the Guggenheim opened a downtown site on Broadway at Prince Street. These events coincided with a kind of bubble-bursting feeling for the more cutting-edge artists, especially those who could no longer afford SoHo's sky-rocketing rents. Many have now moved on to Chelsea and TriBeCa, and SoHo has become a wealthy residential neighbourhood occupied by anyone rich enough to afford the large loft spaces that are prevalent.

There is a cracking restaurant just off the beaten track in MacDougal – Restaurant Provence (page 159) – where you'll get a delicious meal in a romantic setting. For good fare at reasonable prices, locals frequent Jerry's on Prince Street.

However, there are still plenty of art galleries – certainly a higher density than most areas of Manhattan – but the nature of the area has changed quite substantially (and to my mind for the better). Designers, clothes boutiques and dedicated beauty shops have arrived en masse, though the emphasis still lies heavily on style and art in terms of presentation and decor. The Guggenheim has shut up shop to be replaced by **Prada**'s stunning flagship store (page 89). Coffee shops, bars and restaurants that normal mortals can afford are now in better supply and the beauty boutiques with their wooden flooring, high ceilings and gleaming, glistening displays are wonderful places to get expert beauty advice on the cheap.

While the MoMA's **New Museum of Contemporary Art** (page 122) is the only remaining art museum in the area, a

For a well-priced, delicious lunch al fresco, head to the Gourmet Garage on the corner of Broome and Mercer Streets. It has a wonderful deli with ready-made salads to take away.

formidable sense of style remains and can be seen daily at the fashionistas' **SoHo Grand Hotel** haunt (page 188).

LITTLE ITALY

The best subway to **Little Italy** (Map 1) is the N, R, Q, W, 6 to Canal and walk east to Mulberry. Or take the 6 to Spring and walk south. Head along Grand Street towards Mott and Mulberry Streets to **Di Palo's** (page 103), which marks the beginnings of what is left of Little Italy. Di Palo's shop at 210 Grand Street was founded 80 years ago and is still famous for its mozzarella, Italian sausages and salamis. It has its own cheese-ageing room and gets very crowded. A little further on is **Ferrara's** (page 158), the oldest and most popular pastry café in Little Italy.

Ferrara's in Grand Street, near Mulberry, is a perfect spot for a coffee and pastry break, while you'll find the restrooms on the first floor. You'll also get a real slice of the Italian lifestyle.

It has to be said that Little Italy is now little more than a tourist attraction, with the Italians having done a deal with the Chinese community to retain **Mulberry Street** between Hester and Kenmare Streets. It's actually an area that was formerly home to Italians from the Naples area of Italy and, as such, it has taken St Gennaro, the patron saint of Naples, as its own saint. Every year in the third week of September, Italians flock from far and wide to celebrate the Feast of St Gennaro. Food carts line each side of Mulberry Street and there is much laughing, dancing and drinking until the early hours of the morning.

Little Italy is at its finest at the weekend in warm weather when the restaurants put their tables outdoors. Arrive early – around noon – to get a seat outside, or late in the afternoon.

Little Italy's best feature is its wonderful restaurants with outdoor seating where you can watch the world go by while tucking into some great dishes. The restaurants have a reputation for being on the pricey side, but plenty have pasta and pizza specials for a more economical $8.95.

Just a little bit of gruesome history for you – Da Gennaro on the corner of Mulberry and Hester Streets was the original home of **Umberto's Clam House** (which is now further south on Mulberry). This was a favoured haunt of gangster Crazy Joey Gallo and where he was murdered in 1972 while celebrating his birthday.

Further north at 247 Mulberry between Spring and Kenmare Streets is the former home of the **Ravenlight Club** and Mafia headquarters for John Gotti. He was once known as the Teflon Don because no charges could be made to stick and this was where he made the policemen and judges on his payroll come to pay their respects.

The FBI were so determined to put him away they not only bugged the Ravenlight,

Dining al fresco in Little Italy

but also all the parking meters around the streets, but still they got nowhere. Then Gotti's underboss, Sammy Gravano, became a supergrass. He had killed 19 people but got away with all those murders because he did a deal with the FBI that helped them put Gotti away.

NOLITA

NoLiTa stands for North of Little Italy and stretches from Kenmare Street in the south, to Houston in the north and from Crosby Street in the west to Elizabeth Street in the east (Map 2). The best subways are the 6 to Spring Street, the F, V, S to Broadway-Lafayette Street and the F, V to 2nd Avenue.

A fairly new part of town, it's filled with funky coffee shops, bars and restaurants. In a very short space of time Elizabeth, Mott and Mulberry Streets have seen a rapid growth in up-and-coming designers. Ultra cool and cutting edge, some are pricey, but most still charge moderate prices. It's difficult to know how long that will last, though, as many of the boutiques are now frequented by celebrities in search of hip, one-off designs.

LOWER EAST SIDE

One of the seedier parts of town, the **Lower East Side** has a fascinating history, but is now known for its trendy nightclubs and bargain shopping. The Lower East Side stretches from the East River ostensibly to Chrystie Street (though Chinatown is encroaching) and south from Canal Street to East Houston in the north, while Delancey is its main thoroughfare (Map 2). The best way to get there by subway is by taking the J, M, Z or F trains to Delancey or Essex Streets.

In many respects the history of the Lower East Side is the history of America's immigration story which, in turn, has played a pivotal role in the country's development.

The Lower East Side Business Improvement District runs FREE two-hour walking tours of the historic Orchard Street Shopping District at 11am on Sundays from April to December. Call 866-224 0406 for details.

Katz's Deli

At one time this was the most densely populated area in the world with 1,000 inhabitants crammed into a square mile, but more of that later. Almost from the word go, the Lower East Side was a settlement for new arrivals to New York because of its cheap housing and its proximity to where people disembarked. Once these immigrants had established themselves they moved on, leaving space for a new wave of arrivals. Street names such as Essex, Suffolk and Norfolk point to the origins of their first tenants. Since then streets have been named anything from a Kleine Deutschland to a Little Italy or Ireland.

While you're in the neighbourhood, don't miss Katz's Deli (page 160) on East Houston Street at Ludlow Street. It's a real institution.

With each new wave of immigrants came friction between new and old arrivals, which often led to violence. The Protestant English were angry, for instance, when the Roman Catholic Irish built St Mary's on Grand Street in 1828 – and burnt it down. That led to the formation of the **Ancient Order of Hibernians** in 1830 – the organisation that started the St Patrick's Day parade. The Hibernians rebuilt the church and put walls around the outside. It is still in existence, but now runs a kosher soup service for local Jewish people.

Check out **www.lowereastsideny.com** for information on events and discounts.

SWEATSHOPS AND TENEMENTS

Other tenants of the early 1800s were relatively well-off Jews from Germany, who eventually moved further north. This was a pattern that was to be repeated again and again with each new wave of immigrants. But perhaps the saddest were the incredibly poor Jewish immigrants who started arriving from Eastern Europe in the 1860s and '70s. They were forced to eke out a miserly existence by day in sweatshops and had no choice but to live in tenement buildings at night. Whole families were crowded into 1.8m (6ft) square rooms with no heating, running water and often little light. Visit the **Lower East Side Tenement Museum** (page 111) in Orchard Street for their full story.

The Lower East Side was once known as a mugger's paradise. It's no longer so bad, but as in any city, you still need to be careful.

During this period **Hester Street** was the main thoroughfare and it was filled with shops and pedlars selling their wares – meat, fruit and vegetables. The pedlars did very well, though, as they paid no tax and had no overheads, such as rent. Often they made more than three times as much as teachers did. But the shopkeepers were unhappy with the unfair competition and by the 1930s the city had banned pedlars and created the **Essex Market**. Famous for its fresh meats, produce and other products, the market has recently been renovated at a cost of $1.5 million. It is open Monday to Friday 8am–6pm.

A NEW DAWN

The main language in Hester Street between the 1880s and 1920s was Yiddish – a mixture of Hebrew, German and Slavic. The local newspaper, called *Forward*, was published in Yiddish and each edition sold 200,000 copies. Now the area is very quiet. There are still many Jews left, but the new waves of immigrants include Puerto Ricans and Latinos from the Dominican Republic.

If you want to see some real action you need to go to **Delancey** and the big shopping area around Orchard and Ludlow Streets. Here you'll find bargain basement products and cutting-edge designer fashions – many young designers have started in the Lower East Side before moving uptown. Orchard and Ludlow between Delancey and East Houston Streets are also the main drags for the new bars and clubs that have been opening in the area. The best day to experience the Lower East Side is Sunday, when the market is open and the whole area is buzzing with people. A large chunk of it is still closed on Saturday to mark the Jewish Sabbath, but that is gradually changing due to the arrival of the Latinos.

For excellently priced and clean accommodation in Lower East Side, stay at the Howard Johnson Express Inn (page 217) on East Houston.

An outstanding sight on Delancey is Ratner's Dairy Restaurant at 138 Delancey near Essex Street. Although it's still a dairy restaurant, it's now also home to **Lansky Lounge** (page 185), the chic nightspot that celebrates the place where mob boss Meyer Lansky used to hold court. The entrance is at 104 Norfolk Street.

GREENWICH VILLAGE

This is one of the prettiest areas of New York and although the radical free-thinkers have gone, its quaint cobbled and tree-lined streets, shops and Federal and Greek-style buildings are well worth a visit.

Greenwich Village proper (Map 2) is bounded in the north by 14th Street, in the south by Houston, in the east by Broadway and in the west by 7th, where it becomes the West Village, which stretches west to the Hudson River.

When the Dutch first arrived in Manhattan, 'the Village' as it is known in New York, was mostly woodland, but was turned into a tobacco plantation by the Dutch West India Company. Then in the early 1800s people started fleeing from a series of cholera and yellow fever epidemics in the unhygienic Downtown.

When the wealthy moved into their 5th Avenue mansions at the end of the 19th century, though, rents came down and a

GREAT TOURS OF THE VILLAGE

If eating's your bag, then you'll love the **Foods of New York tour** of Greenwich and West Village, which not only shows you the sights, food shops, restaurants and architectural secrets of the area, but will also give you a chance to taste the foods that are unique to this corner of New York. Other great tours are the **Literary Pub Crawl**, which takes you to the watering holes once frequented by the literary giants who lived here, and **Haunted Greenwich Village** shows you places with a legendary past. See the tours section of Chapter 4 for details.

whole new breed of artists, radicals and intellectual rebels moved in, creating a kind of Parisian Left Bank feel to the neighbourhood. Over the years it has been home to such literary lions as Mark Twain, Edgar Allen Poe, Dylan Thomas, Eugene O'Neill and Jack Kerouac.

Now the writers and artists have largely been forced out by the soaring rents – a tiny two-bed apartment costs at least $2,500 a month and to buy a shoebox of a studio is at least $275,000 – and in their place have come upper middle-class Americans for whom making money is the abiding principle. Yet there is still the sense of a community spirit, many restaurants cater mostly to locals rather than tourists (in New York, only Village restaurants seem filled with people who are in no particular rush) and a great variety of Off-Broadway shows and other cultural events can be seen in this neighbourhood.

WASHINGTON SQUARE PARK

If you take the A, B, C, E, F or V subway to West 4th Street and Washington Square, you'll find yourself in what many people consider to be the heart of the Village – and in one of the very few genuine squares in Manhattan. The first thing you'll notice is the Stanford White-designed marble square **Triumphal Arch** at the bottom of 5th Avenue, built in 1892 to commemorate George Washington's inauguration as the first US president.

You may also become aware of how dingy it all looks and I suspect you may be even a little concerned about the 'grungy' nature of many of the people there, but this area is considered 'alternative' rather than dodgy. It's full of locals skating, playing chess and just hanging out, plus students from the nearby **New York University**. It used to be a place where a lot of people took drugs, but that problem is largely in the past.

A little-known fact is that the park was once used by City officials to conduct public hangings until they were moved to Sing Sing penitentiary. Apart from the arch and the people, the other main point of interest in the park is the **Dog Run**. A uniquely New York phenomenon, the idea is that instead of taking your dog for a walk along the roads, you bring them to dog runs where they can literally run around off the lead. It's rather like a parent taking their child to the swings – hilarious and has to be seen to be believed!

North from the park on 6th Avenue between Waverly Place and 9th Street is **Bigelow's Pharmacy**, the oldest traditional chemist in America. Across the street is the beautiful **Jefferson Market Courthouse**, which is now used as a library, and just off 10th Street is one of the most famous rows of mews houses in the Village – **Patchin Place**, which has been home not only to many a writer, including e e cummings and John Reed, but also to Marlon Brando.

Tomoe Sushi, on Thompson Street (page 161), looks pretty unappealing from the outside but has incredible queues – and not without reason. You can get the best sushi in New York here for about a tenth of the price it would cost you at Nobu.

BLEECKER STREET

Effectively the main drag of the Village, this is one of the best places to be in New York, filled as it is with sidewalk cafés, shops, restaurants and clubs. The corner of Cornelia and Bleecker Streets gives you access to some of the best food shops and restaurants in Manhattan. To get here, take the 6 to Bleecker Street or B, D, F, V to Broadway-Lafayette Street.

At 259 Bleecker is **Zito**'s old-fashioned Italian bread shop, which still uses the ovens that were built here in the 1860s and were once used by the whole community. They are particularly famous for focaccia with different toppings, such as onions and olive oil and rosemary, and their prosciutto bread is unique to them.

Next door is **Murray's Cheese Shop** (page 103) with more than 350 cheeses from around the world. Nothing is pre-cut and they have great names such as Wabash Cannonball, Crocodile Tears, Mutton Buttons and Cardinal Sin, a British cows'-milk cheese. They also have 15 different types of olives and sell chorizos, pâtés and breads. Opposite at 260 Bleecker is **Faicco's** (page 103), a landmark shop that has been here since 1900. Their famous range of sausages are made every morning and sold not only to local residents but to many of the local restaurants. They also sell home-cooked ready-made meals and offer a huge deli selection.

Around the corner is Cornelia Street, home to four of the best restaurants in the Village. The **Cornelia Street Café** (page 160) hosts jazz, readings and other events (from $6 to $11), while **Home Restaurant** specialises in American comfort food with a gourmet twist, **Le Gigot** is a traditional country French restaurant and **Little Havana** offers great Cuban food.

Bleecker Street has two more incredible baker shops with their own seating areas. **Pasticceria Bruno** is run by popular chef Biagio. He produces an amazing range of tarts and mousses for $2 to $3 with names like Kiss Cream, Wildberries, Green Apple and Apricot. The café itself has a lot of atmosphere and old world charm. Next door is **Rocco's**, run by Rocco, who used to be a head pastry chef at Bruno's until 1972 when he opened his own place here. An Italian cheesecake made of ricotta cheese is just $12.50 for an entire cake. The interior is much more modern, with steel-framed chairs, mirrors and more seats than Bruno's (page 103).

Christopher Park, Greenwich Village

THE MEATPACKING DISTRICT

The **Meatpacking District** is to be found in the north-western corner of the West Village, south of West 14th Street to West 12th Street and from West Street to Hudson Street on the east side (Map 2). The nearest subway is the A, C, E to 14th Street. Cattle are not actually slaughtered in this area, but large carcasses of beef are cut up in wholesale markets and distributed throughout the city from here.

However, many of the old warehouses are no longer in use and the lofts are being used as nightclubs. One of the trendiest is **Hogs and Heifers** (page 186), which is frequented by a mix of motorcycle groups and celebrities. Many women leave their bras on the ceiling as a memento.

Another great hang-out is **Tortilla Flats** in Washington Street on the corner of West 12th Street. It's a cool, grungy café famous for its hoola-hooping-for-tequila-shots on a Wednesday night. Also home to the wonderful **Florent** restaurant (page 161) is Gansevoort Street. The area was until lately very 'edgy' and still a hang-out for transvestite prostitutes – as depicted in *Sex and the City* when the man-eating Samantha moved here from the Upper East Side. This was also where Carrie's boyfriend Aiden worked at the Furniture Company. But it's rapidly gentrifying, with expensive stores like **Jeffrey's** and Stella McCartney's new shop.

WEST VILLAGE

The **West Village**, on the other side of 7th Avenue, has an amazingly pretty collection of cobbled streets with picturesque homes and lined with trees. These are among some of the oldest remaining houses in New York, many being built in the 1820s and 1850s, and quite a few have the one thing that is so rare in Manhattan – a back garden, albeit tiny. To get here take the 1, 9 to Christopher Street or the A, C, E, to 14th Street, or the L subway to 8th Avenue.

TAKE IT EASY IN THE SPEAKEASY

On the corner of **Bedford Street**, number 86 is one of the most famous former speakeasies in New York. Known as **Chumley's** (page 186) it doesn't have its name advertised anywhere outside, but there is a back entrance on Barrow Street that will take you directly into the bar. The front entrance merely has the old grille, used for checking out potential customers during Prohibition, and the number 86.

In the old days a dumbwaiter took two people at a time to the gambling den upstairs, and the best table in the house was right by the entrance to the cellar, where people could hide if there was a raid. Now Chumley's does fish and chips and shepherd's pie-type food and usually has a roaring fireplace in the winter, while the walls are still lined with all the book jackets donated by many of the writers who once frequented it.

Crossing Bedford is Barrow Street, where you'll find One If By Land. It's in the oldest building housing a restaurant in Manhattan, a former carriage house built in 1726. Great food, service and decor. If you're in the mood for a romantic splurge, this is the place. Tel 212-228 0822.

At the corner of Grove Street is the oldest wooden house in the West Village. Built in 1822, it's the most exclusive cottage in the area and costs $6,000 a month to rent, but you do have your own little garden – what a bargain! All around Grove Street the houses are covered in a network of vines, which blossom in May and have grown in the area for 150 years.

A MATTER OF RIGHTS

Christopher Street, the main drag of the West Village, is the heart of the gay community and a shopping paradise for antique lovers. **Sheridan Square**, one of the Village's busiest junctions, has been the scene of two major riots. First were the New York Draft Riots of 1863, sparked off by the requirement to join the army for the Civil War. The rich could buy their way out, but the poor had no choice and were fearful they would lose their jobs to the newly freed black slaves.

The second riot is the more famous one in 1969 and is known as the Stonewall Riot. This was sparked by the police raiding the Stonewall gay bar and arresting its occupants – an event which frequently occurred at the many gay watering holes in the area. This time the community decided to fight back, and over a period of three nights, the gay community held its ground in the Stonewall as it was surrounded by police. It was the crucial first step made by gay people in standing up for their rights.

Christopher Street is still filled with bars, restaurants and bookstores that are used by gays – though not exclusively – but many members of the gay community have moved on to Chelsea.

Central Park boatyard

NOHO

Wedged between Greenwich Village and the East Village is a small section of streets now known as **NoHo** - North of Houston Street (Map 2). Bounded by Broadway to the west, Bowery to the east, Astor Place to the north and East Houston Street to the south, it's a tiny triangular-shaped area cut off from both of the villages, yet teeming with bars, cafés and shops. The boutiques here are a match for nearby SoHo and some are just as pricey, but for innovative and unique designs, they're streets ahead of many areas, with the exception of NoLiTa.

Get here via the 6 subway to Astor Place or Bleecker Street or the F, V, S to Broadway–Lafayette Street.

EAST VILLAGE

Forget the picturesque cobbled streets of Greenwich and the West Villages. Once you cross The Bowery (otherwise known as Skid Row) and head up to St Mark's Place you are in the heart of the **East Village** (Map 2) and an area more reminiscent of the Lower East Side than a village. No matter where you are in New York, it's easy to spot an East Villager - they have long hair and more metal in their face than a jewellery shop window display. You also know when you've entered the neighbourhood by the many tattoo shops along with boutiques selling punk and leather outfits.

Where Greenwich Village has become upper middleclass, the East Village retains its roots as a Bohemian enclave of free thinkers and non-conformists, though the tramps are gradually being replaced by a more genteel set attracted by newly built apartment blocks and the comparatively reasonable, though not low, rents.

This was once the home of Beat Generation writer Allen Ginsberg (on East 7th Street) and was frequented by Jack Kerouac and other radical thinkers of the 1950s. Amazingly, one of the area's oldest clubs, **CBGB** on The Bowery, is still going strong. The punk-rock club is famous for hosting Blondie, the Ramones, Talking Heads and the Police.

Now the area is most well known for its **second-hand shops**, which can be found all along 7th Street and 2nd and 3rd Avenues. There's a tiny **Little India** on 6th Street, where you'll find a row of curry houses, but the most famous eating outlets are **Stingy Lulu's** and **Yaffa Café**, both on St Mark's Place heading towards Tompkins Square Park (page 163).

The formerly dangerous area of **Alphabet City** (Avenues A, B, C and D) has been much cleaned up, but the muggers and drug pushers still frequent the area beyond B later in the evening. The best subways are the L, N, Q, R, W, 4, 5, 6 to 14th Street–Union Square and the L to 3rd Avenue and 1st Avenue.

CHELSEA

This neighbourhood is only likely to be on your list of places to see if you like art galleries, want to go clubbing or you're gay. However, it's actually worth a visit if you want to see an up-and-coming area in the process of 'gentrification'. Once the enclave of slaughterhouses and the working classes, it has a mixture of sought-after brownstone townhouses and warehouses that have made it a perfect target for artists priced out of SoHo, and although it's still rough around the edges, many of the quaint streets and buildings have been restored.

In the mood for some star-spotting? Try The Park on 10th Avenue, the latest hot spot for real and aspiring film execs.

It is bounded by 6th Avenue (Avenue of the Americas) in the east, the Hudson River in the west, 16th Street in the south and 29th Street in the north. If you get off the A, C, E line at 14th Street and walk north on **8th Avenue**, you'll see the main drag of restaurants, shops, bars and gyms. Along the way you'll notice an abundance of Chippendale-type male bodies - the neighbourhood's gay boys, who love to flaunt their pecs in the local nightclubs.

At the corner of 19th stands the **Joyce Theater**, famous for dance and its fancy Art Deco building. Just a little further north and you're not only in the **Chelsea Historic District** - the blocks around 9th and 10th Avenues at 20th, 21st and 22nd Streets - but at the heart of the new gallery community which lies between 10th and 12th Avenues.

First port of call should be the **Dia**

Center for the Arts, a four-storey, 3,700sq m (40,000sq ft) warehouse, which opened in 1987 and still plays a pivotal role in the art world. Other great galleries nearby include **LFL, Leslie Tonkonow, Max Protetch Gallery, 303 Gallery** and the **D'Amelio Terras Gallery**. Two blocks north on 24th Street is the 1,950sq m (21,000sq ft) **Gagosian Gallery, Barbara Gladstone** and the **Andrea Rosen Gallery**. Photographer **Annie Leibovitz's** studio is on 26th. Appropriately enough, given the area's new-found propensity for art, it now has its first art museum – the **Chelsea Art Museum** (page 116), which can be found on West 22nd Street at 11th Avenue.

CHELSEA HOTEL

One of the most infamous of all of New York's hotels, the red-brick **Chelsea Hotel** (or Hotel Chelsea as it's officially known, see page 213) is not only still going strong but is also in the midst of a great revival. Before Sex Pistols frontman Sid Vicious moved in with his girlfriend Nancy Spungen and allegedly killed her back in the 1970s, famous inhabitants included Mark Twain, Dylan Thomas, William S Burroughs, Arthur Miller and Arthur C Clarke.

Built in 1883 and named an historic landmark in 1966, its lobby walls are covered with plaques commemorating venerated guests and their artworks, while the Spanish **El Quijote** restaurant is famous for its lobster specials.

UNION SQUARE

Take the L, N, Q, R, W, 4, 5, 6 to Union Square at 14th Street (Map 2). This area was once pretty run down and overrun with drug pushers and muggers, but now it's one of the trendiest neighbourhoods in New York. The stretch of Park Avenue South between 14th and 23rd Streets is filled with some truly hip eateries and is known as **Restaurant Row**.

The W Hotel Union Square on Park Avenue South at 17th Street is home to Underbar, one of the hippest new nightclubs in New York (page 194).

BAG YOURSELF A BAGEL

Among the best places for bagels:

Bagelry: 1324 Lexington Avenue between East 88th and 89th Streets on the Upper East Side and many other locations around the city.

Ess-A-Bagel: 359 1st Avenue at 21st Street.

H&H: 80th Street and Broadway and other locations. Ships bagels worldwide.

Murray's Bagels: 500 7th Avenue at West 12th Street.

Pick-A-Bagel: 200 West 57th Street at 7th Avenue and other locations.

Yonah Schimmel's: 137 East Houston Street between Forsyth and Eldridge Streets in the Lower East Side, near to Katz's Deli. Although knishes – pastries stuffed with savory fillings – are the major speciality here.

Along here you'll find **Tammany Hall**, the most corrupt City Hall in New York's history. It was home to Jimmy Walker, ostensibly a popular mayor, but a man who had been elected by the gangsters in the 1920s, which is effectively how organised crime was born in America. The gangsters were impossible to prosecute because they knew all the judges, cops and politicians in New York and virtually lived at Tammany Hall. Walker even had showers installed for them. Eventually, in the face of mounting financial problems in the city, Walker was forced to resign and his successor, Fiorello La Guardia (pronounced Gwar-dia), decided to go after the gangs.

Create an instant picnic by buying farm-fresh produce, homemade breads, cheeses and drinks from the Union Square Farmers' Market every Monday, Wednesday, Friday and Saturday.

In the middle of Union Square is **Luna Park**, a great casual place for a bite to eat in the summer, with outdoor seating (page 220). Further north on Broadway to Madison Square Park, you'll find **Theodore Roosevelt's birthplace** at 28 East 20th

Street. It's not the original building, but it does house some great memorabilia from the former president's life (open Wed to Sun 9am–5pm; $3). Just around the corner is the wonderful, triangular **Flatiron Building** (page 68), at the end of what was once known as **Ladies Mile**, the city's most fashionable shopping district along Broadway and 6th Avenue from 14th Street.

GRAMERCY PARK

Two blocks south and two blocks east of the Flatiron Building on East 20th and 21st at **Irving Place** (Map 3) is one of the prettiest squares in New York City (the nearest subway is the 6 to 23rd Street). The park itself was once a swamp but has now been beautifully laid out, though you won't be able to go in unless you are staying with a resident of the surrounding square or at the **Gramercy Park Hotel**.

The most famous building in the neighbourhood is **The Players** at 16 Gramercy Park, a private club created for actors and theatrical types by actor Edwin Booth when Gramercy Park was the centre of the theatre scene. Booth was the greatest actor in America in the 1870s and 1880s and opened the Gothic Revival-style house as a club in 1888 so that actors and literary types could meet in private to interact. One tragic event overshadowed the end of Booth's life – his brother John Wilkes Booth assassinated Abraham Lincoln.

The Flatiron Building

MADISON SQUARE

It's a weird but true fact that the ugly Madison Square Garden building, constructed above Penn Station on 33rd Street (pages 68–9, 183 and 221), is the latest (and probably least attractive) of the four Madison Square Gardens that have been built in New York. But only the first two were, in fact, located at Madison Square (Map 3), which is where Madison Avenue begins and the site of the recently renovated **Madison Square Park**. Facing the square is Cass Gilbert's **New York Life Building**, which was erected in 1928. In its shadow is **The Little Church Around the Corner** just off 5th Avenue at 29th Street. Its real name is the Episcopal Church of the Transfiguration and its stained glass windows commemorate famous actors such as Edwin Booth, who frequented the church at a time when being an actor was not considered an honourable profession. The nearest subways are the N, R, W, 6 to 28th Street.

34TH STREET

You'll have two major reasons for coming to this part of New York (Map 3) – the divine **Empire State Building** (page 61) and the shopping. **Macy's** is here (page 86), as well as a range of chains and most importantly a lot of retail outlets for the nearby Garment District. This was once a pretty seedy area but, thanks to the efforts of the 34th Street Business Improvement District Partnership (BID), it has been transformed.

Now the streets are constantly maintained, clean and lined with pretty flower tubs and green benches. The BID has even installed some smart green telephones with a semi enclosure to block out some of the street noise. The kiosk at **Herald Square** is in matching green, as is the city's one and only automatic pay toilet right next door. It's pretty swanky and, most importantly, it's clean! The size of the average New York bedroom, you've enough room to swing a cat if you feel like it and 25c gives you 20 minutes inside.

If you plan to do the Empire State, make it your first port of call before the crowds and queues build up. Take the B, D, F, N, Q,

R, V, W to 34th Street and walk one block east to 5th Avenue where you'll find the beautiful Art Deco entrance.

Once you've come back down to earth, take a cheap coffee break at the little-known **Graduate Center** at 365 5th Avenue on the corner of 34th Street, diagonally opposite the Empire State. Here you can buy filtered coffee or a luscious latte with a croissant and sit in relative piece at any time of the day before 4pm, which is when the graduates start pouring in. The building used to be a department store, which is why there are ribbons and ties sculpted into the exterior columns. Now it is used as a research centre for students and holds free concerts. Anyone can sign up to use a computer here for up to two hours for free.

HERALD SQUARE

Head west again to Herald Square, which is named after the now defunct newspaper, and home to the famous **Macy's**, the world's largest retail outlet (the best subways for East 34th Street are the B, D, F, N, Q, R, V, W to 34th Street/Herald Square). Its top-sellers among the Brits are the extremely well-priced Levis and beauty products, while the seventh floor is dedicated to children's goods and it even has a McDonald's – the only department store in town to make such a proud boast.

For the grown-ups there is the wonderful **Cucina & Co** (page 104) in the basement. A combination of buffet foods to eat in and take away, a grill restaurant and a coffee shop, it also has a sandwich station, pasta station and take-aways at incredible prices. Bearing in mind the average New Yorker spends $10 for a sandwich-style lunch and drink, Cucina's $5.49 lunches are amazing value, as are their $5.95–9.95 meal specials.

But don't expect it to look cheap; this is a wonderful space filled with fabulously fresh food in an indoor-market setting. Adjacent to it is **Macy's Cellar**, where a complete dinner for two costs $24.95.

SHOPPERS' PARADISE

Between 5th and 8th Avenues on 34th Street is a shopper's paradise and one of the highlights is the **Sephora** beauty emporium, which has branches all over the city (page 96). With its sparkling floor-to-ceiling windows and stylish displays, this is a pristine shrine to beauty products and fragrances.

Other great shops in the area include **Old Navy**, the high-value end of the **Banana Republic** chain, **Kids R Us, Daffy's** and its amazingly cheap designer selection, plus **HMV, H&M** and **Kmart**.

Fancy a free makeover? They're available during the week at Sephora on 34th Street between 6th and 7th Avenues. Phone 212-629 9135 for an appointment.

PENN STATION

One block south on 33rd Street and 7th Avenue is the entrance to **Penn Station**, short for Pennsylvania Station (subways 1, 2, 3, 9 to 34th Street–Penn Station). Before you enter you'll see a **Lindy's** pastry shop. The original Lindy's in the theatre area was famous for its cheesecake, and this and the other branch (in Times Square), trade off the name but they're pricey and not unique.

As you enter Penn Station, you'll see a handy Duane Reade (think Boots the Chemist) on the left. Walk down to the

Garment District

If you're on the west side of Penn Station you're just a stone's throw from the block-long B&H Photo & Video store on 9th Avenue from 33rd to 34th Street (page 101). It has 625 staff over its four floors selling thousands of items to both amateurs and professionals!

round area that sits under the **Madison Square Garden** building and on your left you'll see the information booth for the **34th Street BID Partnership**. All around are coffee shops, bakeries and a sit-down restaurant called **Kabooz**. None of them is a patch on Cucina & Co or the Graduate Center, though. The restrooms are even worse. Sure, they have running water, but it just happens to be all over the floor. A good alternative is to head for the **Hotel Pennsylvania** on 7th Avenue opposite Penn Station, where you'll find clean WCs situated on the ground floor.

There's a free tour of Penn Station on the fourth Monday of each month starting from the 34th Street Partnership Information Kiosk at 12.30pm, tel 212-484 1222.

The main taxi ranks for Penn Station are on 7th Avenue opposite the Pennsylvania Hotel and on 8th Avenue opposite the majestic Beaux Arts **General Post Office** building. If you want a taxi from here, it's best to walk a block north as the queues can get quite long, or use the A, C, E, 1, 2, 3, 9 subways at 34th Street–Penn Station.

GARMENT DISTRICT

From 34th Street to 42nd Street between 6th and 8th Avenues, you'll find the **Garment District** of New York (Map 3). Having shrunk a little in the past – a lot of work disappeared overseas or moved to the cheap labour available in Chinatown – the area is once again up-and-coming as designers are now choosing to have their clothes manufactured in New York. If you wander around this area – and you may well if you're in search of sample sales – you'll see racks of clothes being pushed around the streets. Some are going to showrooms and warehouses, but as no one manufacturer makes an entire piece of clothing, many of the garments are being shunted from company to company to have different bits sewn on at each place!

Check out the sales section of New York's *Time Out* magazine for up-to-date information on designer sample sales in the Garment District.

MURRAY HILL

It's a testimony to man's desire to tame his environment that the majority of Manhattan is flat. This is a result of the zoning plans created in the early 19th century, when the streets and avenues were laid out north of Downtown, except for the Village. At the same time, the City flattened the majority of Manhattan except for what is now Morningside Heights and Harlem, as nobody believed anyone would live up there! The only other area that has kept its contours is **Murray Hill** (Map 3), a largely residential neighbourhood for New York's gentry, which lies between 5th and 3rd Avenues and 32nd and 40th Streets.

The most famous resident of the area was the multi-millionaire JP Morgan. His son lived in a brownstone on the corner of 37th Street and Madison Avenue, which is now the headquarters of the **Lutheran Church**. JP Morgan lived in a house next door until he had it knocked down to make way for an expansion of his library. Now known as the **Morgan Library** (page 119) it has a unique collection of manuscripts, paintings, prints and furniture, which the financier collected on his trips to Europe. The nearest subways are the 6 to 33rd Street or the 4, 5, 6, 7, S to Grand Central–42nd Street.

MIDTOWN

Technically Midtown starts at 34th Street, but for the purposes of this area guide, I'm starting at the more realistic **42nd Street** (Map 3). From this point up to about 59th

Street are some of the most beautiful and famous shops, hotels and buildings in the world, both to the east and west and on 5th Avenue itself (page 85). At the northern end of the Midtown area, **5th Avenue** is lined with marvellous institutions such as **Saks, Bergdorf Goodman, Tiffany's** (my favourite jewellers), and **Trump Tower** (page 69).

Weird but true, there are few coffee shops or coffee carts on 5th Avenue. If you want a coffee, your best bet is to try one of the side streets leading off to 6th Avenue.

Fabulous hotels in Midtown include the media den of the **Royalton** (page 209), the famous **Algonquin** (page 214) and the chi-chi **Plaza Hotel** (page 205) with its views of Central Park. Opposite **St Patrick's Cathedral** (page 71) on 5th Avenue is the main entrance into the **Rockefeller Center** complex of 19 statuesque buildings with the famous ice-skating rink in the middle of its central plaza (page 65). There's so much to do here, from browsing in the shops, to checking out the architecture or visiting the beautifully restored Art Deco **Radio City Music Hall** (page 65). Further north on 57th Street is **Carnegie Hall** (pages 182–3).

MIDTOWN EAST

The area between 5th Avenue and East River, **Midtown East** (Map 3) has its fair share of New York landmarks. No visit to the city would be complete without a visit to the magnificent, marble-filled **Grand Central Station** (page 68) at 42nd Street, which has been restored to its former glory. It may be overshadowed by the MetLife Building from the outside, but nothing can detract from its gorgeous interior. The ceiling has been painted to show the sky as seen by God from above.

The area along East 45th Street between Vanderbilt and Lexington Avenues is packed with food carts selling everything from steak sandwiches to baked potatoes.

To the east is the stunning **Chrysler Building** (page 67) which many argue is even more beautiful than the Empire State Building, and down by the river is the monolithic **United Nations** building (page 69). And no visit to Park Avenue would be complete without a drink at the **Waldorf Astoria** (page 205). Out of its many cocktail bars, the lobby bar is best for people-watching with a drink.

MIDTOWN WEST

TIMES SQUARE AND THE THEATER DISTRICT

If you arrive at **Times Square** (Map 3) by day when all the lights and motion are less distracting, you may actually notice the lack of a square. Like Greeley and Herald Squares, Times Square is no more than a junction where Broadway crosses 7th Avenue. The **Theater District** starts on the boundary with the Garment District at 41st Street, goes north to 53rd Street and is bounded by 6th and 8th Avenues. The best way to get there is to take the 1, 2, 3, 7, 9 N, Q, R, S, W to Times Square–42nd Street.

Broadway isn't called The Great White Way for nothing. At night, it's at its magnificent best around Times Square, but the best way to see it is from a few blocks north, where you really can appreciate the glittering beauty of all those neon signs.

The Theater District came into being at the end of the 19th century – previously the theatres could all be found in the Union Square area and then Chelsea – when Oscar Hammerstein I (father of the great lyricist) built his opulent but long-gone **Olympia Theater** on Broadway between 44th and 45th Streets. Until then, it had been an unfashionable area known as Long Acre Square, housing the city's stables and blacksmiths.

In 1904, when the *New York Times* set up shop in what is now 1 Times Square, the area was renamed in its honour (it's since moved offices to around the corner). That same year a massive fireworks display on

New Year's Eve became the precursor to the now famous annual countdown watched by millions of people. The surrounding Theater District, home to the Ziegfeld Follies at the **New Amsterdam Theater, Minsky's** and **Gypsy Rose Lee**, blossomed in the 1920s. In fact, so many theatres burst on to the scene that even though many were converted into cinemas in the 1940s, during a clean-up of the burlesque shows by Mayor La Guardia, 30 theatres still remain.

BAD TIMES COME

Sadly, by the 1960s, Times Square had lost its shine and the economic problems of the 1970s and 1980s compounded the situation. If you've ever seen Martin Scorsese's movie *Taxi Driver*, you'll have some idea of the level of drugs, prostitution and seedy strip joints that crowded the area. Crime rose dramatically and until fairly recently it was not a safe place to be.

Things started to change in the early 1990s, helped by the establishment of the **Times Square Business Improvement District**, which worked hard to clean things up and pay for security guards, and the discovery of an ages-old law that prevents sex shops from operating within a certain distance of schools or churches. Since then crime in the area has dropped by 60 per cent and many New Yorkers have even complained of its relative cleanliness. The arrival of the Disney company, which spent millions renovating the **New Amsterdam Theater** to put on *The Lion King* (page 181), was the last nail in the coffin.

In all honesty, I really don't feel these dirt purists should fret too much. To my mind, there is still definitely an edgy vibe to the neighbourhood, while the stream of traffic that puffs its way through each minute and the grunginess of many visitors stops Times Square from being what some people think of as a squeaky-clean environment.

All the same, it's safe enough for the most part, attracts tenants who pay the same rents as on more elegant 5th and Madison Avenues, and has plenty to offer everyone. New hotels have sprung up and corporate companies have moved into the neighbourhood including media giants Viacom, MTV, VH-1 studios, ABC TV's *Good Morning America,* Condé Nast Publications and Reuters news service.

There's the huge new **ESPN Zone**, a 3,900 sq m (42,000 sq ft) sports dining and entertainment complex, **Nasdaq MarketSite** with its massive sign – the largest video screen in the world – and **Madame Tussaud's** (page 63). In between are the **Virgin Megastore** (page 105), the Coco Chanel-style beauty emporium of **Sephora** (page 96) and the **World Wrestling Federation** entertainment and dining complex, which includes a restaurant and hot new nightclub. Oh, and, of course,

Window-shopping on 5th Avenue

For dining after the show with a good chance to spot celebrities, book into Angus McIndoe, 258 West 44th Street. Tel: 212-221 9222.

there are the 30 theatres and nearly 50 cinema screens...

HELL'S KITCHEN/CLINTON

Running up the west side of Midtown from 34th Street to 57th from around 8th Avenue to the river is an area known as **Hell's Kitchen**. In the latter part of the 19th century, a lot of poor Irish immigrants settled here creating a ghetto. They were later joined by blacks, Italians and Latinos and inevitably gangs were formed. The big employers were the docks (see *On the Waterfront*, starring Marlon Brando for an insight into the lifestyle – although set in Brooklyn, it is equally true of all the dock areas), but when container ships came into play many lost their jobs. Other local industries included slaughterhouses and glue and soap factories.

If you have an evening out on the World Yacht (page 171), you'll find yourself walking through Hell's Kitchen/Clinton in search of a taxi. Adopt 'the New York walk' (walk quickly and confidently) and head east to 7th or 6th Avenues where it's easiest to pick up a cab.

A lot of the gangs were put out of business by the police in 1910, but it remained a scary area until fairly recently. It was renamed Clinton in 1959 to hide its violent past – which is long before Bill came on the scene, so there's no link to the former president. Now a lot of people living there work in the Theater District and it's moving up in the world. 9th and 10th Avenues are full of restaurants, the *Intrepid* **Sea-Air-Space Museum** (page 113) is on the river and, on the whole, the area is pretty safe until around 11pm.

UPPER EAST SIDE

One of the most conservative areas of New York, the **Upper East Side** (Map 4) stretches from Central Park South to 98th Street and is centred on 5th, Madison, Park and Lexington Avenues. It came into being after Central Park was finally completed in 1876 and the rich and famous of the Gilded Era – the Whitneys, Carnegies, Fricks, Vanderbilts and Astors – decided to build their mansions alongside. It was a time when neo-classicism was the favourite architectural design, but many of the houses left standing are not the originals as the grandiose properties were built and rebuilt in an ever more opulent style or replaced with apartment blocks.

Jim's Shoeshine on East 59th Street between Madison and Park Avenues is a real institution that has existed since the 1930s.

Two things have always remained the same, though. The neighbourhood is known as the **Silk Stocking District** because of

The Waldorf Astoria

the vast family fortunes represented in the area, and the grand old apartment houses are known as 'white glove' buildings because of the uniforms of the doormen. People still pay a fortune to live there. For instance, Jackie Onassis's former 14-room apartment at 1040 5th Avenue near East 86th Street recently sold for a whopping $9 million. The mansion on the corner of East 86th is one of nine once owned by the Vanderbilts. Now nearby residents include Michael J Fox and Bette Midler.

If you're serious about designer clothes, then you'll be visiting the designer stores that line **Madison Avenue**. If you're clever you won't buy, just gather information on what's new for when you go rummaging through the designer selections at Daffy's or the sample sales (pages 87–8).

This area is also full of museums with a staggering array to choose from. They range from the world's largest and, arguably, most magnificent – the **Metropolitan Museum of Art** (page 108) – to the jewel of the **Frick Collection** (page 114), housed in the magnate's former mansion. Near to the Frick is the joyous **Whitney Museum** (page 125), with its emphasis on contemporary art.

Further north is the beautiful-looking **Guggenheim** (page 115), as well as the **Cooper-Hewitt** (page 117), the **Jewish Museum** (page 117) and the **International Center of Photography**. Finally, up in the borders of East Harlem, populated by Latin Americans, are the **Museum of the City of New York** (page 121) and **El Museo del Barrio** (page 117).

YORKVILLE

Between Lexington Avenue and the East River from East 77th to 96th Streets is the working- to middle-class enclave of **Yorkville** (Map 5) – subway 4, 5, 6 to 86th Street – which has an interesting mix of cultures, singles and families.

Fancy the idea of a picnic by the river? Then stop off at The Vinegar Factory in 91st Street (page 104), where you'll find an extensive selection of cheeses, meats, breads and salads, and head for the nearby Carl Schurz Park.

It was originally populated by German-Hungarians, who moved northwards from their first stopping point in the East Village's Thompkins Square with the arrival of Italian and Slavic immigrants. Now, though, you'd be hard-pressed to find the few remnants of German culture, as most left the neighbourhood during the Second World War to avoid anti-German feelings.

Do like the locals and head to the cosy DT UT coffee bar on 2nd Avenue between 84th and 85th Streets (page 194). For a real American Girl Scouts' adventure, try some 's'mores' (short for 'I want some more') – toasted marshmallows with Hershey chocolate and a biscuit on top.

The most famous resident in the area is the mayor, who lives in the official residence at **Gracie Mansion** (page 68) overlooking the East River and Carl Schurz Park at East 89th Street.

UPPER WEST SIDE

Central Park divides the Upper East and West Sides not only geographically, but in terms of attitude, too. If the East Side is upper crust, conservative old money, then the West Side (Map 5) is more artistic. It's a vibrant neighbourhood filled with bars, restaurants, shops, museums and, of course, the culture of the Lincoln Center.

The area is now anchored by the amazing new **AOL Time Warner Center's** twin towers at Columbus Circle, which house a mixture of offices, hotel, shopping and cultural centres. The $1.7-billion project includes the **Mandarin Oriental Hotel and Spa**, the new home of jazz at the **Lincoln Center** (page 183), broadcast facilities for live transmission of CNN, apartments and **The Palladium**, a massive space for shops, restaurants and entertainment venues (nearest subway is the A, B, C, D, 1, 9 to 59th Street–Columbus Circle). As you navigate the traffic lights to cross the roads at Columbus Circle, you can ponder on the fact that this is where Joe Colombo, the boss of one of the five Mafia families of New York, was shot.

A new place to take a break is Whole Foods, a huge market selling a dazzling array of prepared foods, on the basement level of AOL Time Warner Center. Either dine at one of the tables there or eat in Central Park across the street.

Up Broadway and left down West 63rd Street past the **Empire Hotel** (page 215), you'll find the Lincoln Center. This was once filled with the slums that housed poor Puerto Ricans (the setting for the 1961 movie *West Side Story*) until Robert Moses proposed the building of various cultural centres that include the **Metropolitan Opera House**, the **New York State Theater** and **Avery Fisher Hall**. To see more, join one of the popular backstage tours or enjoy the free lunchtime music supplied by visiting jazz and folk bands during the summer months.

BUILT TO LAST

The Upper West Side is well known for its beautiful buildings including the Beaux Arts **Ansonia Hotel** on Broadway between 73rd and 74th Streets, which has been called home by Babe Ruth and Igor Stravinsky in its time. Starting on the southern tip of Central Park West, which runs all the way up Central Park, is the Art Deco stunner at No 55, which was used as the setting for the film *Ghostbusters*.

On 67th Street near Central Park West is the **Hotel des Artistes** which, as the name suggests, was built for artistic types, who used its studios. Over the years it has been home to such celebrities as Noel Coward and Isadora Duncan. Today you can dine at the elegant **Café des Artistes** there (page 176). Back on Central Park West between 71st and 72nd Streets is the yellow façade of the Art Deco **Majestik** apartment house, which was built in 1930.

Across the way is the famous **Dakota Building**, which was the first apartment block ever to be built on the Upper West Side in 1884, and was named after the distant territory to indicate its remoteness from anything else on the West Side. Of course, since then it has had a long line of famous inhabitants including Leonard Bernstein, Judy Garland and Boris Karloff. Its most famous resident of all, **John Lennon**, was gunned down outside the building by a crazed fan in 1980. His widow Yoko Ono still lives here – she owns several apartments – and donated money to build the Strawberry Fields memorial to the star in Central Park, just across the road.

WHICH MET'S THE MET?

Traditionally the Metropolitan Opera House, with its crystal chandeliers and red-carpeted staircases, has been known as the Met. Increasingly, though, the Metropolitan Museum of Art is being referred to by the same moniker, which is leading to a certain amount of confusion. It probably depends which establishment you stumble across first. My greatest love is for the museum so to me that will always be the Met!

Once you cross West 59th Street going north, 8th, 9th, 10th and 11th Avenues become Central Park West, Columbus, Amsterdam and West End Avenues respectively.

A couple of blocks north between 73rd and 74th is the neo-Renaissance style **Langham**, which was built in 1905, and between 74th and 75th is the **San Remo**, built in 1930, where Rita Hayworth died of Alzheimer's in 1987. Several blocks north, on the corner of 81st Street and Central Park West, stands the elegant **Beresford**. Between them, these grand apartment blocks have housed a huge number of celebrities, including such names as Lauren Bacall, Dustin Hoffman, Steve Martin, and Jerry Seinfeld, who bought Isaac Stern's sprawling apartment home.

MUSEUM HALF MILE

On Central Park West at 77th Street is the **New York Historical Society** (page 123) which was formed in 1804 and was the only art museum in the city until the opening of the Metropolitan Museum of Art in 1872. It was founded to chronicle New York's history but still houses the world's largest collection of Tiffany stained-glass shades and lamps and two million

Just a few blocks from the museums is Zabar's (page 104) on Broadway at West 80th Street, the famous food emporium seen in *Friends*, and Fairway, on West 75th Street. Both are jam-packed with all the ingredients needed for a picnic in nearby Riverside or Central Parks.

manuscripts, including letters sent by George Washington during the War of Independence.

Next door is the real big boy of museums – the **American Museum of Natural History** (page 108) which was the brainchild of scientist Albert Smith Bickmore. It first opened at the New York Arsenal in Central Park in 1869, but by 1874 had moved to these bigger premises. Architect Calvert Vaux, who was also responsible for the Met Museum and largely responsible for Central Park, created the bulk of the building, which has since had a Romanesque-style façade added to it on its 77th Street side and a Beaux Arts-style frontage on the Central Park West side.

This is one of my favourite New York museums. It's crammed with well laid-out exhibitions that really bring the world of science, scientific discovery and expeditions to life, while the **Rose Center** and **Big Bang Theater** attract major crowds to see the 13-billion-year history of the universe.

The Upper West Side's Museum Half Mile also includes the **Children's Museum of Manhattan** (page 146) on 83rd Street between Broadway and Amsterdam Avenue where interactive exhibits keep the wee ones happy.

West 106th Street, at the top end of the neighbourhood, is now known as **Duke Ellington Broadway**. This is where the great musician lived, premiered many of his songs and was buried in 1974. Over 10,000 people came to his funeral and there is a memorial to him on 5th Avenue at West 110th by Central Park's Harlem Meer.

MORNINGSIDE HEIGHTS

Further north the terrain gets hilly as you reach **Morningside Heights** (Map 6) home to the **Cathedral of St John the Divine** (page 70) and **Columbia University**, one of the most exclusive universities in America where a year's tuition fees, room and board will set you back around $38,000. Even so, it has 20,000 students of whom 4,000 are undergraduates. This is a beautiful area, which is bounded by 8th Avenue to the east and West 125th Street to the north.

The *Intrepid* Sea-Air-Space Museum

A great pit-stop in the Columbia University area is Tom's Restaurant on Broadway at 112th Street (page 169). If you recognise the diner's exterior, that's because it was used in *Seinfeld.*

HARLEM

Harlem is a huge area that covers a substantial part of the northern reaches of Manhattan above Central Park, though it has various subsections. What we refer to when we use the name Harlem is actually the African-American area, which stretches from 8th Avenue in the west to 5th Avenue in the east and goes north to the East River (Map 6). The area from East 96th Street east of 5th Avenue going up to the East River is Spanish Harlem, known as El Barrio and populated largely by Puerto Ricans.

Many avenues and streets in Harlem have two names that reflect both historical and more modern influences. For instance, Lenox Avenue is known as Malcolm X Boulevard and 7th Avenue is known as Adam Clayton Powell Junior Boulevard – both named after major African-American activists.

Named after the Dutch town of Haarlem, the area received its first Dutch settlers in the mid-19th century when it was used as farmland and as an escape from the dust and traffic of Midtown. Better-off immigrant families started moving here following the arrival of the railroad link and the building of attractive brownstone townhouses. Then property speculators, eager to take advantage of the new subway heading for Harlem, started building good-quality homes for the upper middle classes in the early 1900s. But they'd got a little ahead of themselves. A couple of mini depressions and Harlem's distance from Midtown Manhattan put the dampers on hopes of a major middle-class movement into the area.

The African-American estate agents spotted a golden opportunity, bought up a whole batch of empty homes cheaply and started renting them out to blacks eager to escape the gang warfare of the West 40s and 50s in Hell's Kitchen and Clinton. This was the beginning of Harlem as the capital of the black world and when African-Americans started migrating from America's southern states, they headed straight here.

Instead of heading for the somewhat touristy Sylvia's Restaurant on 125th, try the M&G Soul Food Diner on West 125th at Morningside Avenue for a truly traditional southern meal to the background sounds of great soul singers (page 169).

And it's no wonder really. Brits are frequently shocked to discover that the blacks may have been freed from slavery by the end of the 19th century, but there was still segregation until the 1960s. Black

Grant's Tomb in Harlem

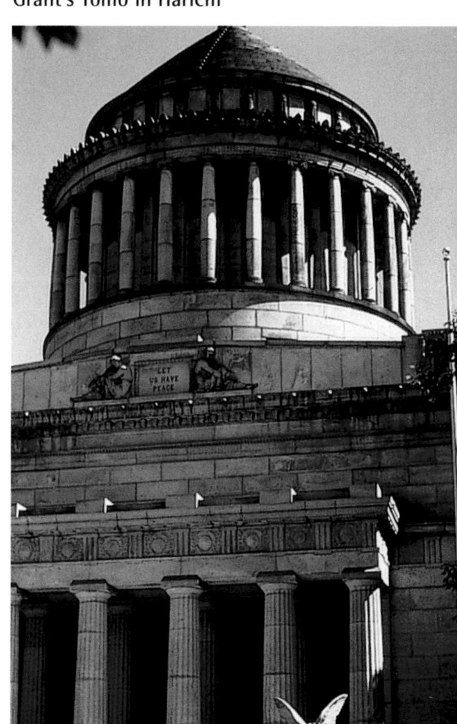

people were not allowed to sit on the same benches as whites, they had to drink at different water fountains and in church they were forced to wait until after the whites for Communion. When great black musicians such as **Duke Ellington** and **Louis Armstrong** went on tour, they had to stay at black-only hotels and eat at black-only restaurants.

Back in Harlem, at least, there was some semblance of belonging and thanks to the influx of political activists, professionals and artists to the area following the opening of the subway lines between 1904 and 1906, many African-American organisations had sprung up by the early 1920s. They included the **National Urban League**, which helped people who were moving into the area to get training for jobs, and the **White Rose Mission**, which helped African-American female migrants coming to New York from the South. They were followed by the political **Universal Negro Improvement Association** and the **Union Brotherhood of Sleeping Porters**, whose leader Phillip Randolph was at one time considered by the government to be the most dangerous black in America.

THE GLORY DAYS OF HARLEM

The 1920s and 1930s were a great time for the neighbourhood, filled as it was with poets, writers, artists, actors and political activists. The combination of prohibition and great jazz musicians such as **Count Basie, Duke Ellington** and **Cab Calloway** made famous nightspots like the **Cotton Club** attractive to the upper middle classes who came in their droves to enjoy Harlem's speakeasies.

But all this was hardly doing anything for the lot of the average African-American who lived in the area. The speakeasies were strictly for whites only and even **WC Handy**, who co-wrote a song with Duke Ellington, was not allowed into the Cotton Club to hear it being played for the first time. Then there was the matter of the racism on **125th Street** – Harlem's epicentre which runs from Frederick Douglas Boulevard to Malcolm X Boulevard. The white-owned shops and hotels here, which were used by the African-Americans, were staffed by whites and it was impossible for blacks to get anything but the most menial jobs.

In 1934 Adam Clayton Powell Junior, preacher at the Abyssinian Baptist Church, organised a boycott of these businesses, entitled Don't Buy Where You Can't Work. The campaign was successful and the shops started hiring blacks. You can still see the remnants of those businesses along 125th.

You can start your experience of Harlem with a tour round the **Apollo Theater** on 125th (page 182), which was the focal point for African-American entertainment between the 1930s and 1970s. Known for its legendary **Amateur Night**, which is now broadcast on TV, it has launched the careers of Ella Fitzgerald, Marvin Gaye, James Brown and even The Jackson Five.

At the corner of 7th Avenue stands the former **Theresa Hotel**, now an office block, but which was once considered to be the Waldorf of Harlem. Back in the days of segregation **Josephine Baker** stayed in the penthouse with its vaulted ceiling and views of both rivers. Malcolm X's Unity organisation was based here in the 1950s and 1960s and in a show of support for African-Americans, Fidel Castro moved his entire entourage to the Theresa when he came to New York in 1960 for a United Nations conference.

A little further down the street is **Blumsteins**, once the largest department store in Harlem. With its dilapidated frontage and peeling paintwork, it's now hard to imagine this as once being the Macy's of the area.

Another major epicentre for Harlem is up on 135th to 137th Streets between Powell Boulevard and Malcolm X Boulevard. You can either walk from 125th Street or take the 2, 3 subway to 135th Street station. Once there you'll find yourself right outside the **Schomburg Center**, which chronicles the history of black people in North America, South America and the Caribbean. Opposite is the **Harlem Hospital Center** where Martin Luther King was operated on after being shot. It was the first hospital in New York to be integrated.

To experience the life and times of Harlem, pick up a copy of *Harlem's Culture: Guide to Great Events,* available at cultural institutions such as the Schomburg Center.

For soul food, try Miss Maude's Spoonbread, Malcom X Boulevard (Lenox Avenue) at 137th Street or visit Manna's Too at 134th Street (or Manna's at 8th Avenue and West 125th Street) for a great selection of well-priced fresh foods and drinks.

A couple of blocks north and you'll find the famous **Abyssinian Baptist Church** at 132 West 138th Street. It was originally founded in 1808, and as the blacks moved from the Lower East Side to Greenwich Village, then up to the West 50s and 60s before finally finding a home in Harlem, the church moved with them. This church was built in 1923 and, with Adam Clayton Powell Junior as its preacher for many years before he became a senator, it was a centre of political activity, particularly in the 1920s.

To experience a gospel choir in action, THE place to go is the Abyssinian Church on 138th Street, but you'll need to arrive early because it gets packed. Another great place is the Second Canaan Baptist on 110th Street and Lenox Avenue.

One block west on 138th and 139th Streets between Powell and Frederick Douglas Boulevards are the four rows of Stanford White houses built in 1891 and known as Striver's Row because this is where the middle and upper classes strove to live. The houses were filled by doctors, lawyers, nurses from Harlem Hospital, jazz musicians and politicians such as Malcolm X. Boxer Harry Wills, known as the Brown Panther, lived here. He was paid $50,000

A terrific variety of tours of Harlem are available from Harlem Heritage Tours (tel 212-280 7888, www.harlemheritagetours.com).

not to fight Jack Dempsey when the mayor banned the fight because he thought a black boxer fighting a white man would lead to riots.

The alleys at the back of these buildings were originally created for parking horses and carriages. Houses were usually built back to back so the alleys are a rarity, but a boon for the current occupants to park their BMWs. You can still see the old signs that say 'Walk your horses' or 'Park your carriages'.

DECLINE AND FALL

Sadly, the good times didn't last long and, from the 1940s to the 1960s, Harlem declined into an urban no-man's land as a result of a lack of government support and racial conflict. The once-fine apartment blocks grew shabbier as landlords were either too unscrupulous or unable to afford to maintain them on the cheap rental income.

If you're concerned about wandering the streets of Harlem by yourself, try either a Big Onion walking tour (page 78) or a Harlem Spirituals bus tour (page 74).

Eventually City Hall and certain businesses started investing in the area. In 1976 the City began reclaiming properties abandoned by landlords who couldn't afford to pay their taxes. You can still buy one of these blocks for $1 if you have the $2 million needed to renovate it. Fortunately, a lot already have been refurbished and with the influx of banks and even Starbucks, a small but important step towards 'gentrification' is taking place.

For some time the brownstones of **Hamilton Heights** and other local neighbourhoods have been targeted by those trying to escape the substantial rents elsewhere in Manhattan. There have been other developments, too. Former president **Bill Clinton** has his offices on 125th Street between Lenox and 5th (the one with the huge Gap advert down the side). He's always been a favourite with African-Americans because he did a lot for racial equality and was invited to move his offices to Harlem from Carnegie Hall. Former baseball star **Magic Johnson** has also been doing much to encourage a sense of pride in the community.

RENAISSANCE

Now many people are predicting a renaissance for Harlem and suggest house prices could sky-rocket within the next few years, though it's unlikely that would help the really poor people. Old nightspots once frequented exclusively by the African-Americans have also been bought up and are being earmarked for renovation, including the **Renaissance Ballroom**, once a neighbourhood institution. Everyone would watch the Harlem Rennies basketball team early in the evening, then clean up to hit the nightclub. It was shut in the 1940s, but is now owned by the Abyssinian Church who are hoping to renovate it.

Another major venue was **Small's Big Apple** jazz club. Its sister establishment, **Small's Paradise**, was a restaurant in the 1930s and 1940s. It was so popular and the dance floor so small that it was said people had to dance on a dime here. It enjoyed a revival from the 1960s and was where Professor du Bois, who once ran the National Association for Advancement of Coloured People, held a birthday party in the 1980s. It closed in the same decade, but is now owned by the Abyssinian Church and there's a chance it may reopen as a tourist centre.

HAMILTON HEIGHTS

The Hamilton Heights neighbourhood (Map 6) is up on the high ground north of Morningside Heights and is effectively the middle-class enclave of Harlem. It takes its name from **Alexander Hamilton**, the first secretary of the treasury to the newly formed United States of America. He lived here from 1802 until he was killed in a duel in 1804.

The area is now the home of **City College**, one of the senior colleges in the New York university system. It was founded in the 19th century to educate the children of the working classes and immigrants and used to be known as the poor man's Columbia. It used to be free, but now it charges $3,200 per year, though that is still a lot cheaper than private universities in America, which charge an average of $27,400 per year.

Further north on West 145th Street off Amsterdam is the area known as **Sugar Hill**, which was made famous in the Duke Ellington song *Take the A Train to Sugar Hill*. Now a conservation area, it is filled with beautiful brownstone townhouses, and was dubbed Sugar Hill because life here was considered to be so sweet.

Battery Park harbour

CHAPTER 4

Seeing the Sights

The major sights are often the number one priority – especially for the first-time visitor – so, to try to make your life a little easier, I have indicated the location of each of the following sights. I suggest that you read Chapter 3 first so you get a good feel for each of the neighbourhoods and that way you can make the most of your time by planning your days in specific areas of the city. For instance, if you plan to see the Empire State Building, bear in mind it is deep in the heart of the 34th Street shopping district. The section entitled Orientation (page 23) will also help you make sense of the streets of New York and get to know the intricacies of the grid system and the distances involved.

PART ONE – THE SIGHTS

This section tells you the Top 10 must-see sights, plus all the major sights in New York. You can either visit them under your own steam or take advantage of the many and varied tours that are listed in the second part of this chapter.

TOP 10 SIGHTS

To help you organise your days better, I have listed what I consider to be the Top 10 sights of Manhattan. Whatever else you do when you are in New York, these are the ones you mustn't miss.

1. **Empire State Building** – 34th Street (page 61)
2. **Statue of Liberty** – ferry from Battery Park (page 60)
3. **Ellis Island Immigration Museum** (with Statue of Liberty page 60)
4. **Central Park** – (pages 127 and 219)
5. **Times Square** – Midtown West (pages 49 and 66)
6. **Rockefeller Center and Radio City Music Hall** – Midtown (page 65)
7. **South Street Seaport** – Financial District (page 66)
8. **Grand Central Station** – Midtown East (page 68)
9. **The Winter Garden** – Battery Park City (page 70)
10. **Cathedral of St John the Divine** – Upper West Side (page 70)

Security at many sights and buildings has been tightened following the tragic events of September 11, so allow extra time for this when planning your schedules.

The Statue of Liberty

A–Z OF SIGHTS

CENTRAL PARK

Think of New York and Central Park is likely to spring to mind. It's the New Yorkers' playground and a wonderful place to spend time during your stay. For a complete description of the park and all its facilities, see page 219. For family fun and activities, see page 127.

ELLIS ISLAND IMMIGRATION MUSEUM AND THE STATUE OF LIBERTY

Battery Park

☎ 212-269 5755
www.statueoflibertyferry.com

🚗 Statue of Liberty and Ellis Island Ferry, which leaves every 20 minutes from Gangway 5 in Battery Park. Subway 1, 9, 4, 5 to Bowling Green

🕘 9am–3.30pm

$ $10 adults, $8 seniors, $4 children (4–12), under 3s free. No credit cards

The Statue of Liberty, one of the biggest attractions in New York, was closed following September 11 but reopened on August 3, 2004. It is reached by a ferry, which also takes you to the Ellis Island Museum where you learn the immigration story of America. Ferry tickets are sold at Castle Clinton, the low circular brownstone building in Battery Park (open 9am–3.30pm). Luggage, including backpacks, is not permitted and the security checks can take up to an hour.

TICKET TO RIDE

The CityPass is an excellent way to avoid long queues and save money if you visit at least three of the participating attractions. These are the American Museum of Natural History, the Empire State Building and New York Skyride, the *Intrepid* Sea-Air-Space Museum, the Guggenheim Museum, the Museum of Modern Art and a harbour tour with the Circle Line. You can buy a CityPass from any of the attractions, which will save you queueing again. Prices are $48 (a saving of $46.50 on normal admission prices) for adults and $34 for 12–17s (saving $35.50). Call 707-256 0490 or visit **www.citypass.com**. You can also buy your CityPass through NYTAB at **www.nytab.com**.

The Statute of Liberty originally came to New York in 1886, as a gift from France. You can enjoy the panoramic views from the observation deck, about 16 storeys above ground, and tour the museum in the pedestal. The rest of the statue will continue to be off-limits, however, including the statue's interior spiral staircases, but you can stroll along the promenade above the star-shaped former fort on which the statue and its pedestal rise some 30 storeys above the harbour.

Don't spoil your day of sightseeing by missing the boat. The last Statue of Liberty and Ellis Island Museum boat leaves at 3.30pm (4pm at weekends) and the museum closes at 5.30pm.

The Statue of Liberty café is extremely small and there are simply not enough loos. There is space to eat outside, but not very much. At Ellis Island, however, you'll find plenty of WCs on all the different levels, a large café and a huge amount of outdoor seating that looks right out over to the Statue of Liberty and the skyscrapers of Lower Manhattan.

The Ellis Island Immigration Museum is the most visited museum in New York, particularly beloved by crowds of Americans who want to see where their immigrant ancestors arrived. In use from 1892 to 1954, it 'processed' up to 10,000 immigrants a day. Each person was examined and then interviewed to find out if they could speak English. An unfortunate two per cent were turned away.

When leaving the Statue of Liberty to go on to Ellis Island DO NOT get on the ferry that takes you to New Jersey. That is on the left. It IS clearly signposted, but it is very easy to get disorientated!

Visitors follow the immigrants' route as they entered the main baggage room and went up to the Registry and then the Staircase of Separation. Poignant exhibits include photos, video clips, jewellery,

FREE SIGHTS AND ATTRACTIONS

1. **Cathedral of St John the Divine** – Upper West Side (page 70)
2. **Central Park** – (pages 127 and 219)
3. **Federal Reserve Bank** – Financial District (page 67)
4. **Gracie Mansion** – Upper East Side (page 68)
5. **Grand Central Station** – Midtown East (page 68)
6. **New York Public Library** – Midtown (page 69)
7. **Rockefeller Center** – Midtown (page 65)
8. **South Street Seaport** – Financial District (pages 66 and 124)
9. **Staten Island Ferry** – Battery Park (page 66)
10. **Times Square** – Midtown West (page 49)
11. **The Winter Garden** – Battery Park City (page 70)
12. **Woolworth Building** – Civic Center/Financial District (page 69)

clothing, baggage and the stark dormitories. The Immigrant Wall of Fame lists half a million names, including the grandfathers of Presidents Washington and Kennedy.

This is a great museum and well worth allocating a good portion of your day to. All the films and the guided tour are free. The Ranger Tours last 45 minutes and leave at 11am, 2pm, 3pm and 4pm. At 2pm there is a re-enactment of a board of inquiry, which decides an immigrant's fate. Immigrants tell their stories in the movie *Island of Hope, Island of Tears*, which runs frequently in two theatres. Free tickets are available at the desk. A play, *Ellis Island Stories*, is also presented frequently. Tickets are $2 and $3.

The museum is very well laid out, has lots of benches everywhere and is so big it never feels too crowded. There is a cashpoint (ATM) in the corridor on the way to the café, which is on your right as you enter the building. The café is a little pricey but you can bring your own picnic and sit outside and enjoy the fabulous views.

The tour, film and play on Ellis Island are free but you need to get tickets for each of them from the information desk (just to the left on your way in). Busiest times are obviously just after a boat has arrived, so try to be the first off the ferry and head straight for the desk.

EMPIRE STATE BUILDING

34th Street

✉ 350 5th Avenue at 34th Street
☎ 212-736 3100
www.esbnyc.com
🚗 Subway B, D, F, Q, N, R, V, W to 34th Street
🕘 9.30am–midnight, last lifts go up at 11.15pm
$ $12 adults, $11 seniors, $7 children (6–11), under 6s free. No credit cards

It is hard to believe that the Empire State, which was for almost 40 years the world's tallest building, was nearly not built at all. Just weeks after its building contract was signed in 1929, the Wall Street Crash brought the financial world to its knees. Fortunately, the project went ahead and was even completed 45 days ahead of schedule, rising to 443m (1,454ft) in 1931. The lobby interior features Art Deco design incorporating rare marble imported from Italy, France, Belgium and Germany.

There are two observation decks, one on the 86th floor and another on the 102nd floor. Sadly, the higher deck is now closed. Your best bet is to arrive as early in the morning as possible to avoid long waits for tickets. Weekends, of course, get really crowded. Once you reach the 86th floor you can enjoy some fabulous views of Manhattan and the outer boroughs and really get your bearings. If you like you can hire the ESB Audio Tour for $5. You buy your tickets on the concourse level below the main lobby, but don't have to use them on the same day.

Fancy a coffee when you're in the Empire State Building? To avoid the pricey snack bars, get back down to ground level and visit Starbucks next door.

The **New York SkyRide** is on the second floor and is open seven days a week 10am–10pm. It simulates a thrilling flight around the skyscrapers and bridges of New York. Entrance $17.50 adults, $16.50 youths (12–17) and seniors, $15.50 children (5–11). For a combined New York Skyride and Empire State Building ticket, the prices are $24 adults, $22 seniors and youths, $18 children. Call 212-279 9777 or visit **www.skyride.com**.

GROUND ZERO – MEMORIAL FOUNDATIONS AT WORLD TRADE CENTER

Financial District

✉ West Street between Liberty and Vesey Streets

☎ **www.groundzero.nyc.ny.us**

🚘 Subway N, R, W to Cortlandt Street; 1, 9 to Rector Street

After a lengthy public consultation, in 2002 the Lower Manhattan Development Corporation (LMDC) began a worldwide search for a suitable design concept for the 6.5-hectare (16-acre) former World Trade Center site. There were 400 submissions from around the globe, which were whittled down to seven and exhibited at the Winter Garden. More than 100,000 visitors saw the exhibition - generating 8,000 comments - and another eight million looked at the plans on the internet. Finally, after three public meetings, Studio Daniel Libeskind's Memory Foundations design was chosen in early 2003.

If you've a CityPass booklet (page 60), you can avoid the ticket queues at the Empire State Building by going directly to the first floor. Walk straight past the crowds on the ground floor and turn right to go up one flight.

NEW YORK PASS

As well as the CityPass, the New York Pass offers discounted entry to over 40 sights as well as giving discounts and extras at a range of shops and restaurants and for some tours, plus free access to the subway and buses. Phone 212-977 8680 or visit **www.newyorkpass.com**.

Originally, Libeskind planned to divide the 'superblock' formed by the World Trade Center into four parts. His plan included a sunken memorial site on the spot where the Twin Towers had stood, and around the memorial he envisioned five irregularly shaped towers of which the tallest would be a 541-m (1,776-ft) towering spire of glass called the Freedom Tower.

Eventually, Libeskind redesigned the towers to be slimmer, taller and squarer, in order to provide more office space. Then, the site developer brought in architect David Childs, who changed Libeskind's glass Freedom Tower into a larger, heavier building but retained the spire. Wind turbines will harness the wind and generate the building's energy. The occupied portion will be 60 storeys high.

Radio City Music Hall

Always carry water around with you whether you are sightseeing or shopping. No matter what the weather, it is incredibly easy to get dehydrated. Take a small bottle and refill along the way.

In January 2004, a jury chose Michel Arad's memorial design, which differed from Libeskind's. It includes a forest of trees planted throughout a plaza around the footprints of the Twin Towers; reflecting pools deep within the footprints, with constantly falling water to mark the voids; exposure of the bedrock-and-slurry wall to reveal the scale of the site and the disaster; and chambers for unidentified remains of the dead, as well as relics of the disaster. Peter Walker, a Californian landscape architect, will design a park on the broad, open street-level plaza.

Santiago Calatrava, designer of the transportation hub, has incorporated Libeskind's Wedge of Light feature. His steel-and-glass train station will allow a shaft of light to fall between its wings without a shadow each year on September 11 between the hours of 8.46am, when the first plane hit, and 10.28am, when the second tower collapsed, in perpetual tribute to altruism and courage.

The design concept will be built in several phases, but will include better street and pedestrian layouts, better connections between subway and PATH train systems, easily accessible shops and restaurants at street level, particularly along Fulton and Church Streets, and better bus and car parking. There will be a mix of office space, shops and other amenities.

MADAME TUSSAUD'S

Times Square

✉ 234 West 42nd Street
☎ 800-246 8872
www.madame-tussauds.com
🚗 Subway A, C, E, 1, 2, 3, 7, 9, N, Q, R, S, W to Times Square/42nd Street
🕘 Daily 10am–8pm. Last tickets 6pm
$ $25 adults, $19 children (4–12)

Madame Tussaud's has been spreading its wings around the globe and has recently opened attractions in Las Vegas, Hong Kong, and this one in New York. If wax models (extremely well done) are your thing, it is worth visiting this sight in the heart of New York's Times Square as the celebs portrayed reflect personalities synonymous with the city, such as Woody Allen, Leonard Bernstein, Jacqueline Kennedy Onassis, John D Rockefeller, Yoko Ono, Donald Trump, Andy Warhol and former mayor Rudolph Giuliani among others.

Nasdaq Marketsite

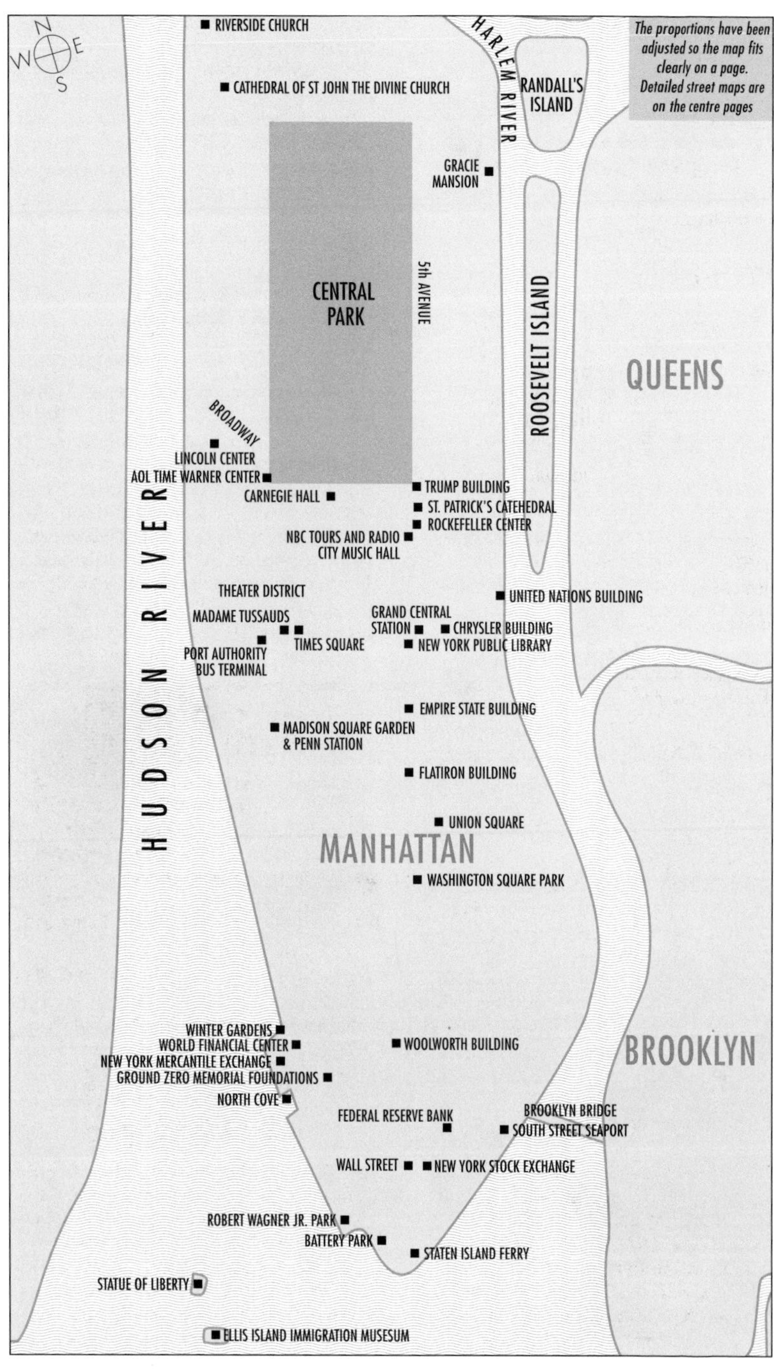

Major sights in Manhattan

NASDAQ MARKETSITE

Times Square

✉ 4 Times Square between 43rd Street and Broadway
☎ 877-627 3271
🚗 Subway 1, 2, 3, 7, N, Q, R, S, W to 42nd Street/Times Square

This wall of light soars seven storeys above Broadway, but it is no longer open to the public for tours.

NBC TOURS

Rockefeller Center/Midtown

✉ Lobby level of 30 Rockefeller Plaza
☎ 212-664 7174
🚗 Subway B, D, F, V to 47th–50th Streets/Rockefeller Center
🕐 Mon to Sat 8.30am–5.30pm
$ $17.75 adults, $15.25 seniors and children (6–16), no children under 6. For a small extra fee, combine with Rockefeller Center Tour (right).

You get a 30-minute look behind the scenes at NBC, the major television network headquartered in New York.

RADIO CITY MUSIC HALL

Midtown at 6th Avenue

✉ 50th Street and 6th Avenue
☎ 212-247 4777
www.radiocity.com
🚗 Subway B, D, F, V to 47th–50th Streets/Rockefeller Center
🕐 Tours Mon to Sat 10am–5pm, Sun 11am–5pm
$ $17 adults, $14 seniors, $10 for under 12s.

While you're at the Rockefeller Center you won't want to miss out on this fabulous building, which has been fully restored to its original Art Deco movie palace glory and is utterly beautiful. This is where great films such as *Gone With The Wind* were given their premieres and it has the largest screen in America. Make a point of visiting the loos – they have a different theme on each floor, from palm trees to Chinese and floral. There are even cigar-theme loos for the boys. The tour takes you around the whole building and you get to meet a Rockette.

To see the Radio City Music Hall, you have to buy your ticket in the morning to find out what time your tour is. It is well worth planning your day around. Or you can now see it as part of the Rockefeller Center Tour.

ROCKEFELLER CENTER

Midtown

✉ Midtown at 5th Avenue – West 48th to West 50th Streets between 5th and 6th Avenues
☎ 212-632 3975
www.RockefellerCenter.com
🚗 Subway B, D, F, V to 47th–50th Streets/Rockefeller Center

Built in Art Deco style in the 1930s, the Rockefeller Center was named after the New York benefactor whose fortune paid for its construction. As well as Radio City Music Hall, it houses opulent office space, restaurants, bars, shopping on several levels and even gardens. To help you find your way round the 19 buildings that make up the complex, collect a map at the lobby of the main building (30 Rockefeller Center). The central plaza, a restaurant in summer, is turned into an ice rink in winter, and a massive Christmas tree with 8km (5 miles) of fairy lights draws huge crowds.

Lovers of the Metropolitan Museum shops can get their fix at one of its branches in the heart of the Rockefeller Center. It's just off the main plaza by the ice rink.

You can either wander around the plaza with the aid of the map or take the 75-minute Rockefeller Center Tour. This takes in The Channel Gardens, Radio City, the ice rink, NBC and more, while giving an insight into the Center's history, architecture and

You must write for tickets for TV tapings months (sometimes years) in advance, but you can join the crowd outside *The Today Show's* walled studio Mon to Fri 7am–10am at 49th Street and Rockefeller Plaza. For other TV shows you can attend, visit www.nycvisit.com. Click on 'Visitors' and 'Things to Do'.

more than 100 pieces of artworks that create the world's most amazing public collection of Art Deco.

Tours hourly Mon to Sat 10am–5pm, Sun 10pm–4pm. Prices $10 adults, $8 children (6–16). Reservations are necessary and can be made by calling 212-632-2975.

SOUTH STREET SEAPORT

Financial District

✉ Water Street to the East River between John Street and Peck Slip
☎ 212-732 7678
🚗 Subway A, C, J, M, Z, 2, 3, 4, 5 to Fulton St/Broadway Nassau

You don't have to go into the South Street Seaport Museum (page 124) to get a feeling of the maritime history of the city – the ships are all around you. So are the shops. The Seaport is a rare New York approximation of a typical American shopping mall. Most shops are open Mon to Sat 10am–9pm, Sun 11am–8pm, and there are dining options at all prices, indoors and out, some with a view of the Brooklyn Bridge. The port is also home to the 150-year-old Fulton Fish Market, which brings the entire area to (somewhat smelly!) life from midnight to 8am. From April to October tours are available at 6am on the first and third Wednesdays of the month, though you must reserve your $12 tickets in advance. Tel 212-748 8590.

STATEN ISLAND FERRY

Battery Park

✉ Ferry Terminal, Battery Park
☎ 718-815 2628
🚗 Subway 4, 5 to Bowling Green; R, W to Whitehall Street
$ Free

Probably the best sightseeing bargain in the world, it passes close to the Statue of Liberty and gives dramatic views of Downtown. Runs regularly 24 hours a day.

TIMES SQUARE AND THE THEATER DISTRICT

Another iconic area of New York and a must-see place. Full details of what to see and do here are given in Chapter 9, Shows, Bars and Nightlife.

THE OUTER BOROUGHS

BRONX ZOO

A wonderful zoo, which combines conservation and ecological awareness with Disney-style rides and a children's zoo. Further details are given on page 233.

NEW YORK BOTANICAL GARDEN

Home to the Bronx River Gorge, it not only gives a fascinating insight into the geological history of New York, but also has acres and acres of beautiful gardens. Further details are given on page 233.

Grand Central Station

HISTORIC RICHMOND TOWN AND ST MARK'S PLACE, STATEN ISLAND

The two top historical sights on Staten Island, both give a unique insight into the New York of yesteryear. Further details are given on page 238.

BUILDINGS OF NOTE

BROOKLYN BRIDGE

This Gothic creation was considered one of the modern engineering feats of the world when it was completed in 1883 after 16 long years of construction, and at the time was both the world's largest suspension bridge and the first to be built of steel.

For a completely different 'insider' view of the modern-day history of Brooklyn Bridge, try Gary Gorman's Brooklyn Bridge VIP Tour (page 77). A former member of the NYPD, he relates fascinating stories of talking down would-be suicide victims.

The original engineer, John A Roebling, died even before the project began and his son, who took over, had to oversee the building from his Brooklyn apartment after being struck down by the bends. In all, 20 people died during the construction of the bridge. Take the A or C train to High Street station and stroll back along the walkway – a great way to see some incredible views of the Downtown skyscrapers.

CHRYSLER BUILDING

Midtown East

✉ 405 Lexington Avenue at 42nd Street

🚗 Subway S, 4, 5, 6, 7 to Grand Central/ 42nd Street

Opened in 1930, this was William van Alen's homage to the motor car. At the foot of the Art Deco skyscraper are brickwork cars with enlarged chrome hubcaps and radiator caps. Inside, see its marble and chrome lobby and inlaid-wood elevators. Its needle-like spire is illuminated at night and the building vies with the Empire State for the prettiest-of-them-all crown.

Just across the way from the Federal Reserve Bank is probably the poshest McDonald's in the world at 160 Broadway. It has doormen, a chandelier and a grand piano upstairs.

FEDERAL RESERVE BANK

Financial District

✉ 33 Liberty Street between William and Nassau Streets

☎ 212-720 6130

www.ny.frb.org

🚗 Subway 2, 3, 5 to Wall Street

Yes, this really is the place where billions of dollars' worth of gold bars are stashed (as stolen by Jeremy Irons in *Die Hard 3*) on behalf of half the countries of the world, and where money is printed. Security, as you can imagine, is tight, but you can still do a free one-hour tour that takes you deep into the underground vaults, providing you phone at least seven days in advance. Your name will be placed on a computer list, but the minimum age is 16. Passport or picture identification is essential.

The UN and Chrysler Buildings

FLATIRON BUILDING

Flatiron District

✉ 175 5th Avenue between 22nd and 23rd Streets

🚗 Subway F, V, N, R, 6 to 23rd Street

The Renaissance palazzo building was the first-ever skyscraper when it was completed in 1902 and is held up by a steel skeleton.

GRACIE MANSION

Yorkville

✉ Carl Schurz Park, 88th Street at East End Avenue

☎ 212-570 4751

🚗 Subway 4, 5, 6 to 86th Street

🕘 Tours March to Nov on Wed only 11am–2pm

$ $7 adults, $4 seniors

Now the official residence of the mayor, you must phone ahead to make an appointment to see it. The tour takes you through the mayor's living room, a guest suite and smaller bedrooms. The best part, though, is the view down the river.

GRAND CENTRAL STATION

Midtown East

✉ East 42nd Street between Lexington and Vanderbilt Avenues

🚗 Subway S, 1, 2, 3, 4, 5, 6, 7, 9, N, Q., R, to Grand Central/42nd Street

Even if you're not going anywhere by train, this huge, vaulted station, which was opened in 1913, is well worth a visit. A $196-million, two-year renovation programme was recently completed and the ceiling once again twinkles with the stars and astrological symbols of the night skies, and the chandeliers, while the marble balusters and clerestory windows gleam in the main concourse. Inside you will find a Mediterranean restaurant, Michael Jordan's Steakhouse and a cocktail lounge modelled on a Florentine palazzo. The lower level dining concourse offers inexpensive meals and take-aways, while main floor shopping outlets include Banana Republic, Godiva

If you go to Grand Central Station on a Friday at 12.30pm, you can go on a tour sponsored by the Grand Central Partnership. Meet outside the station in front of the Whitney Museum offshoot. Tel 212-697 1245

chocolates and Kenneth Cole. Complete your trip to this elegant edifice by tucking in at the Oyster Bar.

MADISON SQUARE GARDEN'S ALL ACCESS TOUR

34th Street

✉ 4 Pennsylvania Plaza

☎ 212-465 6741 **www.thegarden.com**

🚗 Subway A, C, E, 1, 2, 3, 9, D, F, B, V, N, Q, R, W to 34th Street/Penn Station

$ $17 adults, $12 children (12 and under)

This is the round building that sits right on top of Penn Station and the entrance is on 7th Avenue between 32nd and 33rd Streets. It occupies the site of the original Pennsylvania Station, an architectural masterpiece that was even more beautiful than Grand Central Station, but which was razed in the 1960s. (One good thing came out of its destruction, though, the creation of the Landmarks Preservation Commission, which has helped to protect many buildings and areas in New York from developers.)

If you plan to see the Empire State Building, do the New York Skyride and take in Madison Square Garden's one-hour All Access Tour, buy a combination discount ticket for $33 adults, $21 for children (5–11) from either the New York Skyride or Madison Square Garden box offices. You'll save $4.50 and $3.50 respectively.

Madison Square Garden's arena is ten storeys tall, covers 3.24 hectares (8 acres) and is famous for its circular ceiling, which is suspended by 48 bridge-like cables. Every year it hosts 500 events from concerts to boxing, wrestling, basketball and hockey, bringing in five million people. Its most famous residents are the New York Knickerbockers basketball team (known as the Knicks), the New York Rangers ice hockey team and the New York Liberty women's pro basketball team.

Below the arena are the theatre, exhibition centre, box office and two club restaurants. Incidentally, this is actually the fourth Madison Square Garden building. The first two were built at Madison Square on the site of the current New York Life

Building, the third was built on 8th Avenue between 49th and 50th Streets, where the Worldwide Plaza stands. This building opened in 1968 with a gala featuring Bob Hope and Bing Crosby.

During the course of the one-hour tour, you will hear about its history, see the inner workings and the Walk of Fame, and gain access to the locker rooms of both the Knicks and the Rangers.

MORRIS JUMEL MANSION

Harlem

⊠ Roger Morris Park, 65 Jumel Terrace at 160th Street

☎ 212-923 8008
www.morrisjumel.org

🚗 Subway A, C to 163rd Street

🕐 Wed to Sun 10am–4pm

$ $3 adults, $2 seniors and children (over 12)

Built by British colonel Roger Morris in 1765, this is the oldest house in Manhattan. It was confiscated by George Washington in 1776 and briefly used as his war headquarters until the Brits kicked him out of New York. Charles Dickens visited it, and if you want to see a really historical sight so should you.

NEW YORK PUBLIC LIBRARY

Midtown

⊠ 5th Avenue between 40th and 42nd Streets

☎ 212-592 7000

🚗 Subway B, D, F, V, 7 to 42nd Street

Opened in 1911, this is one of the best examples of the city's Beaux Arts architecture. Inside you'll find more than 8.5 million volumes guarded by the twin marble lions of Patience and Fortitude. The steps up to the library are a sun trap during the day and serve as a meeting place. Alternatively, they make a great place for a sandwich or drink stop.

Visit the library on a Monday afternoon from June to August (Tuesdays if it rains) and you can enjoy free outdoor movies and other events at Bryant Park (page 220). Tel 212-512-5799.

NEW YORK STOCK EXCHANGE

Financial District

⊠ 20 Broad Street at Wall Street

☎ 212-656 3000

🚗 Subway 4, 5 to Wall Street; J, M, Z to Broad Street

Amazing fact: the stock exchange was founded by 24 brokers meeting beneath a tree; now more than 1,300 members crowd on to the building's trading floor. It's still an interesting place to visit. At the time of going to press, the stock exchange was closed to the public, though this may change, so call to check.

TRUMP TOWER

Midtown

⊠ 5th Avenue between 56th and 57th Streets

🚗 Subway F, N, R, Q, W to 57th Street

Donald Trump's monument to opulence includes an extravagant pink marbled atrium with waterfalls and plenty of upmarket shops. This is not to be confused with Trump International Hotel and Tower at Columbus Circle.

UNITED NATIONS BUILDING

Midtown East

⊠ 1st Avenue and 46th Street

☎ 212-963 4440 for tour reservations,
www.un.org

🚗 Subway 4, 5, 6, S, 7 to Grand Central/42nd Street

🕐 Mon to Fri 9am–4.45pm, Sat and Sun 10am–4.30pm (not at weekends Jan and Feb)

$ $10 adults, $7.50 seniors, $5.50 students and children (5–14)

Tours of the General Assembly, the Economic and Social Council and other areas every half hour. Despite its fame, this is not the most exciting tour in the world! No children under 5.

WOOLWORTH BUILDING

Civic Center/Financial District

⊠ 233 Broadway at Park Place

🚗 Subway 2, 3 4 to Park Place; N, R to City Hall

There is no official tour of the city's second skyscraper, which was built in 1913 at a cost of $13.5 million, but it's worth taking a sneak look inside the lobby. Incidentally, one-time shop assistant FW Woolworth's building was derided as a 'cathedral of commerce' when it opened, but the millionaire took this as a compliment. Just to prove a point, he can be seen counting his money in the carved ceilings.

WINTER GARDEN AT THE WORLD FINANCIAL CENTER

Battery Park City

✉ 250 Vesey Street at West Street
☎ 212-945 0505
www.worldfinancialcenter.com
🚗 Subway 1, 2, 3, 9, A, C to Chambers Street; N, R to Cortlandt Street

The World Financial Center is actually the main focal point for the northern end of Battery Park City, a strip of land running down the west side of Lower Manhattan from Chambers Street to South Park. It was created by landfill from the digging work required to build the foundations for the World Trade Center. The World Financial Center has a complex of four office towers, but is most famous for the beautiful glass-roofed Winter Garden that looks right over the pretty boats moored in North Cove. Filled with fabulous palm trees, it houses upscale shops including Anne Taylor, Urban Athletics and Gap Kids. Damaged on September 11, it has been repaired and reopened for business. The Hudson River

The Winter Garden is not just a pretty place to enjoy a drink or two – it also holds a series of free concerts and fairs.

Club, which has fabulous views over the harbour, is pricey (around $12 a drink) but is a great place to have Sunday brunch. Or save your cents and enjoy the free summer events held outdoors. Check the website for schedules.

The Woolworth Building

RELIGIOUS BUILDINGS

CATHEDRAL OF ST JOHN THE DIVINE

Upper West Side/Morningside Heights

✉ 1047 Amsterdam Avenue at 112th Street
☎ 212-316 7540
www.stjohndivine.org
🚗 Subway 1 to 110th Street
🕗 Mon to Sat 7am–6pm, Sun 7am–8pm. Public tours Tues to Sat at 11am and on Sun at 1pm
$ Free, but tours cost $5 adults, $4 seniors and students

The world's largest Gothic cathedral has one of the world's biggest rose windows with 10,000 pieces of glass. Even more amazing are the main bronze doors, which weigh 3,000 tonnes each and are only opened for an official visit by the bishop. An Episcopal church built in 1892, its grounds cover 4.9 hectares (12 acres) of land and include a school and accommodation for the clergy. A lot of people will tell you that the church, according to its original plans, is still not complete. The reality is the building never will be 'finished' because the church funds are channelled into helping the poor and needy. Still, it's not as if they are ever going to run out of space. It has a capacity to seat 3,000 people, but because it holds so many art and performing art events, they have chairs rather than pews.

One of the highlights of the cathedral's calendar is the Feast of Assisi when real animals including an elephant and a llama are taken up to the altar to be blessed by the cathedral clergy. Inspired by St Francis of Assisi, whose life exemplified living in harmony with the natural world, the feast usually takes place on the first Sunday in October.

At the back of the cathedral, behind the main altar are seven different chapels, which represent different countries in Europe. These are used for weddings, christenings and the services (at least two a day). The shop is also at the back on the left-hand side and money raised from it is put towards the church's housing and other ministries. There are plenty of WCs at the back of the shop along with drinks machines for general use.

It is appropriate to tip your tour guide around 15 per cent of the cost of the ticket, but don't feel obliged if you've not been over-impressed.

RIVERSIDE CHURCH

Morningside Heights

⌧ Riverside Drive between 120th and 122nd Streets

Subway 1, 9, B, C to 116th Street

Famous for having the world's largest tuned bell and its Carillon Concerts on Sundays at 3pm. You can also go for the great views of Upper Manhattan and the Hudson River. Nearby is the Union Theological Seminary at West 120th and Broadway. Woody Allen uses this façade in many of his movies.

ST PATRICK'S CATHEDRAL

Midtown

⌧ 5th Avenue and 50th Street
www/ny-archdiocese.org/pastoral

Subway 6 to 51st Street and E, V to 5th Avenue/53rd Street

The seat of New York's Roman Catholic Archdiocese, the cathedral was begun in 1857 and the stained-glass windows weren't completed until l930. However, the magnificent results have definitely been worth the wait.

The steps leading up to St Patrick's form a perfect picnic spot for a lunch or snack stop.

PART 2 – THE TOURS

Time is a precious commodity when visiting New York, so you need to make sure that any tour you take pays for itself both financially and in terms of time. Your choice of tours will depend on whether it is your first or second visit or you are a repeat visitor. Newcomers need to get their bearings and two ways of doing this are to take a boat tour and a bus tour. The boat trip goes in a semi-circle around Manhattan from Midtown on one side to Midtown on the other; the bus tour, such as Gray Line's Manhattan Essential New York tour, is known as New York 101 (101 being slang for a first-year university course) because it covers so much of the city in one day. An alternative is the New York Visions tour, which takes a lot less time, is cheaper and is generally more fact-filled.

Bus tours are useful when you want to visit an area such as Harlem or the Bronx, but are unsure of your personal safety, in which case the Harlem Spirituals/New York Visions tours are your best bet. Then there are helicopter tours, which will certainly give you breathtaking views, but won't show you the full ins and outs of each area.

St Patrick's Cathedral

If you take a tour of New York, you are likely to hear the word 'stoop'. This is taken from a Dutch word by original settlers and refers to the steps up to a townhouse, such as a brownstone – another New York term, this time for much sought-after townhouses, though they are as likely to be made out of grey stone as brown stone.

The reality is that the best way to see New York, get to know the city and find those interesting nooks and crannies is on foot, which possibly explains why the Big Onion Walking Tours are so popular – or it could be that they are just so darned good – and why so many people take advantage of the Big Apple Greeters, who can show you any area or sight you wish to visit. Taking a selection of these sorts of tours is definitely a good idea for first and second timers, and given the broad selection of Big Onion tours available, there'll probably be one to interest you each time you go back. There is also a wide choice from bike tours to gangland tours and a reasonable selection of food tours. The following categories of tour have been put in alphabetical order for ease of use. Within each category I have started with what I consider to be the most important or useful tours to go on.

AIR TOURS

LIBERTY HELICOPTER TOURS

Chelsea

✉ VIP Heliport, West 30th Street and 12th Avenue

☎ 212-967 6464
www.libertyhelicopters.com

🚗 Subway A, C, E to 34th Street/Penn Station

Rides over the Hudson River range from $58.50 (5–6 minutes) to $164.50 (16–17 minutes). For $849, eight people can ride in a private helicopter for a tour that flies over the whole of Manhattan.

BIKE TOURS

CENTRAL PARK BICYCLE TOURS AND RENTALS

Colombus Circle

✉ 59th Street and Broadway

☎ 212-541 8759

🚗 Subway A, B, C, D, 1, 2 to Columbus Circle/59th Street

$ $35 adults, $20 children (15 and under) includes bike rental

A two-hour bike tour of Central Park from April to November at 10am, 1pm and 4pm that includes stops at Shakespeare Garden, Strawberry Fields, Belvedere Castle and other sights, plus bike rentals for your own use.

Once you have your bike, don't feel you have to cycle everywhere as you can take bikes on the subway.

CANAL STREET BICYCLE SHOP

Chinatown

✉ 6th Avenue at Canal Street

☎ 212-334 8000

🚗 Subway A, C, E to Canal Street

Rent your bike and head off to the Financial District, which is usually almost deserted on a Sunday.

THE HUB

SoHo

✉ Broome and Thompson Streets

☎ 212-965 9334

🚗 Subway A to Canal

Tandems, recumbents and electric bikes along with standard types. Open daily 11am–11pm, Sun noon–11pm.

METRO BICYCLE

Upper West Side and Upper East Side

✉ 96th Street at Broadway and 87th Street at Lexington

☎ 212-766 9222/212 427 4450

🚗 Subway 1, 2, 3, A, C, B, D to West 96th Street, 4, 5, 6 to East 87th Street

If you want to check out the Upper West Side along the river or the Upper East side, rent here. (They have other locations, too.)

You can also rent bicycles in Central Park. See Chapter 12, page 222.

PONYCABS

SoHo

✉ 517 Broome Street at Thompson Street

☎ 212-254 8844

🚗 Subway C, E to Spring Street, N, R to Prince Street

$ $15 for 30 minutes, $30 an hour

Technically not bicycles, but three-man tricycles or 'pedicabs' (one 'driver' to pedal and two passengers!). So amazing looking that even seen-it-all-before New Yorkers stop to stare. That may be a little off-putting for some, but I found it an excellent way to see SoHo without breaking into a sweat or breaking the bank! You may even be able to hail one of these after the theatre in the Times Square area. Don't forget to tip – 'drivers' earn their money! In good weather only. You can either reserve in advance and arrange a meeting point or turn up at the hub.

BOAT TOURS

CIRCLE LINE

West Midtown

✉ Pier 83, West 42nd Street

☎ 212-563 3200

🚗 Any subway to 42nd Street, then transfer to an M42 bus heading west

$ Prices start from $26 adults, $13 for 12s and under

Choose from a three-hour full island, semi-circle or sunset/harbour lights cruises. Or you can take a three-hour Latin DJ dance cruise, a full-day cruise to Bear Mountain ($45 adults, $30 for 12s and under) or Liberty Island cruises.

Alternatively, you can go for a spin on *The Beast*, a speedboat that takes you on a quick and memorable tour. Sights fly by as you reach a speed of 64kph (40mph) and stop at the Statue of Liberty for photos. May to Oct daily on the hour 10am–7pm ($16 adults, $10 children).

NY WATERWAY

Financial District

✉ Pier 78 at West 38 Street and 12th Avenue

☎ 800-533 3779

🚗 Any subway to 42nd Street, transfer to M42 bus heading west

$ Harbour cruise prices start at $10 adults, $10 children, and go up to $25 adults, $12 children

Offers a wide variety of sightseeing options all the year round, including New York Harbor cruises and evening cruises with on-board entertainment. Also available in the summer are daytrip cruises to Sandy Hook Beach and, for baseball fans, cruise packages that include a round-trip sail on the Yankee Clipper or Mets Express, tickets, souvenirs and the ubiquitous hot dog.

The harbour cruises are very informative and give a great insight into Manhattan and beyond, but it can sometimes be hard to hear when you're on the upper deck. If you want to hear everything, it's probably best to stay inside.

BATEAUX NEW YORK

Chelsea

✉ Pier 61 at Chelsea Piers

☎ 212-352 2022
www.spiritcruises.com

🚗 Subway C, E, 1, 9, 4, 5, 6 to 23rd Street, transfer to cross-town bus heading west

$ Brunch ticket $46, dinner $100–110, tax included

Indulge in a dinner (7pm–10pm daily) or brunch (noon–2pm weekends) while cruising around Lower Manhattan.

WORLD YACHT DINNER CRUISES

Midtown West

✉ Pier 81 at West 41st Street and Hudson

☎ 212-630 8100

🚗 Any subway to 42nd Street, then transfer to an M42 bus heading west

🕘 Daily except for Jan to Mar Fri–Sun only; board at 6pm, sail 7–10pm

$ From $85 for the prix fixe meal, including a three-hour cruise with dancing to live music from Sun to Thurs, $95 on Fri and Sat

With menus created by a selection of New York's best chefs, linen tablecloths, live music, a dance floor and world-class videos, this is an upmarket experience you are sure to enjoy. The cruise lasts three hours and also provides spectacular views of the harbour. Note that the dress code is smart and that jackets are required, so make sure you allow yourself plenty of time to put on your glad rags.

BUS TOURS

HARLEM SPIRITUALS/NEW YORK VISIONS

Midtown

✉ 690 8th Avenue between West 43rd and West 44th Streets

☎ 212-391 0900
www.harlemspirituals.com

🚗 Subway A, C, E, 1, 2, 3, 7, 9, S, N, Q, R, S, W, B, F, D, V to 42nd Street/Times Square

One of the most reputable tour companies in New York, the guides are highly qualified, great founts of knowledge and very friendly, while the buses are modern and comfortable with the all-important air-conditioning. Tours by the Harlem Spirituals include:

Harlem Gospel Tour: A combined walking (though not too far!) and riding tour of Harlem on Sunday and Wednesday during which you attend a church service, hear a gospel choir and have the option of having lunch or brunch at a soul food restaurant. Prices are $46 adults/$79 with meal, $29 children (5–11)/$65 with meal. Tours start at 9am on Wed and 9.30am on Sun, finishing at either 1.30pm or 2.30pm with meal.

Soul Food And Jazz: A chance to relive the heyday of Harlem, thanks to the return of jazz to the area. This combines a walking and riding tour through Harlem's historical sites with a soul food meal and the chance to see a jam session at a local jazz club. Tours are available on Mon, Thur and Sat 7pm–midnight and cost $99 for adults and children.

The New York Visions run: **New York New York** – an excellent four-hour introduction to all the major sights including Times Square, Central Park, Rockefeller Center, Greenwich Village, SoHo, Little Italy, Chinatown and the Wall Street area. Tours leave on Mon and Thur to Sat at 9.30am. Prices are $45 adults, $29 children. Pay an extra $11 (adults and children) and you also get tickets for the ferry to the Statue of Liberty and Ellis Island Immigration Museum (you'll be dropped off at Battery Park) plus an MTA Fun Pass for 24-hour use on the subways and buses (page 27).

Bronx and the Cloisters (a selection of medieval art and architecture) on Sat, **Downtown & Brooklyn** on Tues and the **Triborough Tour** of Manhattan, the Bronx and Brooklyn also on Tues.

Hansom cab ride

GRAY LINE NEW YORK SIGHTSEEING

West Midtown

✉ The Gray Line New York Sightseeing Center, 777 8th Avenue between 47th and 48th Streets
☎ 800-669 0051
www.graylinenewyork.com
🚗 Subway C, E to 50th Street
🕒 Daily 8.30am–5pm
$ $35–89

The oldest sightseeing bus company in New York, it has much to offer, although the average tour guide gives very little information in comparison with the New York Visions tours. Still, if you don't want to be overwhelmed by information on your first visit to New York, then try the Essential New York Tour ($72 adults, $51 children). A double-decker bus tour with 40 hop-on, hop-off stops, it comes with a choice of one-hour harbour cruises or ferry with close-up views of the Statue of Liberty and Ellis Island, a ticket to the Empire State Building and a Fun Pass to New York's subway and bus systems.

Gray Line also offers 'Loops', which run around Downtown, Midtown, uptown and Brooklyn. You can do as few or as many as you like, so you can spend as long as you want in each area, giving you plenty of flexibility. Three hours is $37; best value is a 48-hour pass for $49.

The Showbiz Insiders Tour ($89) is an 8½-hour daily extravaganza giving a behind-the-scenes look at New York's TV and Broadway shows. You'll visit the New Amsterdam Theater, home of *The Lion King,* before taking the Stage Door Tour at Radio City Music Hall and lunch at Planet Hollywood. The tour ends with a private performance given by a current Broadway actor and the opportunity for some photos and autographs.

ON LOCATION TOURS

Upper East Side

☎ 212-209 3370
www.sceneontv.com

The best company in New York for fun and informative bus tours around the sights and attractions seen in two of the city's most famous shows, *Sex and the City* and *The Sopranos,* plus a general TV and movie tour. Details are as follows:

Sex And The City

✉ Bus outside the Plaza Hotel in 5th Avenue at 59th Street
🚗 Subway 4, 5, 6, to 59th Street/ Lexington Avenue, N, R, W to 5th Avenue
🕒 Mon to Fri 3pm, Sat 10am and 3pm, Sun 10.30am and 3pm
$ $35

Here's a chance to check out the stomping grounds of the girls from *Sex and the City* even after the show has ended. During the three-hour bus tour, you'll visit D&G in SoHo, where Carrie shopped for shoes, and the New York Sports Club where Miranda worked out, plus bars such as O'Neil's and Tao where Carrie, Samantha, Charlotte and Miranda did their flirting. Most important of all, you'll get some behind-the-scenes scoops on the show and the actors. This is a really fun experience, which gets into the spirit of the show and gives everyone plenty of browsing and chatting opportunities. You'll also get to eat a cupcake from the famous Magnolia Bakery, though be warned, they are incredibly sweet! By the end, you should be fluent in *Sex and the City*-speak and know your Manhattan Guy (a genetically mutant strain of single man that feeds on Zabar's and midnight shows at Angelika) from your Trysexual (someone

The Blue Note jazz club

who will try everything once) or a 'We' Guy (a man who refers to your potential future relationship by using 'we' statements such as 'we' can cook etc, thus faking a future with you to get what he wants in the present). This tour is busy, so book at least a week in advance.

The Sopranos

✉ Bus departs from the 'Button' statue on 7th Avenue at 39th Street
🚗 B, D, F, V to 42nd Street; N, Q, .R, S, W, 1, 2, 3, 7 ,9, S to Times Square
🕘 Sat and Sun at 2pm
$ $30

Get the 'shakedown' on a tour of 15 sites used in *The Sopranos* including Satriale's Pork Store, the cemetery where Livia Soprano is buried, the Bada Bing nightclub and the diner where Chris was shot. The three-hour tour also includes a guide to New Jersey Mafia-speak, a stop for cannolis – traditional Italian pastries – and six other stops along the way. The tours tend to sell out quickly, so it's best to reserve as far in advance as possible.

Manhattan TV and Movie Tour

✉ Bus departs from Ellen's Stardust Diner, 1650 Broadway at 51st Street
🚗 Subway 1, 9 to 50th Street, N, W, R to 49th Street
🕘 Daily in summer or Thurs to Sun 11am
$ $30

Takes you to 65 different locations seen in TV shows and movies such as *Friends, You've Got Mail, Ghostbusters, The Bill Cosby Show* and Woody Allen's *Manhattan*.

92ND STREET Y

Upper East Side

✉ 1395 Lexington Avenue
☎ 212-996 1100
www.92y.org
🚗 Subway 4, 5, 6 to 86th Street
$ Prices vary

A Jewish organisation that caters to all aspects of Jewish life, it also runs a wide selection of tours covering many secular aspects of city life. They will create a customised tour for you if you prefer.

CEMETERY TOURS

✉ Meet at Jekyll & Hyde Restaurant, 91 7th Avenue South
☎ 212-679 9777/800-394 8633
www.cryptkeepertours.com
🚗 Subway 1, 9 to Sheridan Square
🕘 Mon to Thurs, 7 and 10pm, Sun 3 and 6pm
$ $45

Okay, so technically this is not a bus tour, as your mode of transportation is a hearse, but it still has wheels and travels on roads... As the title indicates, you'll get a three-hour, detailed tour of New York's cemeteries, visiting gravesides of well-known VIPs, celebrities, politicians and sports stars. So, enjoy!

Pace yourself. There's no point in trying to pack so much into your day that you arrive back at your hotel exhausted with your head spinning. Less can often be more!

INSIDER TOURS

Some of the most interesting New York tours are led by residents who have unique inside perspectives that they are willing to share on everything from shopping to the nitty gritty of how the FBI was involved in bringing down Mafia boss 'Teflon Don' John Gotti. Here is a fascinating selection:

GANGLAND TOURS

Lower East Side

✉ Meet at Lansky Lounge, 104 Norfolk Street
☎ 646-610 3661
www.ganglandtours.com
🚗 Subway J, F, M, Z to Delancey Street
🕘 Mon to Thurs, 7 and 10pm, Sun 3 and 6pm
$ $100 per person (minimum three people); $35 each (minimum two people) for a walking tour at a convenient place and time

Take advantage of the fact that it's easy to get a table at a Lower East Side restaurant between 6 and 7pm and eat first, as this tour kicks off at 8.30pm and lasts about an hour and a half. Your 6-ft tall guide Paul Zukowski greets you in his three-piece pinstripe and spats shoes outside Lansky Lounge, the former hangout of gangster Meyer Lansky. While Paul drives you round the Lower East Side and the Village in a white stretch limo, he'll regale you with details of the gangsters who lived, worked and died on the streets of New York. Despite the sometimes grim subject matter, it's absolutely fascinating.

VIP TOUR OF NYPD SITES

☎ 718-769 1495
nyccoptours@aol.com
$ From $75 (individual and group rates on request)

Born in Brooklyn, your guide Gary Gorman is a former cop who shares a lifetime of knowledge and experience on the organisation and workings of the New York Police Department on this three-hour tour by car. You'll be shown all the major sights from the Mounted Unit HQ to the 9th Precinct (used in *Kojak* and *NYPD Blue*) and more. A charming and hugely knowledgeable guide, Gary makes this a brilliant way to spend an afternoon.

FOODS OF NEW YORK

Greenwich Village

☎ 212-209 3370/917-408 9539
www.foodsofny.com
🕘 Tues to Sun 11am–2pm
$ $36.50 per person

A great-value tour, considering the amount of food you eat along the way, with a friendly atmosphere as they only take a maximum of 16.

In the unlikely event you still feel peckish after the food tour, head back to Fish at 280 Bleecker Street where you can have six oysters and a glass of wine or beer at the bar for an unbelievable $8.

In Greenwich Village you'll stop to sample the wares of Zito's old-fashioned bread shop, Murray's famous cheese shop and Faicco's world-famous pork shop, and you'll end up at Vintage New York on Broome Street, where you get the chance to taste five wines from New York State. And, as well as all you'll learn about the food of New York, especially of the Italian community, you'll gain hints about architecture and properties in the Village and visit a real speakeasy. Alternatively, you can choose to go on a tour of the Chelsea Gourmet Food Market and the West Village Meatpacking area (Fri to Sun).

MYSTICAL WORLD OF HASSIDIC JEWS

Brooklyn

✉ Hassidic Discovery Welcome Center, 305 Kingston Avenue
☎ 718-953 5244
www.jewishtours.com
🚗 Subway 3 to Kingston Avenue
🕘 Sun 10am–1pm for individuals or Sun to Fri for groups
$ $36 adults, $18 children (12 and under) includes a delicatessen lunch

It's easy to get to the Hassidic Discovery Welcome Center by the 3 train (the red line), but allow about an hour from Midtown. The subway exit is right by the synagogue and you simply walk a few yards up Kingston Avenue to two brown doors just by a bookshop. There is no dress code, but it would be inappropriate for women to turn up in a sleeveless top.

The Lubavitcher Jews in Crown Heights, Brooklyn, are focused on sharing what they have with the outside world, providing a unique opportunity to get an insight into a Hassidic community. Guided by Rabbi Beryl Epstein – a person with a charming manner and great sense of humour – you'll hear about the history of the Hassidic Jews; visit the synagogue to learn about some of the Jewish customs and traditions; watch a scribe working on a Torah scroll; and see the Rebbe's library, a Matzoh bakery and a Hassidic art gallery. A real insight into a fascinating culture.

The Kingston Avenue subway stop for the Hassidic tour is just one away from Eastern Parkway, the stop for the Brooklyn Museum of Art and the Botanical Gardens – both great places to visit on a Sunday afternoon (pages 230–31).

KRAMER'S REALITY TOUR
West Midtown

✉ The Producer's Club, 358 West 44th Street between 8th and 9th Avenues
☎ 212-268 5525
www.kennykramer.com
🚗 Subway A, C, E to 42nd Street/Penn Station
🕐 Sat at noon, Sun (on holiday weekends) at noon
$ $37.50

The real Kramer behind the *Seinfeld* character has come out of the woodwork and invented his own three-hour tour based on all the *Seinfeld* spots in the city. Kenny Kramer will answer questions, share backstage gossip and the real-life incidents behind the show.

SAVOR THE APPLE
Village and Harlem

✉ PO Box 914, Ansonia Station, New York, NY 10023
☎ 212-877 2903
$ Prices vary

Marlayna gives her personal tours of different parts of the city, but is particularly knowledgeable about Greenwich Village, the East Village and Harlem, where she has many contacts.

SAVORY SOJOURNS
Chelsea

✉ 144 West 13th Street
☎ 212-691 7314
www.savorysojourns.com
$ $85–165

For a unique insight into the fine foods and culinary skills of some of New York's finest restaurants, Savory Sojourns promises to give you an insider's guide to New York's best culinary and cultural destinations followed by a great slap-up meal. Areas covered include Upper East Side, Chinatown, Little Italy, Greenwich Village, Flatiron and Chelsea Market.

WALKING TOURS

BIG ONION WALKING TOURS
Brooklyn

✉ 476 13th Street, Brooklyn, NY 11215
☎ 212-439 1090
www.bigonion.com
🕐 Wed to Sun (June to August), Thurs to Sun (September to May) 1pm. Always call after 9am on the morning of your tour to verify schedule as it will change if the weather is bad
$ $12 adults, $10 students and over 60s

Amazingly informative ethnic, architectural and historic walking tours, which you can just turn up to. Led by American history

Liberty and Broadway junction

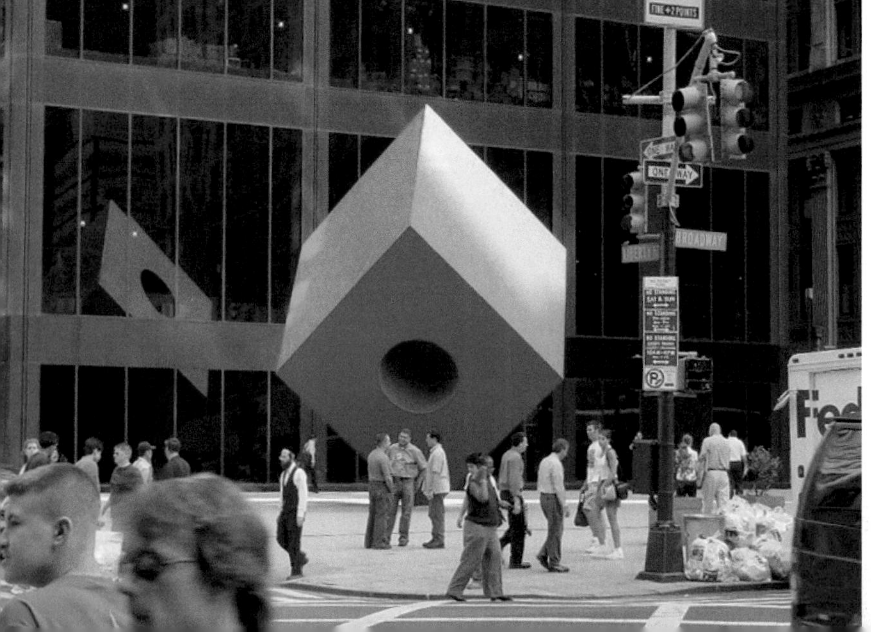

Fishing in East River

graduates, they're not for the faint-hearted – you'll be on your feet for a full two hours – but they are informative and gem-packed. Tours are offered on a rotating basis and begin in different spots. Call the main number to see what's on the schedule. Options include the East Village, Central Park, Gay New York, Financial District, Gramercy Park and Union Square, Greenwich Village, Historic Lower Manhattan, Historic TriBeCa, the Jewish Lower East Side, Presidential New York, Revolutionary New York, Roosevelt Island, SoHo and NoLiTa and the Upper East Side. 'Big Onion' was the nickname given to New York in the 19th century by non-New Yorkers who believed it smelled of the immigrants' heavily spiced cooking!

Some Big Onion tours can get a little crowded. If so, make sure you stand as close to the guide as possible to hear their pearls of wisdom and you'll still get good value for money.

Big Onion's Multi-ethnic Eating Tour: Meet on the corner of Essex and Delancey Streets. Subway J, M, Z to Essex Street, F to Delancey Street.

This is one of the more popular tours, which covers the Lower East Side, Chinatown and Little Italy, and it is offered frequently. You pay a $4 supplement for the food, which includes delicious spicy tofu, mozzarella and Italian sausage, chicken and shrimp and vegetarian dim sum, plus other food favourites of the locals, all eaten outdoors in the streets. The tour also provides a good way to get an insight into areas you may find confusing to wander around in on your own.

If you need to visit the loo before you start this tour, head for the McDonald's diagonally opposite the meeting point.

Circle Line cruise

It gives a fascinating insight into the history of the area and what modern-day life is like – for instance what was once a very high-density Jewish area is now populated by Puerto Rican immigrants. And before the Jews and Chinese, there were the English, Irish and Italians.

You'll end the tour deep in the heart of Chinatown outside a vegetarian food centre and the Chinese Gourmet Bakery. It may be good to stop for a drink before you head off to the nearest subway stations at Canal Street, where you have the choice of the A, C, E, J, M, N, Q, R, W, 6 lines to take you just about anywhere in Manhattan.

Big Onion's Historic Harlem Tour: Meet at the Schomburg Center at 135th Street and Lenox Avenue. Subway 2, 3 to 135th Street.

A brilliant way to get to know a major chunk of Harlem, its history, politics and modern-day life through the eyes of a history graduate.

For a cheap and delicious meal before the Harlem tour, head for Manna's Too on Lenox Avenue at 134th Street. After the tour you'll find yourself outside the Apollo. Just a few metres east is a clean McDonald's with TVs on one wall (and a loo on the opposite side).

You'll hear about Martin Luther King and other African-American activists, local literary salons and gospel churches. You'll learn about the old neighbourhood joints of the Renny and Savoy, how the Apollo and Cotton Clubs were only open to rich white folk looking for an 'authentic black' experience, the campaign to allow black people to work in the shops they bought their food and clothes from, Striver's Row, the architecture and the old black pressure groups, two of whose buildings now house beauty parlours.

Gangs of New York Tour: Meet on the south-east corner of Broadway and Chambers Street at City Hall Park, Sundays at 1pm. Subway 1, 2, 3, 9, A, C to Chambers Street.

This very popular tour is (like the movie of the same name) inspired by Herbert Asbury's 1927 classic book *The Gangs of New York*, which explores every aspect of the city's dark and brutal gang culture that had its epicentre at Five Points.

Led in conjunction with Miramax Films, the tour paints a vivid and detailed picture of life for the immigrants in the 1800s and includes stops at Paradise Square, Murderer's Alley and other sites associated with Bill 'The Butcher' Poole, William Tweed and the police and draft riots. Before you get too carried away with any notions of glamour, just bear in mind that the area then was so unsafe the police refused to go anywhere near it. There was at least one murder a night and ordinary people were so scared of leaving their tenements they even buried their dead in their buildings.

LITERARY PUB CRAWL

West Village

✉ Meet at the White Horse Tavern, 567 Hudson Street at 11th Street
☎ 212-613 5796
🚗 Subway A, C, E, L to 14th Street
🕐 Saturdays at 2 pm

Tour four pubs in the Village area that attracted writers, poets and artists, among them Dylan Thomas, Ernest Hemingway, John Steinbeck, e e cummings, Jack Kerouac, Jackson Pollock and Frank McCourt.

TALK-A-WALK

✉ 30 Waterside Plaza, NY 10010
☎ 212-686 0356
Fax 212-689 3538
$ $9.95

Walking tour guides on cassettes – they're an excellent way to learn about the city. It's best to order them before you leave home and they will be posted to you. There is a choice of four, each looking at the history and the architecture of historic Downtown.

ADVENTURE ON A SHOESTRING

☎ 212-265 2663
🕐 Every day, rain or shine
$ $5

The 'granddaddy' of walking tours, Adventure has been going strong for 41 years, offering 90-minute tours of many Manhattan neighbourhoods as well as outlying areas that are less familiar to tourists, such as Astoria, the Greek section of the borough of Queens, and Hoboken, a new artists' center in New Jersey. Two of the most popular tours are **Haunted Greenwich Village** and **Hell's Kitchen**. Theme tours, such as those based on **Marilyn Monroe's New York** and **Jacqueline Kennedy Onassis's New York** are also favourites.

GREETINGS FROM THE BIG APPLE

It's certainly a novel idea and it's also a winner – the Big Apple Greeters are ready to take you on a personalised and entirely customised tour of any part of New York any day of the week and it costs absolutely nothing. The idea is simple: New Yorkers who are proud of their neighbourhoods and have some spare time will spend between two and four hours with you. They will take you round any area you like and help you do just what you want to do, be it shopping, sightseeing or eating and drinking, rain or shine. Just make your request at least ten working days in advance and confirmation will be awaiting you upon your arrival at your hotel. The service is entirely free and no Big Apple Greeters worth their salt will take a tip, but I found that it was no problem to get them to agree to letting me pay for a spot of brunch or lunch. And they're well worth it. Tel 212-669 8159, fax 212-669 3685, email **bigapple@tiac.net, www.bigapplegreeter.org**

ALLIANCE FOR DOWNTOWN NEW YORK

Financial District

✉ Tours start at the steps of the National Museum of the American Indian, 1 Bowling Green

☎ 212-606 4064
www.downtownny.com

🚗 Subway 4, 5 to Bowling Green

🕐 Thurs and Sat at noon

Free walking tour for individuals and groups exploring the 'birthplace' of New York, including the Customs House, Trinity Church, Wall Street and the Stock Exchange, among others. The Alliance has been doing much work on sprucing up the entire district and employs red-hatted security/cleaners who are there to help you find your way around.

JOYCE GOLD HISTORY TOURS OF NEW YORK

Chelsea

✉ 141 West 17th Street

☎ 212-242 5762
www.nyctours.com

🕐 Various starting times for 2–3 hours

$ $12

Specialists in unusual, in-depth weekend forays into many of the city's distinctive neighbourhoods. Fascinating tours include the East Village, culture and counter-culture, Downtown graveyards and Greenwich Village highlights.

MUNICIPAL ART SOCIETY

Midtown

✉ 457 Madison Avenue between East 50th and East 51st Streets

☎ 212-935 3960/212-439 1049
www.mas.org

🚗 Subway 6 to 51st Street

$ $12 weekdays, $15 weekends

Walking tours taking in both historical and architectural sights. Well-run, informative and very enjoyable. Telephone or visit their website for more information.

BRIT'S GUIDE AWARDS FOR SIGHTSEEING TOURS

Best overview of city:
By bus: New York Visions (page 74)
By boat: Circle Line (page 73)

Most exciting experience:
The Gangland Tour, by stretch limo (page 76)

Best walking tours:
The Big Onion (pages 78–80)

Best for thrills:
The Beast speedboat (page 73)
Liberty Helicopter Tours (page 72)

Most eye-opening experiences:
VIP Tour of NYPD Sites (page 77)
The Mystical World of Hassidic Jews (page 77)

Best for foodies:
Foods of New York around Greenwich Village and Chelsea Gourmet Market (page 77)

Best for free:
Big Apple Greeters (see above)

Best TV Show tours:
Sex and the City (page 75)
Kramer's Reality Tour (page 78)

Most offbeat:
Ponycabs (page 73)

Best musical tours:
Harlem Gospel Tour (page 74)
Soul Food And Jazz (page 74)

ON THE LOOKOUT FOR SEX IN THE CITY?

Hey, we can't guarantee you'll get the fabulous lifestyle of the *Sex and the City* girls Carrie Bradshaw, Samantha Jones, Charlotte York and Miranda Hobbs but we can give you an insight into it.

Shopping

Patricia Field Boutique (page 90): Patricia Field is the designer who created all of the fabulous fashion for the TV series, so anyone who emulates Carrie's style has to pay a visit. You can stock up on the cool bags and jewellery that the cast have worn, in particular the Mia and Lizzie diamond horseshoe necklaces that Carrie has been seen in. In the basement you'll find a bijou beauty counter with a complete guide to the make-up used by Carrie, Charlotte, Samantha and Miranda. Choose your favourite!

Tracey Feith (page 90): When Sarah Jessica Parker wore one of Feith's red and blue silk creations in the series, the shop sold out of the style in days.

Manolo Blahnik (page 92): No true *Sex and the City* experience would be complete without wearing a pair of towering Manolo heels. Check out the SJP ankle-strap stiletto named after the show's star. SATC trivia: SJP is petite as petite can be, yet her shoe size is 7½ (6½ in UK sizes)!

Jimmy Choo (page 92): Another favourite of Carrie's, Jimmy's shoes are so exclusive they are only sold in four Jimmy Choo shoe shops around the globe, plus a few Saks and Bergdorf Goodman stores.

Bars

Monkey Bar: 60 East 54th Street between Madison and Park Avenues. Tel 212-838 2600. Subway E, V to 5th Avenue. Area: Midtown. The venue Mr Big and Carrie chose to discuss how to stay 'just friends' after their affair. It's very upmarket – think dark wood and a resident pianist – plus it has original murals of frolicking monkeys dating back to the 1930s.

Tortilla Flats: 767 Washington Street at West 12th Street. Tel 212-243 1053. Subway 1, 9 Christopher Street. Area: West Village. The ice-breaking date between Carrie and Aidan, accompanied by Miranda and Steve, was filmed at this Mexican party spot. Margaritas are the fashionable tipple here.

Restaurants

Park View at the Boathouse (pages 174–5): The episode where Mr Big and Carrie fell into the boating lake was shot in Manhattan's oasis of calm, Central Park. The Boathouse is often cited as one of the most romantic places in town by those in the know. You can have dinner, rent a boat or act like the locals and sip a drink while the sun goes down over the skyscrapers.

Eleven Madison (page 165): One of New York's hottest eateries, this is where Mr Big chose to tell Carrie he was getting married to Natasha (the stick with no soul) over dinner. Carrie had one too many Cosmopolitans, the girl's favourite cocktail, and fell down the stairs as she walked out.

Nightclubs

Tunnel: Sadly, you can no longer recreate the episode where Carrie and the girls decided they didn't want to stay in on a Saturday night and headed off to a gay club, as it has closed. However, you could try one of the other gay clubs on pages 197–202.

Other locations

The Church of the Transfiguration (page 46): Also known as The Little Church Around The Corner, this was the location for shooting the 'Friar F**k' episode, though on the show it was called the All Souls Center. The Episcopal church – famous for being a haven for actors – got a nice donation towards a wall renovation for its trouble. SATC trivia: nearly all the show's scenes are filmed on location in New York except for when they are in their apartments or eating. The only two places that refused to be used for filming are the Hudson Hotel and the *Intrepid* Sea-Air-Space Museum!

Meisel Gallery: In Prince Street just off West Broadway, this is where Charlotte worked. The show paid $18,000 for the first shoot in the gallery, $28,000 for the second and $37,000 for the third. In the end, the producers decided to find Charlotte a new job!

Also... the **Blue Water Grill** on Union Square and 16th Street (page 164) is where Miranda said she was an 'everything but girl', **Luna Park Café** in the middle of Union Square (page 45) is where Carrie met up with Stamford, and **Faicco's Sausage Store** in Cornelia Street (page 103) is where Samantha wanted to spank her boyfriend before going up to his apartment. For organised tours around the girls' haunts, see page 75.

CHAPTER 5

Shopping

For many people New York equals shopping. Yes, there are jaw-dropping buildings, amazing museums and exciting nightlife, but when it comes down to it New York City is one of the best places in the world to indulge in a spot of retail therapy. You can get a taste of fantastic American service at the fabulous and famous department stores, and shop until you drop for cheaper CDs, clothes, shoes and cameras. Although New York City does have real American malls like the one at the South Street Seaport, it is better known for its many boutiques.

The distinct atmosphere of each New York neighbourhood is reflected in the type of shopping available there. The upper section of 5th Avenue in the Midtown area is where you will find all the top department stores and other posh shops. Even posher – exclusive, actually – is **Madison Avenue**, which is where the top American and European designers such as Prada, Valentino and Versace are based.

New Yorkers in the know head to Aaron's in Brooklyn at 627 5th Avenue (tel 718-768 5400, www.aarons.com) where you can buy in-season women's designer fashions with up to 33 per cent discount.

The Villages are excellent for boutique shops that tend to open late but stay open late, too. In **Greenwich Village** you'll find jazz records, rare books and vintage clothing

5th Avenue at 53rd Street

and the West Village's tree-lined streets are full of fine and funky boutiques and popular restaurants that cater to a young, trendy crowd. On the major shopping streets of Bleecker, Broadway and 8th, you'll find everything from antiques to fashion and T-shirt emporiums. There are plenty of up-and-coming designers and second-hand shops in the **East Village**. Try 9th Street for clothes and 7th for young designers.

The **Flatiron District** around 5th Avenue from 14th to 23rd Streets is full of wonderful old buildings that are brimming with one-of-a-kind shops and designer boutiques. **SoHo** has lots of boutiques selling avant-garde fashion and art, plus restaurants and art galleries, all housed in handsome cast-iron 1850s buildings. West Broadway is the main drag, but other important streets include Spring, Prince, Green, Mercer and Wooster. High-profile recent openings include Prada and Earl Jean.

In **TriBeCa** you will find trendsetting boutiques such as the fantastic Issey Miyake flagship store, art galleries and restaurants in an area that combines loft living with commercial activity.

Last but not least is the **Lower East Side**, which is to bargains what Madison Avenue is to high-class acts. Many of the boutiques offer fashion by young designers – some of whom go on to open outlets in the posher areas – and famous-name gear at huge discounts. This whole area reflects the immigrant roots of New York and stands out as a bargain hunter's paradise particularly when the market is open on Sundays. Orchard Street from Houston to Delancey Streets is well known for leather goods, luggage, designer clothes, belts, shoes and fabrics. Ludlow Street is famous for trendy bars, and boutiques filled with clothes by up-and-coming designers.

TAXES AND ALLOWANCES

US taxes: You will have to add local taxes on to the cost of your purchases – this can add anything from 7 to 9 per cent, depending on where you are buying. (New York sales tax is 8.25 per cent, though it has now been dropped on clothes and shoes costing under $110.)

UK allowances: Your UK duty-free allowance is just £145 and, given the wealth of shopping opportunities, you're likely to exceed this, but don't be tempted to change receipts to show a lesser value as, if you are rumbled, the goods will be confiscated and you'll face a massive fine. In any case, the prices for some goods in America are so cheap that, even once you've paid the duty and VAT on top, they will still work out cheaper than buying the same item in Britain. Duty can range from 3.5 to 19 per cent depending on the item: for example, computers are charged at 3.5 per cent, golf clubs at 4 per cent, cameras at 5.4 per cent and mountain bikes at a massive 15.8 per cent. You pay this on goods above £145 and then VAT of 17.5 per cent on top of that.

Duty free: Buy your booze from US liquor stores – they're better value than the airports – but remember your allowance is 1 litre of spirits and two bottles of wine.

TOP TIPS FOR SHOPPING

To save yourself time and money when shopping in the Big Apple follow these tips:

➡ If you're on a really tight schedule, call ahead and book appointments with the **personal shoppers** at major stores. They're very helpful and their service is absolutely free. Bargain! Call Macy's on 212-695 4400 and Bloomingdale's on 212-705 2000.

➡ Alternatively, you can arrange to go on a shopping tour of everything from Saks Fifth Avenue to discount-hunting at Century 21. Joy Weiner of **Shopping Tours of New York** plans customised shopping tours for groups of one to 15 or more by taxi, limo or minivan. Call 212-873 6791 for more information. Another personal shopping service is provided by **Intrepid New Yorker**, tel 212-534 5071.

➡ You have a right to a **full refund** on goods you return within 20 days with a valid receipt unless the shop has signs saying otherwise. Always check, though, especially if the item is in a sale.

➡ Call in advance for **opening hours**. Smaller shops downtown – in SoHo, the Villages, Financial District and Lower East Side – tend not to open until noon or 1pm, but are often open as late as 8pm. Many are also closed on Mondays.

➡ You can **put items on hold** for a day or two until you make a decision – and if you're still thinking about it the next day you should buy it or you'll be kicking yourself on the flight home.

➡ You can **avoid sales tax** if you arrange to have your purchases shipped outside of

New York State - a facility that is available at larger stores and those that are more tourist orientated.

➡ **Watch out** for 'Sale' signs on the Midtown section of 5th Avenue in the streets 30s and 40s. Here most of the shop windows are filled with signs that say 'Great Sales!', 'Going Out Of Business!' - yet they have been around for years and are still going strong. In fact, most of what is on sale there can be bought cheaper elsewhere and with a guarantee.

The voltage system is different in America so any plug-in electrical goods will not work properly in the UK without an adaptor.

DEPARTMENT STORES

New York has big-name department stores that are as much a sight as a shop. If you want to experience more than one, give yourself plenty of time for browsing in each, carry a bottle of water with you to stop yourself getting dehydrated and take plenty of tea or coffee breaks. Most of the following are in the Midtown area either in or near 5th Avenue. Standard opening times are Monday to Friday 10am–8pm, Saturday 10am–7pm and Sunday noon–6pm.

5TH AVENUE

Bergdorf Goodman: 754 5th Avenue at 57th Street. Tel 212-753 7300. Subway N, R, W to 5th Avenue/59th Street; F to 57th Street.
An air of understated elegance pervades every department - not surprising, given that it has been around for generations of New Yorkers. This department store is not only still going strong, but it is positively booming and has even opened a Bergdorf Goodman Men on the opposite side of the street.

The only major department store NOT to open on a Sunday is Bergdorf Goodman, but it's still well worth a visit on any other day.

Lord and Taylor: 424 5th Avenue at 39th Street. Tel 212-391 3344, **www.maycompany.com**. Subway B, D, F, V to 42nd Street; 7 to 5th Avenue.
Good service but at much cheaper prices. The store is famous for its animated window displays at Christmas time.

Saks Fifth Avenue: 611 5th Avenue at 50th Street. Tel 212-753 4000, **www.saksfifthavenue.com**. Subway E, V to 5th Avenue/53rd Street.
Not only is this one of the finest shopping institutions in New York, it also has fabulous views of the Rockefeller Center and is right next door to the beautiful St Patrick's Cathedral. Saks is a classic and has all the big names. There is a fabulous beauty area on the ground floor where you can get a personal consultation and a makeover.

Takashimaya: 693 5th Avenue between 54th and 55th Streets. Tel 212-350 0100. Subway N, R to 5th Avenue; 4, 5, 6 to 59th Street.
Hugely expensive, but filled with truly gorgeous things laid out in a six-storey townhouse building.

An elegant spot for tea is to be found in The Tea Box, a café in the basement of Takashimaya. It has a superb range of teas and a great selection of teapots to buy.

Tiffany & Co: 727 5th Avenue at 57th Street. Tel 212-755 8000, **www.tiffany.com**. Subway N, R to 5th Avenue/59th Street.
Audrey Hepburn's favourite shop in *Breakfast at Tiffany's*, it surpasses all expectations. One of the few stores that still has lift attendants, who are very happy to explain exactly where everything is. Drool over the golden counters downstairs before taking the lift up to the first floor ('elevator to second' in American-speak) where the more moderately priced silver wing may be able to tempt you to part with wads of cash. And why not? It's well worth it for the exquisite wrapping of each purchase and the divine blue Tiffany drawstring bags!

SHOPPING

MIDTOWN–34TH STREET

Macy's: Herald Square at West 34th Street, 6th Avenue and Broadway. Tel 212-695 4400, **www.macys.com**. Subway B, D, F, N, Q, R, V, W to 34th Street.
This is a beast of a gigantic store, filling as it does an entire city block, so you can be forgiven for getting yourself lost. If you enter from the Herald Square side, you'll find the Visitors' Center on the mezzanine level up to your left. Here you can pick up your free Macy's tote bag or rucksack with any purchase over $35, on production of a special voucher – try the leaflet rack at your hotel. Along the way you'll pass the delightful Metropolitan Museum Shop. A favourite area with Brits is the jeans department and, of course, the beauty counters that throng the ground floor. If you're with children, head for the seventh floor where all their needs are catered for, along with the only McDonald's inside a department store in New York. Don't miss the coffee shops, restaurant and food store run by Cucina & Co (page 104).

Macy's is the venue for a Thanksgiving Day Parade, Fourth of July Fireworks and a Spring Flower Week in April.

UPPER EAST SIDE

Barneys: 660 Madison Avenue at 61st Street. Tel 212-826 8900, **www.barneys.com**. Subway N, R, W to 5th Avenue; 4, 5, 6 to Lexington. Open until 8pm every night.
A truly up-to-the-minute fashion outlet, this store is filled with all the top designers and a good selection of newer ones. There isn't really a Brit equivalent, the nearest being Harvey Nichols, but it doesn't come close. It has eight floors of fashion where there's everything from big name designers to more obscure, but very hip, small labels. There is a branch called Coop on 18th Street in Chelsea, and another one at the World Financial Center in Downtown, but this is the $100-million megastore. Don't miss it!

If you plan to be in New York in August or March, get on down to the Barneys Warehouse Sale – call ahead for locations or check the website.

Bloomingdale's: 1000 3rd Avenue at 59th Street. Tel 212-355 5900, **www.bloomingdales.com**. Subway 4, 5, 6 to 59th Street; N, R to Lexington Avenue. After Saks, this is probably the most famous of all 5th Avenue's department

Macy's department store

stores. You can't go wrong with anything you buy from here. A truly glitzy shop filled with all the right designers, you can now also sample its delights at the new SoHo branch (page 89).

DISCOUNT STORES

Century 21: 22 Cortlandt Street at Broadway. Tel 212-227 9092, **www.c21stores.com**. Subway 1, 2, 4, 5, A, C to Fulton Street/Broadway Nassau. Area: Financial District.
Excellent discounts on everything from adult and children's clothing to goods for the home. Arrive early to avoid the lunchtime rush.

Daffy's: 111 5th Avenue at 18th Street. Tel 212-529 4477, **www.daffys.com**. Subway L, N, R, 4, 5, 6 to 14th Street/Union Square. Area: Union Square.

333 Madison Avenue at 44th Street. Tel 212-557 4422. Subway S, 4, 5, 6, 7 to 42nd Street/Grand Central. Area: Midtown East.

1311 Broadway at West 34th Street. Tel 212-736 4477. Subway B, D, F, N, Q, R to 34th Street. Area: 34th Street.

135 East 57th Street between Lexington and Park Avenues. Tel 212-376 4477. Subway 4, 5, 6 59th Street; N, R Lexington Avenue. Area: Midtown East.
You'll find an amazing range of designer stock from all over the world at all four outlets, and a hunt could result in a real bargain.

Filene's Basement: 620 6th Avenue at 18th Street. Tel: 212-620 3100. Subway F, V, L to 6th Avenue/14th Street. Area: Union Square.
Part of the Boston-based bargain-basement chain. There's also an outlet on Broadway at West 79th Street in the Upper West Side.

INA: 101 Thompson Street between Spring and Prince Streets. Tel 212-941 4757. Subway C, E to Spring Street; N, R, W to Prince Street.
A designer resale stock that changes daily and offers discounts from 30 to 50 per cent per item. You'll be able to get your hands on plenty of model cast-offs, from Manolo shoes to Prada.

Loehmann's: 101 7th Avenue between 16th and 17th Streets. Tel 212-352 0856, **www.loehmanns.com**. Subway 1, 9 to 18th Street. Area: Chelsea.
A five-storey building filled with bargains for men and women. Head straight to the top floor for designer labels such as Donna Karan, Calvin Klein and Versace. The other floors feature accessories, bags, clothing and shoes all at great prices.

Nice Price: 493 Columbus Avenue between 83rd and 84th Streets. Tel: 212-362 1020, **www.clothingline.com**. Subway 1, 2 to 79th Street, B, C to 81st Street. Area: Upper West Side.
This shop is a little on the small side, but well worth the visit.

Tiffany's

HOW TO FIND A REAL BARGAIN

Goods at normal prices in New York are cheaper than here in Britain, but it is possible to find whatever you are looking for at an even better price.

➡ Consult **Insider Shopping**, a phone and internet-based service designed to help you zero in on bargain opportunities. Either dial 212-55-SALES or visit **www.inshop.com** to find out about sales and promotional events at exclusive Manhattan retailers such as Bloomingdale's and Barneys.

➡ If **shopping bargains** are your main reason for visiting New York, then bear in mind that the major sales are held in March and August. The winter sales seem to start earlier and earlier and may even begin before Christmas.

➡ Check out the Sales and Bargains section of *New York Magazine*, the ads in the *New York Times* and the Check Out section of *Time Out*.

➡ Get a copy of *S&B Report* from 108 East 38th Street, Suite 2000, NY, NY 10016.

➡ Bear in mind that many of the vintage clothing outlets are excellent for barely worn designer clothes and some even specialise in never-worn-before sample sales.

➡ Head for the premium shopping bargain outlet of **Woodbury Common**, just an hour out of New York in the Central Valley, tel 845-928 4000. It has discounts of between 25 and 65 per cent at a huge number of factory outlets for designers and department stores such as Ann Taylor, Banana Republic, Barneys, Betsey Johnson, Burberry, Calvin Klein, Christian Dior, Donna Karan, Gap, Giorgio Armani, Gucci, Nike, Saks and Versace. Do you want me to go on? For more information on Woodbury Common, see pages 245–6.

FASHION

You can find everything from top designers to up-and-coming newcomers. The main shopping areas for fashion are the Upper East Side (for posh), SoHo (for designer), the East Village and Lower East Side (for cheap designer). Call ahead for opening times as many shops do not open until late – but they stay open late.

TRIBECA

TriBeCa Issey Miyake: 119 Hudson Street at North Moore Street. Tel 212-226 0100. Subway 1, 2 to Franklin Street.
The new Prada store got the old Guggenheim Museum space in SoHo, Issey Miyake got Frank Gehry, the architect of the amazing Guggenheim Museum in Bilbao. Now serious shoppers mingle with art buffs who come to see the titanium tornado that swirls through this two-storey, 279sq m (3,000sq ft) boutique, plus art by Gehry's son Alejandro. Fortunately, the purpose of the shop (sorry, but that's what it is!) has not been forgotten and the entire Issey collection is here including the Pleats Please, Haat, A/POC and fragrance lines. What's more, the staff are actually helpful. A truly wonderful experience – especially if you can afford $1,600 for a shirt. Otherwise wait for the sales!

SOHO

agnès b: 103 Greene Street between Spring and Prince Streets. Tel 212-925 4649. Subway N, R to Prince Street.
Superb designs for women – simple but stunning and beautifully cut.

Anna Sui: 113 Greene Street between Prince and Spring Streets. Tel 212-941 8406. Subway N, R to Prince Street.
Get the glamour-with-a-hint-of-grunge look with Anna's dresses, skirts, blouses, boots and scarves. The small collection for men includes trousers, shirts and jackets from the outrageously loud to the quite positively restrained.

Banana Republic: 552 Broadway between Spring and Prince Streets. Tel 212-925 0308. Subway N, R to Prince Street.
A classy and reputable chain, famous for classic clothing in feel-good fabrics such as cashmere, suede, velvet and soft cotton at affordable prices. Nevertheless, the best buys are in the frequent sales.

Betsey Johnson: 138 Wooster Street between Houston and Prince Streets. Tel 212-995 5048. Subway C, E to Spring Street; N, R to Prince Street.
A wonderful presentation of a combination of party and working clothes that are thrilling to wear.

Bloomingdale's: 504 Broadway between Spring and Broome Streets. Tel 212-705 2000. Subway N, R to Prince Street.
Aimed at Lower Manhattan's trendy set, this brand-new, six-level SoHo branch of the world-famous store now occupies the former home of Canal Jeans. With plenty of different designer lines, there's something for everyone in this fabulous new fashion emporium.

Burberry: 133 Spring Street between Greene and Wooster Streets. Tel 212-925 9300. Subway C, E to Spring Street.
Don't miss this younger, hipper outlet of the super trendy British company for rainwear, leather, trench dresses, bags, shoes and casual wear.

A great place for a pit stop is at the Universal News and Café Corp at 484 Broadway between Broome and Grand Streets, where you'll not only be able to find a snack, but also check out their magazine range of 7,000 titles!

Catherine Malandrino's: 468 Broome Street at Greene Street. Tel 212-925 6765. Subway 6 to Spring Street.
The designer's own sexy French knitwear in block colours stand alongside more tailored knitted skirts and jackets.

Club Monaco: 520 Broadway at Spring Street. Tel 212-941 1511. Subway 6 to Spring Street.
Once a Canadian company offering high fashion at high street prices, Ralph Lauren loved it so much he bought it.

D&G: 434 West Broadway between Prince and Spring Streets. Tel 212-965 8000. Subway N, R to Prince Street. .
Shop for jeans, suits, bags and dresses to a background of (loud) pop music. *Sex and the City's* Carrie's favourite shop!

Earl Jeans: 160 Mercer Street between Houston and Prince Streets. Tel 212-226 8709. Subway N, R to Prince Street; 6 to Spring Street.
Self-taught California designer Suzanne Costas has not only created jeans that actually fit women, but made them sexy too. Her ultra-low-slung jeans have been the definitive favourites of stars like Cameron Diaz and Kate Moss for some time and now visitors to New York can get their hands on them too.

Hotel Venus: 382 West Broadway between Spring and Broome Streets. Tel 212-966 4066. Subway C, E to Spring Street.
One of Patricia Field's outlets. Her trend-setting club and streetwear are so outrageous they attract a large following among the drag queen and stripper crowd. But don't let that put you off if you fancy a corset, fake fur coat, bodysuit or bikini that's completely OTT. Patricia, by the way, is now known for dressing Sarah Jessica Parker of *Sex and the City.*

J Crew: 99 Prince Street between Mercer and Greene Streets. Tel 212-966 2739. Subway N, R to Prince Street.
American-style men's and women's clothes plus shoes and accessories.

Keiko: 62 Greene Street between Spring and Broome Streets. Tel 212-226 6051. Subway N, R to Prince Street.
Designer swimwear for all tastes – and you may recognise the odd supermodel shopping here.

Le Sportsac: 176 Spring Street between West Broadway and Thompson Streets. Tel 212-625 2626. Subway C, E to Spring Street.
Beloved of Japanese trendoids and US out-of-towners, not to mention Brit hipsters, Le Sportsac offers great nylon bags in every style, size, colour and pattern and they're reasonably priced, too. Worth a visit as the range isn't available in the UK.

Marc Jacobs: 163 Mercer Street between Houston and Prince Streets. Tel 212-343 1490. Subway N, R to Prince Street.
Minimalist and luxury garments displayed in a renovated garage.

Phat Farm: 129 Prince Street between West Broadway and Wooster Street. Tel 212-533 7428. Subway C, E to Spring Street.
If you're into hip-hop baggies, you'll find everything you need here.

Prada New York Epicenter: 575 Broadway at Prince Street. Tel 212-334 8888. Subway N, R to Prince Street.
Art is the byword of this incredible $40 million flagship store for Prada. Once the Guggenheim's SoHo museum, the two-level space has been designed by architect Rem Koolhaas and includes a zebrawood 'wave' in the entry hall and shoe display steps that can be converted into auditorium seating.

Other neat design elements include dressing rooms behind a wall that switches from translucent to transparent (be warned!) and clothes suspended from the ceiling in metal cages. And therein lies one of the main drawbacks of the store from a punter's point of view. Prada's entire collection is to be found here, yet all the empty areas make people feel as if there isn't that much to buy. On top of that, the store has taken being 'cool' so seriously that the staff are positively frosty. Deal with them by either telling yourself that you earn a lot more than they do, or as one woman put it: 'You can have fun by asking the sales people for things from the storage rooms and keep them running!'

Steven Alan: 60 Wooster Street between Spring and Broome Streets. Tel 212-334 6354. Subway 6 to Spring Street.
A small but perfectly formed boutique filled to the rafters with up-and-coming designers such as Kayatone Adeli's cute disco top and Daryl K's hipster trousers.

Stüssy Store: 140 Wooster Street between West Houston and Prince Streets. Tel 212-995 8787. Subway N, R to Prince Street.
Everything you could want if you're after a West Coast look.

NOLITA

Calypso St Barths: 280 Mott Street between East Houston and Prince Street. Tel 212-965 0990. Subway 6 to Spring Street.
A French boutique with a Caribbean influence, this shop is filled with designs from Christiane Celle. There's a riot of sexy silk slip dresses, tie-dye tops and cute beaded cardigans.

Tracey Feith: 209 Mulberry Street between Spring and Kenmare Streets. Tel 212-334 3097. Subway 6 to Spring Street.
Tucked away in the hip NoLiTa, here you can get a dress made to order if you've $550 to burn. Just remember, Sarah Jessica Parker wore one of Feith's red and blue silk creations in *Sex and the City*.

X-Large: 267 Lafayette Street at Prince Street. Tel 212-334 4480. Subway N, R to Prince Street.
Get your urban street clobber here. Sized for boys, but good for girls, too.

LOWER EAST SIDE

Nova USA: 100 Stanton Street at Ludlow Street. Tel 212-228 6844. Subway J, M, Z, F to Delancey Street.
Great for basic but brilliant sportswear, Cameron Diaz and Helena Christensen are just two of the many women who stock up on these casually cool bits of kit when they're in Manhattan.

For info on sample sales in the Lower East Side area, go to www.lowereastsideny.com.

GREENWICH VILLAGE

Patricia Field: 10 East 8th Street between 5th Avenue and University Place. Tel 212-254 1699. Subway A, C, E, F, V, S to West 4th Street.
Once only famous for her outrageous club clobber, Patricia is the designer who creates all the fashion for the girls in *Sex and the*

7th Avenue Garment District

City. So if you want to emulate Carrie, Mia or Lizzie, then come here to stock up on cool bags and jewellery worn by the cast.

Untitled: 26 West 8th Street between 5th and 6th Avenues. Tel 212-505 9725. Subway A, C, E, F, V, S to West 4th Street. Contemporary clothing and accessories from exclusive New York designers as well as the likes of Vivienne Westwood.

MEATPACKING DISTRICT

Alexander McQueen: 417 West 14th Street between 9th Avenue and Washington Street. Tel: 212-645 1797. Subway A, C, E, 8th Avenue.
British fashion guru who made his name at Givenchy before designing for Gucci. The clothes are way out and very expensive.

Stella McCartney: 429 West 14th Street. Tel 212-2551 556. Subway A, C, E to West 14th Street.
The famous daughter of a Beatle has moved on from shaking up fashion at Chloe to launching her own label to great acclaim. Now she's opened her first store in this cool district, where the likes of Liv Tyler and Gwyneth Paltrow shop when in town.

WEST VILLAGE

Lulu Guinness: 394 Bleecker Street between 11th and Perry Streets. Tel 212-367 2120. Subway A, C, E to 14th Street, L to 8th Avenue; 1, 2 to Christopher Street.
Our own home-grown Brit girl Lulu, who started out in Notting Hill, West London, has established herself in the Big Apple. Her vintage-inspired accessories include embroidered and appliquéd bags and purses. If you think you can get it all in the UK, think again – Lulu's produced some fab bags just for New Yorkers.

NOHO

Avirex: 652 Broadway between Bleecker and Bond Streets. Tel 212-925 5456.
Great for flight and varsity jackets.

Dollhouse: 400 Lafayette Street at 4th Street. Tel 212-539 1800. Subway N, R to Prince Street.
As the name suggests, it's all very much for young girls or the young at heart. Nicole Murray specialises in gear for the body-conscious, and prices are excellent.

Urban Outfitters: 628 Broadway between Houston and Bleecker Streets. Tel 212-475 0009. Subway F, V, S to Broadway/Lafayette Street; 6 to Bleecker Street.
The last word in trendy, inexpensive clothes. Also has vintage urban wear. There's one in London now so it's not as special as it used to be, but still worth a visit for its mix of hip clothes, accessories, toys and other whatnots.

EAST VILLAGE

Enelra Lingerie: 48 East 7th Street. Tel 212-4732 454. Subway F, V to 2nd Avenue
Madonna's haunt 20 years ago. Now worth checking out at Halloween when the window displays feature items like full-length latex devil outfits!

Mark Montano: 434 East 9th Street between 1st Avenue and Avenue A. Tel 212-505 0325. Subway 6 to Astor Place.
Drew Barrymore, Johnny Depp and Kate Moss are all fans of the funky designer who uses bright, often vintage fabrics to create designs with style.

A sales tax of 8.25 per cent always used to be added on to all label prices. Now New York City has abolished the sales tax on all clothing and footwear under $110.

Religious Sex: 7 St Mark's Place between 2nd and 3rd Avenues. Tel 212-477 9037. Subway 6 to Astor Place.
If you're feeling outrageous (sequinned thong, anybody?), you'll find the clothes that you're after here.

East Village

CLOTHES SIZES

Clothes sizes for men and women are one size smaller in America, so a dress size 10 in the US is a size 12 in the UK, a jacket size 42 is a UK 44. But it's the opposite with shoes – an American size 10 is our size 9.

Trash and Vaudeville: 4 St Mark's Place between 2nd and 3rd Avenues. Tel 212-982 3590. Subway 6 to Astor Place.
You'll get the East Village look in no time if you step into this punk/grunge paradise. Here you'll find outrageous rubber dresses and shirts, black leather outfits and plenty of studded gear and footwear to match.

CHELSEA

Co-op Store: 236 West 18th Street between 7th and 8th Avenues. Tel 212-716 8816. Subway 1, 2 to 18th Street.
One of the best stores in New York.

After you've been to the Co-op, pop to the Cafeteria at 119 7th Avenue at West 17th Street. It's where you go to see and be seen!

MIDTOWN

Burberry: 9 East 57th Street between 6th and Madison Avenues. Tel 212-925 9300. Subway 4, 5, 6 to 59th Street.
The opening of this fabulous new flagship store reflects the resurgence of the great British classic as a trend-setting force in recent years. There's something for everyone here – men, women, teenagers and even children since the introduction of the new tots' clothing line.

Gianni Versace: 647 5th Avenue between 51st and 52nd Streets. Tel 212-317 0224. Subway E, V to 5th Avenue/53rd Street.
A beautiful shop, housed in the former Vanderbilt mansion, selling beautiful clothes for the rich and famous.

Gucci: 685 5th Avenue at 54th Street. Tel 212-826 2600. Subway E, V to 5th Avenue/53rd Street.
So you may not be able to afford anything on display, but it's essential to know what 'look' you are trying to achieve when you browse through the copy-cat shops downtown.

Jimmy Choo: 645 5th Avenue at 51st Street. Tel 212-593 0800. Subway E, V to 5th Avenue/53rd Street.
Originally part of Jimmy's upscale ready-to-wear 'chain' of stores – think London, Paris, Los Angeles and New York – the designer has sold up most of his shares and gone back to his couture clients. Now the thongs, slingbacks and skinny high-heeled shoes are designed by his daughter Sanda, but still remain the favourites of celebs like Madonna and Sarah Jessica Parker. A pair of women's shoes will set you back $400–600. Men's loafers, sneakers and thongs (flip flops) start at just $250.

Levis: 3 East 57th Street between 5th and Madison Avenues. Tel 212-838 2125. Subway N, R, W to 5th Avenue/59th Street.
If you've ever had trouble finding a pair of jeans that fit you perfectly, come here to be measured and have your jeans custom-made and sent to you.

Liz Claiborne: 650 5th Avenue at East 52nd Street. Tel 212-956 6505. Subway 6 to 51st Street; E, F to Lexington Avenue.
Career and sportswear with plenty of style for women.

Manolo Blahnik: 31 West 54th Street between 5th and 6th Avenues. Tel 212-582 3007. Subway E, V to 5th Avenue/53rd Street.
Anyone serious about their shoe collection wouldn't miss this Mecca for celebs. In fact, Manolo has even designed the SJP – an ankle-strapped stiletto named after Sarah Jessica Parker.

UPPER EAST SIDE

Billy Martin's Western Wear: 220 East 60th Street. Tel 212-861 3100. Subway 6 to 68th Street.
Everything for the posh cowboy.

Calvin Klein: 654 Madison Avenue at 60th Street. Tel 212-292 9000. Subway N, R to Lexington Avenue; 4, 5, 6 to 59th Street.
CK's leading outlet seems to have enjoyed as much attention from the designers as the clothes themselves!

Diesel: 770 Lexington Avenue at 60th Street. Tel 212-308 0055. Subway N, R to Lexington Avenue; 4, 5, 6 to 59th Street.
A massive store in which you'll find everything from denim to vinyl clothing, shoes and accessories.

D&G: 825 Madison Avenue between 68th and 69th Streets. Tel 212-249 4100. Subway 6 to 68th Street.
Shop for jeans, suits, bags and dresses to a background of (loud) pop music.

Donna Karan: 819 Madison Avenue between East 68th and 69th Streets. Tel 866-244 4700. Subway 6 to 68th Street.
A leading American designer who is best known for her elegant, simple outfits for women. The floating staircase is worth popping in for alone.

Emporio Armani: 601 Madison Avenue between 57th and 58th Streets. Tel 212-317 0800. Subway N, R to 59th Street.
Armani's line for younger people.

Giorgio Armani: 760 Madison Avenue at 65th Street. Tel 212-988 9191. Subway 6 to 68th Street.
A huge boutique, which sells all three of Armani's lines. Come here to find well-tailored classics.

Lingerie & Company: 1217 3rd Avenue at 70th Street. Tel 212-737 7700. Subway 6 to 68th Street.
A user-friendly shop for gorgeous undies.

Prada: 841 Madison Avenue at 70th Street. Tel 212-327 4200. Subway 6 to 68th Street.
Check out the season's look before you head for the bargain basement stores.

Ralph Lauren: 867 Madison Avenue at East 72nd Street. Tel 212-606 2100. Subway 6 to 68th Street.
Worth a visit just to see the store – it's in an old Rhinelander mansion and is decorated with everything from Oriental rugs to riding whips, leather chairs and English paintings. The clothes are of excellent quality too.

VINTAGE FASHION

SOHO

Alice Underground: 481 Broadway between Grand and Broome Streets. Tel 212-431 9067. Subway Prince Street N, R, Canal Street, N, R.
A large emporium packed to the rafters with all kinds of retro clothing from the 40s to the 70s, plus accessories like shoes and bags. Be warned, it takes a while to trawl through everything to find a gem.

Transfer International: 594 Broadway, Suite 1002, between Prince and Houston Streets. Tel 212-941 5472, **www.transferintl.com**. Subway N, R to Prince Street.
Specialises in Gucci, Prada, Chanel and Hermès – one of the best places to buy post-worn designer clothes and accessories. They also carry agnès b and Betsey Johnson.

The Americans still measure in feet and inches – good news for older Brits.

NOLITA

Screaming Mimi: 382 Lafayette Street between 4th and Great Jones Streets. Tel 212-677 6464. Subway N, R to NYU 8th Street.
Everything from polyester dresses to denim shirts and tropical prints from the 1960s. There are also jewellery, sunglasses and other accessories, plus a home department upstairs.

LOWER EAST SIDE

Cherry: 185 Orchard Street between Houston and Stanton Streets. Tel 212-358 7131. Subway F, V to 2nd Avenue.
A cool vintage shop, which stocks all manner of goodies and shoes dating back as far as the 1940s.

GREENWICH VILLAGE

Stella Dallas: 218 Thompson Street between Bleecker and West 3rd Streets. Tel 212-674 0447. Subway A, C, E, F, V, S to West 4th Street.
An amazing vintage shop full of girly chiffon and other items.

EAST VILLAGE

Love Saves The Day: 119 2nd Avenue at East 7th Street.Tel 212-2283 802. Subway 6 to Astor Place.
Packed full of objects of real retro desire such as biker jackets last worn by fans of Evel Knievel or Barry Sheene. As well as clothes, there are gems such as 1950s' *Playboy* magazines and hardback manuals of John Travolta's work-out routines for *Saturday Night Fever*.

Tokyo Joe: 334 East 11th Street between 1st and 2nd Avenues. Tel 212-473 0724. Subway 6 to Astor Place.
The pre-worn designer offerings are

advertised on a blackboard outside the shop every day.

Tokio: 7 East 7th Street between 1st and 2nd Avenues. Tel 212-353 8443. Subway 6 to Astor Place; N, R to 8th Street.
Plenty of vintage and downtown designer gear.

CHELSEA

Out Of Our Closet: 136 West 18th Street between 6th and 7th Avenues. Tel 212-633 6965. Subway 1, 2 to 18th Street.
Used designer fashions in excellent condition at a fraction of the price.

UNION SQUARE

Cheap Jack's: 841 Broadway between 13th and 14th Streets. Tel 212-777 9564. Subway L, N, Q, R, 4, 5, 6 to Union Square/14th Street.
A huge selection, but on the pricey side.

UPPER EAST SIDE

Gentlemen's Resale: 322 East 81st Street between 1st and 2nd Avenues. Tel 212-734 2739. Subway 6 to 77th Street.
Top-notch designer suits at a fraction of the original price.

BROOKLYN

Domsey's Warehouse: 496 Wythe Avenue at South 9th Street. Tel 718-384 6000. Subway J, M, Z to Marcie Avenue Station.
Well worth the trip for an excellent selection of vintage fashion.

BEAUTY STORES AND SPAS

Everyone knows New York is the place to find fabulous fashion bargains, but not so well known are the great beauty buys to be had, too. In the first instance, most make-up – particularly the gorgeous American brands such as Philosophy, Hard Candy, Benefit and Laura Mercier – is a lot cheaper in the Big Apple. The exceptions are the 'prestige' French brands such as Décleor, Christian Dior and Chanel, which are generally cheaper in the UK (they have to be imported to America).

Stores in SoHo tend to open some time between 10am and noon and stay open until 7pm Monday to Saturday, while most open from noon to 6pm on Sundays.

Even better, though, are the beauty boutiques themselves. Almost all brands have their own dedicated stores where you can browse to your heart's content, have make-up lessons – some free, some redeemable against purchases, the rest very well priced – or just enjoy yourself trying out foundations and colours. Best of all, you needn't traipse all over Manhattan to find your one favourite store – all have

Club Monaco

dedicated boutiques in the picturesque area of SoHo and its environs of NoLiTa, north SoHo and the West Village. To get to SoHo use either the N, R subway lines to Prince Street or the 6, C, E to Spring Street.

BEAUTY

Aveda: 233 Spring Street between 6th Avenue and Varick Street. Tel 212-807 1492. As befits the beauty line entirely based on the gentle and nurturing Ayurvedic system, this is a tranquil setting in which to choose your favourite hair and skincare products. Made from natural plant and flower extracts, Aveda's holistic approach is carried through all products including the make-up ranges and massage oils.

Face Stockholm: 110 Prince Street at Greene Street. Tel 212-966 9110. Fans of the cosmetic company can go mad in this glittery emporium, filled as it is with the full range of colours and brushes. You can have your make-up done here or take a lesson. Phone for an appointment or just drop in.

5S: 98 Prince Street between Greene and Mercer Streets. Tel 212-925 7880. A make-up and skincare line by Japanese company Shiseido, the products reflect the ancient philosophies of the islands and are organised into five senses of well-being including energising and nurturing.

Fresh: 57 Spring Street between Lafayette and Mulberry. Tel 212-925 0099. Soaps, lotions and potions with lovely fragrances based on natural ingredients from the Boston-based company.

Helena Rubinstein Beauty Gallery: 135 Spring Street between Greene and Wooster Streets. Tel 212-343 9963. Help yourself to a free cup of water or apple juice before perching on a seat at one of the spacious make-up counters, where you can spend as much or as little time as you like trying out products. Or head to the Force C Premium counter where you can have an orange juice while examining Rubinstein's vitamin-C laden products including the Prodigy bestseller (think $125 for 50ml). You can also make an appointment to see the in-house dermatologist or visit the HR Express area for nail services, quick brow waxing and facials. Make-up lessons are pretty pricey at $100, but are redeemable against purchases that you make. Downstairs is home to the tiny but famous Helena Rubinstein spa (page 97).

Kiehl's: 109 3rd Avenue between 13th and 14th Streets. Tel 212-677 3171. One of New York's most famous establishments, the crowds still flock to this emporium in the Union Square area for its luxurious moisturisers and lip balms.

Tracie Martyn is considered by many to be the best facialist in New York, using a massage technique that people say can leave you looking 10 years younger. Tel 212-2069 333.

MAC: 113 Spring Street between Greene and Mercer Streets. Tel 212- 334 4641. As with many of the beauty boutiques in SoHo, the wonder of this flagship store for MAC is as much in the architecture, lighting and displays as in the products. In fact, it's such a wonderful place, it has become a big favourite with celebs such as Britney Spears, Gwyneth Paltrow and Alanis Morissette.

It sells all MAC products including the MAC Pro range used by make-up artists on fashion shows and movie shoots, which are only available in a few outlets around the

The MAC boutique in SoHo

SHOPPING

globe. During your visit, you can either plump for a 45-minute makeover for $40, complete with useful tips, or turn up with nothing but foundation on your face and let the artists finish off your make-up for free.

Make-Up Forever: 409 West Broadway between Prince and Spring Streets. Tel 212-941 9337.
A French line specialising in ultra-bright colours thanks to the triple pigment formula used in all its lipsticks and eyeshadows. This is a funky little shop decked out to look like the make-up area of a film set. The well-trained staff are happy to advise on colours and products, while a $50 makeover is redeemable against purchases including the company's best-selling silicon-based foundation.

Sephora: 555 Broadway between Prince and Spring Streets. Tel 212-625 1309.
One of many New York outlets of this pristine clean French beauty chain, which has become a sure-fire hit thanks to its incredibly broad range, sparkling presentations and low-key staff who can provide plenty of help and advice when requested. This is the best place to get your favourite American brands such as Benefit, Hard Candy, Nars and Philosophy.

Shiseido Studio: 155 Spring Street between West Broadway and Wooster Street. Tel 212-625 8820.
A 350sq m (3,800sq ft) learning centre where you can have free skincare lessons and test a selection of more than 330 cosmetics and fragrances.

Shu Uemura: 121 Greene Street between Prince and Spring Streets. Tel 212-979 5500.
Like MAC, Shu Uemura is another make-up range much loved by industry professionals thanks to its quality and texture. The Japanese cosmetics company, based on Eastern philosophies, is famous for its colour and tools – this is the place to come for everything from brushes to eyelash curlers.

A quiet space, slightly off the main drag of Spring Street, the boutique has an open, friendly atmosphere that makes browsing here a delight. You can also get a free 30-minute make-up lesson from one of the professional make-up artists on Thursday and Friday 11am–5pm or on Saturday 11am–1.30pm. The Saturday lessons are very popular, though – they are usually booked up a month in advance – so go in the week.

HANDS AND FEET

Jin Soon Natural Hand & Foot Spa: 56 East 4th Street between Lafayette and Bowery. Tel 212-473 2047.
When in town, actress Julianne Moore always books a full foot treatment with Jin Soon Choi. Expect rose petals and botanicals with the ultra pampering $30 pedicure. The tiny NoLiTa spa became such a Mecca for celebs and those wanting perfect hands and feet that a second, larger, Jin Soon Spa has been established in the West Village at 23 Jones Street between Bleecker and West 4th Streets. Tel 212-229 1070. Check out the 'floating room' where gorgeous orange silk hangs over a small pond.

Rescue: 21 Cleveland Place between Kenmare and Spring Streets. Tel 212-431 3805.
Famous for intensive treatments, this nail specialist also has an outlet in NoLiTa at 8 Center Market Place between Grand and Broome Streets. Tel 212-431 0449.

For excellent manicures with no frills for just $5, head to the East Village where a plethora of salons dot the streets of Marks Place and 2nd Avenue. Generally New Yorkers pay around $25 for both a manicure and pedicure.

HAIR

Arista Hair Salon & Spa: 138 5th Avenue between 19th and 20th Streets. Tel 212-242 7979.
A tiny but pricey venue for all aspects of hair, beauty and grooming – this is where Carrie and Co paid a whopping $50 each for their pedicure party in *Sex and the City*.

Devachan: 2nd Floor, 558 Broadway between Prince and Spring Streets. Tel 212-274 8686.
Small salon where celebs come to get perfect locks and an amazing scalp massage. It also doubles as a spa.

Prive: The Soho Grand, 310 West Broadway between Canal and Grand Streets. Tel 212-274 8888.
Home of Laurent D, who looks after Gwyneth's hair when she's in town. His haircuts start at around $200.

Nelson: Around Spring Street area. Tel 212-343 1373.
Known as the Edward Scissorhands of SoHo, he cuts people's hair on the street, producing acceptable choppy, sexy cuts.

SPAS

Acqua Beauty Bar: 7 East 14th Street between 5th Avenue and Union Square West. Tel 212-620 4329.
This hip beauty parlour in the ultra trendy Union Square area offers a full menu of nail, body and face treatments from just $12 for a manicure and $60 for 'amazing' facials – or splash out on the $150 package!

Bliss 57: 2nd Floor, 568 Broadway between Houston and Prince Streets.
Tel 212-219 8970.
One of New York's most famous spas, this is the place where you can get it all and in the fastest possible time. You can have a manicure at the same time as your facial and even an underarm wax too. Therein, lies its downside, though – for some, it can seem too swift and impersonal.

Helena Rubinstein Spa: 135 Spring Street between Greene and Wooster Streets.
Tel 212-343 9963.
The gorgeous Beauty Gallery is at street level, but tucked away below is the luxurious and tranquil oasis of a spa much beloved by celebs such as Sarah Jessica Parker and J Lo. Facials include the Power A, for deep pore cleansing, and Force C for ultra pampering of the skin. Other treatments include self-tanning, sugar scrubs, full waxing and cellulite busting.

Inspirations/Rose Alcido Spa:
525 Broadway at Spring Street.
Tel 212-966 2611.
A teeny space famous for Rose's signature Golden-Spoon facial. Following a full facial, two hot spoons are used to massage the face, giving an intense, penetrating treatment.

John Masters Organic Spa: 77 Sullivan Street between Spring and Broome Streets.
Tel 212-343 9590.
Outstanding full-body massages and facials for those who like to ensure all aspects of their life are organic.

The Mezzanine Spa at Soho Integrative Health Center: 62 Crosby Street between Broome and Spring Streets.
Tel 212-431 1600.
Dr Laurie Polis founded this tiny spa at her office. Body treatments include volcanic mud therapy, while the Diamond Peel involves suction and microcrystals to exfoliate the face.

Monique K Skin Care: 345 East 9th Street between Avenues A and B.
Tel 212-673 2041.
For an excellent deal on superb facials, head to this East Village hideaway. Owned by Monique K, once head facialist at the famous Georgette Klinger Salon (page 98), you get the same quality facials at much better prices.

Oasis Day Spa: 108 East 16th Street between Irving Place and Park Avenue.
Tel 212-254 7722.
Get off the beaten track for a truly relaxing experience at one of New York's best-kept secrets. Here you'll escape all elements of hustle and bustle in a sweet-smelling space where you are given your own massage slippers and a comfy robe. Fab therapies include a deep-penetrating Lava Stone Massage for $110, the Body Glow Salt Rub for $50 or an exquisite facial with customised face mask and warm hand mitts for $90.

Prema Nolita: 252 Elizabeth Street between Houston and Prince Streets.
Tel 212-226 3972.
Thought to be the smallest spa in town, Celeste Induddi and her two partners have just one treatment room, but sell their own Prema line plus celeb faves Jurlique and Anne Semonin.

Sam-C Spa and Margolin Wellness Center: 2nd Floor, 166 5th Avenue at 21st Street. Tel 212-675 9355.
A doctor-meets-spa centre in Chelsea, owned and run by chiropractor Dr Margolin and celebrated masseur Sam-C. Famous treatments include the Hydrotherapy Tub in which you are immersed in a large, very hot tub of pulsating water while a therapist massages your head and applies cold compresses, and the Sam-C Massage, a unique, intensive body massage. Other treatments include chiropractic, reflexology, acupuncture, body scrubs, steam shower and mud wraps.

MIDTOWN

You can also find excellent beauty boutiques, nail parlours and spas dotted throughout the rest of Manhattan. Here's a selection:

BEAUTY

Sephora: 636 5th Avenue between 50th and 51st Streets. Tel 212-245 1633.
The Rockefeller Center is home to the flagship Manhattan Sephora store.

HANDS AND FEET

Pinky Nail Fifty Six Corp: 240 East 56th Street. Tel 212-446 9553.
A fab chain of nail salons where manicures start at $10 and pedicures at $20. This location is particularly well known for its cleanliness and friendliness.

HAIR

Oscar Blandi Salon at the Plaza: 768 5th Avenue at Central Park South.
Tel 212-593 7930.
A sumptuous slice of Mediterranean style, this is where celebrity hairdresser Oscar tends to the tresses of clients such as Jennifer Lopez, Gwyneth Paltrow, Uma Thurman and Heather Graham among others. Mere mortals can still get an appointment, though, and walk out with a fashionable, yet wearable style. Nail and make-up services are also available.

Ouidad: 846 7th Avenue between 54th and 55th Streets. Tel 212-333 7577.
Named after the owner, this hair salon specialises in cutting and styling curly hair. In fact, they take curly hair so seriously you won't be allowed in without it! The dedicated team spend up to four hours styling and taming your locks and the salon has its own range of products.

Times Square

PERFUMES

Caswell-Massey: 518 Lexington Avenue at East 48th Street. Tel 212-755 2254.
An apothecary founded in 1752, which once provided scents for George Washington and Dolly Madison. Today it continues to make a glorious range of floral scents such as freesia, lilac and rose. You can buy gift sets with perfumes and soaps, or buy individual bottles.

SPAS

Avon Center Spa: 6th Floor, Trump Tower, 725 5th Avenue between 56th and 57th Streets. Tel 212-755 2866.
An incredible space and a wonderful opportunity to enter the spanking Trump Tower for a face and body treatment. Eliza Petrescu is famous for her eyebrow waxings.

Bliss 57: 3rd floor, 19 East 57th Street between 5th and Madison Avenues. Tel 212-219 8970.
Sarah Jessica Parker's favourite spa, which also sells its own skincare range, BlissLabs.

Elizabeth Arden Red Door Salon & Spa: 691 5th Avenue between 54th and 55th Streets. Tel 212-546 0200.
For the ultimate beautifier nothing beats the Pomegranate Warm Stone Facial, which promises to firm up skin and deflect damage-inducing free radicals in a trice with the help of a pomegranate paste.

Georgette Klinger Salon: 501 Madison Ave between 52nd and 53rd Streets.
Tel 212-838 3200.
Georgette is one of New York's most famous facialists and the foundation of her work is purification. Each facial is comprehensive and tailor-made for individual needs, starting with a thorough skin analysis. Deep cleansing and steaming rid the skin of underlying impurities, a gentle massage adds skin tone and individualised face masks finish off the refining process.

Green Tea Spa: 141 West 35th Street between Broadway and 7th Avenue. Tel 212-564 6971.
Nestled in the 34th Street district right next to Macy's is this large Japanese spa in which you are served antioxidant rich green tea in a clean, minimalist environment. Treatments include waxing, facials, manicures, pedicures and massages. For the perfect pick-you-up-in-an-instant opt for the 10-minute neck massage for $10.

UPPER EAST SIDE

BEAUTY

Face Stockholm: 687 Madison Avenue at 62nd Street. Tel 212-207 8833.
Another outlet of the fab beauty company. You'll also find another one of these boutiques on the Upper West Side at 226 Columbus Avenue between 70th and 71st Streets.

Fresh: 1061 Madison Avenue between 80th and 81st Streets. Tel 212-396 0344.
A Boston-based company specialising in beauty products made from natural ingredients such as honey, milk, soy, sugar and even Umbrian clay.

L'Occitane: 1046 Madison Avenue at 80th Street. Tel 212-396 9097.
Ultra-luxurious bath and beauty products from the famous French company.

HANDS AND FEET

Bloomie Nail Corp: 1320 Madison Avenue at 92nd Street. Tel 212-426 5566.
Another city-wide nail chain where no appointments are necessary (see also Pinky's, opposite), here you can have anything from your basic manicures to paraffin pedicures and massages.

SPAS

Ajune: 1294 3rd Avenue between 74th and 75th Streets. Tel 212-628 0044.
Simply decorated, clean-looking spa. Try its classic Ginger Massage, which involves lying down on a giant hot water bottle contraption and being massaged firmly but gently with a warm ginger cream.

ANTIQUES AND FLEA MARKETS

In balmy weather, nothing beats strolling through the treasure trove of antiques, collectables and one-off pieces at any of New York's outdoor markets or in some of the unusual individual shops.

SOHO

The SoHo Antiques Fair: Broadway and Grand Street.
Antiques and collectables all year round.

WEST VILLAGE

Susan Parrish Antiques: 390 Bleecker Street between Perry and West 11th Streets. Tel 212-645 5020.
American quilts from the 1800s to 1940.

EAST VILLAGE

Irreplaceable Artefacts: 216 East 125th Street between 2nd and 3rd Avenues. Tel 212-777 2900.
An excellent selection of actual architectural bits and bobs.

CHELSEA

The Annex Antiques Fair & Flea Market: 26th Street and 6th Avenue.
Tel 212-243 5343.
Browsers come year-round to pick through several parking lots full of vintage clothing, furniture, pottery, glassware, jewellery and

Bloomingdale's

art. Get there early for the best finds. Weekends only.

Chelsea Antiques Building: 110 West 25th Street. Tel 212-929 0909.
This 12-storey building houses 90 galleries of antiques and collectables with merchandise ranging from Japanese textiles to vintage phonographs and radios.

The Garage: 112 West 25th Street. Tel 212-647 0707.
The Garage is exactly that – a two-storey parking garage that transforms into another bustling venue at the weekend.

The Showplace: 40 West 25th Street. Tel 212-633 6010.
Like an indoor extension of the outdoor market (which is open on weekends only), with a small café downstairs.

MADISON SQUARE

Old Print Shop: 150 Lexington Avenue between East 29th and East 30th Streets. Tel 212-683 3950.
This is the place to search out Americana up to the 1950s.

MIDTOWN EAST

Lillian Nassau: 220 East 57th Street between 2nd and 3rd Avenues. Tel 212-759 6062.
Come here for art nouveau lamps and glassware, especially original Tiffanys.

Manhattan Arts & Antiques Center: 1050 2nd Avenue between East 55th and East 56th Streets. Tel 212-355 4400.

UPPER EAST and WEST SIDES

Green Flea Indoor/Outdoor Market: West 84th Street between Columbus and Amsterdam Avenues on Saturday 10am–5.30pm and at Columbus Avenue between 76th and 77th Streets on Sunday 10am–5.30pm. Tel 212-721 0900.
Antiques, collectables, bric-a-brac, handmade pottery and discount clothing.

BOOKS

Books are big business in New York and book readings are a popular form of entertainment. For a real slice of the New York lifestyle, there are a number of places that specialise in readings: **The Drawing Center** (35 Wooster Street between Grand and Broome Streets, tel 212-219 2166) gives readings related to the exhibitions; **The Poetry Project** at St Mark's Church (131 East 10th Street, tel 212-674 0910) has three evening readings a week, Monday and Wednesday at 8pm, and Friday at 10.30pm; The **92nd Street Y** (1395 Lexington Avenue, tel 212-996 1100) also has a great series of lectures and readings, as does **The Dia Center for the Arts** (548 West 22nd Street, tel 212-989 5912). Also check out Barnes & Noble (below) for more.

NOLITA

Tower Books: 383 Lafayette Street at 4th Street. Tel 212-228 5100. Subway B, D, F, Q to Broadway/Lafayette; 6 to Bleecker Street.
Contemporary fiction and a huge magazine section.

GREENWICH VILLAGE

Shakespeare & Co: 716 Broadway at Washington Place. Tel 212-529 1330. Subway N, R to 8th Street; 6 to Astor Place.
This is an excellent bookstore. Unlike many a Barnes & Noble, where the staff sometimes don't appear to recognise joined-up writing, all the assistants here are graduates and will be genuinely helpful.

WEST VILLAGE

Three Lives Bookstore: 154 West 10th Street off 7th Avenue. Tel 212-741 2069.
A delightful shop with a charming ambience, known for attentive staff with encyclopaedic knowledge.

EAST VILLAGE

St Mark's Bookshop: 31 3rd Avenue on the corner of 9th Street. Tel 212-260 7853. Subway 6 to Astor Place.
An excellent bookstore with a broad range of books. The bulletin board in the front gives details of local literary events.

UNION SQUARE

Barnes & Noble: 105 5th Avenue at 18th Street. Tel 212-807 0099, **www.bn.com**. Subway L, N, R, 4, 5, 6 to 14th Street/ Union Square.
This is the original store of one of the largest chains of bookstores in America and, as well as a massive selection of books, it also sells CDs and videos. Barnes & Noble are responsible for putting many independent bookstores out of business, but are well worth a visit. Many have coffee shops and seating areas for you to look through books before buying. You'll see branches everywhere.

Strand Book Store: 828 Broadway at 12th Street. Tel 212-473 1489, **www.strandbooks.com**. Subway L, N, R, 4, 5, 6 to 14th Street/Union Square.
This whole area used to be famous for antiquarian bookshops, but the Strand is the only one left. The store has over two million second-hand and new books on any subject you'd care to name – all at around half the published price.

MIDTOWN

Rizzoli: 31 West 57th Street between 5th and 6th Avenues. Tel 212-759 24241. Subway N, R, W to 5th Avenue/59th Street; F to 57th Street.
This trendy store has a good stock of art, fashion and design publications and is popular with those in the media and with design students.

MIDTOWN EAST

Borders Books & Music: 461 Park Avenue at 57th Street. Tel 212-980 6785. Subway N, R to Lexington Avenue; 4, 5, 6 to 59th Street.
Excellent outlets for books, CDs, videos and more obscure books, too.

Urban Center Books: 457 Madison Avenue, between East 50th and East 51st Streets. Tel 212-935 3595. Subway 6 to 51st Street or E, F to 5th Avenue.
Housed in the pretty Villard Houses, this bookstore is a treasure trove for anyone interested in architecture and buildings.

CAMERAS AND ELECTRONICS

Have a clear idea of what you're looking for before buying – pick up a copy of Tuesday's *New York Times* to check out prices in the science section first. Of course, you can always find electrical items at really cheap prices in the Chinatown stretch of Canal Street, but you won't get a guarantee.

FINANCIAL DISTRICT

J&R Music World: 33 Park Row between Ann and Beekman Streets. Tel 212-732 8600, **www.jandr.com**. Subway A, C, E to Broadway-Nassau Street.
Check out the weekly ads in the *New York Post* and *Village Voice* to get an idea of what's on offer. The store also sells jazz, Latin and pop music.

US video tapes are not compatible with British machines unless the latter has the PAL mark.

GREENWICH VILLAGE

The Wiz: 726 Broadway between Washington and Waverly Places. Tel 212-677 4111, **www.thewiz.com**. Subway N, R to 8th Street; 6 to Astor Place.
The last word in bargain-basement buys. Phone for the location of other branches.

MADISON SQUARE

Fotografica: 112 West 20th Street between 5th and 6th Avenues. Tel 212-929 6080. Subway F, V to 23rd Street.
A vast stock of used camera equipment at trade prices. Owner Ed Wassel will be happy to order anything not in stock.

34TH STREET–PENN STATION

B&H Photo & Video: 420 9th Avenue between West 33rd and West 34th Streets. Tel 212-444 6600, **www.bhphotovideo.com**. Subway A, C, E to 34th Street/Penn Station.
A massive three-storey, block-long store, which stocks every conceivable piece of electronic imaging, audio, video and photo equipment you've ever heard of. All the staff are professionals in their own right and really know their onions. They're helpful, too, which is why this emporium is an excellent place to go for everyone from novices to professionals.

Willoughby's: 136 West 32nd Street between 6th and 7th Avenues. Tel 212-564 1600, **www.willoughbys.com**. Subway B, D, F, Q, N, R, V, W, 1, 2, 3 to 34th Street.
Reputedly the world's largest collection of cameras and all things audio, but the service isn't brilliant so make sure you know what you want before you go.

CHILDREN

All these stores are to be found in Midtown – most in the Times Square area.

FAO Schwarz: 767 5th Avenue at 58th Street. Tel 212-644 9400, **www.fao.com.** Subway N, R to 5th Avenue.
The most famous children's store in the world, it's not only huge, but is also an entertainment centre in its own right with giant, oversized displays that take your breath away, plus every conceivable toy your child could want.

If you stay at the Ritz-Carlton Hotel in Battery Park City, you'll be entitled to a 10 per cent discount at FAO Schwarz.

The Disney Store: 711 5th Avenue at 55th Street. Tel 212-702 0702, **www.disney.com**. Subway E, F to 5th Avenue. Also at 218 West 42nd Street. Tel 212-302 0595. Subway 1, 2, 3, 9, N, R to Times Square/ 42nd Street.
If it comes with a pair of ears, then you'll find it here!

Toys R Us: 1514 Broadway at 44th Street. Tel 212-225 8392, www.toysrus.com. Subway N, Q, R, S, W, 1, 2, 3, 7 to Times Square.
Move over FAO Schwarz, it's time to make room for the amazing new toy emporium in the heart of the rejuvenated Times Square district. The three-storey, glass-enclosed building is home to an 18m (60ft) Ferris wheel, a giant roaring dinosaur and a life-size Barbie townhouse. If you are here with kids, it's a must-see.

Hershey's Times Square: 48th Street and Broadway. Tel 212-581 9100. Subway N, R, S, 1, 2, 3, 7, 9, A, C, E to 42nd Street–Times Square.
The Cadbury's of America now has a massive chocolate haven in Times Square. Enter (at your peril) under the 65-m (215-ft) tall, 18-m (60-ft) wide giant Hershey bar to find every kind of Hershey sweet under the sun, as well as clothing, toys and giant chocolate greetings cards.

Warner Brothers Studio Store: 1 Times Square. Tel 212-840 4040. Subway N, R, 1, 2, 3, 7 to Times Square.
The last word in items that feature Bugs Bunny, Daffy Duck, Tweety and Sylvester. There are four floors with clothes for adults as well as children, toys and original cartoon drawings (cels).

Times Square Toys R Us

FOOD

LITTLE ITALY

Di Palo's: 206 Grand Street at Mott Street. Tel: 212-226 1033. Subway J, M, N, Q, R, W, Z, 6 to Canal Street.
One of the last remaining Italian speciality food stores in Little Italy, it was founded 80 years ago and is particularly famous for its mozzarella and Italian sausages and salami. It even has its own ageing room for cheeses.

LOWER EAST SIDE

Russ & Daughters: 179 East Houston Street between Allen and Orchard Streets. Tel 212-475 4880. Subway F to 2nd Avenue. Along with Katz's Deli (page 160), this is one of the most famous outlets in the Lower East Side. Established in 1914, it sells every possible kind of fish, caviar, pickled vegetables and bagels.

GREENWICH VILLAGE

Take the subway A, C, E, F, V, S to West 4th Street and you can explore a whole area of foodie shops.

Aphrodisia: 264 Bleecker Street between 6th and 7th Avenues. Tel 212-989 6440. Known for its huge selection of bulk herbs, spices, teas and pot-pourris.

Balducci's: 424 6th Avenue at West 9th Street. Tel 212-673 2600.
One of the most famous gourmet food emporiums in New York. You can find everything from fresh vegetables and fruit to edible flowers and hung game.

If you'd like a taste of the foods sold in some of the shops in the Village, go on the Foods of New York tour, which also introduces you to great restaurants in the area (page 77).

Faicco's Sausage Store: 260 Bleecker Street between 6th and 7th Avenues. Tel 212-243 1974.
A landmark Italian speciality food shop established in 1900, it is known for its own sausages that are made daily (and sold to many of the neighbouring restaurants), its homemade mozzarella cheese, again made daily, plus rice balls made with three cheeses and rolled in breadcrumbs. Other specialities include prosciutto balls, potato croquettes, fried ravioli and stuffed breads.

Murray's Cheese Shop: 257 Bleecker Street between 6th and 7th Avenues.
Tel 212-243 3289.
The owner travels all over the world to bring back a fascinating selection of more than 350 cheeses with amazing names such as Wabash Cannonball, Crocodile Tears, Mutton Buttons and Cardinal Sin, a British cow's milk cheese. They also sell olives, chorizos, pâtés and breads.

Pasticceria Bruno: 245 Bleecker Street between 6th and 7th Avenues.
Tel 212-242 6031.
An Italian–French bakery run by one of the top 10 pastry chefs in New York. It does miniature and large fruit tarts, mousses, cookies, sorbets, ice-cream cakes and homemade chocolates, and you can sit down to try any of them with a nice cup of tea or coffee.

Rocco's: 243 Bleecker Street between 6th and 7th Avenues. Tel 212-242 6031.
Famous for its fresh cannolis (an Italian pastry filled with cream), it sells large and small sizes of everything from Italian cheesecakes to chocolate, hazelnut and lemon cakes. You can eat in, too, with a cup of delicious coffee.

Christmas at Cartier

Zito's: 259 Bleecker Street between 6th and 7th Avenues. Tel 212-929 6139.
Just about the oldest bread shop in New York, its ovens date back to the end of the 19th century and it is now famous for its old-world-style Italian breads. The focaccias come with many different toppings from onions and olive oil to rosemary. Their prosciutto bread is exclusive to them.

CHELSEA

Chelsea Market: 75 9th Avenue between 15th and 16th Streets. Tel 212-243 6005. Subway A, C, E, 14th Street.
You'll find everything you need here for a gourmet feast, from fishmongers and bakers to wine merchants, and even florists for table decorations. Check out Buon Italia for great cheeses, sauces and all manner of Italian fodder.

34TH STREET

Cucina & Co: The basement of Macy's (page 86), 151 West 34th Street, 6th Avenue and Broadway. Tel 212-868 2388. Subway B, D, F, N, Q, R, V, W to 34th Street.
One of the most fabulous grocer's markets in New York, now famous for its supplies of lobster and caviar.

UPPER EAST SIDE/YORKVILLE

The Vinegar Factory: 431 East 91st Street between York and 1st Avenues. Tel 212-987 0885. Subway 4, 5, 6 to 86th Street.
One of the most famous markets in the city. Here you'll find stacks of cheeses, meats, breads, salads and cakes – in fact, everything you need to create your own perfect picnic.

UPPER WEST SIDE

Zabar's: 2245 Broadway at 80th Street. Tel 212-787 2000. Subway 1, 2 to 79th Street.
Just about the most famous food store in New York and also considered to be one of the finest. It has a tremendous range of cheeses, fresh fruit and veg, meats, fish and even bagels. In fact it's so famous it's even featured in *Friends*.

DRINK

SOHO

Vintage New York: 482 Broome Street at Wooster Street. Tel 212-226 9463. Subway 6 to Spring Street.
SoHo is home to a complete first in New York City – a shop that can sell both wine and food. And the reason why is because it is owned by a vineyard from New York State, which means it can open on Sundays and sell alcoholic wine and food together – both of which are otherwise illegal in New York. All the wines come from New York State vineyards and you can have five tastes for just $5.

You can only buy wine and spirits from liquor stores and to make your life even more difficult, the liquor stores do not sell mixers or even beer!

LOWER EAST SIDE

Schapiro's Winery: 124 Rivington Street between Essex and Norfolk Streets. Subway J, M, Z, F to Essex/Delancey Street.
The Schapiro family have been running this winery since 1899 and it's decorated with old casks and bottles. It's the city's only kosher wine and spirits warehouse and sweet wine is made on the premises. There is a free tour at 2pm on Sunday. Hourly tastings take place Monday to Thursday 11am–5pm and on Friday before 3pm.

EAST VILLAGE

Astor Wines & Spirits: 12 Astor Place at Lafayette Street. Tel 212-674 7500. Subway 6 to Astor Place.
Has a wide range of wines and spirits.

UNION SQUARE

Union Square Wine and Spirits: 33 Union Square West between 16th and 17th Streets. Tel 212-675 8100. Subway 4, 5, 6, L, N, Q, R, W to Union Square.
A great selection, good prices and the staff know their wines.

MIDTOWN EAST

Park Avenue Liquor Shop: 292 Madison Avenue between 40th and 41st Streets. Tel 212-685 2442. Subway 4, 5, 6, 7 to Grand Central/42nd Street.
Specialises in Californian wines and European bottles. Discounts are given with bulk purchases.

Schumer's Wine & Liquor: 59 East 54th Street between Park and Madison Avenues. Tel 212-355 0940. Subway E, F to Lexington Avenue, 6 to 51st Street.

With a great range of American and European wines, they also stock a good selection of spirits and champagne.

UPPER EAST SIDE/YORKVILLE

Sherry-Lehmann: 679 Madison Avenue between 61st and 62nd Streets. Tel 212-838 7500. Subway 4, 5, 6 to 59th Street.
The most famous wine shop in New York. A huge selection and well situated for that Central Park picnic.

Best Cellars: 1291 Lexington Avenue between 86th and 87th Streets. Tel 212-426 4200. Subway 4, 5, 6 to 86th Street.
One of the best value stores in the city for fine wines under $10.

Don't be fooled by the bottles of wine you may see in certain food shops in New York. They are either non-alcoholic or low alcohol as it is illegal for food stores to sell wine. However, this rule does not apply to beer.

MUSIC

GREENWICH VILLAGE

Tower Records: 692 Broadway at 4th Street. Tel 212-505 1500, **www.towerrecords.com**. Subway N, R to 8th Street.
An excellent range of CDs and tapes. Around the block from the Village shop on Lafayette Street is the knockdown Tower Clearance shop.

SMOKER'S CORNER

Amazingly enough, the best shop to buy your ciggies from is a chain of chemists called **Duane Reade** – the New York equivalent of our Boots!

THEATER DISTRICT

Virgin Megastore: 1540 Broadway between 45th and 46th Streets. Tel 212-921 1020, **www.virgin.com**. Subway N, Q, R, S, W, 1, 2, 3, 7 to 42nd Street/Times Square.
A huge emporium with everything from CDs to tapes and vinyl. Open until 1am.

UPPER WEST SIDE

Tower Records: 1961 Broadway at 66th Street. Tel 212-799 2500. Subway 1, 9 to 66th Street/Lincoln Center.
The Lincoln Center branch also has an excellent range of CDs and tapes.

SPECIALITY AND GIFT SHOPS

SOHO

Broadway Panhandler: 477 Broome Street between Greene and Wooster Streets. Tel 212-66 3434. Subway N, R, W to Prince Street.
All things for the kitchen, from the latest gadgets to classic pieces such as steel saucepans and Alessi toasters. There are hundreds of items to choose from and it's a must-visit for any domestic gods or goddesses when in town. Famous chefs often give in-store demonstrations.

JEWELLERY

Want a true sparkler? Then look no further than the 47th Street **Diamond District** where the little gems are traded, cut and set. More than 2,600 independent businesses are to be found in a single block between 5th Avenue and the Avenue of the Americas (6th Avenue). Many have booths in jewellery exchanges such as the **World's Jewelry Exchange** at 50 West 47th Street (tel 212-997 0111). Clustered near the Diamond District are a prestigious group of internationally renowned jewellers including **H Stern** (645 5th Avenue, tel 212-688 0300) and **Martinique Jewellers** (1555 Broadway between 46th and 47th Streets, tel 212-869 5765).

Other jewellers of note include **Wempe** (700 5th Avenue at 55th Street, tel 212-397 9000) and **Tourneau** (500 Madison Avenue at 52nd Street, tel 212-758 6098), which are both famous for fine watches. **Fortunoff** (681 5th Avenue at 54th Street, tel 212-758 6660) offers discounts on a large variety of jewellery items, including engagement rings, pearls, brand-name watches and gold bracelets and necklaces. **Robert Lee Morris** (400 West Broadway, tel 212-431 9405) in SoHo is one of only two or three American jewellery designers with an international reputation.

WEST VILLAGE

Flight 001: 96 Greenwich Avenue between Jane and 12th Streets. Tel 212-691 1001. Subway 1, 2, 3, 9 to 14th Street.
A travel accessories shop that looks like a sleek 1960s' airport lounge, it stocks fabulously cool carry-on items such as digital cameras, spray-on vitamins and WAP-activated global travel guides. It also has a range of very practical but funky luggage that will stand out from the rest.

MXYPLYZYK: 125 Greenwich Avenue at 13th Street. Tel 212-989 4300. Subway 1, 2, 3, 9 to 14th Street.
Kitschy-cool gifts and whatnots including Devil Ducks (with horns – glow-in-the-dark or plain red) and tractor-seat stools for when you're tired of serious shopping.

Tea and Sympathy: 108–110 Greenwich Avenue between 12th and 13th Streets. Tel 212-807 8329. Subway 1, 2, 3, 9 to 14th Street.
Filled with all things the Brit abroad loves, this is a combination of a shop and café offering sausage rolls, fish and chips and 'proper' tea. Liz Hurley orders food for her fashion shoots, David Bowie had his 50th birthday bash here and Kate Moss and Rupert Everett are regulars.

GREENWICH VILLAGE

Village Comics: 214 Sullivan Street between West 3rd and Bleecker Streets. Tel 212-777 2770. Subway C, E to West 4th Street.
If comics are the name of the game for you, then there's a good chance you'll find a back issue of what you're looking for. It also has a mail order service.

CHELSEA

IS: 136 West 17th Street between 6th and 7th Avenues. Tel 212-620 0300. Subway A, C, E, 1, 9 to 14th Street.
A designer stationery store with a distinctly hip edge, it has classy personalised notepaper in fluorescent colours and citrus-coloured notebooks in funky 1960s-style graphics.

Canal Street, Chinatown

CHAPTER 6

Museums

New York has an incredible wealth of museums and other cultural institutions and thanks to the relatively small size of Manhattan it is possible to see many of them in a short visit. And you don't need to be an art lover or culturally inclined to enjoy them. Several of Manhattan's finest museums are based around Museum Mile, a stretch along 5th Avenue north to 89th Street, where you'll find the Metropolitan Museum of Art and the Guggenheim Museum. All the institutions work hard to attract visitors and have a range of programmes and events designed to bring even the driest subject matter to life.

As befits a city that is famed for regenerating itself, none of the museums sits on its laurels. There is a constant wave of refurbishment and renewal that inspires people to keep returning. Recently, for instance, the American Museum of Natural History has finished a $25-million programme to update its Hall of Ocean Life using state-of-the-art technology, the Museum of Modern Art (MoMA) has reopened after a multi-million dollar refurbishment and expansion, when exhibitions were moved out to Queens, and the Brooklyn Museum of Art has completed its new glass entrance pavilion and public plaza. The Museum of Jewish Heritage and the Morgan Library are still in the process of renovation and extension work.

On top of this a raft of new museums have opened, including the Museum of Sex, the American Folk Art Museum, Chelsea Art Museum and the Annette Green Museum dedicated to the history of perfumes, while the Skyscraper Museum's permanent home has been open to the public for a year. Construction is under way for a new Jewish Children's Museum in Brooklyn and the United States Golf Association is soon to open a golf museum complete with interactive exhibitions and a putting space in the former Russian Tea Room on West 57th Street.

Of course, it does mean there is a lot to choose from and, especially if you're on your first visit to New York, you'll want to ensure you don't waste any time. For this reason, I've given you my Top 10 first, which includes the major institutions and covers everything from art to natural history. It should also be noted that many cultural institutions in New York go to great lengths to make themselves accessible to children and details of events and programmes for youngsters and families can be found in Chapter 7, Children's New York.

The American Museum of Natural History

MAJOR MUSEUMS

METROPOLITAN MUSEUM OF ART

Upper East Side

✉ 5th Avenue at 82nd Street
☎ 212-535 7710 or 212-879 5500
www.metmuseum.org
🚗 Subway 4, 5, 6 to 86th Street
🕒 Tues to Thurs and Sun 9.30am–5.15pm, Fri to Sat 9.30am–8.45pm. Closed Mondays, Jan 1 and Dec 25
$ Suggested price $12 adults, $7 students and seniors, under 12s free with an adult. Same-day entrance to The Cloisters (page 117) is included in the price

New York is filled with fine museums, yet this really is the mother of them all and you could easily spend a well-paced day here. But with 5,000 years of art spread over 139,500sq m (1.5 million sq ft), it's best to admit that you won't be able to see it all in one visit. And therein lies your perfect excuse to return to the city! If you can, visit the website in advance to get a good feel for the layout. Think about what you really want to see and write out a list of priorities, allowing a reasonable amount of time to absorb what each gallery has to offer.

Don't miss the Metropolitan's fabulous outdoor café on the second floor for stunning views of Central Park. It's generally open from May to early September.

One of the things I really wanted to do on my first visit was to see an aspect of American culture, so I headed for the **American Wing** to be wowed by the collection of Tiffanys along with US arts and crafts and glorious neo-classical sculptures in the garden court. It's one of the Met's most popular areas, with three floors and 25 rooms filled with more than 1,000 paintings by American artists, 600 sculptures and 2,500 drawings. The two real musts are the **Egyptian Art** exhibits and the **Temple of Dendur**, which was built by Egypt to thank the American people after the US helped rescue monuments threatened by the Aswan Dam. Other greats include the **Greek** and **Roman** displays, the **Japanese** and **Chinese** exhibits and the **medieval** art.

The wonderful thing about this museum is that you can wander by yourself, hire an Audio Guide for the day ($6 adults, $4 under 12s), which you can use in any order you choose, or take advantage of a plethora of free tours, talks and lectures.

The hour-long tours leave from the front hall at 10.15am, 11.15am, 1.15pm, 2.15pm and 3.15pm. Check the calendar on the website in advance for information on the one-hour gallery talks or lectures, which focus on either a special exhibition or one of the permanent collections. The free lectures tend to be held at 6pm on a Friday or 3pm on a Sunday, while free films tend to be held from Tuesday to Friday at 2pm (plus 7.30pm on Friday) and on Saturday at 1.15pm. You do not need to make reservations except for the Saturday afternoon film.

For comprehensive information on family programmes, see page 147.

AMERICAN MUSEUM OF NATURAL HISTORY

Upper West Side

✉ Central Park West at 79th Street
☎ 212-769 5000
www.amnh.org
🚗 Subway B, C to 81st Street–Museum of Natural History; 1, 9 to 79th Street
🕒 Sun to Thurs 10am–5.45pm, Fri 10.30am–5pm, Sat 10.30am–5pm. The Rose Center stays open until 8.45pm each evening
$ Suggested price $12 adults, $9 students and seniors, $7 under 13s

Like the Metropolitan, this is an epic of a museum, best seen in parts rather than attempting the whole. It provides an amazingly detailed yet comprehensive overview of life on Earth and beyond and has undergone an enormous amount of growth and redevelopment over the last few years.

One of its most famous permanent exhibitions is the **Milstein Hall of Ocean Life**, which has just been given a $25-million redesign using the latest marine technology and a $15-million donation by museum trustee Irma Milstein and her husband Paul (hence the new name). Using the hall's massive blue whale as its centrepiece, lights, video and sound effects create the illusion of being immersed in the ocean to provide a dynamic and breathtaking view of life under the sea.

Other permanent exhibits include the

dinosaur collection, the $50-million gem collection including the famous Star of India blue sapphire, the Native American section and the seven continents. Along the way, much fun is to be had using the many interactive computer exhibits, for instance, to travel back in time to trace the roots of evolution.

In addition to the main museum, there is the **Rose Center for Earth and Space** – a spectacular museum within a museum, which incorporates the newly revamped **Hayden Planetarium** as its centrepiece. This is the place to come to learn about both the inner workings of Earth and the outer reaches of the universe. The **Big Bang Theater** gives a dramatic recreation of the first minutes of the origins of the universe and is found inside a 26.5-m (87-ft) wide sphere that appears to float in a glass-walled ceiling.

Here you will also find the **Space Theater**, billed as the most technologically advanced in the world, which shows incredibly realistic views of outer space. The two films are *Passport to the Universe* in which Tom Hanks narrates an amazing journey from Earth to the edge of the universe and *The Search For Life: Are We Alone?* Narrated by Harrison Ford, this film takes you on an incredible journey in a search of the answers.

Admission for one film including museum entrance: $21 adults, $15.50 students and seniors, $12.50 under 12s. Admission to both films including museum entrance: $30 adults, $22 students and seniors, $18 under 12s.

The **IMAX Theater** also shows a wonderful range of breathtaking movies examining different aspects of life on earth. Admission including museum entrance: $17 adults, $12.50 students and seniors, $10 under 13s. For information on showing times and to reserve tickets in advance, either visit the website or phone 212-769 5200.

If you take the B or C train to 81st Street you can go straight into the American Museum of Natural History from the subway. Just follow the tiled signs in the mosaic wall to avoid the crowds, heat or cold.

TOP 10 MUSEUMS

No matter how long you intend to stay in New York, it's useful to plan exactly what you want to see. As you get to know the city, you'll form your own opinions but, in the meantime, here are my favourites. They cover a broad spectrum, from the history of New York City to art and the world's amazing natural history, and each is a true delight in itself.

And don't miss the **Butterfly Conservatory**, full of stunning tropical butterflies, which is open every year from the beginning of October to the end of May. Walk among the lush vegetation and flowering plants to see some of the 500 free-living butterflies, but do remember it's 27°C (80°F) inside, so leave your coat in the cloakroom. Admission: $7 adults, $5 students and seniors, $4 under 13s.

For more information on family programmes, see page 147.

ELLIS ISLAND IMMIGRATION MUSEUM

Battery Park

This is featured in the major sights to visit while you are in New York in Chapter 4. See pages 60-1.

LOWER EAST SIDE TENEMENT MUSEUM

Lower East Side

- ✉ 90 Orchard Street between Broome and Delancey streets
- ☎ 212-431 0233 **www.tenement.org**
- 🚗 Subway F to Delancey Street; B, D, Q to Grand Street; J, M, Z to Essex Street
- 🕒 Visitor Center open daily 11am–5.30pm. However, the museum can only be visited via a tour
- $ $9 adults, $7 students for one-hour tour; $8 adults, $6 students for 45-minute tours. Under 5s go free

After they had gone through Ellis Island, what happened to many of those millions of immigrants? They ended up in tenements on the Lower East Side of New York and this is the museum that tells their poignant stories. You'll get the chance to see four re-created apartments in a typical, five-storey tenement giving a good insight into the living conditions of the seekers of the American Dream.

Before you take one of the walking tours at the Lower East Side Tenement Museum, it is well worth watching the slide show and film.

The museum consists of several tenement houses – essentially America's first public housing, predating almost every housing law in the US – that are only accessible via the tours. These houses contain several apartments, faithfully restored and complete with furniture and clothes. It's a must-see in order to understand not only this neighbourhood, which continues to function as a launching pad for fresh generations of artists and retailers, but also the American success story.

The tour **Piecing It Together: Immigrants in the Garment Industry** examines the life of the Polish Levine family, who ran a garment shop in their apartment in the early 1900s, plus the stories of other immigrants involved in the garment industry from the 1930s to the present day. The tour **Getting By: Weathering the Great Depressions of 1873 and 1929** focuses on the German-Jewish Gumpertz family in the 1870s and the Sicilian-Catholic Baldizzi family in the 1930s and how they forged new lives for themselves in America.

For information on family activities at the museum, see pages 148–9.

MOMA's temporary home is to close on September 23, 2004, and the grand reopening at West 53rd Street is not scheduled to take place until November 20. So check dates carefully to avoid disappointment or a wasted journey.

MUSEUM OF MODERN ART (MOMA)

Midtown

- ✉ 11 West 53rd Street between 5th and 6th Avenues
- ☎ 212-708 9400 **www.moma.org**
- 🚗 Subway E, V to 5th Avenue
- 🕒 Sat to Tues and Thurs 10.30am–5.45pm, Fri 10.30am–8.15pm
- $ $12 adults, $8.50 students and seniors, free for under 16s if with an adult. On Fri 4.30–8.15pm, pay what you wish.

After an absence of over two years, during which it moved to a temporary home in Long Island City (page 237), the new Museum of Modern Art reopens at West 53rd Street in midtown Manhattan on November 20, 2004. The reopening coincides with the 75th anniversary of the museum's first arrival on this site, and the latest renovations constitute the largest building project in the museum's history. Designed by Yoshio Taniguchi, the new museum will occupy over 630,000 sq ft.

Lower East Side Tenement Museum

Opposite: Metropolitan Museum of Art

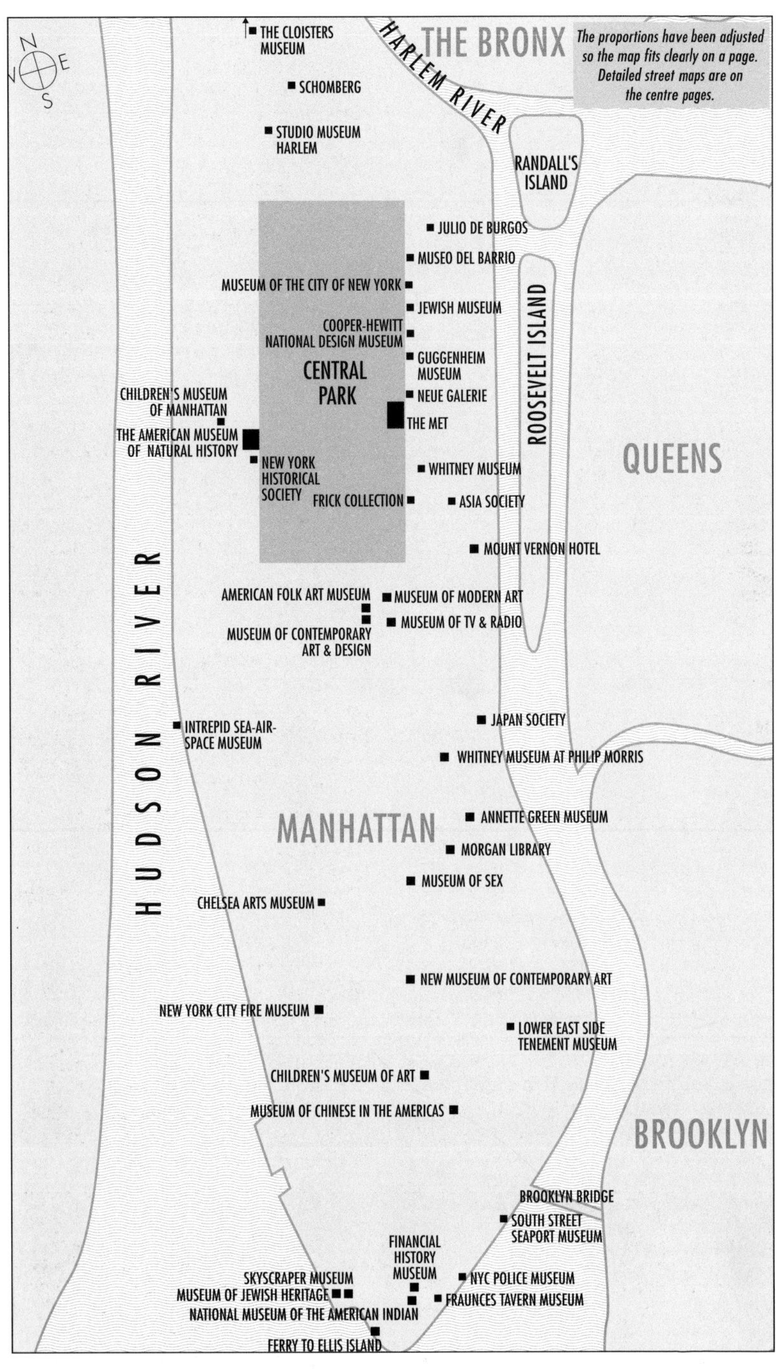

Museums in Manhattan

Founded in 1929 by three private citizens, including Abby Rockefeller, this was the first museum to devote its entire collection to the modern movement. Since then it has retained its pioneering sense of the new, and was the first museum to see architecture, design, photography and film as art forms. The museum's collection, which started with a gift of eight prints and one drawing, dates from the 1880s to the present day and now encompasses more than 100,000 works.

Many of the icons of modern and contemporary art are here including Van Gogh's *The Starry Night*, Monet's *Water Lilies*, Picasso's *Les Demoiselles* and Andy Warhol's *Gold Marilyn Monroe*. The collection includes paintings, sculptures, drawings, photographs, films, film stills and videos. Films are screened daily in the two cinemas (cost included in the museum entrance price, though you need to get a special ticket to reserve your place). Free gallery talks are given at 1pm and 3pm every day except Wednesday and on Friday at 6pm and 7pm, or for $4 you can take a personalised audio self-guided tour.

For information on family events, see page 148.

MUSEUM OF SEX

Madison Square Park

✉ 233 5th Avenue at 27th Street
☎ 212-689 6337
www.museumofsex.com
🚗 Subway 6, N, R, W to 28th Street
🕐 Mon to Fri 11am–6.30pm, Sat 10am–9pm, Sun 10am–6.30pm
$ $17 adults, $14 students and seniors or $12 before 2pm. Minimum age 18 and IDs will be checked

Times Square may have been cleaned up, but the prostitutes are back in Manhattan in force at New York's newest and, let's face it, most audacious museum. Not for the fainthearted, the inaugural exhibition examined how New York City transformed sex in America by exploring the histories of prostitution, burlesque, birth control, obscenity and fetish. This and other exhibitions use selections from private and public collections never shown before and if you're in any doubt as to whether this is the museum for you, just bear in mind that some of the material was once confiscated and classified as obscene.

Special package holiday breaks that include a ticket to the Museum of Sex are available for guests staying at the nearby Gershwin Hotel. Check out www.gershwinhotel.com for details.

The main collections of the museum include serious works of art by contemporary artists and a massive collection of film, videos, magazines, books and artefacts acquired over 20 years by Ralph Whittington, the former curator of the Library of Congress. Blow-up dolls never had it so good! Clearly the entrance fee is designed to put off casual thrill-seekers and the museum does strictly enforce the minimum age requirement. Despite the subject matter, it is a serious institution with an important message about past and present sexual subcultures and our modern attitudes to sex and sexuality.

INTREPID SEA-AIR-SPACE MUSEUM

Clinton

✉ USS *Intrepid*, Pier 86, west end of 46th Street at the Hudson River
☎ 212-245 0072
www.intrepidmuseum.org
🚗 Subway A, C, E to 42nd Street, then take the M42 bus to 12th Avenue
🕐 April 1 to Sept 30 Mon to Fri 10am–5pm, Sat, Sun and holidays 10am–7pm. October 1 to March 31 daily 10am–5pm. Closed Dec 25. Last admission one hour before closing.
$ $10 adults, $5 under 12s

THE INSIDE STORY

If you haven't got much time, try a one-hour tour of museums. From January to March and July to September, the **Insider's Hour** gives you a quick peek around the most diverse art collections and interactive exhibits. Participating institutions include the Metropolitan Museum of Art (page 108), Lower East Side Tenement Museum (page 111), *Intrepid* Sea-Air-Space Museum (page 113), American Museum of Natural History (page 108), Museum of Modern Art (page 111), Museum of Jewish Heritage (page 120) and National Museum of the American Indian (page 121).

A thoroughly enjoyable museum, which appeals to all ages and sexes. All the staff are very friendly and there are former members of the crew around the ship who are happy to give an insight into its history and life on board. *Intrepid* was one of 24 Second World War US aircraft carriers and despite incidents of serious damage to these ships, none of them was ever sunk. *Intrepid*'s worst moment came on November 25, 1944, when two kamikaze pilots hit the ship five minutes apart, killing 69 men and seriously injuring 85 others.

The only way to see the submarine at *Intrepid* is on a tour and long queues build up very quickly, so get there early and see it before anything else.

The second plane exploded on the hangar deck and the ship burned for about six hours, but *Intrepid* made it back to America for repairs and returned to the war. Stories of life on board are told by veterans at film screenings throughout the ship and there are also plenty of hands-on exhibits to keep children happy. One of the best exhibits is the F-18 navy jet flight simulator, which costs an extra $5, but is great fun.

FRICK COLLECTION

Upper East Side

⊠ 1 East 70th Street at 5th Avenue
☎ 212-288 0700
www.frick.org
Subway 6 to 68th Street
Tues to Thurs and Sat 10am–6pm, Fri 10am–8.45pm, Sun 1–6pm
$ $12 adults, $8 seniors, $5 under 16s who must be with an adult, children under 10 not admitted

When it opened to the public in 1935, the limestone mansion that was built for coal and steel industrialist Henry Frick quickly became a popular attraction in New York. The Frick now offers an intimate look into what was once a grand home in the last days of America's Gilded Age. Its artwork and objects from the 14th to the 19th centuries, such as fine French furniture, bronzes, Chinese porcelains and Limoges enamels, are arranged as if the Fricks still lived here. The walls are lined with Holbeins, Vermeers, Rembrandts, Turners, Gainsboroughs and Van Dycks.

Now you can really soak up the ambience with a glass of wine from the bar in the Garden Court when the Frick stays open late on Friday evenings.

This is the closest that the Americans will come to creating the atmosphere of an English stately home, and the serenity of this bijou museum is lovely. Get a preview by looking at the virtual-reality tour on the Fricks website.

The Frick Collection

SOLOMON R GUGGENHEIM MUSEUM

Upper East Side

✉ 1071 5th Avenue at 89th Street

☎ 212-423 3500
www.guggenheim.org

🚗 Subway 4, 5, 6 to 86th Street

🕘 Sat to Wed 9am–6pm, Fri 9am–8pm

$ $15 adults, $8 students and senior citizens, under 12s free

The Guggenheim Museum in New York is probably best known for its beautiful building, which was designed by Frank Lloyd Wright and is now one of the youngest buildings in the city to be designated a New York City landmark. It houses one of the world's largest collections of Kandinsky, as well as works by Chagall, Klee, Picasso, Cézanne, Degas, Gauguin and Manet. It also has Peggy Guggenheim's entire collection of cubist, surrealist and abstract expressionist art. Tours are free. For information on family events, see page 148.

Check out the Guggenheim's sculpture gallery for some of the best views of Central Park.

SKYSCRAPER MUSEUM

Battery Park

✉ The Ritz-Carlton Hotel, 2 West Street between Battery Place and West End.

☎ 212-968 1961
www.skyscraper.org

🚗 Subway 1, 9 to South Ferry; N, R, W to Whitehall Street; 4, 5 to Bowling Green

$ Entrance to the museum when it has an exhibition is generally free, though it is suggested that you give a donation of $2

Finally in its new home in the same building as the Ritz-Carlton in Battery Park, this is one of New York's most apt museums, celebrating as it does the city's rich architectural heritage and examining what historical forces and which individuals shaped the different skylines of its past. Through exhibitions, programmes and publications, the museum offers a fascinating insight into how individual buildings were created, complete with detailed information about how the contractors bid for the work, what was involved and how the building work was executed, all with comprehensive photographic illustrations.

At the beginning of June, don't miss the wonderful Museum Mile Festival. On the first Tuesday of the month all nine museums along 5th Avenue – including the Met – are free to the public. The road is closed and the traffic is replaced by live bands, street entertainers and outdoor art activities for children.

Since 1997, the museum has presented exhibitions in temporary spaces – two vacant banking halls on Wall Street in the heart of New York's historic Financial District – including Downtown New York, Building The Empire State and Big Buildings. The exhibitions are surprisingly moving as they manage to convey the very real human sacrifices and energy put into creating these incredible edifices. Most moving of all was its recent homage to the Twin Towers, which marked the entire 30-year history of the World Trade Center.

South Street Seaport Museum

A-Z OF THE REST

AMERICAN FOLK ART MUSEUM

Midtown

✉ 45 West 53rd Street between 5th and 6th Avenues
☎ 212-265 1040
www.folkartmuseum.org
🚗 Subway E, V to 5th Avenue–53rd Street
🕘 Tues to Sun 10am–6pm, except Fri 10am–8pm
$ $9 adults, $5 students and seniors, under 12s and members free

The first entirely new museum building in New York since 1966, the museum's $18-million structure was designed by award-winning architects Tod Williams and Billy Tsien. From a punter's point of view, this new museum provides an excellent opportunity to get to grips with American folk art. It also gives an insight into America's history and cultural heritage from the perspective of these arts.

Be prepared to prove you're a student if you want to make the most of discounted admissions to the museums.

AMERICAN MUSEUM OF THE MOVING IMAGE

Queens

It's only a short trip to Queens and worth a visit here if you are into films. See page 236.

ANNETTE GREEN MUSEUM

Murray Hill

✉ 145 East 32nd Street between Lexington and 3rd Avenues
☎ 212-725 2755
http://fragrance.org/museum_info.html
🚗 Subway 6 to 33rd Street
🕘 Open by appointment only Mon to Fri 10am–noon and 1–4pm
$ $5 adults, $2.50 students and seniors

America's first-ever perfume museum is owned and run by the Fragrance Foundation and aims to give an insight into the importance of scent in our lives. Exhibits include the Lure and Lore of Perfume Classics, which explains our continuing love affair with traditional fragrances such as Chanel No 5 and Obsession.

ASIA SOCIETY

Midtown East

✉ 725 Park Avenue at 70th Street
☎ 212-288 6400
www.asiasociety.org
🚗 Subway 6 to 68th Street
🕘 Tues to Sun 11am–6pm, Fri 11am–9pm
$ $7 adults, $5 students and senior citizens, members and under 16s free

Founded in 1956 by John D Rockefeller III with his collection of Asian art, the society aims to build an awareness of the 30 Pan-Asian countries, which include Japan, New Zealand, Australia and the Pacific Islands. To this end it runs films, lectures and seminars in conjunction with its exhibitions and even has a regular schedule of Asian musicians who play at the museum.

BROOKLYN CHILDREN'S MUSEUM

New York's first children's museum, it has a great programme of events and workshops and is particularly worth the trip if you are on a family holiday. See page 149.

BROOKLYN MUSEUM OF ART

One of the largest museums in the world and has recently undergone a facelift. It is easy to reach in Brooklyn if you have the time to plan it into your schedule. See page 230.

CHELSEA ART MUSEUM

Chelsea

✉ 556 West 22nd Street at 11th Avenue
☎ 212-255 0719
www.chelseaartmuseum.org
🚗 Subway C, E to 23rd Street
🕘 Wed to Sun noon–6pm
$ $5 adults, seniors and students free

In the heart of Chelsea's new gallery district, this new medium-sized, three-storey museum provides a venue for abstract work by artists who have not been exhibited in New York before and for midsize travelling shows from Europe and smaller American museums. It is also the new home of the Miotte Foundation, which is dedicated to the conservation of Informal Art (abstract) works by Jean Miotte, who has had a studio in SoHo since 1978.

CHILDREN'S MUSEUM OF ART

Little Italy

A wonderful children's museum, see page 146 for more details.

CHILDREN'S MUSEUM OF MANHATTAN

Upper West Side

The CMOM is entirely dedicated to children under the age of 10 – and their families. See page 146.

THE CLOISTERS

Washington Heights

✉ Fort Tyron Park, Fort Washington Avenue at Margaret Corbin Plaza, Washington Heights
☎ 212-923 3700
www.metmuseum.org
🚗 Subway A to 190th Street
🕘 March to Oct Tues to Sun 9.30am–5.15pm, Nov to Feb Tues to Sun 9.30am–4.45pm
$ Suggested donation $12 adults (includes free same-day admission to the Metropolitan Museum of Art – page 108), $7 students, under 12s free if with an adult

It's a long way north to The Cloisters. If you want to make the most of your time in the vicinity, combine a visit with a walking tour of Harlem (page 80).

Rockefeller cash allowed the Metropolitan Museum to buy this beautiful red-tiled Romanesque building 70 years ago. Now it is used purely to display examples of medieval art and architecture, including five cloisters – hence the name – from ruined French monasteries dating from the 12th to the 15th centuries. It is stunning to look at and houses some really exciting exhibits. For details about family events, see page 147.

COOPER-HEWITT NATIONAL DESIGN MUSEUM

Upper East Side

✉ 2 East 91st Street at 5th Avenue
☎ 212-849 8400
🚗 Subway 4, 5, 6 to 86th Street
🕘 Tues 10am–9pm, Wed to Sat 10am–5pm, Sun noon–5pm,
$ $5 adults, $3 students and seniors. Free on Tues 5–9pm

The only American museum devoted entirely to historical and contemporary design, the Cooper-Hewitt covers everything from applied arts and industrial design to drawings, prints, textiles and wall-coverings. Take time to look at the exterior of the building itself, which was designed in a Georgian style for tycoon Andrew Carnegie.

EL MUSEO DEL BARRIO

Spanish Harlem

✉ 1230 5th Avenue at 104th Street
☎ 212-831 7272
www.elmuseo.org
🚗 Subway 6 to 103rd Street
🕘 Wed to Sun 11am–5pm
$ Suggested donation $5 adults, $3 students and seniors, under 12s free with an adult

Opened in 1969 by a group of Puerto Rican parents, teachers and artists, it houses 8,000 objects of Caribbean and Latin American art from pre-Colombian times to date. Exhibits include musical instruments, miniature houses, dolls and masks.

GETTING IN FREE

No charge is made for admission to the following museums so they make a great addition to your itinerary:

National Museum of American Indian (page 121)

Schomburg Center for Research In Black Culture (page 124)

Ellis Island – you pay for the ferry ride! (pages 60–1)

Whitney Museum of American Art at Philip Morris (page 125)

In addition to this, many museums offer times – usually on a Friday or Tuesday evening – when you can gain access free or pay a voluntary donation of whatever you wish:

Free Friday nights

American Folk Art Museum 6–9pm (page 116)

Asia Society 6–9pm (page 116)

Frick Collection after 6pm on certain Fridays (page 114)

Free Tuesdays from 5–9pm

Cooper-Hewitt National Design Museum (page 117)

Jewish Museum (page 119)

FORBES MAGAZINE GALLERIES

Financial District

✉ 60–62 5th Avenue
☎ 212-206 5548
www.forbescollection.com
🚗 Subway F, L, N, V to 14th Street
🕐 Tues, Wed, Fri and Sat 10am–4pm
$ Free

The Forbes Magazine Galleries at the magazine's headquarters showcase The Forbes Collection™ of home and business furnishings, decorative accessories, gifts, jewellery, books, toy boats, miniature soldiers, presidential manuscripts and fine art.

FRAUNCES TAVERN MUSEUM

Financial District

✉ 54 Pearl Street at Broad Street, 1st and 2nd floors
☎ 212-425 1778
www.frauncestavernmuseum.org
🚗 Subway J, M, Z to Broad Street; 4, 5 to Bowling Green; 1, 2 to Wall Street
🕐 Mon to Fri 10am–4.45pm, Sat and Sun noon–4pm.
$ $3 adults, $2 children and seniors, under 6s and members free

When New York was (briefly) capital of America, the Fraunces Tavern housed the Departments of Foreign Affairs, Treasury and War and was where George Washington delivered his famous farewell speech to his officers. Now, nestled among the skyscrapers of the Financial District, this 18th-century Georgian building, along with four adjacent 19th-century buildings, houses a fine museum dedicated to the study of early American history and culture. Although well preserved, an awful lot of restoration work has been done to keep its 1783 façade.

Don't miss the cosy restaurant at the Fraunces Tavern Museum – it serves lovely food in a stately tourist environment.

Fraunces Tavern Museum

ISAMU NOGUCHI GARDEN MUSEUM

The Japanese sculptor's art can be seen at this museum in Queens. See page 237.

JAPAN SOCIETY

Midtown East

✉ 333 East 47th Street between 1st and 2nd Avenues
☎ 212-832 1155
www.japansociety.org
🚗 Subway E, V to Lexington Avenue–53rd Street; 6 to 51st Street
🕐 Tues to Fri 11am–6pm, Sat and Sun 11am–5pm
$ $5 adults, $3 students and seniors

The perfect place to feed your yearnings for all things Japanese from textiles and modern photography to historical ceramics, paintings, glass and metalworks. The ideal combination of Zen and now.

JULIA DE BURGOS LATINO CULTURAL CENTER AND TALLER BORICUA GALLERY

Spanish Harlem

✉ 1680 Lexington Avenue at 106th Street
☎ 212-831 4333
🚗 Subway 6 to 110th Street
🕐 Tues to Sun noon–6pm except Thurs 1–7pm

Another excellent location to see works by Latino artists. Around the museum, look out for pavement artwork by James de la Vega, a young local artist.

JEWISH MUSEUM

Upper East Side

✉ 1109 5th Avenue at 92nd Street
☎ 212-423 3200
www.thejewishmuseum.org
🚗 Subway 4, 5, 6 to 96th Street
🕐 Mon to Wed 11am–5.45pm, Thurs 11am–8pm, Fri 11am–3pm, Sun 10am–5.45pm
$ $8 adults, $5.50 students and seniors, children free. Free admission on Tuesdays from 5–9pm

Impressive annual exhibitions. The core exhibit is called The Jewish Journey and sets out how the Jewish people have survived through the centuries and explores the essence of Jewish identity. Many of the objects were actually rescued from European synagogues before the Second World War. It covers 4,000 years of history with an emphasis on art and culture both ancient and modern.

MERCHANT'S HOUSE MUSEUM

East Village

✉ 29 East 4th Street
☎ 212-777 1089
www.merchantshouse.com
🚗 Subway 6 to Astor Place
🕐 Thurs to Mon 1pm–5pm
$ $5 adults, $3 students and children free.

Built in 1832, this was home to prosperous merchant Seabury Tredwell and his family for over 100 years and is the city's only preserved 19th-century home – complete with original furnishings and decor. Tours every half hour Sat and Sun.

MORGAN LIBRARY

Midtown East

The bijou Morgan Library will be closed until early 2006.

✉ 29 East 36th Street between Madison and Park Avenues
☎ 212-685 0008
www.morganlibrary.org
🚗 Subway 6 to 33rd Street

A gem of a museum, housed in an Italianate building that was once J Pierpont Morgan's library. The collection contains medieval and Renaissance manuscripts; drawings and prints from the 14th century onwards, including works by Rubens, Degas, Blake and Pollock; ancient Middle Eastern seals and tablets; and original handwritten music manuscripts by Beethoven, Bach, Brahms and Schubert. The shop has some great upmarket souvenirs and child-friendly games. Keep it in mind for your next visit.

MOUNT VERNON HOTEL MUSEUM AND GARDEN

Upper East Side

✉ 421 East 61st Street between 1st and York Avenues
☎ 212-838 6878
🚗 Subway 4, 5, 6 to 59th Street
🕐 Tues to Sun 11am–4pm; closed in August and some holidays
$ $4 adults, $3 students and seniors, under 12s free

An amazing structure that dates back to the colonial era, this was once the coach house of the daughter of America's second president, John Adams. An early 18th-century building, it has been lovingly

The Jewish Museum

restored by the Colonial Dames of America who will sometimes be on hand to talk about the furnishings and park at the back.

MUSEUM OF AMERICAN FINANCIAL HISTORY

Financial District

⊠ 28 Broadway at Bowling Green Park
☎ 212-908 4110
www.financialhistory.org
Subway 4, 5 to Bowling Green, N, R to Rector Street
$ Suggested donation $2

Housed appropriately enough in the former headquarters of John D Rockefeller's Standard Oil, this recently opened museum traces the growth of the world's largest financial superpower. It has the largest public museum archive of financial documents in the world and exhibits include rare $100,000 bills. Wow!

MUSEUM OF CHINESE IN THE AMERICAS

Chinatown

⊠ 2nd floor, 70 Mulberry Street on the corner of Bayard Street
☎ 212-619 4785
www.moca-nyc.org
Subway N, R, 6 to Canal Street
Tues to Sun noon–5pm
$ $3 adults, $1 for 12s and over and seniors, free for under 12s

A fascinating little museum tucked away on the first floor of the community centre. It contains photographs and personal belongings and talks are given on the history of Chinese immigrants to both North and South America.

MUSEUM OF CONTEMPORARY ART AND DESIGN

Midtown

⊠ 40 West 53rd Street between 5th and 6th Avenues
☎ 212-956 3535
www.americancraftmuseum.org
Subway E, V to 5th Avenue
Daily 10am–6pm, Thurs 10am–8pm
$ $8 adults, $5 students and seniors, under 12s free

Along with the neighbouring American Folk Art Museum, this museum, formerly known as the American Craft Museum, gives a perfect insight into American arts and crafts. It has everything from wood and metal to clay, glass and fibre. Plans are for the museum to be moved to a permanent home in the new AOL Time Warner complex at Columbus Circle this year (2005).

MUSEUM OF JEWISH HERITAGE: A LIVING MEMORIAL TO THE HOLOCAUST

Battery Park City

⊠ 8 First Place between West Street and Battery Place
☎ 212-509 6130 for tickets in advance
www.mjhnyc.org
Subway 1, 9 to South Ferry; N, R, W to Whitehall Street; 4, 5 to Bowling Green
Sun to Wed 9am–5pm, Thurs 9am–8pm, Fri and eve of Jewish holidays 9am–3pm in winter, 9am–5pm in summer. Sat and Jewish holidays closed
$ $7 adults, $5 students, under 6s free.

Joy, tradition, tragedy and unspeakable horror are the powerful themes of this museum, which tells the moving story of 20th-century Jewish life from the perspective of those who lived it. Created as a living memorial to the Holocaust, it puts the tragedy into the larger context of modern Jewish history and includes 24 original films that feature testimonies from Steven Spielberg's Survivors of the Shoah Visual History Foundation, as well as the museum's own video archive.

It is worth renting an audio guide at the Museum of Jewish heritage, narrated by Meryl Streep and Itzhak Perlman, cost $5.

Before entering the museum, take a look at the six-sided shape of the tiered roof, a symbolic reminder of the six million who died in the Holocaust and of the Star of David. The biggest drawback with this museum is that it can feel inaccessible to non-Hebrew speakers, who simply don't understand much of the language used. Another problem is the size of the plaques – many are too tiny and the introductory film is too haphazard to give a really coherent understanding of the Holocaust. Maybe some of the problems will be ironed out by the opening of the new four-storey, 6,510-sq m (70,000-sq ft) east wing, which will contain a theatre, memorial garden, resource centre, family history centre, more gallery space, event hall and café.

MUSEUM OF TELEVISION AND RADIO

Midtown

✉ 25 West 52nd Street between 5th and 6th Avenues
☎ 212-621 6600
www.mtr.org
🚗 Subway E, F to 5th Avenue; B, D, F, Q to 47th–50th Streets/Rockefeller Center
🕘 Tues to Sun noon–6pm, Thurs noon–8pm, Fri theatre programmes until 9pm
$ $10 adults, $6 students and seniors, $5 under 13s

In addition to the exhibits, the museum also has a daily programme of screenings in two cinemas and two presentation rooms. Pick up a copy of the schedules in the lobby on your way in. You can also make an appointment with the library to check out the museum's collection of over 100,000 radio and TV programmes before accessing them on the custom-designed database.

MUSEUM OF THE CITY OF NEW YORK

Spanish Harlem

✉ 1220 5th Avenue at 103rd Street
☎ 212-534 1672
www.mcny.org
🚗 Subway 6 to 103rd Street
🕘 Sun noon–5pm, Wed to Sat 10am–5pm. Pre-registered groups only Tue 10.30am–noon. Closed on major holidays
$ Suggested donation $12 families, $7 adults, $4 children, students and seniors

The Museum of the City of New York is very relaxed about defining your family. Groups can buy a family ticket at the Museum of the City of New York even if they are not related.

The entire breadth of New York's history and the people who played parts in its development are celebrated in this fascinating museum. Prints, photographs, paintings and sculptures and even clothing and decorative household objects are used to tell the story of New York City. The museum is particularly noted for its Broadway memorabilia.

NATIONAL ACADEMY OF DESIGN

Midtown

✉ 1083 5th Avenue 10128
☎ 212-369 4880
www.nationalacademy.org
🚗 Subway 4, 5, 6 to 86th Street
🕘 Weds to Thurs 10am–5pm, Fri 10am–6pm, Sat and Sun 11am–6pm
$ $8 adults, children free

Both a museum and a design school of fine art with the largest collection of 19th- and 20th-century American art in the country, comprising more than 5,000 works.

NATIONAL MUSEUM OF THE AMERICAN INDIAN

Bowling Green/Financial District

✉ George Gustave Heye Center, US Custom House, 1 Bowling Green between State and Whitehall Streets
☎ 212-668 6624
www.americanindian.si.edu
🚗 Subway 4, 5 to Bowling Green; 1, 9 to South Ferry
🕘 Daily 10am–5pm except Thurs 10am–8pm
$ Free

The first museum dedicated entirely to Native American history, art, performing art and culture. The collection includes fabulous leather clothing, intricately beaded head-dresses, sashes, hats and shoes, explaining the white man's influence on Indian culture, as well as their own centuries-old traditions. Despite the size and grandness of the beautiful building, it only has 500 pieces on display and thus seems quite small. However, it is very well laid out and the explanations of each piece have usually been given by Native Americans.

NEUE GALERIE MUSEUM FOR GERMAN AND AUSTRIAN ART

Upper East Side

✉ 1048 5th Avenue at 86th Street
☎ 212-628 6200
www.neuegalerie.org
🚗 Subway 4, 5, 6 to 86th Street
🕘 Fri to Mon 11am to 7pm
$ $10 adults, $7 students and seniors. Under 12s not permitted, under 16s only with an adult.

Opened in November 2001, this museum was founded by the late German Expressionist art dealer Serge Sabarsky and chairman of the MoMA board Ronald S Lauder. It does exactly what it says on the tin by exhibiting fine and decorative arts of

Germany and Austria from the first half of the 20th century. A real bonus is the building itself – a wonderful Louis XIII-style, Beaux Art landmark.

While you're on the Museum Mile, take a pit stop at the fabulous Sabarsky Café in the Neue Galerie, which is open every day except Wednesday.

NEW MUSEUM OF CONTEMPORARY ART

SoHo

✉ 583 Broadway between Houston and Prince Streets

☎ 212-219 1222

www.newmuseum.org

🚗 Subway F, S to Broadway/Lafayette Street; N, R, W to Prince Street; 6 to Bleecker Street and Prince Street

🕐 Tues to Sun noon–6pm, Thurs noon–8pm

$ $6 adults, $3 students, under 18s free. $3 Thursdays 6–8pm

When they say 'contemporary', they really mean it. All the works exhibited are by living artists, often looking at social issues through modern media and machinery. The area downstairs at the museum is open free to the public and contains the bookstore, a spacious reading room and an exhibition space for interactive projects, installations and performances.

NEW YORK CITY FIRE MUSEUM

West SoHo

✉ 278 Spring Street between Varick and Houston Streets

☎ 212-691 1303

www.nycfiremuseum.org

🚗 Subway 1, 9 to Houston Street; C, E to Spring Street

🕐 Thurs to Sat 10am–5pm, Sun 10am–4pm

$ $4 adults, $2 students and seniors, $1 under 12s

Technically not a children's museum, though the bright shiny engines are an undoubted hit with youngsters and the young at heart. Housed in the old quarters of Engine 30, here you will find artefacts and fire engines depicting 200 years of city fire-fighting.

NEW YORK CITY POLICE MUSEUM

Bowling Green/Financial District

✉ 100 Old Slip at South Street

☎ 212-477 9753

www.nycpolicemuseum.org

🚗 Subway 4, 5 to Bowling Green; 2, 3, 4, 5 to Wall Street

🕐 Tues to Sat 10am–5pm

$ Suggested donation $5 adults, $3 seniors, $2 under 19s, under 6s free

Having opened in January 2000, this is one of the very latest attractions in the Downtown area and it's a little corker. It is now permanently housed in the former 1st Precinct building – the oldest cop shop in New York. Highlights include the Mounted Unit – one of the oldest and most prestigious within the NYPD – and the K-9

The National Museum of the American Indian

dog unit. In addition to the police memorabilia – a line-up of guns, uniforms and badges – there's even the Tommy gun with its original violin case that was used to kill mobster Frankie Yale. Plus, you can have a go at playing detective yourself in the interactive crime scene area. View the NYPD Hall of Heroes, which now has a memorial to the 23 policemen and women who lost their lives in the attack on the World Trade Center in 2001.

THE NEW YORK CITY TRANSIT MUSEUM

Brooklyn Heights

A great little museum that is particularly popular with children. See page 229.

THE NEW YORK HALL OF SCIENCE

Queens

A great science museum with demos. See page 236.

NEW YORK HISTORICAL SOCIETY

Upper West Side

✉ 2 West 77th Street at Central Park West
☎ 212-873 3400
www.nyhistory.org
🚗 Subway B, C to 81st Street; 1 to 79th Street
🕘 Tues to Sun 11am–6pm
$ $8 adults, $6 students and seniors, under 12s free

When this jewel was formed in 1804 it was the only art museum in the city until the opening of the Metropolitan Museum of Art in 1872. The Historical Society was founded to chronicle New York's history and is home to the world's largest collection of Tiffany stained-glass shades and lamps, two million manuscripts, including letters sent by George Washington during the War of Independence, and a lock of his hair.

New York Hall of Science

P.S. 1 CONTEMPORARY ART CENTER

Long Island City, Queens

A ground-breaking modern art museum. See page 237.

QUEENS COUNTY FARM MUSEUM

Floral Park, Queens

A fun, working historical farm with hayrides. See page 237.

SCHOMBURG CENTER FOR RESEARCH IN BLACK CULTURE

Harlem

✉ 515 Malcolm X Boulevard at 135th Street
☎ 212-491 2200
www.schomburgcenter.org
🚗 Subway 2, 3 to 135th Street
🕐 Mon to Wed noon–8pm, Thurs to Sat 10am–6pm
$ Free. Tours by appointment

To see the Schomburg Center at its best, phone or check out the website in advance to find out about film screenings and jazz concerts.

Established in 1926 by Arthur Schomburg, the museum has more than five million items including books, photographs, manuscripts, art works, films, videos and sound recordings that document the historical and cultural development of black people in the United States, the Caribbean, the Americas, Africa, Europe and Asia.

The research unit is open to anyone, while there are exhibitions on art dating back to the 17th century that include masks, paintings and sculptures. Incidentally, the corner of Malcolm X Boulevard, where the Schomburg sits, was once home to Harlem's Speaker's Corner where people used to come and talk about their political beliefs and organisations.

SOUTH STREET SEAPORT MUSEUM

Financial District

✉ 207–211 Water Street at Beekman Street
☎ 212-748 8600
www.southstseaport.org
🚗 Subway A, C to Broadway/Nassau Street; 2, 3, 4, 5, J, Z, M to Fulton Street
🕐 April 1 to Sept 30 daily 10am–6pm; Oct 1 to Mar 31 Wed to Mon 10am–5pm
$ $6 adults including all tours, films, galleries and museum-owned ships

A sprawling mass of galleries, 19th-century buildings, a visitors' centre and a selection of ships, all of which give an insight into life in the olden days of New York. The museum is also the venue for a series of free outdoor summer concerts held almost nightly.

STUDIO MUSEUM IN HARLEM

Harlem

✉ 144 West 125th Street between 7th and Lenox Avenues
☎ 212-864 4500
🚗 Subway A, B, C, D, 2, 3, 4, 5, 6 to 125th Street
🕐 Mon to Fri 10am–6pm
$ $5 adults, $3 students and seniors, $1 children

Works of art by African-American, African and Caribbean artists.

VAN CORTLANDT HOUSE MUSEUM

The Bronx

Fascinating former family plantation estate-turned museum. See page 234.

WHITNEY MUSEUM OF AMERICAN ART

Upper East Side

✉ 945 Madison Avenue at 75th Street
☎ 212-570 3676 or 1-800-WHITNEY
www.whitney.org
🚗 Subway 6 to 77th Street
🕐 Tues to Thurs, Sat and Sun 11am–6pm, Fri 1–9pm
$ $12 adults, $10 students, under 12s free. First Friday of every month 6–9pm pay what you wish, plus musical performances

The Whitney may be housed in one of the most ghastly looking buildings in the world – a grey, granite series of cubes designed by Marcel Breuer – but it has a world-class collection of 20th-century art. Yet it all came about almost by accident. Gertrude Vanderbilt Whitney offered her entire collection to the Metropolitan but was turned down, so she decided to set up her own museum. As a result, in 1931, the Whitney was founded with a core group of 700 art objects.

Subsequently, the museum's holdings have been greatly enriched by other purchases and the gifts of other major

BRIT'S GUIDE MUSEUM AWARDS

Most unmissable museum:
Metropolitan Museum of Art (page 108)

Most hands-on museums:
American Museum of Natural History (page 108)
Intrepid Sea-Air-Space Museum (page 113)
Children's Museum of Manhattan (page 146)

Most audacious museum:
Museum of Sex (page 113)

Most amazing museum building:
Solomon R Guggenheim (page 115)

Most unattractive museum building:
Whitney Museum of American Art (page 125)

Most fun bijou museum:
Museum of the City of New York (page 121)

Most tear-jerking museums:
Lower East Side Tenement Museum (page 111)
Museum of Jewish Heritage (page 120)

collectors. It now has a permanent collection of 12,000 works including paintings, sculptures, drawings, prints, photographs and multimedia installations and is still growing.

As well as the wide range of artists in its collection, the Whitney has huge bodies of works by artists such as Alexander Calder, Edward Hopper, Georgia O'Keefe, Gaston Lachaise and Agnes Martin.

Although the Midtown branch (below) is known for exhibitions of works by contemporary artists, the main museum still likes to mount cutting-edge exhibitions. To make the most of your visit, you can take an audio tour.

The shop in the basement, next to the restaurant, is filled with funky and colourful gifts. There's some great stuff for kids including soap crayons that will wash off baths and tiles and colourful blocks of soap that can be moulded into sculptures.

WHITNEY MUSEUM OF AMERICAN ART AT PHILIP MORRIS

Midtown

✉ 120 Park Avenue at 42nd Street
☎ 212-878 2550
🚗 Subway S, 4, 5, 6, 7 to 42nd Street/ Grand Central
🕘 Mon to Fri 11am–6pm, Thurs 11am–7.30pm. The Sculpture Court is open Mon to Sat 7.30am–9.30pm, Sun 11am–7pm
$ Free

The midtown branch of the Whitney is devoted to exhibitions of individual contemporary artists.

ESSEX
HOUSE

CHAPTER 7

Children's New York

A visit to New York for a child is incredibly exciting. From the towering buildings to the bright lights of Times Square, it's a visual feast for kids as well as adults. The prospect of tackling New York with a young child, however, may seem a little daunting, yet the city is surprisingly well geared up to the challenge. Restaurants are welcoming, hotels are accommodating and a whole array of outdoor and indoor activities – particularly in the summer – provide an unlimited supply of entertainment. A word of warning: visiting any of the incredible children's stores with a real-life child in tow is likely to lead to plastic card meltdown!

CENTRAL PARK

⊠ From Central Park South at 59th Street in the Midtown area to 110th Street in Harlem

☎ **www.centralpark.org**

Top of the pile for all-round entertainment, with a small but perfectly formed Wildlife Conservation Center and Children's Petting Zoo, the fun carousel, ice-skating at the Wollman Rink and the Discovery Center at Belvedere Castle, plus a whole host of activities, make for an all-round winner. For more information on Central Park, see pages 219–20.

As you enter through the Grand Army Plaza at the southern end of the park at 59th Street, you will find the following:

CAROUSEL

⊠ Mid-park at 64th Street and 5th Avenue

☎ 212-879 0244

🚗 Subway N, R to 5th Avenue; 6 to 68th Street

🕘 10.30am–6pm daily; closes at 5pm in winter

$ 90c a ride

A carousel has been on this site since 1871 when the original was powered by a blind mule and a horse, which walked a treadmill in an underground pit. Fortunately, no animals have to be put through such torture any more as the current electrical ride was donated by the Michael Friedsam Foundation in 1951. It features some of the largest hand-carved horses in the US.

CHILDREN'S ZOO AND WILDLIFE CENTER

⊠ Mid-park at 64th Street and 5th Avenue

☎ 212-861 6030
www.wcs.org

🚗 Subway N, R to 5th Avenue; 6 to 68th Street

🕘 10am–5pm daily; closes at 4.30pm in winter

$ $6 adults, $1 under 13s, under 3s free

A small but perfectly formed zoo and conservation centre that is just the right size for little people to enjoy. Exhibits include a polar bear, Tamarin monkeys and red pandas, plus other endangered species. There is a guided tour at 2.30pm, while you can watch the sea lions being fed at 11.30am, 2pm and 4pm, and the penguins at 10.30am and 2.30pm.

THE DAIRY

⊠ Mid-park at 65th Street

☎ 212-794 6564

🚗 Subway N, R to 5th Avenue; 6 to 68th Street

🕘 11am–5pm daily; closes at 4pm in winter

$ Free

A 19th-century-style building overlooking the Wollman Rink with an interactive

Central Park Zoo

SUMMER IN THE CITY

Puppet shows, free storytellings, films and workshops in libraries – these form just a part of what's on offer throughout the summer, so you'll be hard pressed to find a moment's peace! To find out what's going on where and when, pick up a copy of *Events For Children* from any branch of the New York Public Library. Most are free or very good value for money.

Here is an outline of some of the many activities available for children in summer:

Central Park
The park is a year-round winner, but summertime is when it really comes into its own. Specific children's events abound, including those organised by **Arts in the Park** (tel 212-988 9093), while the whole family can enjoy offerings put on by the **Central Park SummerStage** (tel 212-360 2777, **www.summerstage.org**) and **New York Shakespeare Festival** (tel 212-260 2400, **www.publictheater.org**).

Bryant Park Summer Film Festival (tel 212-512 5700)
Perfect for adults and children alike, head to Bryant Park on a Monday night and pull up a chair, or lay out a rug, to enjoy a free outdoor film on the massive screen. Remember to take some snacks and drinks. Children can let off a little steam before or after at the nearby carousel.

New York Philharmonic Young People's Concerts (Avery Fisher Hall, 10 Lincoln Center Plaza, tel 212-875 5000)
A series of summer concerts where children get to meet the musicians and try out their instruments for an hour before the concert. You'll also be in the right spot for the Lincoln Center's free Out-of-Doors Festival, with events throughout August.

International Festival of Puppet Theatre (tel 212-794 2400, **www.hensonfestival.org**)
A biennial puppet festival held at various venues throughout the city in September (next one 2006) produced by the Jim Henson Foundation.

Lincoln Center Out-of-Doors (Lincoln Center Plaza, Broadway at 65th Street, tel 212-875 5108)
A free festival for all ages running throughout August with specific events for children. They include the Iced Tea Dance where children get to dance with professionals, a Homemade Instrument Day in which children can make their own instruments and play them and a Play Day.

the park. It also houses a reference library and an exhibit about the history and design of the park.

BELVEDERE CASTLE DISCOVERY CENTER

✉ Mid-park at 79th Street
☎ 212-772 0210
🚗 Subway B, C to 81st Street
🕘 Tues to Sun 10am–5pm; closes 4pm in winter
$ Free

Sitting on a Vista Rock, this is the highest point in the park and gives great views in all directions. The new Henry Luce Nature Observatory includes exhibits on flowers, trees and birds in the park. The Center is a popular venue and the starting point for many fun events such as:

Discovery Kits (call 212-772 0210 for reservations): The Central Park Conservancy lends a backpack with binoculars, guidebook, maps and sketching materials for bird-watching in the Ramble and other locations. For children aged 6 and up, though those under 12 must be with an adult.

Experimental Science and Nature Fun (call 212-772 0210 to register): Learn about botany, geology, weather and animal habitats through science experiments and short demonstrations at various points in the park. Open to all ages.

Woods and Water Exhibit (tel 212-772 0210): A colourful, hands-on exhibit sponsored by the Central Park Conservancy which focuses on the rich variety of plants and animals in the park.

INDEX to MAP PAGES
LEGEND
92
Highways/Interstate
3
Throughroutes
Main Roads
Other Roads
Railways
Places of Interest
Bus/Rail Stations
Parks
SOHO
Districts
MAP 8
MAP 7
MAP 6
MAP 5
MAP 4
MAP 3
MAP 2
MAP 1
MAP 11
MAP 9
MAP 10
Queens
New York
Manhattan
Brooklyn
N
Upper New
York Bay

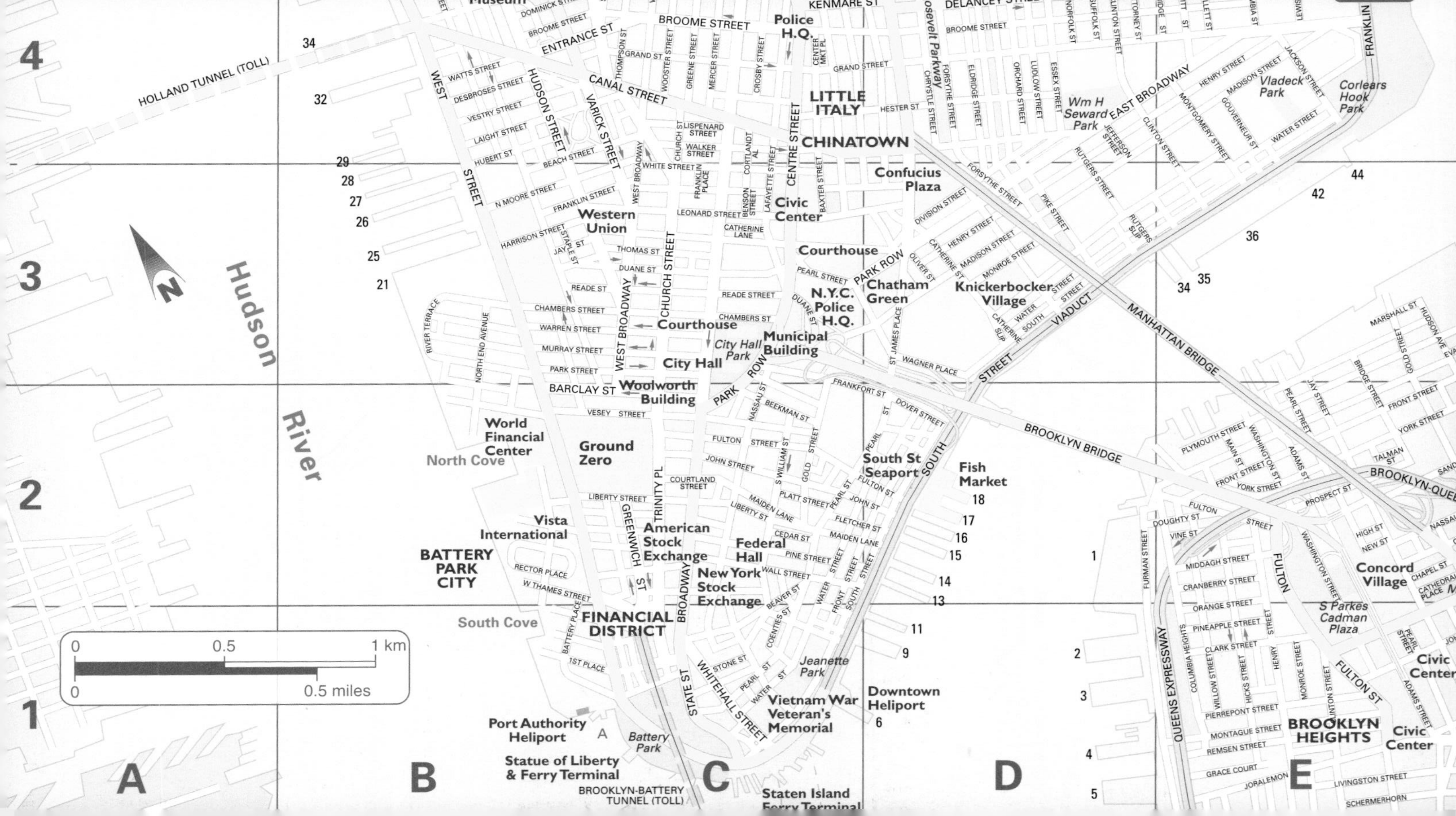
Hudson River
North Cove
South Cove
BATTERY PARK CITY
World Financial Center
Ground Zero
Vista International
FINANCIAL DISTRICT
American Stock Exchange
New York Stock Exchange
Federal Hall
Woolworth Building
City Hall
City Hall Park
Courthouse
Municipal Building
N.Y.C. Police H.Q.
Chatham Green
Knickerbocker Village
Confucius Plaza
Civic Center
Western Union
CHINATOWN
LITTLE ITALY
Police H.Q.
Museum
South St Seaport
Fish Market
Downtown Heliport
Vietnam War Veteran's Memorial
Jeanette Park
Battery Park
Port Authority Heliport
Statue of Liberty & Ferry Terminal
BROOKLYN-BATTERY TUNNEL (TOLL)
Staten Island Ferry Terminal
HOLLAND TUNNEL (TOLL)
BROOKLYN BRIDGE
MANHATTAN BRIDGE
Wm H Seward Park
Vladeck Park
Corlears Hook Park
BROOKLYN HEIGHTS
Concord Village
S Parkes Cadman Plaza
Civic Center
QUEENS EXPRESSWAY
0
0.5
1 km
0.5 miles
A
B
C
D
E
1
2
3
4

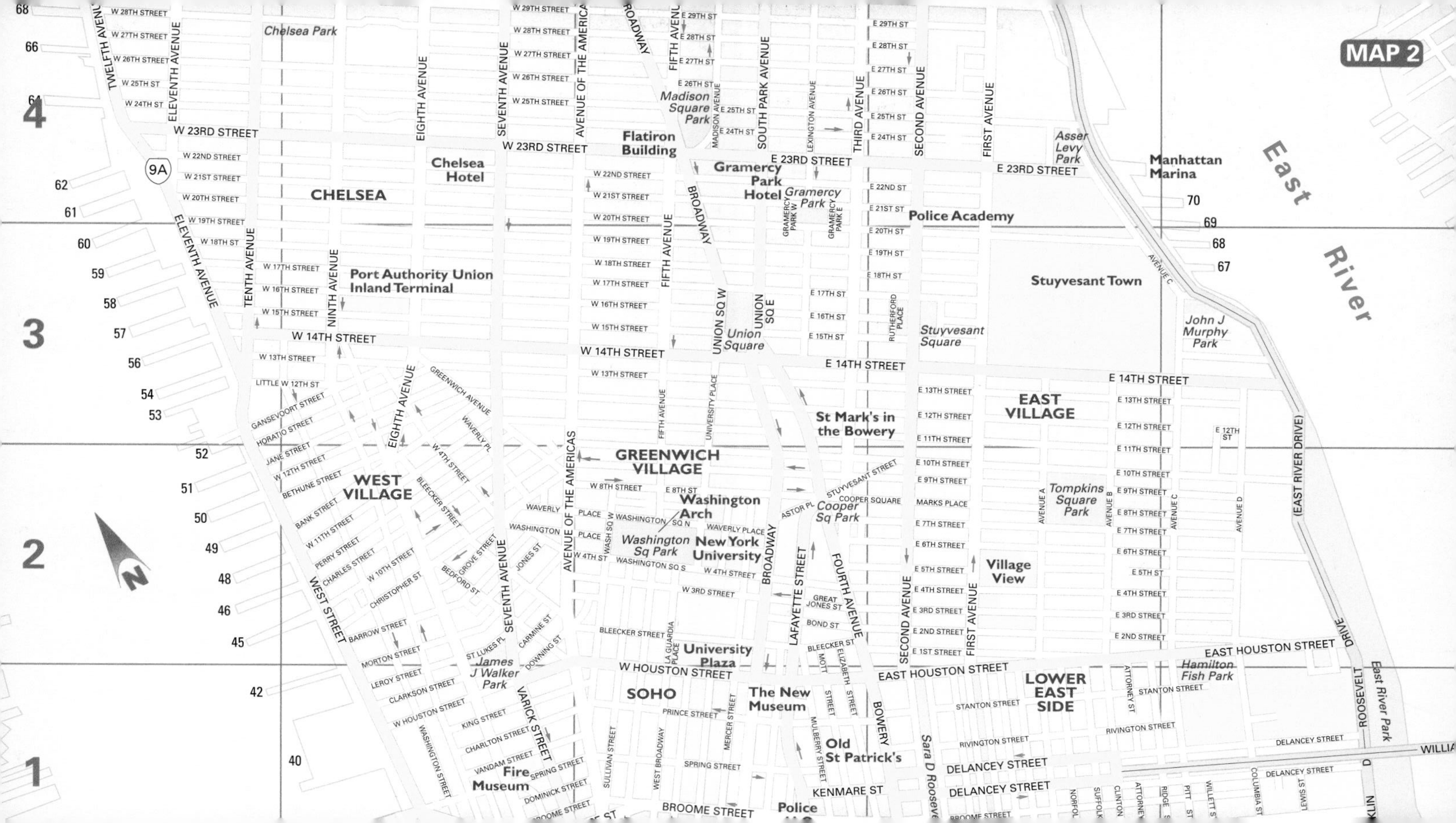

MAP 2
CHELSEA
Chelsea Park
Chelsea Hotel
Port Authority Union Inland Terminal
Flatiron Building
Madison Square Park
Gramercy Park Hotel
Gramercy Park
Police Academy
Stuyvesant Town
Asser Levy Park
Manhattan Marina
East River
John J Murphy Park
Stuyvesant Square
Union Square
WEST VILLAGE
GREENWICH VILLAGE
EAST VILLAGE
St Mark's in the Bowery
Washington Arch
Washington Sq Park
New York University
Cooper Sq Park
Tompkins Square Park
Village View
University Plaza
SOHO
The New Museum
LOWER EAST SIDE
Hamilton Fish Park
Old St Patrick's
James J Walker Park
Fire Museum
East River Park
TWELFTH AVENUE
ELEVENTH AVENUE
TENTH AVENUE
NINTH AVENUE
EIGHTH AVENUE
SEVENTH AVENUE
AVENUE OF THE AMERICAS
FIFTH AVENUE
BROADWAY
SOUTH PARK AVENUE
LEXINGTON AVENUE
THIRD AVENUE
SECOND AVENUE
FIRST AVENUE
W 23RD STREET
E 23RD STREET
W 14TH STREET
E 14TH STREET
W HOUSTON STREET
EAST HOUSTON STREET
WEST STREET
BLEECKER STREET
LAFAYETTE STREET
FOURTH AVENUE
BOWERY
DELANCEY STREET
KENMARE ST
BROOME STREET
(EAST RIVER DRIVE)
ROOSEVELT DRIVE
AVENUE A
AVENUE B
AVENUE C
AVENUE D
9A

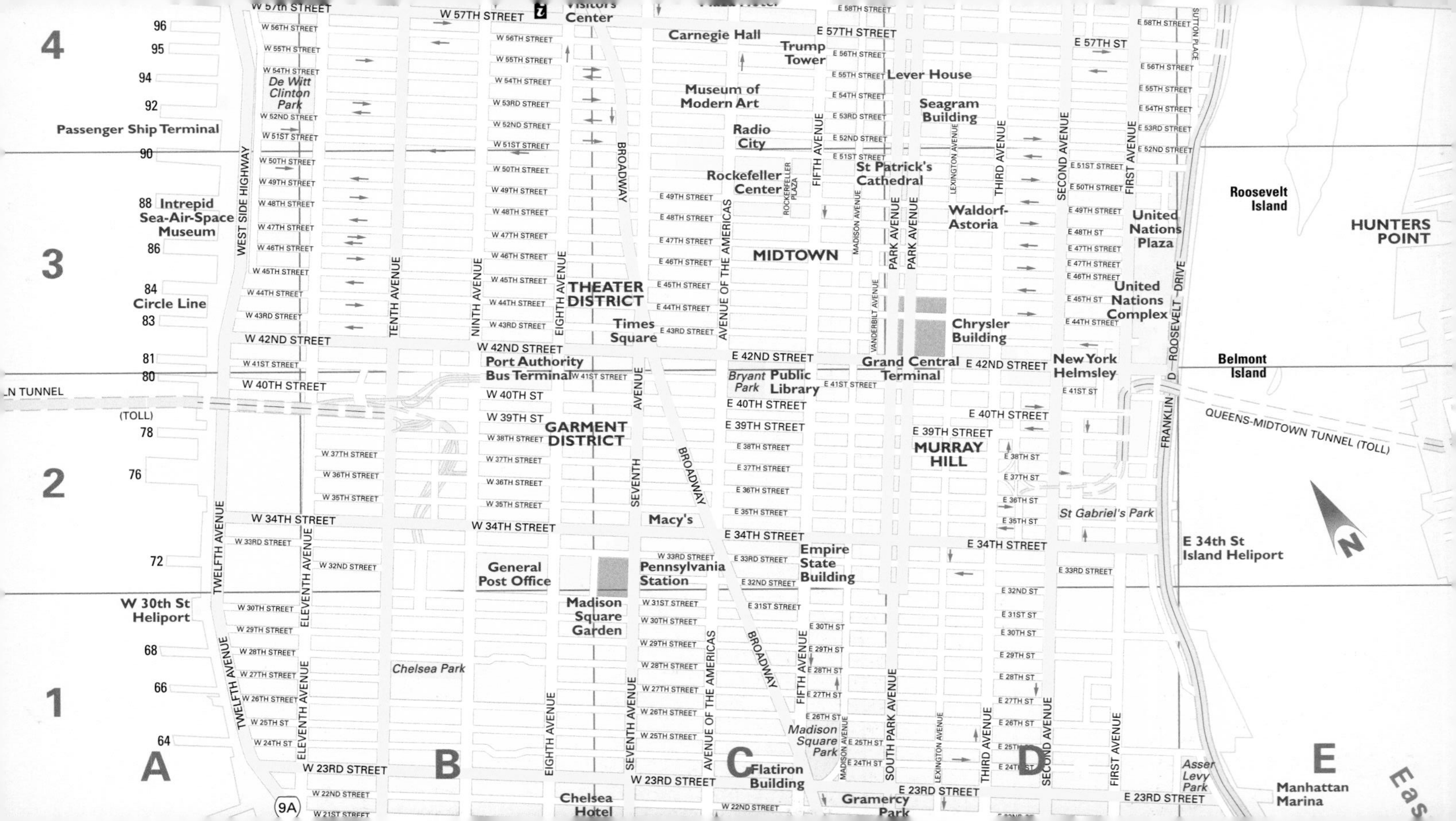

4
3
2
1
A
B
C
D
E

Passenger Ship Terminal
Intrepid Sea-Air-Space Museum
Circle Line
W 30th St Heliport
De Witt Clinton Park
Chelsea Park
Visitors Center
Carnegie Hall
Trump Tower
Lever House
Museum of Modern Art
Seagram Building
Radio City
Rockefeller Center
ROCKEFELLER PLAZA
St Patrick's Cathedral
Waldorf-Astoria
United Nations Plaza
United Nations Complex
MIDTOWN
THEATER DISTRICT
Times Square
Chrysler Building
Port Authority Bus Terminal
Grand Central Terminal
New York Helmsley
Bryant Park
Public Library
GARMENT DISTRICT
MURRAY HILL
St Gabriel's Park
Macy's
Empire State Building
General Post Office
Pennsylvania Station
Madison Square Garden
Madison Square Park
Flatiron Building
Chelsea Hotel
Gramercy Park
Asser Levy Park
Manhattan Marina
E 34th St Island Heliport
Roosevelt Island
Belmont Island
HUNTERS POINT
East

96
95
94
92
90
88
86
84
83
81
80
78
76
72
68
66
64
9A

TWELFTH AVENUE
WEST SIDE HIGHWAY
ELEVENTH AVENUE
TENTH AVENUE
NINTH AVENUE
EIGHTH AVENUE
SEVENTH AVENUE
BROADWAY
AVENUE OF THE AMERICAS
FIFTH AVENUE
MADISON AVENUE
VANDERBILT AVENUE
PARK AVENUE
SOUTH PARK AVENUE
LEXINGTON AVENUE
THIRD AVENUE
SECOND AVENUE
FIRST AVENUE
SUTTON PLACE
FRANKLIN D ROOSEVELT DRIVE
QUEENS-MIDTOWN TUNNEL (TOLL)
LINCOLN TUNNEL (TOLL)

W 57TH STREET
W 56TH STREET
W 55TH STREET
W 54TH STREET
W 53RD STREET
W 52ND STREET
W 51ST STREET
W 50TH STREET
W 49TH STREET
W 48TH STREET
W 47TH STREET
W 46TH STREET
W 45TH STREET
W 44TH STREET
W 43RD STREET
W 42ND STREET
W 41ST STREET
W 40TH STREET
W 40TH ST
W 39TH ST
W 38TH STREET
W 37TH STREET
W 36TH STREET
W 35TH STREET
W 34TH STREET
W 33RD STREET
W 32ND STREET
W 31ST STREET
W 30TH STREET
W 29TH STREET
W 28TH STREET
W 27TH STREET
W 26TH STREET
W 25TH STREET
W 25TH ST
W 24TH ST
W 23RD STREET
W 22ND STREET
W 21ST STREET

E 58TH STREET
E 57TH STREET
E 57TH ST
E 56TH STREET
E 55TH STREET
E 54TH STREET
E 53RD STREET
E 52ND STREET
E 51ST STREET
E 50TH STREET
E 49TH STREET
E 48TH STREET
E 48TH ST
E 47TH STREET
E 46TH STREET
E 45TH STREET
E 45TH ST
E 44TH STREET
E 43RD STREET
E 42ND STREET
E 41ST STREET
E 41ST ST
E 40TH STREET
E 39TH STREET
E 38TH STREET
E 38TH ST
E 37TH STREET
E 37TH ST
E 36TH STREET
E 36TH ST
E 35TH STREET
E 35TH ST
E 34TH STREET
E 33RD STREET
E 32ND STREET
E 32ND ST
E 31ST STREET
E 31ST ST
E 30TH ST
E 29TH ST
E 28TH ST
E 27TH ST
E 26TH ST
E 25TH ST
E 24TH ST
E 23RD STREET
E 22ND STREET

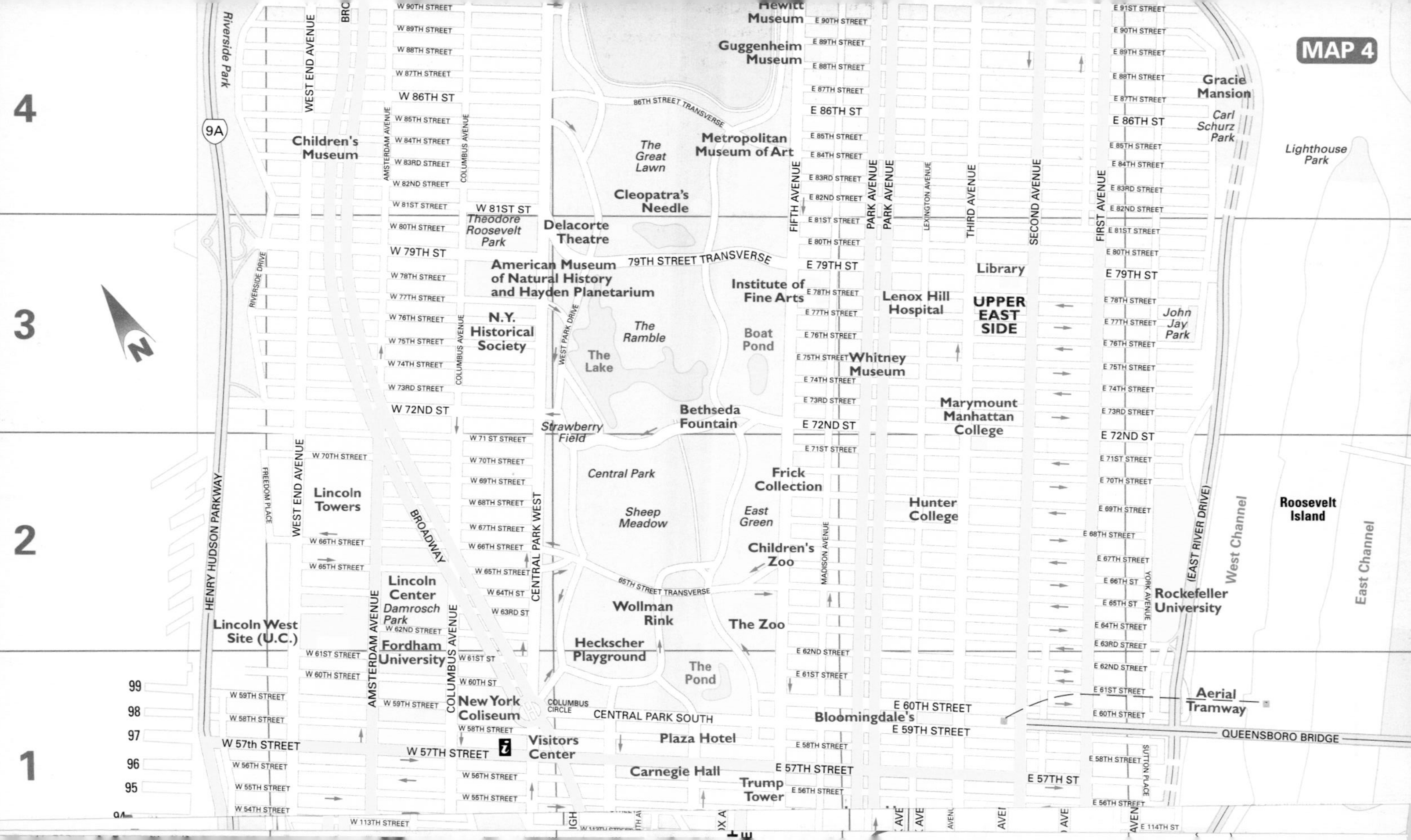

MAP 4
1
2
3
4
Riverside Park
9A
HENRY HUDSON PARKWAY
RIVERSIDE DRIVE
FREEDOM PLACE
WEST END AVENUE
Children's Museum
Lincoln Towers
Lincoln West Site (U.C.)
AMSTERDAM AVENUE
BROADWAY
COLUMBUS AVENUE
Lincoln Center
Damrosch Park
Fordham University
New York Coliseum
Visitors Center
COLUMBUS CIRCLE
CENTRAL PARK WEST
CENTRAL PARK SOUTH
Theodore Roosevelt Park
American Museum of Natural History and Hayden Planetarium
N.Y. Historical Society
Delacorte Theatre
79TH STREET TRANSVERSE
86TH STREET TRANSVERSE
65TH STREET TRANSVERSE
WEST PARK DRIVE
The Great Lawn
Cleopatra's Needle
The Ramble
The Lake
Boat Pond
Strawberry Field
Bethesda Fountain
Central Park
Sheep Meadow
East Green
Children's Zoo
Wollman Rink
The Zoo
Heckscher Playground
The Pond
Hewitt Museum
Guggenheim Museum
Metropolitan Museum of Art
Institute of Fine Arts
Frick Collection
Whitney Museum
Plaza Hotel
Carnegie Hall
Trump Tower
Bloomingdale's
FIFTH AVENUE
MADISON AVENUE
PARK AVENUE
LEXINGTON AVENUE
THIRD AVENUE
SECOND AVENUE
FIRST AVENUE
YORK AVENUE
SUTTON PLACE
Lenox Hill Hospital
Library
UPPER EAST SIDE
Marymount Manhattan College
Hunter College
John Jay Park
Rockefeller University
Gracie Mansion
Carl Schurz Park
Lighthouse Park
(EAST RIVER DRIVE)
West Channel
Roosevelt Island
East Channel
Aerial Tramway
QUEENSBORO BRIDGE
W 57th STREET
W 57TH STREET
W 72ND ST
W 79TH ST
W 81ST ST
W 86TH ST
E 57TH STREET
E 57TH ST
E 59TH STREET
E 60TH STREET
E 72ND ST
E 79TH ST
E 86TH ST
99
98
97
96
95

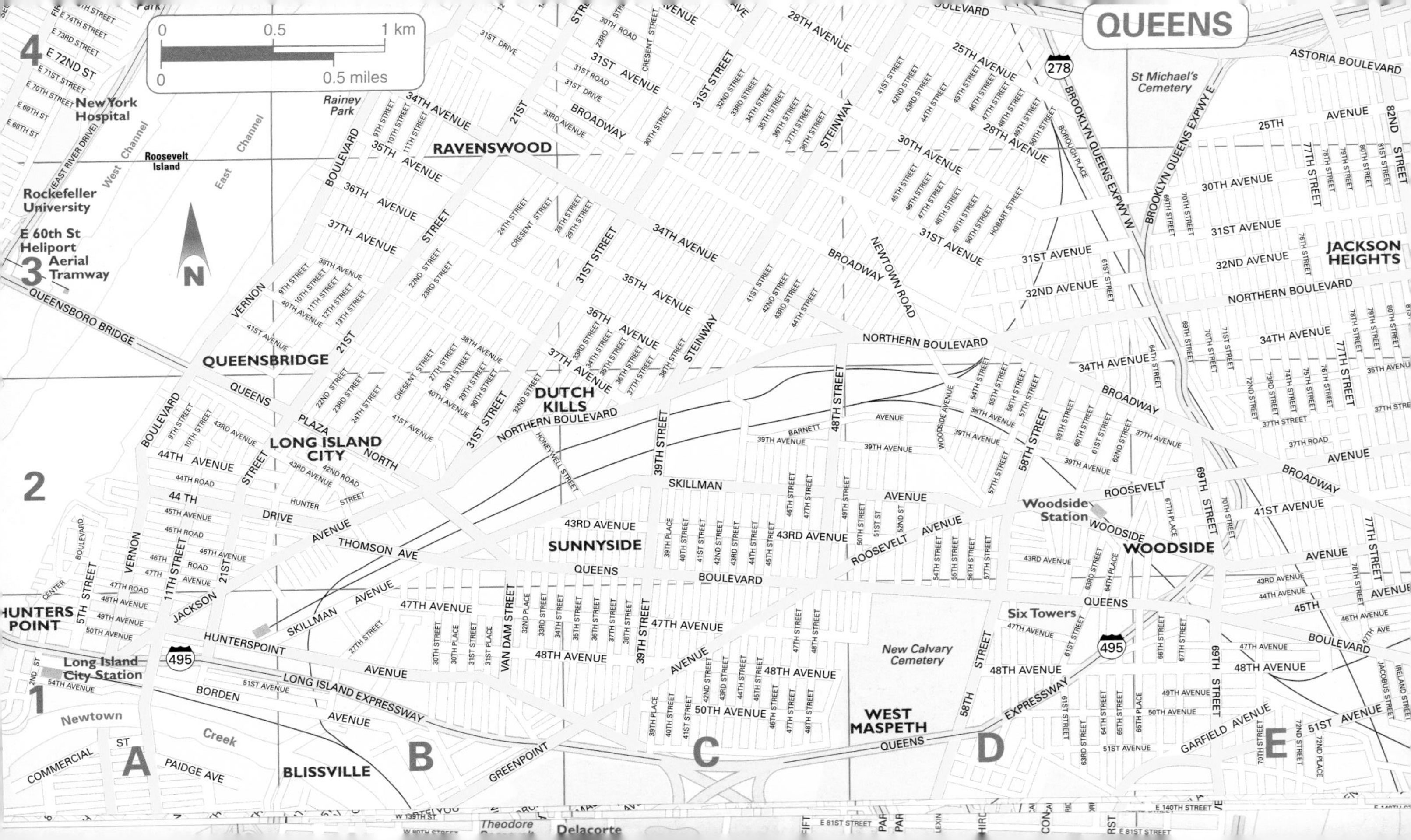

QUEENS
1
2
3
4
A
B
C
D
E
HUNTERS POINT
Long Island City Station
Newtown Creek
BLISSVILLE
LONG ISLAND CITY
QUEENSBRIDGE
RAVENSWOOD
DUTCH KILLS
SUNNYSIDE
WEST MASPETH
New Calvary Cemetery
Six Towers
Woodside Station
WOODSIDE
JACKSON HEIGHTS
St Michael's Cemetery
Rainey Park
Roosevelt Island
West Channel
East Channel
E 60th St Heliport
Aerial Tramway
Rockefeller University
New York Hospital
QUEENSBORO BRIDGE
LONG ISLAND EXPRESSWAY
BROOKLYN QUEENS EXPWY W
BROOKLYN QUEENS EXPWY E
495
278
N
0
0.5
1 km
0
0.5 miles

MANHATTAN STREET INDEX

Single bold number refers to map number

Alpha numerics refer to those within specified map

QUEENS STREET INDEX

Brooklyn Street Index

SWEDISH COTTAGE MARIONETTE THEATRE

✉ Mid-park at 81st Street
☎ 212-988 9093
🚗 Subway B, C 81st Street
🕘 Tues to Fri 10.30am and noon, Sat 1pm
$ Suggested donation $5 adults, $4 children

Formerly a 19th-century Swedish schoolhouse, this cottage was moved to Central Park in 1876 and now holds various marionette plays for children throughout the year.

NORTH MEADOW RECREATION CENTER

✉ Mid-park at 97th Street
☎ 212-348 4867
🚗 Subway B, C, 6 to 96th Street
🕘 Mon to Fri 9am–7pm, Sat and Sun 10am–6pm
$ Free

Open to all ages, the centre provides free Field Day Kits which include everything you need to equip a family for a day in the park. The kits contain a basketball, ten cones, three bats, horseshoe set, playground ball, football, frisbee, skipping rope and hula-hoops. Call in advance to register.

CHARLES A DANA DISCOVERY CENTER

✉ North East Corner at the Harlem Meer
☎ 212-860 1370
🚗 Subway 2, 3, 6 to 110th Street
🕘 Daily 11am–5pm, closes 4pm in winter
$ Free

One of the park's many visitor centres, it is also the park's only environmental educational centre with children's workshops year-round. Free to all, the centre sponsors workshops, musical performances and park tours and also loans fishing poles for fishing in the well-stocked Meer. Its Catch-and-Release fishing programme is open to all ages and gives people the chance to fish for large-mouth bass, catfish, golden shiners and bluegills.

If you need a babysitter, contact the Baby Sitters' Guild for licensed childcare at 60 East 42nd Street, No 912, tel 212-682 0227, www.babysittersguild.com.

TOP SIGHTS FOR KIDS

Circle Line Sightseeing Cruise (page 73)
Statue of Liberty (page 60)
Empire State Building (page 61)
Times Square (page 49)
Central Park (pages 127 and 219)

CIRCUSES

BIG APPLE CIRCUS

Midtown West

✉ Damrosch Park, Lincoln Center
☎ 212-307 4100
🚗 Subway 1, 9 to 66th Street–Lincoln Center
$ Ticket prices vary

A totally family-friendly circus, it has a regular winter season from October to January in Central Park and travels to other parks in the city during the spring.

RINGLING BROS AND BARNUM & BAILEY CIRCUS

Midtown West

✉ Madison Square Garden, 7th Avenue at 32nd Street
☎ 212-465 6741
www.ringling.com
🚗 Subway A, C, E, 1, 2, 3, 9 to 34th Street–Penn Station
$ $25–75

An extremely popular circus, America's original and most famous company keeps children and adults glued to their seats with

RESTAURANTS

Restaurants in New York are very well geared up to families. Most have excellent value children's menus with plenty of choice and also provide colouring books and crayons to keep little ones occupied. But it is more than that – Americans generally welcome children with pleasure.

The **Pizzeria Uno** chain has good food, great value and friendly service. Some of the city's finest dining establishments such as the **Bull & Bear** at the Waldorf Astoria (page 167), **The View** at the Marriott Marquis (page 174) and the Ritz-Carlton's **Rise** bar and restaurant at Battery Park (page 187) have proved welcoming to kids. While these top-notch eateries do not tend to have specific children's menus, they go to a lot of trouble to accommodate their requests.

a triple extravaganza of thrilling acts taking place in three rings at once.

UNIVERSAL BIG TOP CIRCUS

Midtown West

✉ Venues vary

☎ 1-800 316 7439 or book through TicketMaster on 212-307 7171

$ $13–25

For thrills with a difference, try this African-American troupe, which provides circus standards to hip-hop, R&B and salsa music.

MUSEUMS

New York is brilliant when it comes to providing exciting and engaging museums and museum activities for children. They not only have plenty of dedicated children's museums, but many of the adult museums are genuinely interesting for children, too, while others provide a host of entertaining and lively activities.

CHILDREN'S MUSEUM OF ART

Little Italy

✉ 182 Lafayette Street between Broome and Grand Streets

☎ 212-274 0986

🚗 Subway N, R to Prince Street, B, D, F, Q to Broadway–Lafayette Street; 6 to Spring Street

$ $6, free for infants under 1

Under 7s can have an artistic ball with art computers, an art playground and a giant floor-to-ceiling chalkboard. There are also regular performing arts workshops led by local artists. A visit here is the perfect way to combine a shopping trip to SoHo for you with fun for the kids!

The Whitney Museum

CHILDREN'S MUSEUM OF MANHATTAN

Upper West Side

✉ 212 West 83rd Street between Broadway and Amsterdam Avenue

☎ 212-721 1234

www.cmom.org

🚗 Subway 1, 9 to 86th Street

🕘 Wed to Sun (and school holidays) 10am–5pm

$ $6 adults and children, $3 seniors, free for infants under 1

The CMOM is entirely dedicated to children under the age of 10. This is a fabulous place and almost worth a visit even if you don't have kids! Its mission statement is to inspire children and their families to learn about themselves and our culturally diverse world through a unique environment of interactive exhibits and programmes.

After you've explored CMOM, cross the street for a light snack and drinks at Café Lalo, which serves up great cakes and is featured in the Meg Ryan and Tom Hanks movie *You've Got Mail.*

And they certainly achieve it with their inspiring exhibits, such as the zany and fun-filled Body Odyssey, which shows children just what they're made of. Youngsters aged five and over can rush through the blood tunnel, hold their noses and slime around in the digestive tract, or take deep breaths and wind their way down the windpipe. On the way, they will learn about where burps come from, what makes a cut stop bleeding and where shed skin goes.

Other exhibits include WordPlay for tots aged six months to four years. The Time Warner Media Center helps children aged six and above to get behind the scenes of a professionally equipped TV studio and produce their own show, and the CMOM Theater takes children into a magical world of dance, music, theatre and puppetry.

MUSEUM ACTIVITIES

Major New York museums put their wealth of resources to great use by offering fab events and activities that both entertain and educate children from as young as four years old to their teens. Full details of all the following museums appear in Chapter 6, but here is an outline of what they specifically offer children and families.

METROPOLITAN MUSEUM OF ART

This magnificent museum uses various means to make its resources as accessible to children as possible – for free – and provides printed gallery guides and museum hunts at the **Uris Information Desk** on the ground floor near the 81st Street entrance. In addition, a whole series of workshops and programmes are available both through the week and at weekends. For exact times and dates, check out the calendar section of the website (**www.metmuseum.org**) or call 212-650 2304. Programmes include:

Hello Met!: Children from 5 to 12 and their families are given a stimulating introduction to the Met's encyclopaedia collection through sketching and a short film. Sunday 2–3pm.

Start With Art: Children aged 3 to 7 (plus an adult) meet at the Uris tiered seating area to explore art at the Met through storytelling, sketching and games. Tuesday and Thursday 2.30–3.30pm; Wednesday and Friday 3.30–4.30pm.

Look Again!: The history, meaning and cultural aspects of art in the museum are explored through chats, drawing and, from time to time, performances for children from 5 to 12 (plus an adult) on Saturday and Sunday.

Art Evening for Families: Conversation and sketching help visitors aged from 6 to 12 explore the museum's art collection. Saturday 6–7pm.

THE CLOISTERS

The northern Manhattan branch of the Metropolitan Museum, which is devoted to the art and architecture of medieval Europe, also has a series of free workshops for children from 4 to 12, usually on a Saturday 1–2pm. Subjects include medieval feasts and celebrations and stories from the Middle Ages. For further details see page 117, phone 212-650 2280 or visit **www.metmuseum.org/calendar**.

AMERICAN MUSEUM OF NATURAL HISTORY

This museum is a mine of entertaining exhibits and interactive displays filled as it is with ever-popular dinosaurs, an amazing new ocean life display, thousands of dollars worth of sparkling gems and a whole array of interactive devices that bring so many aspects of the natural world to life. In addition, each weekend it offers workshops on anything from **Mummies**, in which 8- and 9-year-olds can make their own miniature mummies, to **Space Camp**, where 7- to 9-year-olds can learn what it takes to become an astronaut, and **Stories of the Sky**, in which 4- to 6-year-olds (with an adult) take a trip to a fun, inflatable planetarium and learn about the ancient tales of the sun, moon and stars through music, games and storytelling.

Avoid the restaurants at the American Museum of Natural History and head round the corner to Pizzeria Uno in Columbus Avenue at 81st Street (page 177) where you'll find far more friendly family fare at excellent prices.

Ticket prices tend to be between $25 and $30, Saturday sessions generally run from noon–1.30pm and Sunday sessions from 10.30am. Check out **www.amnh.org** first to see which activities will be available during your visit to the city.

The museum also runs field trips, such as bird watching, bug (insect) hunts or flower inspections in the adjacent Central Park.

Coney Island parade

TOP 5 HOTELS FOR FAMILIES

Ritz-Carlton at Battery Park (page 204)
The Four Seasons (page 205)
Westin New York Times Square (page 213)
Le Parker Meridien (page 209)
The Wellington (page 214)

MUSEUM OF MODERN ART

The Family Programs at the MoMA introduce children and their parents to the world of modern art through guided walks, art workshops, artist talks and film screenings. For a list of scheduled activities, phone 212-708 9805 or email familyprograms@moma.org

The Gallery Talks: Saturday morning sessions for children aged 4 to 10, which offer lively interactive discussions in the museum's galleries before it opens to the public and include:

One-at-a-Time: Families can explore the permanent collection and special exhibitions. **Tours for Fours** is especially designed for 4-year-olds and introduces families to painting, sculpture, photography and works on paper.

Family Art Workshops: Children aged 5 to 10 and their parents explore artworks in the museum, then create their own art in a hands-on workshop.

THE WHITNEY MUSEUM

The Whitney has worked hard to make itself accessible to young children. Free guides are provided for families to introduce children and adults to selected works of art and encourage new ways of learning about art together. The **From the Ground Up!** guide helps families to explore the architecture of the building and includes in-museum and take-home activities. **People, Places and Spaces** is the Whitney's first family audio guide to works from the Whitney's permanent collection and is included with the admission fee.

Every Saturday noon–1pm the **Look Out! Families Explore American Art** session for children aged 7 to 11 explores different parts of the museum through sketching activities. It's best to reserve a place by calling 212-570 7745. **Family Fun! Workshops** are held every second Saturday of the month 9–11am and feature gallery tours and art projects for children aged 5 to 10 and their families. Registration is necessary, call 212-570 7745. You can also call this number for further information about other family workshops.

BRILLIANT MUSEUMS FOR ALL THE FAMILY

Intrepid Sea-Air-Space Museum (page 113)
New York City Fire Museum (page 122)
New York City Police Museum (page 122)
Lower East Side Tenement Museum (page 111)
New York City Transit Museum – Brooklyn (page 229)
And a brilliant sight:
Historic Richmond Town – Staten Island (page 238)

TOP SHOPS FOR CHILDREN

New York has some fantastic shops dedicated to children. The two not to be missed are the classic, long-established toy store **FAO Schwarz** (page 101) and the much newer but equally incredible **Toys R Us** flagship store in Times Square (page 102). Other fun places include the **Warner Brothers Studio Store** (page 102) and, of course, **The Disney Store** (page 102).

THE SOLOMON R GUGGENHEIM MUSEUM

In addition to special free family days, the Guggenheim runs a series of fascinating paid-for workshops. They include **Art and Technology Workshops**, in which 7- to 13-year-olds get real hands-on experience, **My iMovie**, when they get to use digital cameras to create short animated videos, and **Portraiture in Photoshop**, in which they study paintings in the museum before creating portraits of their family using Photoshop 6.0. For further details and to book a place, call 212-423 3587.

THE LOWER EAST SIDE TENEMENT MUSEUM

The best tour for children is the 45-minute **Confino Family Apartment tour**, which aims to bring history to life. The apartment recreates the life of the Sephardic Jewish Confino family from Kastoria in Greece in 1916. Teenager Victoria Confino welcomes visitors as if they were newly arrived immigrants and she were teaching them

Holiday-time tours at the Lower East Side Tenement Museum sell out quickly, so book as far in advance as possible.

how to adapt to life in America. Along the way you can touch any items in the apartment, try on period clothing and foxtrot to music played on an authentic wind-up Victrola. Price $9, free for under 5s.

FUN STOPS

MADAME TUSSAUD'S

✉ 234 West 42nd Street between 6th and 7th Avenues
☎ 800-246 8872
www.madame-tussauds.com
🚗 Subway A, C, E to 42nd Street/Times Square
🕘 Daily 10am–8pm
$ $25 adults, $19 children, free for under 4s

The New York version of London's famous waxworks is an enjoyable outing for kids. They'll get to see all their favourite stars from Michael Jordan to Tom Cruise.

SONY WONDER TECHNOLOGY LAB

✉ Sony Plaza, East 56th Street between Madison and 5th Avenues
☎ 212-833 8100
www.sonywondertechlab.com
🚗 Subway E, V to 5th Avenue/53rd Street
🕘 Tues–Wed 10am–6pm, Thurs 10am–8pm, Sun noon–6pm, closed Mon
$ Free, but you must book your time in advance

Four floors of interactive exhibits with robots and lots of hi-tech entertainment. Adults will love playing here as much as kids. Reservations only though, so be sure to book well in advance.

BROOKLYN

Brooklyn is a wonderful place to spend time with children. The neighbourhood is not only home to a raft of great museums for adults, it also has its own children's museums, a zoo, a boating lake and wildlife activities in the massive Prospect Park. On top of that, there is the famous Coney Island entertainments centre at the southern end of the borough.

BROOKLYN CHILDREN'S MUSEUM

Y 145 Brooklyn Avenue at St Mark's Avenue
S 718-735 4400
www.brooklynkids.org
🚗 Subway 1 to Kingston Avenue
🕘 Mon to Fri 9am–5pm, Wed to Fri 2–5pm, Sat and Sun 10am–5pm
$ Suggested donation $4

A fabulous place for children, this was once part of the Brooklyn Museum of Art until it set up on its own in 1899. Now children can have a ball here playing with synthesisers, operating water wheels to dam a stream, dancing on the keys of a walk-on piano and playing instruments from around the world. There are daily workshops, with a summertime rooftop performance on Fridays at 6pm.

PROSPECT PARK

A massive park brimming with activities for adults and children (see Chapter 14, A Taste of the Outer Boroughs) where you could easily spend a day enjoying the activities and chilling out.

LEFFERTS HOMESTEAD CHILDREN'S MUSEUM

✉ Prospect Park, Flatbush Avenue
☎ 718-965 6505
www.brooklynkids.org
🚗 Subway Q, S to Prospect Park
🕘 Mon to Fri 9am–5pm, Wed to Fri 2–5pm, Sat and Sun 10am–5pm
$ Suggested donation $4

Right by the main Grand Army Plaza entrance to Prospect Park stands this restored 18th-century farmhouse, once owned by original Dutch settlers in Brooklyn. Children can play with cooking tools, hunt for barnyard implements or play with toys from the era. Families can also take part in craft activities such as candle-making, sewing, butter-churning and making fire with a flint and steel. At weekends throughout the summer, stories are told under a tree, plus hoop games to play and gardening to do.

PROSPECT PARK ZOO

✉ Prospect Park, Flatbush Avenue
☎ 718-965 6505
www.brooklynkids.org
🚗 Subway Q, S to Prospect Park
🕘 Mon to Fri 9am–5pm, Wed to Fri 2–5pm, Sat and Sun 10am–5pm
$ Suggested donation $4, or $6 for a family of four

Again close to the Grand Army Plaza entrance to Prospect Park, this is Brooklyn's only zoo. It features nearly 400 animals and more than 80 species in an environment that gives children close-up views of some of the world's most unusual ones. They include prairie dogs, wallabies, tamarins, baboons, a red panda, plus a vibrant band of birds, reptiles and amphibians.

THE CAROUSEL

Right next door to the zoo and museum is the magnificently carved carousel, which features 51 horses, a lion, giraffe, a deer and two dragon-pulled chariots. It is also one of the few carousels in the world that is wheelchair accessible.

AUDUBON CENTER AT THE BOATHOUSE

✉ Lincoln Road/Ocean Avenue entrance to Prospect Park
☎ 718-965 6505
www.brooklynkids.org
🚗 Subway Q to Parkside Avenue; S to Prospect Park
🕐 End of May to first Mon in Sept Thurs to Sun and holidays noon–6pm; Sept to Nov until 5pm and Dec to May until 4pm

The beautiful 1905 Beaux Art boathouse was reopened in 2002 following an extensive restoration. With its elegant arches, decorative tiles and classical balcony, its design was based on a 16th-century Venetian library. Now an official Historic New York City Landmark, it is home to the new state-of-the-art Audubon Center, which is dedicated to preserving wildlife and natural education. You can take tours along nature trails into the surrounding acres of natural habitat, see interactive bird and wildlife exhibits or participate in family activities such as craftwork, music and technology sessions.

THE WOLLMAN RINK

✉ Prospect Park, Ocean Avenue entrance
☎ 718-965 6505
www.brooklynkids.org
🚗 Subway Q to Parkside Avenue; S to Prospect Park
🕐 Pedal boating hours: mid-May to end of May Thurs to Sun and holidays noon–5pm; June to Sept until 6pm and Oct to Nov until 5pm

Located between the lake and Concert Grove, the Wollman provides fun for all seasons. In the winter (from November to March/April) it provides 2,475sq m (26,600sq ft) of ice for skating, while in the summer you can hire pedal boats when it once again becomes a beautiful lake. Not part of the original plans for Prospect Park, this was built in 1960 and is now the home ground for the Brooklyn Blades amateur men's and women's ice-hockey teams.

Family time at Bryant Park

CONEY ISLAND, BROOKLYN

NEW YORK AQUARIUM FOR WILDLIFE CONSERVATION

✉ Surf Avenue at West 8th Street
☎ 718-265 3400
🚗 Subway D, F to West 8th Street–NY Aquarium
🕐 Mon to Fri 10am–5pm, Sat and Sun 10am–7pm
$ $11 adults, $7 under 13s and seniors, free for under 2s

Most famous for its beluga whale family, the aquarium has another unusual exhibit showing the creatures that live in New York's famous East River. Sharks, dolphins and a re-creation of the Pacific coastline also feature.

The New York Aquarium is just a short stroll away from Astroland amusement park, so if the weather turns bad you can take shelter in the Aquarium.

ASTROLAND

✉ 1,000 Surf Avenue at West 8th Street
☎ 718-372 0275
🚗 Subway D, F to West 8th Street–NY Aquarium
🕐 Last week of May to last week of Sept noon–midnight (depending on weather); phone for winter opening
$ $2 for each children's ride or $15 for 10

Undoubtedly tacky, Coney Island's amusement park has definitely seen better days, but that doesn't stop children from having fun. There are rides for every age.

CHAPTER 8

Restaurants

New Yorkers take their restaurants very seriously – not surprising, given that many New York apartments have tiny kitchens if they have one at all.

Of course, like everything American, big is best and in the case of restaurants big doesn't necessarily refer to size but to the reputation of the chefs, many of whom are now celebrities in their own right. In fact, many have become so highly regarded that getting into their establishments is a difficult task. If your heart is set on a meal at a trendy or landmark New York restaurant, book well ahead.

New Yorkers swear by the *Zagat Survey* as the best guide for foodies. It lists hundreds of top restaurants reviewed by members of the public, and you can buy it in most UK bookshops for £8.99, or visit www.zagat.com.

The number of restaurants in New York precludes me from giving all but a 'best of the best' kind of listing here. I have gone for the well known, the excellent and the trendy and added a few neighbourhood joints for good measure. And don't worry about spending a fortune because in many cases good food comes at excellent prices in the Big Apple. The price rating here is for a three-course meal without wine.

$	Under $35 per head
$$	Under $65 per head
$$$	$65 and up!

TOP 10 RESTAURANTS

Considering how many thousands of eating establishments there are in New York and how many of them serve up wonderful food in delightful environments, it's difficult to narrow them down to a Top 10. Yet all the restaurants listed below have earned their stripes for getting all the elements of fine dining and hospitality right: consistently excellent and innovative cuisine, attentive service and an enjoyable ambience in a wonderful setting. They obviously have prices to match, but for a once-in-a-holiday treat they won't disappoint.

LE CIRQUE 2000 $$–$$$

French–American
Midtown East

✉ New York Palace Hotel, 455 Madison Avenue between 50th and 51st Streets
☎ 212-303 7788
🚗 Subway 6 to 51st Street

Make no bones about it, this is THE best restaurant in all of New York. Others may come and go, but Sirio Maccioni's family-run restaurant has always remained an unswerving symbol of thrilling, cosmopolitan New York – entirely due to its gastronomic mastery matched only by its amazing style and ambience. Former mayor Rudolph Giuliani agreed and in an official proclamation to mark the restaurant's 25th anniversary stated: 'As one of the most glamorous and hospitable restaurants in New York, Le Cirque 2000 has maintained the perfect balance between high quality food and service. In recognition of this important anniversary I hereby proclaim Tuesday March 24, 1998, in the city of New York as Le Cirque 2000 Day.'

Le Cirque

RESTAURANTS

RESTAURANTS WITH VIEWS

2 West: American Fusion, Battery Park, $-$$$ (page 155)
American Park at the Battery: Gourmet American, Battery Park, $$$ (page 155)
Jean Georges: French, Midtown West, $$$ (page 153)
Park View At The Boathouse: American-seafood, Central Park, $$-$$$ (page 174)
Rainbow Room: Continental, Rockefeller Plaza, $-$$$ (page 166)
River Café: Gourmet American, Brooklyn, $$$ (page 178)
The View: Continental, Times Square, $$-$$$ (page 174)
Water Club: American, East Village, $-$$$ (page 170)
World Yacht Dinner Cruises: Gourmet American, Midtown West, $$$ (page 171)

The restaurant moved to its current venue in 1997 and is now an integral part of the glitteringly beautiful New York Palace Hotel (page 205) in elaborate rooms, complete with intricate mosaics, stained-glass windows and ornately decorated ceilings. Famous New York restaurant designer Adam Tihany has created a fun yet genteel contemporary dimension to the restaurant by adding bold-coloured, high-backed chairs with clown buttons down the back, multi-coloured ladder lamps, geometric carpets and jewel-toned, one-arm armchairs. The end result is a stunning yet whimsical, grand yet inviting setting that transports you to a fantasy realm in which to enjoy some of the best cuisine in the world.

Originally entirely French cuisine, the restaurant has broadened its scope to include Italian and American accents using the freshest meat, poultry, fish and vegetables. This is definitely one place where it would be a waste of stomach space to load up on the bread. With changing menus including such delicious starters as Martini Trifle 'Le Cirque' with avocado, peas, tomato and jumbo shrimp (served in a cocktail glass!) or frutti di mare salad with octopus carpaccio, arugula (rocket) and linguine, crustacean vinaigrette followed by entrées such as grilled halibut with cream of fresh peas and star anise, pea shoots, white asparagus and frog's legs or black Angus steak in a Napoleon of braised and crispy potatoes, you'll definitely need space left for a melt-in-the-mouth dessert. You can't go wrong with any of them, but a real winner has been the chocolate fondant – a warm, creamy chocolate cake and orange confit. You get the picture!

Of course, going à la carte will make serious inroads into your holiday budget, but the three-course fixed-price lunch is a surprisingly accessible $44, while the fixed-priced five-course dinner is $90 per person.

AUREOLE $$$

French
Upper East Side

✉ 34 East 61st Street between Madison and Park Avenues
☎ 212-319 1660
🚗 Subway 4, 5, 6 to 59th Street; N, R to Lexington Avenue

Always among the top 10 restaurants in New York, the courtyard garden is the restaurant's best-kept secret. Tucked behind the brownstone that houses Aureole, away from the hustle and bustle of the street, it's an idyllic spot for outdoor dining and always incredibly romantic in candlelight. Inside is a curvaceous balcony, elegant decor and hot-house flower arrangements.

Celebrity chef Charlie Palmer – considered the king of New York chefs – frequently changes the menu, but delicious concoctions have included wood-grilled lamb mignons with lentil cakes, pan-seared foie gras steak and fricassée of lobster with Provençal artichokes. Expensive, but worth it to experience dining in one of the best restaurants in town.

Wine is incredibly expensive in New York. If you buy a glass for $6 you're doing well, and even in mid-range restaurants it can set you back $12. Do as New Yorkers do, have a glass of wine or cocktail before you go out and drink beer with your meal or just stick to the one glass of wine.

DANIEL $$–$$$

French
Upper East Side

✉ 60 East 65th Street between Park and Madison Avenues
☎ 212-288 0033
🚗 Subway 6 to 68th Street; F to Lexington Avenue/63rd Street

A grand, elegant place with soaring ceilings, gilded columns, plush wall hangings and upholstery, plus fine art and mosaics – a wonderful backdrop to a romantic interlude. It is the perfect setting for celebrity chef Daniel Boulud's sumptuous haute cuisine. Classic dishes have included the signature potato-wrapped paupiette of sea bass with leeks and red wine sauce; tuna tartare with caviar and a lemon coulis; and seared foie gras with sliced kumquats. It's fine dining with excellent service that will transport you as close to heaven as a mortal can get! A jacket is required to start the journey.

FOUR SEASONS $$$

Continental
Midtown East

✉ 99 East 52nd Street between Lexington and Park Avenues
☎ 212-754 9494
🚗 Subway 6 to 51st Street; E, F to Lexington/3rd Avenue

You have a choice between the Grill Room or the Pool Room at this landmark restaurant, and whichever you opt for will make you feel like one of New York's movers and shakers – this is where they come for their power lunches. The continental dishes are exquisite, the setting elegant and the service impeccable. Pricey? You bet.

JEAN GEORGES $$$

French
Midtown West

✉ Trump International Hotel, 1 Central Park West between 60th and 61st Streets
☎ 212-299 3900
🚗 Subway A, B, C, D, 1, 9 to 59th Street/Columbus Circle

Celebrity chef Jean-Georges Vongerichten's exquisite French dishes are served in an elegant and subtle landmark restaurant that is both romantic and relaxed. Designed by Adam Tihany in a contemporary Art Deco style, the upscale crowd also gets to enjoy superb views of Central Park, while in good weather it's possible to sit outside. Dish highlights in a continally changing menu have included asparagus with rich morel mushrooms, Arctic char baked with wood sorrel and Muscovy duck steaks with sweet and sour jus. It's an unbeatable combination, so plan ahead, book your table and get a rich uncle to take you pronto!

LA CARAVELLE $$$

French
Midtown

✉ Shoreham Hotel, 33 West 55th Street between 5th and 6th Avenues
☎ 212-586 4252
🚗 Subway F to 5th Avenue; B, Q to 57th Street

Owned by welcoming husband-and-wife team André and Rita Jammet, this paragon of classic French cuisine opened in 1960 and has been going strong ever since. The elegant, contemporary decor provides a delightful backdrop for some of the finest dining and service in the city. Dishes have included truffled pike quenelles in a lobster sauce and crispy duck with cranberries.

Don't be too put off by the prices of these landmark restaurants – many offer fixed price menus and the cheapest is for lunch, when it's also easier to get a table. Go on, treat yourself!

LE BERNARDIN $$$

French
Midtown West

✉ 155 West 51st Street between 6th and 7th Avenues.
☎ 212-554 1515
www.le-bernardin.com
🚗 Subway V, F, B, D to Rockefeller Center

Ranked number one in the 2004 *Zagat Survey*, this is a truly marvellous restaurant. It's primarily a seafood extravaganza, although you can put in a request for pasta or lamb. It's very pricey, the prix fixe lunch alone is $47, dinner $89 per person, but it's more than worth it as the mouthwatering dishes are sublime. Chef Eric Ripert's cuisine is regarded by NY gourmets as very inventive. He provides an almost raw menu, which has featured delicacies such as tuna or lemon-splashed scallops with olive oil and chives. From the cooked menu, tasty treats have included layers of crab, avocado and potatoes with a spiced sauce, or baked snapper in spicy sour broth. The dining room itself is also a pleasure to experience, featuring crisp white linen, rich furnishings and a wood-panelled bar with smart blue and gold striped chairs for lounging in pre- and-post dinner.

LESPINASSE $$$

Asian–French
Midtown East

✉ St Regis Hotel, 2 East 55th Street between 5th and Madison Avenues
☎ 212-339 6719
🚗 Subway 4, 5, 6 to 59th Street

A palatial interior with enough chandeliers, quality paintings, regal chairs and fine china to look right at home at Versailles – and please the New York elite who frequent the super classy St Regis Hotel establishment. The multi award-winning French dishes with delicious Asian touches have included herbed risotto and mushroom fricassée, grilled red snapper with mustard greens, a sautéed veal chop with spinach and wine-simmered onions, and braised beef short ribs with potato mousseline. A jacket and tie are basic requirements for what is one of the best restaurants in Manhattan.

PICHOLINE $$$

Mediterranean
Upper West Side

✉ 35 West 64th Street between Broadway and Central Park West
☎ 212-724 8585
🚗 Subway 1, 9 to 66th Street/Lincoln Center

A beautiful restaurant serving exquisite Mediterranean dishes in a refined and elegant setting. Opt to make it one of your 'special' treats while in the city so you can sample the amazing cheese trolley – yes trolley, not board. Each day more than 50 different cheeses, out of a total of 70 varieties, are on offer and if you don't know which to choose, all the waiters are well versed in what cheeses go well with what wines and for what kind of palates. Take advantage of their considerable knowledge. A tradition to be savoured.

21 CLUB $–$$$

Gourmet American
Midtown

✉ 21 West 52nd Street between 5th and 6th Avenues
☎ 212-582 7200
🚗 Subway F to 5th Avenue

Despite its name, this landmark restaurant has never been a club, but during Prohibition it was a speakeasy, starting life in Greenwich Village before moving to its Midtown location in 1929. West 52nd Street between 5th and 6th Avenues was known then as the 'wettest block in Manhattan' because there were at least 38 speakeasies.

One of the most discreet was the 21 Club, which purposefully remained a tiny, clandestine retreat behind the iron gate of its townhouse façade, to avoid both the gangsters and police raids. Its success depended on an employee, who was assigned to spot gangsters, policemen and revenue agents through the peephole and was so skilful that 21 escaped most raids and troubles except for one in 1930. After that the owners had a new security system designed to create false stairways and walls to hide its 2,000 cases of fine wines. It involved the building of a 2-tonne door to the secret cellar, made out of the original bricks to look like a wall. The cellar is still

View from the Four Seasons

going strong and now houses $1.5 million of wine, much of which is owned by the celebrities and power brokers who call the 21 Club their own. Actress Liz Taylor and former President Gerald Ford still keep their bottles here.

Once Prohibition ended in 1932, many of the former speakeasies went out of business, but the 21 turned itself into a fine dining establishment that has been attracting celebrities and movers and shakers ever since. Patrons have included Joe DiMaggio, Aristotle Onassis, Franklin D Roosevelt, Humphrey Bogart, Ernest Hemingway and Jackie Gleason. The night before I enjoyed lunch here, Margaret Thatcher had been at a private function and Joan Collins had dined in the main restaurant.

The 21 classics include creamy chicken hash, English game pot pie and the 21 burger. The menu may also feature mussels marinière, Maine lobster salad, hickory-fired filet mignon with stoneground corn and cèpes, or grilled swordfish with white bean purée, cucumbers and spicy paprika sauce. Prix fixe lunch and dinner menus make the restaurant accessible to all and between 2.30 and 5pm there is a special In Between menu with such dishes as mahi mahi wrap with avocado, mango and arugula served with potato soufflés for a mere $17.

AREA-BY-AREA GUIDE TO RESTAURANTS

BATTERY PARK AND BATTERY PARK CITY

AMERICAN PARK AT THE BATTERY $$$

Gourmet American

✉ Battery Park by the river
☎ 212-809 5508
www.americanpark.com
🚗 Subway 1, 9 to South Ferry

A superb American restaurant in an elegant, glass building that shows off the spectacular views of the Hudson and East Rivers and the Statue of Liberty from every table. In good weather you can eat outside on the terrace. Sumptuous American dishes may include sautéed day-boat sea scallops, whole roasted black sea bass and stuffed free-range chicken breast.

GIGINO AT WAGNER PARK $

Italian

✉ 20 Battery Place at Hudson River
☎ 212-528 2228
🚗 Subway 1, 9 to South Ferry

Great little café/diner near the Museum of Jewish Heritage in the relatively new Robert Wagner Junior Park. Good for a coffee and sarnie pit stop with great views of the Statue of Liberty.

If you want an even cheaper pit stop than Gigino while in Battery Park City, opt for items from the well-priced snack cart in Wagner Park.

HUDSON RIVER CLUB $$$

Gourmet American

✉ 4 World Financial Center, 250 Vesey Street at West Street
☎ 212-786 1500
🚗 Subway 1, 2, 3, 9, A, C to Chambers Street

Specialising in American cuisine from the Hudson Valley, the delicious food is matched by the spectacular views of the North Cove Harbour and the Statue of Liberty. If you don't want to splash out on an expensive meal, at least treat yourself to a $12 drink at the bar. Sunday brunch is a real favourite with the Wall Streeters who live in the area, so if you'd like to join them, book in advance.

2 WEST $-$$$

American fusion

✉ 2 West Street between Battery Place and West End
☎ 212-344 0800
🚗 Subway 1, 9 to Rector Street

The lobby-level restaurant of the Ritz-Carlton has fabulous views of the Hudson River and Statue of Liberty, plus outdoor

21 Club

seating for al fresco dining in the warmer months. The menu offers a choice of American classics plus some global fusions including chicken pot au feu and soba noodles with seafood stir-fry. The lunch menu also offers quick and easy Bento Boxes with Italian and Spanish themes.

FINANCIAL DISTRICT AND SOUTH STREET SEAPORT

KOODO SUSHI $$

Japanese

✉ 129 Front Street on the lower level of Seaport Suites Hotel between Pine and Wall Streets
☎ 212-425 2890
🚗 Subway 1, 2, 4, 5 to Wall Street

This place doesn't look like much, but it's quite new and has one of the best sushi chefs in town. The fish is impeccable, but the chef really shines in his daily specials – take hostess Michelle's advice on this.

MARKJOSEPH STEAKHOUSE $$

Steakhouse

✉ 261 Water Street between Peck Slip and Dover Street
☎ 212-277 0020
www.markjosephsteakhouse.com
🚗 Subway: 1, 2, 4, 5, A, C, J, M, Z to Fulton Street/Broadway Nassau

A quite recent opening, this restaurant has made its mark as one of the best steakhouses in the city. The porterhouse steak is so tender some people have said it 'could be eaten through a straw'. Team it with the delicious hash browns. Wearing a jacket is advisable.

Sometimes the only way to get into a very popular restaurant is to go very early or very late in the evening. Ask what times are available when you book.

QUARTINO $$

Italian

✉ 21 Peck Slip at Water Street
☎ 212-349 4433
🚗 Subway 1, 2, 4, 5, A, C, J, M, Z to Fulton Street/Broadway Nassau

Northern Italian fare in a very charming, high-ceilinged, wooden-tabled restaurant. The small menu includes delicious and well-priced thin-crust pizzas and just one or two daily specials. Everything is very fresh and wholesome and nothing is fried. Again, like MarkJoseph's, it's just a stone's throw from the main tourist drag of Fulton Street, but is remarkably unexplored by anyone but locals.

TRIBECA

CHANTERELLE $$

French

✉ 2 Harrison Street at Hudson Street
☎ 212-966 6960
www.chanterelleny.com
🚗 Subway 1, 9 to Franklin Street

'If this restaurant were any more romantic it would be illegal', gushes one of the entries in New York's *Zagat Survey*. It's true that it's a premier spot in the city for a romantic night out, and the great food matches the ambiance. The $38 prix fixe lunch is one of the best bargains in NY.

HARRISON $$

Continental

✉ 355 Greenwich Street at Harrison Street
☎ 212-274 9310
www.theharrison.com
🚗 Subway 1, 2 to Franklin Street

Created by the owners of the hip Red Cat in Chelsea (page 164), this chic restaurant serves up delicious Continental cuisine in an elegant setting.

LE ZINC $

Bistro

✉ 139 Duane Street between West Broadway and Church Street
☎ 212-513 0001
🚗 Subway A, C, 1, 2 to Chambers Street

A casual, well-priced bistro. Here you'll get French food infused with Asian and Hungarian. Delicious stuff.

MONTRACHET $$$

Bistro

✉ 239 West Broadway between Walker and White Streets
☎ 212-219 2777
www.myriadrestaurantgroup.com
🚗 Subway 1, 2 to Franklin Street

One of the best French bistros in the city and well known for excellent service. Decor is tired but charming.

RESTAURANTS

NOBU $$$

Japanese

✉ 105 Hudson Street at Franklin Street
☎ 212-219 0500
www.myriadrestaurantgroup.com
🚗 Subway 1, 9 to Hudson Street

A wonderful Japanese restaurant serving excellent cuisine mostly to celebrities. If you can get in you'll enjoy the decor and dining. Your best bet is to book weeks ahead to get a chance of a table, or go at lunchtime.

NOBU NEXT DOOR $$

Next to the celebrity haunt is an outlet for mere mortals who can sample some of the food everyone is raving about. Still very much worth a visit.

ODEON $$

American-French

✉ 145 West Broadway between Duane and Thomas Streets
☎ 212-233 0507
🚗 Subway 1, 9 to Chambers Street

A *très* hip hangout that still attracts celebrities for its cool atmosphere and American-French cuisine. You'll need to book ahead. A great late night stop as it stays open until 2am.

TRIBECA GRILL $$

Asian

✉ 375 Greenwich Street at Franklin Street
☎ 212-941 3900
www.myriadrestaurantgroup.com
🚗 Subway 1, 9 to Franklin Street

Robert De Niro and Drew Nieporent's popular American restaurant. The $20 prix fixe lunch attracts major crowds.

CHINATOWN

There are hundreds of tiny restaurants lining the Chinatown streets and mostly serving good-value food from various regions in China. Here are four to get you started.

BIG WONG $

Cantonese

✉ 67 Mott Street between Bayard and Canal Streets
☎ 212-964 0540
🚗 Subway J, M, N, Q, R, W, A, Z, 6 to Canal Street

Cheap, tasty food particularly the noodles with duck, shrimp or chicken, and congee. Don't expect much of the decor or service.

DIM SUM GO GO $

Dim sum-vegetarian-Chinese

✉ 5 East Broadway between Catherine and Oliver Streets
☎ 212-732 0797
🚗 Subway J, M, Z, 6 to Canal Street; F to East Broadway

One of the more popular restaurants in the area thanks to its delicious dim sum.

JOE'S SHANGHAI $

Chinese-Shanghai

✉ 9 Pell St between Bowery and Doyers Street
☎ 212-233 8888
www.joesshanghai.com
🚗 Subway J, M, N, R, Z, 6 to Canal Street

A Chinese restaurant known for the most fabulous soup dumplings in New York.

Well-priced steaming hot food is the trademark of the restaurants in Chinatown. But don't expect elegance in the decor or politeness in the waiters – it simply isn't available!

NEW YORK NOODLE TOWN $

Hong Kong-style noodle house

✉ 281/2 Bowery at Bayard Street
☎ 212-349 0923
🚗 Subway J, M, Z, N, Q, R, W, 6 to Canal Street

Noodles, of course, are one speciality and come in fragrant broths with dumplings or stir-fried with vegetables, meat or seafood. Another speciality is the delicious, succulent barbecued meat.

LITTLE ITALY

Mulberry Street from Hester to Kenmare Street and along Grand Street to Mott Street is all that remains of a once thriving Italian community. Thankfully, though – especially for anyone who feels relieved to have escaped the madness and mayhem of Chinatown – the tiny area is incredibly vibrant and filled with ambient pizzerias and trattorias, many with pavement tables and some even with gardens at the back.

Of course, the area gets packed with tourists, but locals also eat here so the food is 100 per cent authentic. The restaurants all have plenty in common – fading decor, if any, large portions of piping hot Italian classics, friendly service and great value for money. If you're really on a budget, stick to the excellent fixed-price menus, then just sit back and watch the world go by.

It's hard to go wrong with any of the restaurants, but here is a round-up of seven of the best moving northwards along Mulberry from Hester to Grand Street: **Il Fornaio** (132a Mulberry, tel 212-226 8306); **Sal Anthony's SPQR** (133 Mulberry, tel 212-925 3120); **Pellegrino's** (138 Mulberry, tel 212-226 3177); **Angelo's** (146 Mulberry, tel 212-966 1277); **Taormina** (147 Mulberry, tel 212-219 1007); **Il Palazzo** (151 Mulberry, tel 212-343 7000) and **Da Nico** (164 Mulberry, tel 212-343 1212). By the way, Taormina was once the local hangout of former Mafia boss 'Teflon Don' John Gotti (page 38). To get to Little Italy take subway 6 to Spring or Bleecker Streets.

FERRARA PASTRIES & CAFÉ $

Italian café

✉ 195 Grand Street between Mulberry and Mott Streets
☎ 212-226 6150
🚗 Subway S to Grand Street

This is the oldest surviving pastry joint in an area that was once teeming with cannoli caverns. A spacious area, it serves up delicious drinks and cakes and provides plenty of entertaining people-watching.

If you've been wandering around Chinatown for a while and don't want a meal but do need a WC, Ferrara's has a lovely clean one on the first floor (up the stairs at the back). Keep the owners happy, though, by at least buying something to take away.

Le Zinc

NOLITA

CAFÉ HABANA $

Cuban

✉ 17 Prince Street at Elizabeth Street
☎ 212-625 2001
🚗 Subway N, R to Prince Street; 6 to Spring Street

A hot little restaurant filled with beautiful people eating spicy Cuban food – think chicken tacos with coriander and tomato salsa. Delish!

EIGHT MILE CREEK $

Australian

✉ 240 Mulberry Street between Prince and Spring Streets
☎ 212-431 4635
www.eightmilecreek.com
🚗 Subway N, R to Prince Street; 6 to Spring Street

Just a few steps north of Little Italy the laid-back Aussies have arrived serving up cuisine from Down Under. Good Aussie food is both deliciously exotic and pricey – and this tiny restaurant is no exception.

SOHO

BALTHAZAR $$

Bistro

✉ 80 Spring Street between Broadway and Crosby Streets
☎ 212-965 1414
🚗 Subway N, R to Prince Street

A classy French brasserie, with a genuinely French ambience, serving up good food to a trendy crowd. Great oysters.

BLUE RIBBON $$

Eclectic

✉ 97 Sullivan Street between Prince and Spring Streets
☎ 212-274 0404
🚗 Subway C, East to Spring Street

This restaurant gets packed at any time of the day or night so don't decide to come here if you are on a tight schedule. If you're not, the eclectic and seafood dishes are definitely worth the wait.

Weird but true: some of the smaller restaurants don't take credit cards. Check in advance.

CANTEEN $$
American–Asian
✉ 142 Mercer Street at Prince Street
☎ 212-431 7676
🚗 Subway N, R to Prince Street
A super-stylish restaurant that attracts a trendy crowd but is not at all snooty. The American-Asian food isn't cheap but it is delicious.

FANNELLI CAFÉ $
American
✉ 94 Prince Street at Mercer Street
☎ 212-226 9412
Contemporary crowds pack an old saloon-style bar and dining room serving American food. It does an excellent selection of sandwiches for lunch.

FIAMMA OSTERIA $
Italian
✉ 206 Spring Street between 6th Avenue and Sullivan Street
☎ 212-653 0100
🚗 Subway C, E to Spring Street
A bi-level restaurant which is very fancy, in a Hollywood type of way. The food is very good and uncomplicated, think grilled octopus with pepperand mint and veal chops with sage.

LUCKY STRIKE $$
French
✉ 59 Grand Street between West Broadway and Wooster Street
☎ 212-941 0479
www.luckystrikeny.com
Restaurateur Keith McNally's hot spot has become a watering hole for models, celebrities and club kids as well as SoHo's art crowd. The menu is French, chocolate and Lucky martini.

MERCER KITCHEN $$
French–eclectic
✉ Mercer Hotel, 99 Prince Street at Mercer Street
☎ 212-966 5454
www.jean-georges.com
Jean-Georges Vongerichten (he of Jean Georges fame) oversees the eclectic French-inspired cuisine that is served to a trendy crowd in a chic environment.

RESTAURANT PROVENCE $$
French
✉ 38 MacDougal Street at Prince Street
☎ 212-475 7500
One of the hidden gems of SoHo, this is a beautifully rustic restaurant with a fountain in the garden. The food is country-style French cooking and the most expensive main course is $25. Try the prix fixe brunch for $19.50 or make a reservation for about 6.30pm to get a table in the garden.

THOM $$
American
✉ 60 Thompson Street between Spring and Broome Streets
☎ 212-431 0400
www.60thompson.com
🚗 Subway C, E to Spring Street
Based in the newest SoHo hotel, this is a fashionable restaurant in its own right and serves up delicious American cuisine at reasonable prices.

VERUKA $$
International
✉ 525 Broome Street between Thompson Street and 6th Avenue
☎ 212-625 1717
Upbeat late-night joint serving an international menu. You don't have to eat here, you can just hang out in the lounge.

ZOE $$
Californian
✉ 90 Prince Street between Broadway and Mercer Street
☎ 212-966 6722
Fabulous Californian-style American food in a beautiful environment. Dishes include pan-seared skate with pistachio and scallion couscous, stuffed aubergine and lemon-caper emulsion or rotisserie Long Island duck breast with mushroom and goats' cheese turnover, ginger-maple Brussels sprouts and juniper sauce. The amazing range of breads include everything from soda to focaccia and come with butter that includes sesame seeds, poppy seeds, salt and pepper and garlic, plus their own spread made with white beans.

Little Italy at night

LOWER EAST SIDE

aKa $

American

✉ 49 Clinton Street between Rivington and Stanton Streets

☎ 212-979 6096

www.akacafe.com

🚗 Subway F to Lower East Side/2nd Avenue

Once a dress shop, this small but perfectly formed café turns out inventive and tasty dishes from its shoebox-sized kitchen. Try the open-faced lamb tongue sandwich with almond butter and redcurrant jelly for just $8. No single dish costs more than $13.

ALIAS $

American

✉ 76 Clinton Street at Rivington Street

☎ 212-505 5011

🚗 Subway F to Lower East Side/ 2nd Avenue

Just down the street from aKa, this place is a touch more 'evening'. It has lower lighting, tablecloths and a small but serious wine list, yet remains funky with laid-back clients and staff. Chef Scott Ehrlich turns out some pretty big tastes from his mini kitchen but at far less than Midtown pricing.

KATZ'S DELICATESSEN $

American–Jewish

✉ 205 East Houston Street at Ludlow Street

☎ 212-254 2246

🚗 Subway F to 2nd Avenue

A real institution, this deli has been here since 1888. The sandwiches may sound pricey at around $9, but I defy you to finish one. Luckily, there are plenty of brown paper bags around to take your leftovers away with you as everybody else does. Stick to the sandwiches though – the soups are a bit disappointing. You take a ticket on the way in, order your food at the counter and have your ticket filled out, then you pay for it all as you leave.

If the canteen-style seating at Katz's seems familiar to you, it's because that sex scene with Meg Ryan and Billy Crystal in *When Harry Met Sally* was filmed here.

GREENWICH VILLAGE

BABBO $

Italian

✉ 110 Waverly Place between MacDougal and 6th Avenues

☎ 212-777 0303

🚗 Subway A, B, C, D, E, F, Q to Washington Square

An Italian newcomer that is already famous for its 'tasting' menu, which allows you to sample a little bit of everything.

CORNELIA STREET CAFÉ $$

Eclectic

✉ 29 Cornelia Street between Bleecker and West 4th Streets

☎ 212-989 9319

A fabulous neighbourhood restaurant, which serves lunch and dinner seven days a week. Specials include homemade seafood cakes, herb-crusted salmon, lobster ravioli and Thai bouillabaisse. It's also famous for its jazz club in the basement, which begins at 9pm and costs just $5 for the whole evening (page 193).

GOTHAM BAR AND GRILL $$$

Gourmet American

✉ 12 East 12th Street between 5th Avenue and University Place

☎ 212-620 4020

🚗 Subway L, N, R, 4, 5, 6 to Union Square/14th Street

Always highly rated by *Zagat*, the excellent American cuisine is served up in a superb environment to a stylish crowd.

JOHN'S PIZZA $

Italian

✉ 278 Bleecker Street between 6th and 7th Avenues

☎ 212-243 1680

A great place for brick-oven pizzas.

TANGERINE $$

Thai

✉ 228 West 10th Street between Bleecker and Hudson Streets

☎ 212-463 8585

www.tangerinebarandrestaurant.com

🚗 Subway 1, 9 to Christopher Street/ Sheridan Square

Decor and food both beautifully presented. Curries, yellow, green and masaman, are delicious, however, for a tastebud sensation try the combination plates, which come piled high with meat, seafood and vegetable treats.

TOMOE SUSHI $$

Japanese

✉ 172 Thompson Street between Bleecker and West Houston Streets

☎ 212-777 9346

This place looks pretty grotty outside but has an incredible queue and not without reason. You can get the best sushi in New York here for about a tenth of the price it would cost you at Nobu.

MEATPACKING DISTRICT

FLORENT $

French

✉ 69 Gansevoort Street between Greenwich and Washington Streets

☎ 212-989 5779

www.restaurantflorent.com

🚗 Subway A, C, East to 14th Street

Open 24 hours at the weekend, this French restaurant is a popular late-night spot with club crowds.

A new trend when dining out in New York is to order a selection of starters to eat as a kind of Greek meze and skip the main course altogether.

MARKT $$

Belgian

✉ 401 West 14th Street at 9th Avenue

☎ 212-727 3314

🚗 Subway L to 8th Avenue; A, C, East to 14th Street

A stylish Belgian brasserie with a popular bar. Great mussels and good beer selection.

OLD HOMESTEAD $$

American

✉ 56 9th Avenue between 14th and 15th Streets

☎ 212-242 9040

www.oldhomesteadsteakhouse.com

🚗 Subway L, A, C, E to 14th Street/ 8th Avenue

An original chophouse joint that opened in 1868 and is still serving massive portions of good ol' steak and chips – at, some would say, equally inflated prices.

WEST VILLAGE

CAFÉ DE BRUXELLES $$

Belgian

✉ 118 Greenwich Avenue at West 13th Street

☎ 212-206 1830

🚗 Subway A, C east to 14th Street

Another friendly Belgian bistro serving great grub and beer.

GARAGE RESTAURANT $

American

✉ 99 7th Avenue South between Barrow and Grove Streets

☎ 212-645 0600

🚗 Subway 1, 2, 3, 9 to Christopher Street

A friendly spot for American food in a great location; it also has live jazz.

Save a fortune on buying wine with your meal by taking a bottle with you to Grange Hall. They charge $10 corkage – incredibly cheap by New York standards.

GRANGE HALL $$

American

✉ 50 Commerce Street at Barrow Street

☎ 212-924 5246

🚗 Subway 1, 9 to Christopher Street

In one of the Village's prettiest streets, this restaurant serves up American fare with an organic twist. It's inexpensive, unpretentious fun and serves large helpings.

ITHAKA $$

Greek

✉ 48 Barrow Street between 7th Avenue South and Bedford Streets

☎ 212-727 8886

A former 1851 row house, which now accommodates a superb Greek restaurant with its own Mediterranean sea mural in the conservatory garden area. Known for large portions, a real locals' favourite.

PHILIP MARIE $$

American

✉ 569 Hudson Street at West 11th Street

☎ 212-242 6200

www.philipmarie.com

🚗 Subway 1, 9 to Christopher Street

Hearty American fare. Try the newcomer's parsley salad with country ham, dried tomatoes and Wisconsin cheese.

NOHO

FIVE POINTS $

American

✉ 31 Great Jones Street between Lafayette Street and Bowery

☎ 212-253 5700

🚗 Subway B, V, S to Broadway/Lafayette; 6 to Bleecker Street

Named after the once-infamous gangland area, this is a popular neighbourhood restaurant with a friendly bar, so there's no need to worry. For a good, tasty meal, try out the Maine scallop with oxtail sauce or the beef 'n' reef pasta bowl.

INDOCHINE $$

Vietnamese–French

✉ 430 Lafayette Street between Astor Place and 4th Street

☎ 212-505 5111

🚗 Subway 6 to Astor Place

This celebrity haunt serves delicious Vietnamese-French food in tiny portions.

EAST VILLAGE

ANGELICA KITCHEN $

Vegetarian

✉ 300 East 12th Street between 1st and 2nd Avenues

☎ 212-228 2909

🚗 Subway L, N, Q, R, W, 4, 5, 6 to 14th Street/Union Square

A shock for anyone that thinks veggie food is boring. This cool spot serves up very tasty soups, chilli and noodle dishes. No alcohol.

CHEZ ES SAADA $$

Moroccan

✉ 42 East 1st Street between 1st and 2nd Avenues

☎ 212-777 5617

www.chezessaada.com

🚗 Subway 6 to Bleecker Street

Moroccan basement restaurant that gets packed with beautiful people. Open late.

Zoe in SoHo

GARDEN DINING

Aureole: French, Upper East Side, $$$ (page 152)
Barbetta Restaurant: Northern Italian, Midtown West, $$$ (page 170)
Bottino: Italian, Chelsea, $$ (page 163)
Remi: Italian, Midtown, $$$ (page 167)
Restaurant Provence: French, SoHo, $$ (page 159)
Tavern on the Green: Gourmet American, Central Park West, $$$ (page 175)

There are more restaurants for the Village and Chelsea in Chapter 10, plus many of the bars referred to in Chapter 9 serve meals, too.

FRANK $

Italian

✉ 88 2nd Avenue between 5th and 6th Streets

☎ 212-420 0202

🚗 Subway 6 to Astor Place

A tiny Italian restaurant with a real parlour feel, it serves good Tuscan fare at reasonable prices.

KHYBER PASS $

Afghan

✉ 34 St Mark's Place between 2nd and 3rd Avenues

☎ 212-473 0989

🚗 Subway 6 to Astor Place

For delicious and incredibly cheap fare look no further than this Afghan restaurant with a few Iranian dishes thrown in for good measure. Think tangy, mouthwatering Indian cuisine.

During Summer Restaurant Week, which runs from the last week of June and often lasts until the end of August, over 150 restaurants offer three-course meals for around $20, excluding tip, tax and drinks. Check out NYC & Co at www.nycvisit.com.

LA PALAPA $$

Mexican

✉ 77 St Mark's Place between 1st and 2nd Avenues

☎ 212-777 2537

www.lapalapa.com

🚗 Subway E, V to Lexington Avenue/53rd Street

Superb Mexican cuisine with shrimp dishes and baked cod with guajillo, garlic and achiote barbecue sauce to choose from. The restaurant is dark and sultry.

STINGY LULU'S $

American diner

✉ 129 St Mark's Place between 1st and Avenue A

☎ 212-674 3545

🚗 Subway 6 to Astor Place

A great American diner, which also doubles as a music venue and serves food until 4am.

YAFFA CAFÉ $

American diner

✉ 97 St Mark's Place between 1st and Avenue A

☎ 212-677 9000

🚗 Subway 6 to Astor Place

A classic American diner with a grungy East Village twist.

CHELSEA

BOTTINO $$

Italian

✉ 246 10th Avenue between 24th and 25th Streets

☎ 212-206 6766

www.bottinonyc.com

🚗 Subway C, E to 23rd Street

This is the place to go if you want to see the chic art dealers in recreational mode. You can tuck into the delicious Tuscan cuisine in either the minimalist dining room or the back garden. If you don't have time to stop and eat, grab a sarnie to take away from the next-door Bottino to Go.

BRIGHT FOOD SHOP $

American–eclectic

✉ 216 8th Avenue at 21st Street

☎ 212-243 4433

www.kitchenmarket.com

🚗 Subway C, E to 23rd Street

A classic neighbourhood diner with a twist – it serves south-western and Asian versions of American classics.

CAFETERIA $

American diner

✉ 119 7th Avenue at 17th Street

☎ 212-414 1717

🚗 Subway 1, 9 to 18th Street

Another diner experience, only this time filled with the beautiful people who use the 24-hour joint before and after hitting the local clubs.

Bottles of water can cost $10 at some of the pricier restaurants. Save your money! New York has access to the finest and cleanest tap water, direct from the Catskill Mountains upstate.

THE PARK $$

Mediterranean

✉ 118 10th Avenue at 17th Street

☎ 212-352 3313

🚗 Subway C, E to 23rd Street

Restaurant Row, 46th Street and 9th

BEST FOR DINING AND DANCING

Cornelia Street Café: Greenwich Village (page 160)

Garage Restaurant: West Village (page 161)

Metronome: Madison Square (page 165)

Rainbow Room: Rockefeller Plaza (page 166)

Supper Club: Times Square (page 170)

Swing 46 Jazz & Supper Club: Times Square (page 193)

The View: Times Square (page 174)

World Yacht Dinner Cruises: from Midtown West (page 171)

Once a mechanic's garage, this is one of the 'in' spots for film-industry executives. It's a huge industrial bar-cum-restaurant space with a kind of African safari camp interior serving Mediterranean food.

THE RED CAT $$

Mediterranean–American

✉ 227 10th Avenue between 23rd and 24th Streets

☎ 212-242 1122

🚗 Subway C, E to 23rd Street

One of the earlier arrivals in Chelsea, along with the original galleries, this is a real staple with the art pack. It serves up Mediterranean-influenced American food, but you can just go for a cocktail.

UNION SQUARE

BLUE WATER GRILL $$$

Seafood

✉ 31 Union Square West between 14th and 15th Streets

☎ 212-675 9500

www.brguestrestaurants.com

🚗 Subway L, N, Q, R, W, 4, 5, 6 to Union Square

Not only brilliant for people and celeb-watching, this is a Mecca for all those who love their seafood. Dishes include pan-roasted Pacific mahi mahi with lobster,

NEW YORK FOODS AND FOOD TERMS

Arugula: The American name for rocket, used in salads.

Bialy: A cousin of the bagel, it originates from Bialystock in Eastern Europe and is kosher Jewish food. The dough is not as chewy as a bagel and there is no hole in the middle, just a depression in which garlic and onions are put. Without any tasty extras such as cream cheese, this is truly boring food.

Bagels: As opposed to bialys, these are the delicious Jewish creations, which are at their very best when filled with smoked salmon and cream cheese (page 45).

Cannoli: Tubular-shaped biscuit bells with fresh cream on the inside, these come from Italy and are truly delicious.

Cilantro: American name for the fresh leaves of coriander.

Halva: Sweetened, crushed sesame paste. It originates from all around the Mediterranean, Turkey and Arabia.

Konja: A Chinese dessert, which you can buy in bags – they are individual mouth-size pots of lychee jelly.

Lox: Thinly sliced pieces of smoked salmon, generally sold with a 'schmear' of cream cheese. It tastes the same as a smoked salmon and cream cheese bagel but works out much cheaper.

Morels: Deliciously meaty mushrooms from Oregon.

Pie: Used to refer to an entire pizza. Most are much larger than the ones we eat in the UK, so people tend to buy by the slice or share a whole 'pie'.

Scallion: Spring onion.

Schmear: Spreading of cream cheese on a bagel.

You can find a list of more general US foods and food terms on page 20.

RESTAURANTS

mashed potatoes and grilled asparagus and ginger-soy lacquered Chilean sea bass with Chinese broccoli, sticky rice and wasabi vinaigrette. It also has an oyster bar and a 150-seat jazz club for nightly entertainment and dining. Or you can go on Sundays for the wonderful jazz brunch which is served from 10.30am.

CHAT 'N' CHEW $

American diner

✉ 10 East 16th Street between 5th Avenue and Union Square West
☎ 212-243 1616
🚗 Subway L, N, R, 4, 5, 6 to Union Square/ 14th Street

Classic 1950s' American diner with huge servings of meat loaf et al.

MESA GRILL $$

South-western

✉ 102 5th Avenue between 15th and 16th Streets near Union Square
☎ 212-807 7400
www.mesagrill.com
🚗 Subway L, N, R, 4, 5, 6 to Union Square/ 14th Street

Delicious and inventive south-western cuisine from chef Bobby Flay. A real winner, so give it a try if you are in the area.

REPUBLIC $

Asian

✉ 37 Union Square West between 16th and 17th Streets
☎ 212-627 7172
www.thinknoodles.com
🚗 Subway L, N, R, 4, 5, 6 to Union Square/ 14th Street

Also in Upper West Side. Specialists in excellent, quick, noodle-based pan-Asian dishes in a canteen-style environment.

STRIP HOUSE $

American

✉ 13 East 12th Street between 5th Avenue and University Place
☎ 212-627 7172/212-328 0000
www.theglaziergroup.com
🚗 Subway L, N, Q, R, W, 4, 5, 6 to 14th Street/Union Square

You can eat succulent beef here, especially, of course, the New York 'strip'. Lots of other cuts are available as well as some fish, all served in the glorious surroundings of leather banquettes and velvet.

GRAMERCY PARK

ELEVEN MADISON $$$

French–American

✉ At the corner of Madison Avenue at 24th Street
☎ 212-889 0905
🚗 Subway 6, N, R to 23rd Street

With a soaring ceiling, marble floors and French-influenced dishes, this is one of New York's hottest restaurants. It's expensive but not snooty and the service is attentive, as seen in *Sex and the City*.

GRAMERCY TAVERN $$$

Gourmet American

✉ 42 East 20th Street between Broadway and Park Avenue South
☎ 212-477 0777
🚗 Subway N, R to 23rd Street

Another real winner and again always highly ranked by the *Zagat Survey* – an excellent American restaurant.

MADISON SQUARE

METRONOME $$

Mediterranean

✉ 915 Broadway at 21st Street
☎ 212-505 7400
www.metronomenyc.com
🚗 Subway N, R to 23rd Street

The cheaper alternative to the Supper Club (page 170), it serves Mediterranean food in a beautiful candlelit setting and has great jazz from Wednesday to Saturday.

TABLA $$$

American Indian

✉ 11 Madison Avenue at 25th Street
☎ 212-889 0667
🚗 Subway N, R to 23rd Street

Danny Meyer's bi-level restaurant serving American Indian cuisine is a big hit and attracts a trendy crowd. Downstairs is cheaper, you'll be pleased to know.

MIDTOWN

44 $$

Gourmet American

✉ Royalton Hotel, 44 West 44th Street between 5th and 6th Avenues
☎ 212-944 8844
www.ianschragerhotels.com
🚗 Subway B, D, F, Q to 42nd Street

A *très* trendy joint in the Philippe Starck-designed Royalton, serving new American cuisine. A favourite with posh magazine editors.

CHINA GRILL $$

Chinese

✉ CBS Building, 60 West 53rd Street between 5th and 6th Avenues
☎ 212-333 7788
🚗 Subway B, D, F, V to 47th–50th Streets/ Rockefeller Center

Classy establishment serving eclectic food in a fairly noisy setting. Has a bar that gets pretty crowded.

db BISTRO MODERNE $$$

French–American

✉ City Club Hotel, 55 West 44th Street between 5th and 6th Avenues
☎ 212-391 2400
🚗 Subway B, D, F, V, S, 4, 5, 6, 7 to 42nd Street

The latest showcase for one of New York's superstar chefs, Daniel Boulud. It got lots of press for the $29 hamburger, and became an instant scene. Located in the very star-chic City Club Hotel, this is one of the few really good places to eat close to the Theater District.

DIWAN $$

Indian

✉ 148 East 48th Street between Lexington and 3rd Avenues
☎ 212-593 5425
🚗 Subway 6 to 51st Street

An upmarket Indian with more unusual dishes than your average vindaloo or tandoori – butter chicken and sea bass in fenugreek sauce, for example.

HARD ROCK CAFÉ $

American

✉ 221 West 57th Street between Broadway and 7th Avenue
☎ 212-489 6565
www.hardrock.com
🚗 Subway B, D to East 7th Avenue

Classic burger and chips 'cuisine' in a noisy, rock 'n' roll environment.

Al fresco dining in SoHo

HARLEY DAVIDSON CAFÉ $

American

✉ 1370 6th Avenue at 56th Street
☎ 212-245 6000
🚗 Subway B, Q to 57th Street

Home-style American comfort foods like meatloaf and chicken pot pie. The memorabilia includes a huge floor road map of Route 66.

LA CARAVELLE $$$

See Top 10 Restaurants, page 153

NORMA'S $–$$

American

✉ Le Parker Meridien Hotel, 118 West West 57th Street between 6th and 7th Avenues
☎ 212-708 7460
www.leparkermeridien.com
🚗 Subway B, D, E to 7th Avenue

An all-day breakfast joint with a complete difference – it's *très* chi-chi, beautifully decorated and serves some of the most inventive 'breakfast' food going! Specialities include molten chocolate French toast with pineapple chutney, caramelised onion corned beef hash with poached eggs and a serious stack of strawberry and rhubarb pancakes. They also offer desserts and fresh fruit smoothies.

OPIA $$

French

✉ 130 East 57th Street at Lexington Avenue
☎ 212-688 3939
🚗 Subway: 4, 5, 6, N, R, W to 59th Street/Lexington Avenue

Antoine Blech, formerly of the great neighbourhood bistro Orienta, is the very welcoming host at this nifty and trendy hideaway for beautiful people in the Habitat Hotel. The French-inspired cuisine is absolutely delicious.

RAINBOW ROOM $–$$$

Continental

✉ 65th Floor, 30 Rockefeller Plaza
☎ 212-632 5100
www.cipriani.com
🚗 Subway B, D, F, V to 47th–50th Streets/Rockefeller Plaza

This legendary Art Deco landmark makes a fantastic location for dinner – complete with delicious Continental food. The opulent interior is matched only by the views and – get this – you can experience it all at a reasonable price if you opt for the fixed-price theatre menu served from 5.30pm. For a slice of real Hollywood glamour, find out when the Ballroom is open to the public for dinner dances.

REMI **$$$**
Italian
✉ 145 West 53rd Street between 6th and 7th Avenues
☎ 212-581 4242
🚗 Subway N, R to 49th Street; B, D, east to 7th Avenue
To New Yorkers, this special restaurant is like a taste of Venice with its enchanting Atrium Garden that offers foreign films and live music to accompany dinner al fresco. It also has rotating art exhibitions all year long in the Rialto Room. The food is delicious and you can even get Remi take-aways.

ROCK CENTER CAFÉ **$$**
American
✉ 20 West 50th Street between 5th Avenue and Rockefeller Plaza
☎ 212-332 7620
🚗 Subway B, D, F, Q to 47th–50th Streets/Rockefeller Plaza
A Mecca for tourists, thanks to the scenic setting, though the American dishes are a little disappointing.

SEAGRILL **$$$**
Seafood
✉ 19 West 49th Street between 5th Avenue and Rockefeller Plaza
☎ 212-332 7610
www.restaurantassociates.com
🚗 Subway B, D, F, Q to 47th–50th Streets/Rockefeller Center
Surrounded by lush greenery, the outdoor tables, topped with striped umbrellas in summer, offer fine views of the Rockefeller Center. In winter, the outdoor seating is replaced by the famous skating rink. The seafood specialities include Chilean sea bass with wilted spinach, grilled lobster with homemade fettucine and coriander-crusted swordfish. Note that the refurbished restaurant's dress code has changed to exclude jeans, shorts and trainers.

SEPPI'S **$$**
French–Italian–Turkish
✉ 123 West 56th Street between 6th and 7th Avenues
☎ 212-708 7444
www.leparkermeridien.com
🚗 Subway B, D, E to 7th Street
Perfect for Carnegie Hall goers. An eclectic range of dishes such as a classic Italian osso bucco with saffron risotto, duck breast with sweet potato gratin and Turkish mushroom dumplings in garlic yogurt sauce are served in an informal, laid-back environment.

21 CLUB **$$–$$$**
See Top 10 Restaurants, page 154

UPSTAIRS AT 21 **$$**
Gourmet American
✉ 21 West 52nd Street between 5th and 6th Avenues
☎ 212-582 7200
🚗 Subway F to 5th Avenue
Now you can get many of the 21 Club's classic dishes in a less formal but equally well-serviced restaurant – and see out of windows into the bargain! It has quickly become a favourite with the trendy jet set.

MIDTOWN EAST

ASIA DE CUBA **$$**
Asian–Cuban
✉ Morgan's Hotel, 237 Madison Avenue between 37th and 38th Streets
☎ 212-726 7755
www.ianschragerhotels.com
🚗 Subway 6 to 33rd Street; 4, 5, 6, 7 to Grand Central/42nd Street
The Philippe Starck interior guarantees a trendy crowd for the fusion Asian and Cuban food.

BULL AND BEAR **$$–$$$**
Steakhouse
✉ The Waldorf Hotel entrance on Lexington Avenue at 49th Street
☎ 212-872 4900
www.waldorfastoria.com
🚗 Subway 6 to 51st Street
A landmark restaurant renowned for its excellent hospitality and unashamedly masculine decor that pays homage to stock market symbols the bull and the bear. This is the number one restaurant in New York for delicious, melt-in-the-mouth, prime, aged Black Angus beef dishes, yet has plenty to offer the less carnivorously inclined.
Chef Eric Kaplan has introduced a range of

The Bull and Bear

eclectic, mouthwatering dishes that include yellowfin tuna mignon; Maryland crabcakes with remoulade sauce and corn salsa; and shrimp Creole with andouille sausage and rice. For something lighter opt for one of the salads such as lobster salad with mango, avocado and corn and grilled filet mignon and vegetables, roasted potatoes and balsamic vinegar.

CAVIAR RUSSE $$$

Caviar

✉ 2nd floor, 538 Madison Avenue, between 54th and 55th Streets

☎ 212-980 5908
www.caviarrusse.com

🚗 Subway F to 5th Avenue

Posh caviar and cigar lounge where you can see how the other half live.

CHIN CHIN $$

Chinese

✉ 216 East 49th Street between 2nd and 3rd Avenues

☎ 212-888 4555

🚗 Subway 6 to 51st Street

One of New York's finest Chinese restaurants, it frequently plays host to the city's power crowd.

DOCKS OYSTER BAR $

Seafood

✉ 633 3rd Avenue at 40th Street

☎ 212-986 8080
www.docksoysterbar.com

🚗 Subway 4, 5, 6, 7 to Grand Central/ 42nd Street

This raw fish and seafood speciality restaurant also has a popular bar.

EUROPA GRILL $$

Mediterranean

✉ 599 Lexington Avenue at 53rd Street

☎ 212-755 6622

🚗 Subway E, F to Lexington/3rd Avenue

A welcoming restaurant, which has been designed in natural elements of wood, stone and earth tones to create a soothing and tranquil environment. Lincoln Engstrom, formerly of the River Café (page 178), is the chef and he has created delicious and stylish Mediterranean dishes. They include poussin stuffed with ricotta salata and zucchini, peppers and sage, pomegranate-marinated lamb with crispy panisse and fresh mint, and lemon-cured pork loin served with soft polenta.

FOUR SEASONS $$$

See Top 10 Restaurants, page 153

ISTANA $$

Mediterranean

✉ NY Palace Hotel, 455 Madison Avenue at 51st Street

☎ 212-303 6032

🚗 Subway 6 to 51st Street

A little-known but excellent restaurant serving Mediterranean cuisine in the incredibly beautiful environs of the former Villard Houses that are also home to Le Cirque 2000 (page 151).

LA GRENOUILLE $$$

French

✉ 3 East 52nd Street between 5th and Madison Avenues

☎ 212-752 1495
www.la-grenouille.com

🚗 Subway 6 to 51st Street

A sophisticated temple for Francophiles, the exquisite French food is well worth the money. If money's no object, go for dinner, otherwise go for a more economical lunch.

LE CIRQUE 2000 $$–$$$

See Top 10 Restaurants, page 151

LESPINASSE $$$

See Top 10 Restaurants, page 154

OYSTER BAR $$

Seafood

✉ Grand Central Station, lower level, between 42nd Street and Vanderbilt Avenue

☎ 212-490 6650
www.oysterbarny.com

🚗 Subway 4, 5, 6, 7 to Grand Central/ 42nd Street

It seems only appropriate to have a landmark restaurant like this in the landmark that is Grand Central Station. It's fame stems from the generations of connoisseurs who have consumed 1,000 dozen oysters every day at the counters of this atmospheric saloon.

PALM $$

Seafood–steakhouse

✉ 837 2nd Avenue between 44th and 45th Streets

☎ 212-687 2953
www.thepalm.com

🚗 Subway 4, 5, 6, 7 to Grand Central/ 42nd Street

A family-run business and now the epicentre of a multi-million pound empire of Palm restaurants the length and breadth of North America, this establishment

THE AMERICAN DINER

We don't have a real equivalent of an American diner in the UK but the closest is probably a cross between a transport café and a Garfunkels – i.e. diners are relatively cheap, have a homey feel to them but are a lot smarter than your average café. They specialise in American comfort food – pancakes, waffles, crispy bacon, eggs, grill foods, meatloaf – the kind of things that we would choose for a brunch. Go to just about any American city or town and you'll find a good smattering of diners. The one exception is Manhattan where they're very thin on the ground. At all costs avoid the touristy Brooklyn Diner on West 57th Street – it's too expensive to give you the real diner experience. Some of the few diners in New York include:

SoHo

Moondance: 80 6th Avenue between Grand and Canal Streets. Tel 212-226 1191. A cracking spot for a cheap meal, it gets packed at the weekends when it's open 24 hours a day.

NoLiTa

Jones Diner: 371 Lafayette Street at Great Jones Street. Tel 212-673 3577. Pretty dingy-looking from the outside, this is one of the cheapest and best places in the area to get very basic grills and sarnies.

Chelsea

Empire Diner: 210 10th Avenue between West 22nd and West 23rd Streets. Tel 212-243 2736. A real New York institution and a great pit-stop for clubbers as it's open 24 hours a day. The interior is fabulous with its Art Deco style and the people are pretty gorgeous, too.

Garment District

Cheyenne Diner: 411 9th Avenue at 33rd Street. Tel 212-465 8750. In the heart of the Garment District and just around the corner from Penn Street Station, this is a great place to fill up.

Midtown West

Market Diner: 572 11th Avenue at West 43rd Street. Tel 212-695 0415. One of the most famous diners in Manhattan, this is where clubbers go to get breakfast or fill up before the evening run.

Midtown East

Comfort Diner: 214 East 45th Street between 2nd and 3rd Avenues. Tel 212-867 4555. A classic retro diner known for its friendliness and also its staples of meatloaf and fried chicken.

Upper East Side

Comfort Diner: 142 East 86th Street at Lexington Avenue. Tel 212-369 8628. The Upper East Side/Yorkville branch of the friendly diner.

Morningside Heights

Tom's Restaurant: 2880 Broadway at 112th Street. Tel 212-864 6137. The exterior was made famous by its use in *Seinfeld*. If you come here you'll be sharing the space with Columbia University students, who enjoy the cheap comfort food.

Harlem

M&G Soul Food Diner: 383 West 125th Street at Morningside Avenue. Tel 212-864 7326. This is the southern soul food version of a diner and a great venue for a meal in Harlem. You'll also enjoy the background soul music.

celebrated its 75th anniversary in 2001. Thanks to the double steak speciality, it had earned its reputation as one of New York's greatest steakhouses by the 1930s. In the 1940s, lobster was introduced setting the seal on the surf-and-turf trend.

Palm continues to be a Mecca for celebrities and the wheelers and dealers of Manhattan, who come not only for the giant steaks and jumbo Maine lobsters but also for the Italian classics and wide choice. Palm Too across the road (840 2nd Avenue, 212-697 5198) was opened to take the overspill and now has its own loyal customers.

VONG $$$
Thai–French
✉ 200 East 54th Street at 3rd Avenue
☎ 212-486 9592
www.jean-georges.com
🚗 Subway E, F to Lexington/3rd Avenue
Another of Jean-Georges Vongerichten's masterpieces, this Thai–French restaurant has sunken tables and deep booths that keep the trendy crowd happy.

WATER CLUB $–$$$
Seafood
✉ 500 East 30th Street at East River
☎ 212-683 3333
www.thewaterclub.com
🚗 Subway 6 to 28th Street, near Madison Square
Another delightful and special venue from the owner of the River Café (page 178), this restaurant also specialises in seafood. Although on the pricey side – but worth it for the fine cuisine – the weekend brunch option at a prix fixe of $20 is an excellent way to sample some delicious dishes while gazing out across the East River.

MIDTOWN WEST

BARBETTA RESTAURANT $$$
Italian
✉ 321 West 46th Street between 8th and 9th Avenues
☎ 212-246 9171
www.barbettarestaurant.com
🚗 Subway A, C, East to 42nd Street
During the summer, the rather special Barbetta garden is one of the city's most sought-after sites for dining, with its century-old trees and the scented blooms of magnolia, wisteria, jasmine and gardenia. Barbetta is the oldest Italian restaurant in New York and features cuisine from Piedmont in the north-west region of Italy.

THEATER DISTRICT

From 6th Avenue in the east to 9th Avenue in the west and from West 40th Street to West 53rd Street, the Theater District is as good a place as any to get a pre-theatre meal. As well as the many theatres, there are hundreds of restaurants and you'd be hard-pressed to go wrong.

The main drag for eateries is between 8th and 9th Avenues on West 46th Street and is known as Restaurant Row.

HUDSON CAFETERIA $$
Asian
✉ The Hudson, 356 West 58th Street between 8th and 9th Avenues
☎ 212-554 6000
www.ianschragerhotels.com
🚗 Subway A, B, C, D, 1, 2 to 59th Street/Columbus Circle
The restaurant at Ian Schrager's newest hotel is a haven for people and celeb-watching and you'll enjoy the Asian cuisine.

JEAN GEORGES $$$
See Top 10 Restaurants, page 153

LE BERNARDIN $$$
See Top 10 Restaurants, page 153

PETROSSIAN $$$
Caviar–Russian
✉ 182 West 58th Street at 7th Avenue
☎ 212-245 2214
🚗 Subway N, R to 57th Street
Take advantage of the $20 prix fixe lunch to enjoy caviar, foie gras and smoked salmon.

SUPPER CLUB $$$
Gourmet American
✉ 240 West 47th Street between Broadway and 8th Avenue
☎ 212-921 1940
🚗 Subway 1, 9 to 50th Street
At this special place, you'll find fine dining combined with swing dancing and a cabaret – the show is a mix of Cab Calloway, the Blues Brothers and other swing acts. The food is also delicious, particularly the lobster and steak, and I defy anyone to hate the New York cheesecake – so much lighter than European cheesecake, it just melts in your mouth. Stupendous!

The Hudson Cafeteria

WORLD YACHT DINNER CRUISES $$$

Gourmet American

✉ Pier 81, West 41st Street at Hudson River

☎ 212-630 8100

🚗 Subway A, C, East to 42nd Street

A beautiful, four-course dining experience with the best views of Midtown and Lower Manhattan plus the Statue of Liberty as you cruise the river and the bay. Dishes have included Chilean sea bass, rosemary-roasted chicken with scallions, bean purée and sweet garlic jus, red snapper with anchovy paste, topped with sweet and spicy cilantro-chipotte rouille, and herb-roasted rack of lamb served with arugula and couscous, and the chefs are some of the finest around New York. The prix fixe meal, including a three-hour cruise and live music for dancing, costs $67 from Sunday to Thursday, $75 on Friday and $79 on Saturday.

THEATER DISTRICT

BLUE FIN $

Seafood

✉ W Times Square Hotel, 1567 Broadway at 47th Street

☎ 212-918 1400

www.brguestrestaurants.com

🚗 Subway N, R, W to 49th Street

The Blue Fin made a big splash when it opened in 2000. It serves up fresh fish in theatrical surroundings. Sushi is available on the first floor.

ELLEN'S STARDUST DINER $

American diner

✉ 1650 Broadway at 51st Street

☎ 212-956 5151

🚗 Subway 1, 9 to 50th Street

Tourists and children love this 1950s-style diner thanks to its kitsch-retro decor and the singing waitresses. It's great fun, but you wouldn't want to eat here too often – think burgers, chips and anything else that's greasy!

FIREBIRD $$

Caviar–Russian

✉ 365 West 46th Street between 8th and 9th Avenues

☎ 212-586 0244

🚗 Subway A, C, East to 42nd Street

The opulent Russian decor creates a fabulous setting for tucking into the caviar and blinis. There is a prix fixe pre-theatre dinner, which is excellent value at $20.

FRANKIE AND JOHNNIE'S $$

Steakhouse

✉ 269 West 45th Street between Broadway and 8th Avenue

☎ 212-997 9494

www.frankieandjohnnies.com

🚗 Subway A, C, E, N, R to 42nd Street

This is considered to be one of the longest-running shows on Broadway, having first opened as a speakeasy in 1926. Now it still retains its intimate hideaway aura and archetypal New York reputation as a classic steakhouse, known for its generous portions.

Firebird

RESTAURANT REFERENCE GUIDE

Name	Area	Style	Price range	Page
44	Midtown	gourmet American	$$	165
2 West	Battery Park	American Fusion	$-$$$	155
21 Club	Midtown	gourmet American	$-$$$	154
aKa	Lower East Side	American	$	160
Alias	Lower East Side	American	$	160
Alouette	Upper West Side	bistro	$$	176
American Park	Battery Park	gourmet American	$$$	155
Angelica Kitchen	East Village	Vietnamese-French	$$	162
Angelo's	Little Italy	Italian	$	158
Asia de Cuba	Midtown East	Asian-Cuban	$$	167
Aureole	Upper East Side	French	$$$	152
Babbo	Greenwich Village	Italian	$	160
Balthazar	SoHo	bistro	$$	158
Barbetta Restaurant	Midtown West	Italian	$$$	170
Big Wong	Chinatown	Chinese	$	157
Blue Fin	Theater District	seafood	$	171
Blue Grotto	Upper East Side	Mediterranean	$	175
Blue Ribbon	SoHo	eclectic	$$	158
Blue Water Grill	Union Square	seafood	$$$	164
Bottino	Chelsea	Italian	$$	163
Bright Food Shop	Chelsea	American-eclectic	$	163
Bull & Bear	Midtown East	steakhouse	$$-$$$	167
Café de Bruxelles	West Village	Belgian	$$	161
Café des Artistes	Upper West Side	French	$$	176
Café Habana	NoLiTa	Cuban	$	158
Café Sabarsky	Upper East Side	bistro	$	176
Cafeteria	Chelsea	diner	$	163
Canteen	SoHo	American-Asian	$$	159
Carlyle	Upper East Side	French	$$$	176
Caviar Russe	Midtown East	caviar	$$$	168
Cello	Upper East Side	seafood	$$$	176
Chanterelle	TriBeCa	French	$$	156
Chat 'n' Chew	Union Square	diner	$	165
Chez Es Saada	East Village	Moroccan	$$	162
Cheyenne Diner	Garment District	diner	$	169
Chin Chin	Midtown East	Chinese	$$	168
China Grill	Midtown	Chinese	$$	166
Cornelia Street Café	Greenwich Village	eclectic	$$	160
Comfort Diner	Midtown East	diner	$	169
Comfort Diner	Upper East Side	diner	$	169
Da Nico	Little Italy	Italian	$	158
Daniel	Upper East Side	French	$$-$$$	153
db Bistro Moderne	Midtown	French-American	$$$	166
Dim Sum Go Go	Chinatown	Chinese	$	157
Diwan	Midtown	Indian	$$	166
Dock's Oyster Bar	Midtown East	seafood	$	168
Eight Mile Creek	NoLiTa	Australian	$	158
Eleven Madison	Gramercy Park	French-American	$$$	165
Ellen's Stardust Diner	Theater District	diner	$	171
Empire Diner	Chelsea	diner	$	169
Europa Grill	Midtown East	Mediterranean	$$	168
Fannelli Café	SoHo	American	$	159
Ferrara Pastries & Café	Little Italy	Italian café	$	158
Fiamma Osteria	SoHo	Italian	$	159
Firebird	Theater District	caviar-Russian	$$	171
Five Points	NoHo	American	$	162
Florent	Meatpacking District	French	$	161
Four Seasons	Midtown East	Continental	$$$	153
Frank	East Village	Italian	$	162
Frankie & Johnnie's	Theater District	steakhouse	$$	171
Garage Restaurant	West Village	American	$	161
George & Gina's Restaurant	Harlem	Puerto Rican	$$	177
Gigino at Wagner Park	Battery Park	American	$	155
Gotham Bar & Grill	Greenwich Village	gourmet American	$$$	160
Gramercy Tavern	Gramercy Park	gourmet American	$$$	165
Grange Hall	West Village	American	$$	161
Grimaldi's	Brooklyn	pizzeria	$	178
Hard Rock Café	Midtown	American	$	166
Harley Davidson Café	Midtown	American	$	166
Harrison	TriBeCa	Continental	$$	156
Hudson Cafeteria	Midtown West	Asian	$$	170
Hudson River Club	Battery park	gourmet American	$$$	155
Il Fornaio	Little Italy	Italian	$	158
Il Palazzo	Little Italy	Italian	$	158
Indochine	NoHo	Vietnamese-French	$$	162
Istana	Midtown East	Mediterranean	$$	168
Ithaka	West Village	Greek	$$	161
Jean Georges	Midtown West	French	$$$	153
Joe's Shanghai	Chinatown	Chinese	$	157
John's Pizza	Greenwich Village	pizzeria	$	160
Jones Diner	Notlia	diner	$	169

Name	Area	Style	Price range	Page
Katz's Delicatessen	Lower East Side	American-Jewish	$	160
Koodo Sushi	Financial District	Japanese	$$	156
Kyber Pass	East Village	Afghan	$	162
La Caravelle	Midtown	French	$$$	153
La Grenouille	Midtown East	French	$$$	168
La Palapa	East Village	Mexican	$$	163
Le Bernardin	Midtown West	French	$$$	153
Le Cirque 2000	Midtown East	French-American	$$-$$$	151
Le Zinc	TriBeCa	bistro	$	156
Lespinasse	Midtown East	French-Asian	$$$	154
Lucky Strike	SoHo	French	$$	159
M&G Soul Food Diner	Harlem	diner	$	169
Manna's Restaurant	Harlem	southern	$	177
Market Diner	Midtown West	diner	$	169
MarkJoseph Steakhouse	South Street Seaport	steakhouse	$$	156
Mark's	Upper East Side	French-American	$$$	176
Markt	Meatpacking District	Belgian	$$	161
Mars 2112	Theater District	American	$	174
Mercer Kitchen	SoHo	French-eclectic	$$	159
Mesa Grill	Union Square	south-western	$$	165
Metronome	Madison Square	Mediterranean	$$	165
Moondance	SoHo	diner	$	169
Montrachet	TriBeCa	bistro	$$$	156
New York Noodle Town	Chinatown	Chinese	$	157
Nobu	TriBeCa	Japanese	$$$	157
Nobu Next Door	TriBeCa	Japanese	$$	157
Norma's	Midtown	American	$-$$	166
Odeon	TriBeCa	American-French	$$	157
Old Homestead	Meatpacking District	American	$$	161
Opia	Midtown	French	$$	166
Ouest	Upper West Side	French-American	$$	176
Oyster Bar	Midtown East	seafood	$$	168
Palm	Midtown East	seafood/steakhouse	$$	168
Palm New York West Side	Theater District	seafood/steakhouse	$$-$$$	174
Park View at the Boathouse	Central Park	American-seafood	$$-$$$	174
Pellegrino's	Little Italy	Italian	$	158
Petrossian	Midtown West	caviar-Russian	$$$	170
Philip Marie	West Village	American	$$	161
Picholine	Upper West Side	Mediterranean	$$$	154
Pizzeria Uno	Upper West Side	pizzeria	$	177
Planet Hollywood	Theater District	American	$	174
Quartino	South Street Seaport	Italian	$$	156
Rainbow Room	Midtown	Continental	$-$$$	166
Rao's	Harlem	Italian	$	177
Remi	Midtown	Italian	$$$	167
René Pujol	Theater District	bistro	$$	174
Republic	Union Square	Asian	$	165
Restaurant Provence	SoHo	French	$$	159
River Café	Brooklyn	gourmet American	$$$	178
Rock Center Café	Midtown	American	$$	167
Rosa Mexicana	Upper East Side	Mexican	$$	176
Ruby Foo's	Upper West Side	Asian	$$	177
Sal Anthony's SPQR	Little Italy	Italian	$	158
Seagrill	Midtown	seafood	$$$	167
Seppi's	Midtown	French-Italian-Turkish	$$	167
Serafina Fabulous Grill	Upper East Side	Italian	$$	176
Spazzia	Upper West Side	Mediterranean	$$	177
Stingy Lulu's	East Village	diner	$	163
Strip House	Union Square	American	$	165
Supper Club	Midtown West	gourmet American	$$$	170
Sylvia's	Harlem	southern	$	178
Tabla	Madison Square	American-Indian	$$$	165
Tangerine	Greenwich Village	Thai	$$	160
Taormina	Little Italy	Italian	$	158
Tavern on the Green	Central Park	gourmet American	$$$	175
The Park	Chelsea	Mediterranean	$$	163
The Red Cat	Chelsea	Mediterranean-American	$$	164
The View	Theater District	Continental	$$-$$$	174
Thom	SoHo	American	$$	159
Tom's Restaurant	Morningside Heights	diner	$	169
Tomoe Sushi	Greenwich Village	Japanese	$$	161
TriBeCa Grill	TriBeCa	Asian	$$	157
Upstairs at 21	Midtown	gourmet American	$$	167
Veruka	SoHo	international	$$	159
Vong	Midtown East	Thai-French	$$$	170
Water Club	Midtown East	seafood	$-$$$	170
World Yacht Dinner Cruises	Midtown West	gourmet American	$$$	171
Yaffa Café	East Village	diner	$	163
Zoe	SoHo	Californian	$$	159

Due to a new law that now bans smoking in all indoor public spaces, it is now no longer possible to smoke even at a restaurant's bar. Some restaurants with outdoor seating will be able to set aside tables for smoking, though.

MARS 2112 $

American

✉ 1633 Broadway at 51st Street
☎ 212-582 2112
www.mars2112.com
🚗 Subway 1, 9 to 51st Street

This theme restaurant offering will literally take you out of this world to Mars via the space shuttle. Fortunately, the food is pretty American Earthbound so you won't be eating little green men. Of course, it comes with the ubiquitous shop where you can buy your own Martian doll.

PALM NEW YORK WEST SIDE $$–$$$

Seafood–steakhouse

✉ 250 West 50th Street between 7th and 8th Avenues
☎ 212-333 7256
🚗 Subway 1, 9 to 50th Street

A sister restaurant to the incredibly successful Palm restaurant (page 168), this has very quickly become a hot spot for celebrities, theatre-goers and tourists.

PLANET HOLLYWOOD $

American

✉ 1540 Broadway at West 45th Street
☎ 212-333 7827
🚗 Subway N, Q, R, S, W, 1, 2, 3, 7 to Times Square

Brilliant Hollywood memorabilia with the standard American burger fare.

RENÉ PUJOL $$

Bistro

✉ 321 West 51st Street between 8th and 9th Avenues
☎ 212-246 3023
🚗 Subway C, East to 50th Street

A great French bistro serving delicious food in a delightful setting.

THE VIEW $$–$$$

Continental

✉ Top floor, Marriott Marquis Hotel, 1535 Broadway at 45th Street
☎ 212-704 8900
🚗 Subway N, R, S, 1, 2, 3, 7, 9 to Times Square/42nd Street

New York's revolving restaurant attracts lovebirds and tourists in droves but serves up a high standard of Continental cuisine. As expected, the views over Manhattan are spectacular – particularly at sunset, though the service could be improved upon.

CENTRAL PARK

PARK VIEW AT THE BOATHOUSE $$–$$$

American–seafood

✉ Central Park Lake, Park Drive North at East 72nd Street

South Street Seaport

☎ 212-517 2233
🚗 Subway 6 to 68th Street/Hunter College
One of the most wonderful locations in New York. Set right by the lake with its blue rowing boats, the restaurant's sparkling lights add to the romantic atmosphere, while the mostly seafood menu is delicious. There is also a roaring open fireplace in the bar for those wintry days, when you can almost feel as if you really were deep in the countryside.

TAVERN ON THE GREEN $$$

Gourmet American

✉ Central Park at West 67th Street
☎ 212-873 3200
www.tavernonthegreen.com
🚗 Subway B, C to 72nd Street
Looking at the glitzy razzmatazz that is the Tavern, it's hard to imagine this building started life in 1870 as a house for the sheep that roamed Central Park. By the early 1930s, Parks Commissioner Robert Moses had spotted its potential as a restaurant. He banished the sheep to Brooklyn's Prospect Park and, in 1934, opened what was known as The Restaurant with a coachman in full regalia at the door and the blessing of Mayor Fiorello La Guardia.

In the 1970s, famous restaurateur Warner LeRoy spent $10 million turning it into a spectacle in its own right, creating the Crystal and Terrace Rooms with his lavish use of brass, stained glass, etched mirrors, antique paintings and prints and chandeliers – including genuine Baccarat crystal and stained-glass Tiffanys. The Tavern on the Green took the city by storm when it opened in 1976. Celebrities, politicians and anyone who was anyone flocked to it to see and to be seen here.

You don't have to eat at the Tavern to enjoy its fabulous garden. From May to October you can sip a cocktail in the garden bar.

Now the Tavern pulls in out-of-towners, who've all been told by their friends to visit this unique sight, and the restaurant has a staggering turnover of $34 million a year! And what a riot of colours and textures its clients are greeted with. The food is classic gourmet American with typical main courses including sautéed crabcakes; roast prime rib of beef with Yorkshire pudding, Yukon-gold mashed potatoes and creamy horseradish; and grilled pork porterhouse with peach and apple chutney.

UPPER EAST SIDE

AUREOLE $$$

See Top 10 Restaurants, page 152

BLUE GROTTO $

Mediterranean

✉ 1576 3rd Avenue between 88th and 89th Streets.
☎ 212-426 3200
🚗 Subway 4, 5, 6 to 86th Street
This is more Yorkville than 'silk stocking' Upper East Side, which is reflected in the

The Tavern on the Green

reasonable prices. It's popular with the locals and serves Italian and Mediterranean-style cuisine in a lounge-like space.

CAFÉ SABARSKY $

Bistro

⌧ 1048 5th Avenue at 86th Street

☎ 212-288 0665

Subway 4, 5, 6 to 86th Street

This is not just in a fabulous location – all but opposite the Metropolitan Museum of Art, yet quietly tucked away in the new Neue Galerie Museum for German and Austrian Art (page 121) – but is a wonderful pit stop for light breakfasts, lunch and afternoon tea. You'll also love its elegant decor to match the Austrian-German art theme of the museum itself.

CARLYLE $$$

French

⌧ Carlyle Hotel, 35 East 76th Street at Madison Avenue

☎ 212-744 1600

Subway 6 to 77th Street

An old establishment that attracts an older 'silk stocking' clientele, but if you want to see how the other half lives, try the fine French cuisine for breakfast or a delicious brunch. Divine.

CELLO $$$

Seafood

⌧ 53 East 77th Street between Madison and Park Avenues

☎ 212-517 1200

Subway 6 to 77th Street

This is very upmarket and very smart – jackets required – but if you're in the mood for seafood, it is the place to go. Famed chef Laurent Tourondel's creations include marinated Chilean sea bass with honey and parsnip purée.

DANIEL $$–$$$

See Top 10 Restaurants, page 153

MARK'S $$$

French–American

⌧ The Mark, 25 East 77th Street at Madison Avenue

☎ 212-879 1864

www.mandarinoriental.com

Subway 6 to 77th Street

Excellent French-American cuisine. The prix fixe lunch and pre-theatre deals are great value – just make sure you give yourself time to soak up the ambience.

ROSA MEXICANA $$

Mexican

⌧ 1063 1st Avenue at 58th Street

☎ 212-753 7407

Subway 4, 5, 6 to 59th Street

Extremely popular Mexican eaterie that is known as much for its margaritas as for its delicious food.

SERAFINA FABULOUS GRILL $$

Italian

⌧ 393 Lafayette Street at 4th Street or 1022 Madison Avenue at 79th Street

☎ 212-702 9595

www.serafinarestaurant.com

Subway 4, 5, 6 to 59th Street

Famous for thin-crust pizzas that have been voted the best in the world by gourmets, this is a haunt of both Prince Albert of Monaco and Ivana Trump. Toppings include Al Porcini with porcini mushrooms, fontina cheese and mozzarella and Al Caviale with salmon caviar, potatoes and crème fraîche. The signature focaccias, two layers of stuffed dough with delicious fillings, range from Scottish smoked salmon, asparagus and Italian Robiola cheese to truffle oil and Robiola.

UPPER WEST SIDE

ALOUETTE $$

Bistro

⌧ 2588 Broadway between 97th and 98th Streets

☎ 212-222 6808

Subway 1, 2, 3, 9 to 96th Street

This French bistro attracts the crowds despite having a very simple menu.

CAFÉ DES ARTISTES $$

French

⌧ 1 West 67th Street between Columbus Avenue and Central Park West

☎ 212-877 3500

Subway 1, 9 to 66th Street

A reasonably priced, fine dining establishment that serves up wonderful French cuisine in a romantic setting.

OUEST $$

French–American

⌧ 2315 Broadway between 83rd and 84th Streets

☎ 212-580 8700

www.ouestny.com

Subway 1, 2 to 86th Street

Once you can get your tongue around the restaurant's name – it's simply called West! – you'll be ready to enjoy the French-American cuisine created by Valenti.

PICHOLINE $$$

See Top 10 Restaurants, page 154

PIZZERIA UNO $

Italian

✉ Columbus Avenue at 81st Street
☎ 212-595 4700
www.unos.com
🚗 Subway B, C to 81st Street

Okay, so this is a chain restaurant, but it actually provides good quality food for those wanting a simple, but tasty, meal at a very good price. This one is a great little neighbourhood joint offering an excellent range of family-friendly dishes just around the corner from the American Museum of Natural History (page 108). There is an excellently priced children's menu, plus crayons. What more could you ask after tramping round dinosaur exhibits?

RUBY FOO'S $$

Asian

✉ 2182 Broadway at 77th Street
☎ 212-724 6700
www.brguestrestaurants.com
🚗 Subway 1, 9 to 79th Street

Beautiful Asian decor combined with delicious Asian food. Dim sum is a speciality of the house.

SPAZZIA $$

Mediterranean

✉ 366 Columbus Avenue at West 77th Street
☎ 212-799 0150
🚗 Subway 1, 9 to 79th Street

This restaurant serves delicious Mediterranean food just a stone's throw away from the American Museum of Natural History (page 108).

HARLEM

GEORGE & GINA'S RESTAURANT $$

Puerto Rican

✉ 169 East 106th Street between Lexington and 3rd Avenues
☎ 212-410 7292
🚗 Subway 6 to 103rd Street

A Puerto Rican restaurant deep in the heart of Spanish Harlem.

MANNA'S RESTAURANT $

Southern-style buffet

✉ 486 Lenox Avenue/Malcolm X Boulevard at 134th Street
☎ 212-234 4488
🚗 Subway 2, 3 to 135th Street

Not so much a restaurant as a great, cheap pit stop used by the locals. There are two huge buffets of hot and cold food plus salads and fruit, which you can buy by the plastic tub and either take away or eat at one of the simple, canteen-style tables. Fresh fruit and salad items cost $3.99 a pound and meats cost $4.99 a pound as opposed to around $8.99 in the Midtown area. The hot buffet includes a tremendous range of chicken, including southern-style, lamb, beef stews, meatloaf, ribs, vegetables and many different rices. There are also many salads to choose from, including the ubiquitous Caesar's salad, and fruits such as melon, watermelon, orange and papaya. It also has a fresh fruit and vegetable juice bar. Open Monday to Saturday 7am–8pm and Sundays 10am–7pm.

RAO'S $

Italian

✉ 455 East 114th Street at Pleasant Avenue
☎ 212-722 6709
www.raos.com
🚗 Subway 6 to 116th Street

An institution that you'll only get into if you come across the handful of people who actually have access to this eight-table

CELEBRITY HAUNTS

All of the restaurants in the Top 10 guide on pages 151–5, plus the following:

Blue Water Grill: Union Square (page 164)

db Bistro Moderne: Midtown (page 166)

Eleven Madison: Gramercy Park (page 165)

44: The Royalton Hotel, Midtown (page 165)

Indochine: NoLiTa (page 162)

Lucky Strike: SoHo (page 159)

Mark's: Upper East Side (page 176)

Nobu: TriBeCa (page 157)

Odeon: TriBeCa (page 157)

Palm New York West Side: Theater District (page 174)

Park View at the Boathouse: Central Park (page 174)

Serafina Fabulous Grill: Upper East Side (page 176)

Norma's at the Parker Meridian

Italian restaurant! Famous for its sauces, which Sinatra used to have flown to him around the world. Now the jukebox plays all the crooner's favourites.

If you can't get in to Rao's, you can still taste their fabulous sauces, by buying them either direct from the restaurant or from Faicco's Sausage Store in Bleecker Street, Greenwich Village (page 103).

SYLVIA'S $

Southern soul food

⊠ 328 Lenox Avenue between 126th and 127th Streets
☎ 212-996 0660
www.sylviassoulfood.com
Subway 2, 3 to 125th Street

Southern home-style cooking – aka soul food. Sylvia's place is a New York institution and famous for its Sunday gospel brunch, but you need to book a few weeks ahead as it's always very busy.

If you need a break around 110th Street, drop in for a cuppa and a delicious cake at Make My Cake, 103 West 110th Street at Lenox Avenue/Malcom X Boulevard. Tel 212-932 0833.

BROOKLYN

GRIMALDI'S $

Italian

⊠ 19 Old Fulton Street between Front and Water Streets
☎ 718-858 4300
www.grimaldis.com
Subway A, C to High Street/Brooklyn Bridge

Considered the best place in New York to get a delicious pizza at a great price.

RIVER CAFÉ $$$

Gourmet American

⊠ 1 Water Street under the Brooklyn Bridge
☎ 718-522 5200
Subway A, C to High Street/Brooklyn Bridge

This is a really special restaurant. For unrivalled views of New York's magnificent Lower Manhattan skyline, this is the place to come and the food matches up to the location. Superb dishes include braised Maine lobster, crisp black sea bass, seared diver sea scallops, grilled, aged prime sirloin of beef and pan-roasted chukar partridge.

Park View at the Boathouse

CHAPTER 9

Shows, Bars and Nightlife

BROADWAY SHOWS

One of the first things you discover about Broadway, as we Brits think of it, is that it is just one tiny stretch of almost the longest thoroughfare on the island of Manhattan. The Theater District, as it is known, is a congregation of theatres between Broadway and 8th Avenue from about 44th to 52nd Streets (take the N, R, Q, W, 1, 2, 3, 7, 9, S lines to 42nd Street/Times Square). This is Broadway. You'll also see and hear the terms 'Off Broadway' and 'Off-Off Broadway' (yes, really), which refer to uptown and downtown theatres, particularly in Greenwich Village, East Village and SoHo. These theatres are well worth a visit, as they may be offering rarely seen revivals, the innovative work of new playwrights, or productions featuring hilarious, off-the-wall humour, but they do change frequently, so I have only included a sample selection.

Of course, Broadway productions also change all the time, but many of the big shows – the ones that most Brits are interested in – do stay around for a little longer. I have included reviews of those shows I believe will be available for the next couple of years, but for a completely up-to-date guide to what's on at the theatre, pick up the *New York Times*, which has comprehensive listings of dance, classical music, opera, Broadway, Off Broadway and Off-Off Broadway every day. Other papers and magazines that you can check out include the *New Yorker*, *Village Voice* and *New York Press*. If you want to check before you go, visit the Keith Prowse or Theatre Direct websites given below.

Look for discount coupons for Broadway shows at neighbourhood information stands and barrows throughout Manhattan.

BOOKING YOUR TICKETS

You can book tickets in advance in the UK through either your travel agent or Keith Prowse (tel 01232 232425). An alternative is to use the TicketMaster website at **www.ticketmaster.com**.

If booking in New York, try Theatre Direct (tel 800-334 8457, **www.broadway.com**); Broadway Line, which also offers tours (tel 212-302 4111); Americana Tickets & Travel (tel 212-581 6660); and Premiere Ticket Service (tel 212-643 1274).

Watch out for ticket touts – an increasing number of the tickets they sell are fakes.

For cheaper tickets, go to the **Theater Development Fund/OOOTS** booths. The less crowded (but less convenient) downtown booth is at 108 Front Street at John Street, open Mon to Sat 11am–6pm, Sun 11am–3.30pm; matinee tickets bought here are for the following day's performance. The booth in the middle of Times Square at 47th Street is open Mon to Sat 3–8pm, Wed and Sat 10am–2pm for matinee tickets and Sun 11am–7pm. It gets very busy so arrive early for the best selection, then spend the day in Midtown (see Chapter 3, The New York Neighbourhoods).

Broadway

Discounts range from 25 per cent to 50 per cent but bear in mind that the booths only accept cash or travellers' cheques. Have plenty of options ready in case there are no tickets for your first show choice. If you are flexible about what you would like to see, you can decide to go to a show at the very last minute, since TKTS Midtown is open right until showtime.

MUSICALS

All the Broadway and Off Broadway shows listed here have one interval. The suggested ages given are for guidance only.

AIDA

✉ Palace Theater, 1554 Broadway at 47th Street
☎ 212-307 4747
🕐 Tues 7pm, Wed to Sat 8pm, matinees Wed and Sat at 2pm, Sun at 3pm

Elton John and Tim Rice teamed up to create the musical score for this new version of the operatic classic. Set in ancient Egypt, it's a great story of loyalty and betrayal, courage and love as three people are forced to make choices that will change their lives and the course of history.

Awards: 4 Tony Awards 2000
Length of show: 2 hours 30 minutes
Age: 12 and over

The Hit Show Club (630 9th Avenue between 44th and 45th Streets, tel 212-581 4211) and Broadway Bucks (226 West 47th Street between Broadway and 8th Avenue, l0th floor) distribute coupons that can be redeemed at the box office for one-third or more off regular ticket prices. If you don't see them in your hotel, pick them up from the offices.

AVENUE Q

✉ John Golden Theater, 252 West 45th Street between Broadway and 8th Avenue
☎ 212-239 6200
🕐 Tues to Sat 8pm, Sat and Sun 1pm

A bright and entertaining show with people and puppets about the struggles with life when you're straight out of college. Funny and urbane. Has been called a mix of *Sesame Street, The Simpsons* and *Sex and the City.*

Length of show: 2 hours 15 minutes
Age: 18 and over (don't let the puppets fool you)

BEAUTY AND THE BEAST

✉ Lunt-Fontanne Theater, 205 West 46th Street between Broadway and 8th Avenue
☎ 212-307 4747
🕐 Wed to Sat 8pm, Sun 6.30pm, matinees Wed and Sat 2pm, Sun 1pm

The wonderful, award-winning Disney version with music by Alan Menken and lyrics by Tim Rice and the late Howard Ashman. It tells the age-old story of how a young woman falls in love with a stubborn but charming beast.

Awards: 1 Tony Award 1994
Length of show: 2 hours 30 minutes
Age: From the very young to the very old

Many theatres have started scheduling Tuesday performances at 7pm, an hour earlier than customary, to accommodate those who have to travel far or want to dine afterwards.

CHICAGO

✉ Ambassador Theater, 219 West 49th Street between Broadway and 8th Avenue
☎ 212-239 6200
🕐 Tues 7pm, Wed to Sat 8pm, Sun 7pm, matinees Sat and Sun 2pm

This great musical with wonderful dancing is the winner of six Tony Awards and has other productions throughout the world, but many still consider this one to be the best. *Chicago* tells the story of a chorus girl who kills her lover and then escapes the noose and prison with the help of a conniving lawyer. If greed, corruption, murder and treachery are your bag, then this is the musical for you.

Awards: 6 Tony Awards 1997
Length of show: 2 hours 30 minutes
Age: 12 and over (parental guidance)

HAIRSPRAY

⊠ Neil Simon Theater, 250 West 52nd Street between Broadway and 8th Avenue

☎ 212-307 4100

◷ Tues 7pm, Wed to Sat 8pm, matinees Wed and Sat 2pm, Sun 3pm

A fabulous production based on John Waters's cult 1988 movie, it tells the story of how a bumbling Baltimore teenager is turned from social outcast to star when she gets the chance to dance on the popular *Corny Collina Show* (well, it is set in 1962!). But then her troubles really start... Hilarious – and the girls have hair that Marge Simpson would be proud of!

Length of show: 2 hours 40 minutes

Age: 12 and over

THE LION KING

⊠ New Amsterdam Theater, 214 West 42nd Street at Broadway

☎ 212-307 4747

◷ Tues 7pm, Wed to Sat 8pm, Sun 6.30pm, matinees Wed and Sat 2pm, Sun 1pm

With the original music from Elton John and Tim Rice (which won them Oscar and Grammy awards) combined with new music from Hans Zimmer and Lebo M, Disney tells the story of Simba, a lion cub who struggles to accept the responsibilities of adulthood and his destined role as king.

Awards: 6 Tony Awards 1998

Length of show: 2 hours 45 minutes

Age: From the very young to the very old

MAMMA MIA!

⊠ Cadillac Winter Garden Theater, 1634 Broadway at 50th Street

☎ 212-239 6200

◷ Wed to Sat 8pm, Sun 7 pm, matinees Wed, Sat and Sun 2pm

If you haven't had a chance to see this fabulously uplifting musical in London, then why not try it in New York? Set on a mythical Greek island, it tells the story of a single mum and her daughter on the eve of her daughter's wedding – and comes with 22 cracking ABBA songs.

Length of show: 2 hours 30 minutes

Age: 5 and over

THE PHANTOM OF THE OPERA

⊠ Majestic Theater, 247 West 44th Street between Broadway and 8th Avenue

☎ 212-239 6200

◷ Tues 7pm, Mon and Wed to Sat 8pm, matinees Wed and Sat 2pm

Set in 19th-century Paris, this is Andrew Lloyd Webber's famous musical of Gaston Leroux's novel. It tells the timeless story of a mysterious spectre, who haunts the Paris opera house, spooking the owners and falling in love with a beautiful singer.

Awards: 7 Tony Awards 1998

Length of show: 2 hours 30 minutes

Age: 5 and over, depending on whether your child may be scared of the mask.

For fantastic views of Times Square, treat yourself to a drink at the Broadway Lounge on the eighth floor lobby level of the Marriott Marquis Hotel at 1535 Broadway.

THE PRODUCERS

⊠ St James Theater, 246 West 44th Street between Broadway and 8th Avenue

☎ 212-239 6200

◷ Tues 7pm, Wed to Sat 8pm, matinees Wed and Sat 2pm, Sun 3pm

Based on Mel Brooks's zany 1968 movie, this tells the story of a down-on-his-luck theatre producer who hatches a plot to raise cash from a Broadway flop scam.

Awards: 11 Tony Awards 2001

Length of show: 2 hours 40 minutes

Age: 12 and over

RENT

⊠ Nederlander Theater, 208 West 41st Street between 7th and 8th Avenues

☎ 212-307 4100

◷ Mon to Sat 8pm, matinees Wed and Sat 2pm

The Tony Award- and Pulitzer Prize-winning musical is based on Puccini's opera *La Bohème*, but is set in New York's East Village. It tells the story of struggling young artists living on the edge in the search for glory.

Awards: 4 Tony Awards 1996

Length of show: 2 hours 45 minutes

Age: 16 and over due to adult themes

WICKED

✉ Gershwin Theater, 222 West 51st Street between Broadway and 8th Avenue
☎ 212-307 4100
🕐 Tues 7pm, Wed to Sat 8pm, matinees Wed and Sat 2pm, Sun 3pm

A prequel to the classic story of the *Wizard of Oz* focusing on Glinda the Good Witch and the Wicked Witch of the West that also addresses adult themes.

Awards: 12 Tony nominations 2004
Length of show: 2 hours 45 minutes
Age: 10 and over

OFF BROADWAY

BLUE MAN GROUP: TUBES

✉ Astor Place Theater, 434 Lafayette Street at Astor Place
☎ 212-254 4370
🕐 Tues and Thurs 8pm, Fri 7pm, 10pm, Sat 4pm, 7pm and 10pm, Sun 1pm, 4pm and 7pm

One of the most successful Off Broadway shows. Take a trio of post-modern clowns, cover them in blue rubber and allow them to be outrageous with sound and art and you have this wonderful avant-garde extravaganza that is both hilarious and challenging to watch.

Length of show: 2 hours
Age: 15 and over

Carnegie Hall

Queues for the Times Square OOOTS booth start long before it opens, so arrive early to get a good choice. But even if you arrive at the last minute, you may catch a show, because the booth stays open right until showtime.

I LOVE YOU, YOU'RE PERFECT, NOW CHANGE

✉ Westside Theater, 407 West 43rd Street between 8th and 9th Avenues
☎ 212-239 6200
🕐 Tues to Sat 8pm, Sun 7pm, matinees Sat and Sun 2pm

For a thoroughly modern take on the whole notion of dating and romance, you can't go wrong with this comedy. It's a kind of *Seinfeld* set to music.

Length of show: 2 hours
Age: adult

MAJOR MUSIC VENUES

APOLLO THEATER

Harlem

✉ 253 West 125th Street between Adam Clayton Powell Jnr and Frederick Douglas Boulevards
☎ 212-749 5838
🚗 Subway A, B, C, D, 2, 3 to 125th Street

This venue started life as a burlesque house for whites only when Harlem was actually a white neighbourhood, but it very quickly changed and became a theatre for blacks with live entertainment. The Amateur Night has been a launching pad for Stevie Wonder and James Brown. When Ella Fitzgerald came here she planned to dance, but at the last moment she decided to sing and, as the saying goes, a star was born. Wednesday's Amateur Night is still going strong and is shown on NBC at 1am on Saturday night/Sunday morning.

CARNEGIE HALL

Midtown West

✉ 154 West 57th Street at 7th Avenue
☎ 212-247 7800
🚗 Subway B, D, E, N, R, Q, W to 57th Street

Built in the Beaux Arts style under the patronage of Andrew Carnegie, this is perhaps one of the most famous classical

Pace yourself during the day so you've enough juice left to enjoy one of the many theatre productions in the evening.

concert venues in New York and a real landmark. Check the listings sections of newspapers or *Time Out* for details of visiting artists or take a guided tour by phoning the number above.

MADISON SQUARE GARDEN

34th Street

✉ 7th Avenue at 32nd Street

☎ 212-465 6741

🚗 Subway A, C, E, 1, 2, 3, 9, B, D, F, N, Q, R, V, W to 34th Street/Penn Street Station

New York's biggest and most famous rock venue, which doubles up as a sports stadium. Also the **Theater at Madison Square Garden**, which is underneath, plays host to big-name stars who want to share some intimacy with their audience.

RADIO CITY MUSIC HALL

Midtown

✉ 1260 6th Avenue at 50th Street

☎ 212-247 4777

🚗 Subway B, D, F, V to 47th–50th Street/Rockefeller Center

Recently renovated, this home to the Rockettes in its Art Deco splendour also plays host to some big-name stars.

LINCOLN CENTER

Upper West Side

✉ 65th Street at Columbus Avenue

☎ 212-875 5400

🚗 Subway 1, 9 to 66th Street/Lincoln Center

The major venue for classical music in New York, the Lincoln Center, a collection of buildings that includes the home of the Metropolitan Opera, was built on slums that were featured in the film *West Side Story*. The **Alice Tully Hall** (tel 212-875 5050) houses the Chamber Music Society of Lincoln Center; the **Avery Fisher Hall** (tel 212-875 5030) is home to the New York Philharmonic; the **Metropolitan Opera House** (tel 212-362 6000); the **New York State Theater** (tel 212-870 5570), is the base of New York City Opera; and the **Walter Reade Theater** (tel 212-875 5601), is home to the Film Society of Lincoln Center. Jazz at Lincoln Center is at the AOL Time Warner Center (page 193).

You can take a behind-the-scenes tour of the Lincoln Center, which is really the only way to see beyond the ornate lobbies of the buildings, unless you're paying big bucks for a performance. The tours are fabulous and give a really good insight into the workings of the various venues. They start at 10.30am, 12.30pm, 2.30pm and 4.30pm each day from the ticket booth in the main part of the Center and cost $12.50, students and seniors $9, children (12 and under) $6. You can also go on a **Backstage Tour** of the Metropolitan on Mon, Tues, Thurs, Fri

The Lincoln Center

and Sun at 3.45pm and Sat at 10am. The tours are very popular so it's best to book in advance on 212-875 5350.

Standing room tickets to the Met go on sale on the day of the performance for $15.

In addition to the tours, you can enjoy the Lincoln Center environment with a series of jazz and folk bands that entertain the crowds for free during the summer. The Autumn Crafts Fair is held in the first week of September.

BARS

Here's a selection of bars to drop into while you are out and about in the city, including some of the hotel bars that stand out from the crowd and lounges that stay open into the early hours.

SOHO and TRIBECA

47 East Houston Street between Mott and Mulberry Streets. Tel 212-343 7251.
Serving drinks at decent prices in *très chic* SoHo, this dark and rather grungy basement bar is a watering hole for artists and locals.

Café Noir: 32 Grand Street at Thompson Street. Tel 212-431 7910.
Moroccan comfort food meets Spanish tapas in this little urban oasis. Think tagines, stews and pitchers of sangria. There's also an extensive wine list and the occasional live jazz session.

Merc Bar: 151 Mercer Street between Prince and Houston Streets. Tel 212-966 2727.
A long-time fixture of the SoHo scene, this cool bar attracts an attractive crowd to its luxuriously deep sofas. It's at its best in summer when worn leather chairs get an airing on the sidewalk – a great place to sit and people-watch. Be warned: the drinks are pricey at $10-plus.

Velvet Restaurant and Lounge: 223 Mulberry Street between Prince and Spring Streets. Tel 212-965 0439.
A truly discreet lounge bar that takes darkness to new depths. The giant sofas and adjoining parlour where you can play games of chess and backgammon add to the chilling-out factor.

Void: 16 Mercer Street at Canal Street. Tel 212-941 6492.
Once the preferred watering hole of cybergeeks and short-film-and-video nerds, Void has since matured into a mellow neighbourhood bar with internet hook-ups. A giant video screen fills one wall of the bar and there are film screenings here sometimes. On other nights you'll be entertained by either a DJ or a jazz band.

CINEMAS

You don't just head to Times Square for theatrical shows, you can see some great blockbuster movies at any of the many sparkling new and renovated cinemas in the area. For complete listings of movies and cinemas near your hotel, check *Time Out*.

AMC Empire 25: 234 West 42nd Street between 7th and 8th Avenues, tel 212-398 3939. This has 25 screens on five levels and has devoted seven screens on the top floor, known as the Top of the Empire, to repertory classics and independent films. You can catch a pre-show snack in the 42nd Street Food Court, which has everything from pizzas to Chinese and barbecued spare ribs.

Loews 42nd Street E Walk: 243 West 42nd Street between 7th and 8th Avenues, tel 212-840 7761. The new Loews E Walk, with 13 screens and all-stadium seating, is billed as a modern-day movie palace. A one-storey high, hand-painted mural honours the local landmarks of Broadway and Times Square.

Loews Astor Plaza: 44th Street between Broadway and 8th Avenue, tel 212-505 6395. Another great Theater District venue for movies.

The Angelika Film Center: 18 West Houston Street, tel 212-777 FILM. A good selection of the latest art films is shown here, as well as at the Lincoln Plaza Cinemas, 1886 Broadway at 62nd Street, tel 212-757 2280. The Angelika has a café and the Lincoln Plaza Cinemas sell sandwiches and pastries.

LOWER EAST SIDE

Good World: 3 Orchard Street between Canal and Hester Streets. Tel 212-925 9975. A mellow bar with a semi-regular DJ and an attractive young crowd. Stars that have been spotted here include Keanu Reeves, Bjork, Courtney Love and Matt Dillon. Best time to go is Sun to Thurs and order the Scandinavian-style Good World, an elderberry-infused caipirinha.

Inoteka: 98 Rivington Street at Ludlow Street. Tel 212 614-0478.
The staff at this wine bar are ingratiating and knowledgeable. The crowd is a mixture of neighborhood denizens and drop-ins from uptown, creating a good atmosphere.

Kush: 183 Orchard Street between Houston and Stanton Streets. Tel 212-677 7328.
Get a taste of paradise by sipping a few cocktails and nibbling on tasty bar snacks like mixed olives and salted almonds in this Moroccan oasis. The decor is fab with wonderful tiling and whitewashed walls lit by candles.

Lansky Lounge: 104 Norfolk Street between Delancey and Rivington Streets. Tel 212-677 9489.
Once the former boardroom of infamous 1920s' gangster Meyer Lansky, the Jewish genius who masterminded many of Bugsy Siegal's and Lucky Luciano's biggest moves, the Lansky Lounge has a real speakeasy vibe. Swing, Latin and lounge music nights draw good crowds, and don't forget to sample the superb flavoured martinis – the Diplomat is a favourite. The prices can be a bit steep, though, and in observance of the Jewish Sabbath it is closed on Friday.

Max Fish: 178 Ludlow Street between Houston and Stanton Streets.
Tel 212-529 3959.
Part art gallery, part pick-up joint and part downtown party venue, this institution draws a hip but unpretentious crowd of artists, musicians and bohos. You'll get cheap drinks here, and it still has one of the best jukeboxes in town.

Milk and Honey: 134 Eldridge Street between Broome and Delancey.

No, we didn't forget the phone number: this bar is open only to insiders who manage to get hold of it. First arrivals bemoan the fact that now 'everyone' knows how to get in. Other than the challenge of entering, what does the place have to offer? Its hot reputation and deftly mixed drinks.

Many of the hip bars get packed out on Friday and Saturday nights with the people who live outside Manhattan. If you want to experience the scene without tourists, choose another night.

Orchard Bar: 200 Orchard Street between Houston and Stanton Streets.
Tel 212-673 5350.
One of the best lounges on the Lower East Side, the decor at the Orchard Bar is very different (think rocks for seats and bamboo shoots hanging from the walls). Cutting-edge DJs, cheapish drinks and a trendy crowd of artists and musicians mean it gets packed at the weekends so if you want to try it out, you'll need to plan ahead.

Smithfield: 115 Essex Street between Rivington and Delancey Streets.
Tel 212-475 9997.
The closest you'll get to a local in Manhattan. This glass-bricked bar offers everything from pints of Guinness to vodka shots, each served up with a great story by bartender and co-owner Stuart Delves. Very entertaining.

GREENWICH VILLAGE

Cafe Wha?: 115 MacDougal Street between West 3rd and Bleecker Streets.
Tel 212-254 3706.
Village hang-out since the beginning of time. There is something fun and exciting on every night of the week here, including live Brazilian dance parties on Mondays, funk on Tuesdays and comedy nights on Saturdays. Best of all, the bill for drinks and snacks won't inhale the entire contents of your wallet. Get there before 10pm if you want to get a table.

Madame X: 94 West Houston Street between Thompson Street and La Guardia Place. Tel 212-539 0808.
There's a real London Soho den-of-iniquity feel to this joint, bathed as it is in red and lit by the glow of lanterns. Known for serving pretty potent cocktails and rare imported beers. In summer, head for the black door at the rear and you'll find the new outdoor alcove, where red lights above the benches bring the boudoir theme outside. Best of all, you'll probably be able to find a free corner.

MEATPACKING DISTRICT

APT: 419 West 13th Street at 10th Avenue. Tel 212-414 4245.
A real hit with trendy New Yorkers since the day it opened, this intimate bar/club makes you feel like you are somewhere extra special. The dark, candlelit first floor is furnished like an apartment, complete with bed, dining table and chairs and sofas, offering comfortable lounging. Charming staff serve up tasty cocktails, such as Moscow Mules and Appletinis, for around $10. The wood-walled room downstairs has a more modern vibe, and punters propping up the long bar often end up shaking their stuff to the DJ's hip tunes. Book in advance for the weekend.

Hogs & Heifers: 859 Washington Street at West 13th Street. Tel 212-229 0930.
The hogs are the motorcyclists and the heifers are the dames, who are known for hanging their bras on the ceiling. There's no more bar dancing here, so there'll be no repeats of Drew Barrymore's performance.

Lotus: 409 West 14th Street between 9th and 10th Avenues. Tel 212-243 4420.
Three storeys devoted to nightlife, including a bar, restaurant and club. Jennifer Lopez, Bruce Willis and Britney Spears have been seen here, but the celeb scene has hardly cooled off since it opened in 2000. Avoid the weekend crush by going midweek. Try their Tartini – a Cosmo with Chambord.

Rise at the Ritz-Carlton Hotel

WEST VILLAGE

Chumley's: 86 Bedford Street between Grove and Barrow Streets.
Tel 212-675 4449.
A former literary speakeasy, it's still a great place to drink and have a spot of shepherd's pie while you look over the book jackets that line the wall. Yes, they were all donated by the authors who used to frequent the establishment such as Jack Kerouac and F Scott Fitzgerald. You'll find their signatures imprinted in some of the older tables. There's even a roaring fire giving a cosy atmosphere in the winter.

NOHO

Joe's Pub: 425 Lafayette Street between 4th Street and Astor Place.
Tel 212-539 8770.
This newish cabaret continues to be a real hot spot. An extension of the Public Theater, Joe's brings you live music, spoken-word performances and a crowd jam-packed with the trendiest types around. Stars spotted here include Ethan Hawke, Minnie Driver, Janeane Garofalo and Camryn Manheim. The drink to order is the Lady Macbeth – 115ml (4fl oz) of champagne and 115ml (4fl oz) of ruby port. Strong stuff!

EAST VILLAGE

Angel's Share: 8 Stuyvesant Street between East 9th and East 10th Streets.
Tel 212-777 5415.
Dedicated to the art of mixology, this little gem of a bar will rustle up any cocktail you desire. Part of its charm is the fact that it's so hard to find, you'll feel like you've stumbled across a city secret. Take the stairs to the second floor and veer left past the restaurant to the door at the rear. Inside you'll find a dark, intimate bar where classy city dwellers take their first dates.

Beauty Bar: 231 East 14th Street between 2nd and 3rd Avenues. Tel 212-539 1389.
Deb Parker's theme bar is equipped with 1960s-style hairdryers and chairs, real manicurists, great drinks and a heavy dose of the hip and beautiful.

KGB: 85 East 4th Street between 2nd and 3rd Avenues. Tel 212-505 3360.
As the name suggests, it is decorated with deep-red walls, portraits of Lenin and Brezhnev, propaganda posters and an oak bar preserved from the time when the place was a front for the Communist party. The crowd is a mix of actors, writers and drunks

who love the private-parlour feel of the place. Up-and-coming writers and successful authors often do readings for free, so call in advance to see who's on.

Korova Milk Bar: 200 Avenue A between 12th and 13th Streets. Tel 212-254 8838.
The Milk Bar is decorated in a wacky retro-futuristic style that pays homage to Stanley Kubrick's *A Clockwork Orange*. It attracts a sci-fi crowd who love its surreal quality and the ice-cream drinks.

CHELSEA

Kanvas: 219 9th Avenue between 23rd and 24th Streets. Tel 212-727 2616.
The latest favourite Chelsea hang-out is owned by two firefighters, who have furnished a couple of giant loft rooms with comfy banquettes, subtle lighting and a chilled line in music. There's also gallery space on both floors so you can snap up some art while you're sipping your sour apple martini, the bar's speciality.

FLATIRON DISTRICT

Tiki Room: 4 West 22nd Street between 5th and 6th Avenues. Tel 646-230 1444.
Retro Hawaiian, this 1960s-inspired bar has tropical flowers, a giant rattan lampshade, images of beaches on the flat screen TVs above the bar and lots of coconut and pineapple-laden fare. A Top 40 sound track provides the sounds.

MIDTOWN

Campbell Apartment Bar: Gallery Level, Grand Central Station. Tel 212-953 0409.
This apartment used to be the office/salon of the 1920s' tycoon John W Campbell. The beamed ceiling, huge leaded-glass window and the massive stone fireplace make a unique, almost castle-like space. But the dark wood, couches and club armchairs create an intimate place for a drink.

Russian Vodka Room: 265 West 52nd Street between Broadway and 8th Avenue. Tel 212-307 5835.
A brilliant vodka bar that doesn't require you to take out a second mortgage. There are cheap smoked fish platters, delicious cocktails and marvellous vodka infusions. It tends to attract the publishing crowd.

UPPER EAST SIDE

Rooftop at the Met: 5th Avenue and 81st Street. Tel 212-535 7710.
There's a stunning view and you'll get to admire the exhibits at the Metropolitan Museum of Art along the way up. Known as a great singles pick-up joint, this bar is nicest at sunset. The terrace is open during the summer.

HOTEL BARS

Hotel bars are currently the hippest place to sip a cocktail in New York. Your only problem will be which one to choose.

FINANCIAL DISTRICT/BATTERY PARK

Rise at the Ritz-Carlton Hotel: 2 West Street between Battery Place and West End. Tel 212-344 0800. Subway 1, 9 to Rector Street; 4, 5 to Bowling Green.
A big hit with both visitors and the Wall Street crowd is the 14th floor bar of the newly opened Ritz-Carlton Hotel. They go for the comfy, plush chairs with fabulous views of the harbour, Statue of Liberty and amazing sunsets. The bar specialises in a series of colourful martinis served in gorgeous corkscrew-stemmed glassware and 710ml (25fl oz) margarita, sangria and mojitos, which are a perfect size for sharing. If you fancy a nibble, then either go for the dim sum or signature 'tiers' – platters of food for up to four people. They include the Pacific Union with sesame chicken, cured salmon and seared beef with dipping sauces and The New Yorker, which comes with mini burgers, pastrami sandwiches and shrimp cocktail with homemade crisps.
You can sit inside or outside and, best of all, the service is excellent.

The Grand Bar at the SoHo Grand

TRIBECA

Church Lounge at TriBeCa Grand Hotel: 2 6th Avenue at White Street. Tel 212-519 6600. Subway A, C, E to Canal Street.
The Wall Street crowd has made this upscale bar an after-work hang-out. It's meant to look like a living room – if your living room were full of beautiful people. Sanctum Lounge with DJs, open Thursday to Sunday only, is the even more exclusive adjunct.

SOHO

The Grand Bar and Salon at the SoHo Grand Hotel: 310 West Broadway between Grand and Canal Streets. Tel 212-965 3000. Subway A, C, E to Canal Street.
A chic gathering place that has attracted the rich and famous, such as Matt Damon and Venus Williams, since its opening a few years ago. It was at the forefront of the lounge-as-living-room trend and is filled with a mix of comfy, retro chic furnishings that serve as great perches for drinking and watching the multi-lingual crowd – mostly dressed in classic New York black. Sit back, nibble on the snacks and feel the energetic we're-at-the-centre-of-the-universe buzz.

Thom's Bar at the 60 Thompson Hotel: 60 Thompson Street between Broome and Spring Streets. Tel 212-219 2000. Subway 6, C, E to Spring Street.
A sophisticated decor of dark wood, soft violet seats, brown leather club chairs and white Venetian plaster walls make for pleasant surroundings. The entertainment is provided by the chic crowd who know that this boutique hotel is the only place to be seen midweek. Drinks are surprisingly cheap, like flavoured vodka for $7.50.

GREENWICH VILLAGE

North Square at the Washington Square Hotel: 103 Waverly Place at MacDougal Street. Tel 212-254 1200. Subway A, B, C, D, E, F, V to West 4th Street/Washington Square.
The small, cosy basement space's classic bar and luxurious leather chairs are a reminder of another era, while beautifully stencilled windows offer a glimpse of the current street scene. It attracts a large European crowd, who find it the perfect spot to pore over a map and a Martini, but locals – as well as the occasional celeb – can also be found enjoying the laid-back atmosphere.

GRAMERCY PARK

Gramercy Park Hotel Bar: 2 Lexington Avenue, Gramercy Park at 21st Street. Tel 212-475 4320. Subway 6 to 23rd Street.
A home-from-home for media types from around the world. The bar is narrow and maybe a little dark, but friendly and unpretentious. Notable for reasonably priced drinks and the cheese snacks that are served with boundless generosity.

MIDTOWN

Asia de Cuba at the Morgans Hotel: 237 Madison Avenue between 37th and 38th Streets. Tel 212-726 7755. Subway 4, 5, 6, 7 to 42nd Street/Grand Central.
A packed first-floor bar that overlooks the super-trendy restaurant. Heaving with an attitude-heavy Upper East crowd, it's a sleeker, more sophisticated version of the bar that opened in London's St Martin's Lane Hotel and should be at the top of your must-go-there list. If you like your drinks deliciously expensive and served in punchbowl-size glasses, you'll love it.

Cellar Bar at the Bryant Park Hotel: 40 West 40th Street between 5th and 6th Avenues. Tel 212-642 2136. Subway B, D, F, V, 7 to 42nd Street/Bryant Park.
A must-do for any fashionista, because this new boutique hotel on the block has been adopted by the fashion pack. Expect to see models, designers and magazine editors propping up the bar, but don't even think about dropping in during fashion week – you won't be able to move for the wafer-thin clientele.

Fiftyseven Fiftyseven at the Four Seasons Hotel: 57 East 57th Street between 5th and Park Avenues. Tel 212-758 5700. Subway N, R, Q, W to 5th Avenue.
The Four Seasons is dynamic in early evening when celebs rub shoulders with power-broking businessmen and hip hotel guests, while a pianist provides the background music. Be sure to sample some of the 15 types of martini on offer.

Sky bar at La Quinta Manhattan: 17 West 32nd Street between Broadway and 5th Avenue. Tel 212-736 1600. Subway N, R, W to 28th Street.
A cross between a backyard deck and a funky beach bar, this partially enclosed rooftop watering hole is packed year-round with international visitors who appreciate the casual atmosphere and towering views of the Empire State Building.

MIDTOWN EAST

Oasis at W New York: 541 Lexington Avenue at 49th Street. Tel 212-755 1200. Subway 6 to 51st Street.
An oasis of tranquillity, the bar heats up when the fashion, art and music crowd descends for cocktails before dinner at the hotel's Heartbeat restaurant. The ambience is Californian and casual with clever touches that include a waterfall and backgammon tables disguised as tree stumps. Also at the hotel is the Whiskey Blue, overseen by Randy Gerber, otherwise known as Cindy Crawford's husband. The hip clientele enjoy cosy sofas that are great for people-watching and a top-notch sound system that plays until the wee small hours.

Villard at the New York Palace Hotel: 455 Madison Avenue between 50th and 51st Streets. Tel 212-303 7757. Subway E, V to 5th Avenue; 6 to 51st Street.
Extravagant and romantic, an 18th-century French-style getaway right in the heart of the city.

Wet Bar at W New York – The Court Hotel: 130 East 39th Street between 5th and Madison Avenues. Tel 212-592 8844. Subway 4, 5, 6, 7, S to 42nd Street.
George Clooney, Whoopi Goldberg and D'Angelo Marc Anthony have all been spotted in this sleek and uncluttered setting, which plays host to professionals and hotel guests. Try their apple martini.

MIDTOWN WEST

Ava Lounge at the Majestic Hotel: 210 West 55th Street between Broadway and 7th Avenue. Tel 212-956 7020. Subway 1, 9 to 50th Street; N, Q, R, W to 49th Street.
A swish retro duplex penthouse lounge with great views over the Late Show studios. In summer time the upstairs terrace lounge is THE place to be, while in winter opt for the library-style bar lounge on the lower level. Great music and a laid-back but chi-chi vibe make both bars a perfect place for a drink or two.

Halcyon Lounge at the RIGHA Royal Hotel: 151 West 54th Street between 6th and 7th Avenues. Tel 212-468 8888. Subway N, R to 57th Street.
An elegant setting for pre-theatre cocktails and nightly entertainment.

Hudson Hotel Bar at the Hudson Hotel: 356 West 58th Street between 8th and 9th Avenues. Tel 212-554 6000. Subway A, B, C, D, 1, 9 to 59th Street/Columbus Circle.
This Ian Schrager and Philippe Starck Mecca for the in-crowd provides wonderful theatre. There's a glowing glass floor, flashy DJ and dark and enticing Games Room. In the summer, the after-work crowd head to the Private Park – the hotel garden – and sip cocktails next to giant watering cans. Pure, surreal magic.

King Cole Bar at the St Regis Hotel: 2 East 55th Street. Tel 212-339 6721. Subway E, V to 5th Avenue at 53rd Street.
The specialities of the (very upscale) house are the Bloody Marys and the mural behind the bar, by noted American illustrator Maxfield Parrish.

Living Room at the W Times Square Hotel: 1567 Broadway at 47th Street. Tel 212-930 7444. Subway 4, 5, 6, L, N, Q, R, W to 14th Street.
Another of the cool W Hotel bar scenes, a magnet for fashion models (many agencies are in the area) and other pretty people.

Lobby Bar at the Royalton: 44 West 44th Street between 5th and 6th Avenues. Tel 212-869 4400. Subway B, D, F, V to 42nd Street; 7 to 5th Avenue.
The first of the Philippe Starck-designed hotels is still holding its own against all newcomers and its long, narrow bar continues to be a place to see and be seen. The loos are wonderful, too.

It's incredibly easy to walk past the Royalton, or '44' as it's known – there is no sign outside, just large wooden doors.

Mobar at the Mandarin Oriental: 59th Street at Columbus Circle. Tel 212-207 8880. Subway A, B, C, D, 1, 9 to Columbus Circle.
In the dazzling new AOL Time Warner Center, the sleek lobby lounge is drawing the crowds. The cocktails are $15 but the spectacular view of Central Park from the 35th floor (not to mention celebrity sightings) is free.

The Oak Bar at the Plaza Hotel: 5th Avenue at Central Park South. Tel 212-759 3000. Subway N, R, W to 5th Avenue.
This bar is perhaps most famous for its wall murals by painter Everett Shinn – Cary Grant sat beneath one in a scene from

Hitchcock's *North by Northwest.* Today, the bar attracts a mature, business-like crowd, although sightings of Kevin Costner and Al Pacino have been reported. Specialities are the views of Central Park, and the world's largest raisins for nibbling with drinks.

The Oak Room at the Algonquin: 59 West 44th Street between 5th and 6th Avenues. Tel 212-840 6800. Subway B, D, F, V to 42nd Street; 7 to 5th Avenue.
Once world-famous as the New York literary set's salon of choice, this handsome room provides an intimate and civilised setting for some of the country's leading jazz and cabaret artists, who are usually booked for extended runs. The clientele is clubby and patrician, but anyone can buy dinner or drinks here.

Pen-Top Bar at the Peninsula Hotel: 700 5th Avenue, 23rd Floor. Tel 212-903 3097. Subway E, V to 5th Avenue/53rd Street; N, R, W to 5th Avenue/59th Street.
The view is breathtaking and the prices can be, too, but in beautiful weather, you'll feel as if you're in the centre of the universe – like the power brokers who surround you.

THEATER DISTRICT

The Broadway Lounge at the Marriot Marquis Hotel: 1515 Broadway at Times Square. Tel 212-704 8900. Subway N, Q, R, S, W, 1, 2, 3, 7, 9 to 42nd Street/Times Square.
This bar has a magnificent view of Times Square. It is a huge space with ceiling-to-floor windows.

The Marriot Marquis

UPPER EAST SIDE

Café Carlyle at the Carlyle Hotel: 35 East 76th Street at Madison and Park Avenues. Tel 212-744 1600. Subway 6 to 77th Street.
A highly glamorous bar and restaurant that specialises in cabaret. Woody Allen currently (up to Dec 2004) plays on clarinet with The Eddie Davis New Orleans Jazz Band on Monday nights and Bobby Short, a New York favourite, plays piano during spring and the autumn. $75 per person cover charge.

Mark's Bar at the Mark Hotel: 25 East 77th Street at Madison Avenue. Tel 212-744 4300. Subway 6 to 77th Street.
This bar has been described as a cosy tearoom that feels like a luxury train carriage. It never gets too noisy and patrons, who perch on forest-green sofas and floral slipper chairs, are treated like guests in an elegant private home. The bar attracts a youngish fashion set, but the crowd can be diverse, depending on the evening.

NIGHTCLUBS

This category includes live music venues and late night lounges as well as mainly dance clubs. Hours vary with the event at most clubs, so check out the listings in the *Village Voice, Paper, New York Press* and *New Yorker.* Three websites provide information on which venues and which nights the parties are: **www.papermag.com**, **www.newyork.citysearch.com** and **www.clubnyc.com**.

The best way to make sure you enjoy a good night's clubbing, follow these rules:

➡ On Friday and Saturday nights, the clubs are packed with crowds from boroughs outside Manhattan. For a quieter night, go on Thursday. Sunday is the big night for Manhattanites, so you'll get the real vibe then, along with the crowds.

➡ Call ahead early in the evening to find out if there's a cover charge, when to arrive and how to dress. Also find out if there's a party theme on the night that you plan to go. Clubs can change nightly – for example, catering to straights one night, gays the next.

➡ The real nightlife doesn't get going until after midnight, so get some zeds in before you go out.

➡ Carry some ID with you just in case – it would be terrible if you couldn't get a drink and you're over 21.

TOP 10 CLUBS AND LOUNGES

(in alphabetical order)

APT (dance): Meatpacking District (page 186)

Asia de Cuba: Midtown (page 188)

Bowery Ballroom: East Village (page 192)

Bungalow 8: Chelsea (page 193)

Cielo: Meatpacking District (page 192)

Crobar: Chelsea (page 193)

Lit: East Village (page 192)

Pangaea: NoHo (page 192)

Pianos: Lower East Side (page 191)

SoHo: 323: SoHo (page 191)

➡ Large groups of men don't stand much hope of getting into straight clubs – you'll have more chance if you're with a woman.

CHINATOWN

Happy Endings: 302 Broome Street at Forsyth Street. Tel 212-334 9679. Subway 6, N, R to Canal Street.
A brothel-turned-bar with a DJ in the basement dance room and a mixed lounge scene that attracts hip young things.

SOHO

Don Hill's: 511 Greenwich Street at Spring Street. Tel 212-219 2850. Subway 6, C, E to Spring Street; N, R to Prince Street. Open nightly 9pm–4am.
A Mecca for fashion and music celebs, this is a great place to find dance and live music nights. Even the mixed nights have a big gay crowd. The big night is Brit-Pop Tiswas on Saturdays.

NV: 289 Spring Street at Hudson Street. Tel 212-929 NVNV. Subway 6, C, E to Spring Street; N, R to Prince Street. Open Wed to Sun 10pm–4am.
The crowd is trendy and friendly, while the music is a great mix of everything from house and disco to hits from the 1980s. The upstairs has dance-floor energy while the much larger downstairs keeps a mellow lounge atmosphere.

Clubs come and go and go in and out of fashion pretty quickly. Keep up to date through www.clubplanet.com.

SoHo: 323: 323 West Broadway. Subway 6, C, E to Spring Street; N, R to Prince Street. Tel 212-334 2232.
New York party animals who love the South Beach (Florida) scene are flocking to this new spot, opposite the SoHo Grand. Even before its official opening, it hosted post-premiere parties for the TriBeCa Film Festival, and Eva Mendes, David Duchovny, and Robert De Niro were among the first celebrities on site. There's a sleek, clean lounge and a dark, loft-like upstairs bar. The drink to go for is Twos & Threes – champagne and lychee purée with a touch of Chambord.

LOWER EAST SIDE

Pianos: 158 Ludlow Street between Rivington and Stanton Streets. Tel 212-505 3733. Subway F, J, M, Z to Delancey Street/ Essex Street.
A former piano shop turned clean, white-washed bar space that attracts trendy fashionistas plus the NYU students from the area. Local and national up-and-coming rock bands play in the somewhat dingy back room, while there's also a more intimate lounge upstairs.

Plant: 217 East 3rd Street between Avenues B and C. Tel 212-375 9066. Subway F, V to Lower East Side/2nd Avenue.
Considered one of the coolest bars in town, you can party to underground sounds on Friday and techno sounds on Saturday. Mary Jane's Tropical Sundays is devoted to house, breaks and jazz. The Pep Sounds Wednesday night party has broken beat, nu-jazz and similar rhythmic sounds.

Sapphire Lounge: 249 Eldridge Street between Houston and Stanton Streets. Tel 212-777 5153. Subway F to 2nd Avenue.
Pretension and attitude are left at the door in this tiny dance club that plays a great mix of hip-hop, reggae, acid jazz, R&B and disco classics. Opens at 7pm.

Metropolitan Opera House

Slipper Room: 167 Orchard Street between Rivington and Stanton Streets. Tel 212-253 7246. Subway F, M, J, Z to Delancey Street/Essex Street.
Adding some real showbiz panache to the Lower East Side, this glitzy retro lounge is the venue for genuinely good cabaret as well as some far out, gender-bending burlesque. A great evening out.

GREENWICH VILLAGE

Nell's: 246 West 14th Street between 7th and 8th Avenues. Tel 212-675 1567. Subway A, C, E to 14th Street; L to 8th Avenue.
Attracts a straight crowd who go for the jazz and funky soul upstairs and the reggae and R&B downstairs. Sometimes there are live acts, so call in advance to see who's on.

Roxy: 515 West 18th Street between 10th and 11th Avenues. Tel 212-645 5156. Subway A, C, E to 14th Street; L to 8th Avenue.
A huge venue with plenty of different themes such as Roller Disco Wednesday, Old School Friday, and Hunky Gay Saturday.

SOBs: 204 Varick Street at Houston Street. Tel 212-243 4940. Subway 1, 9 to Houston Street.
The name stands for Sounds Of Brazil, which says it all. It's the place to come for the last word in Latin music from salsa to samba and even reggae.

MEATPACKING DISTRICT

Cielo: 18 Little West 12th Street between 9th Avenue and Washington Street. Tel 212-645 5700. Subway A, C, E, to 14th Street; L to 8th Avenue.
The dance floor is sunken but the fabulous sound system hits the heights. This is one of the hottest spots in the city, and the good news and bad news is that it draws the big crowds.

One: 1 Little West 12th Street at 9th Avenue. Tel 212-255 9717. Subway A, C to 14th Street; L to 8th Avenue.
It's big (465sq m/5,000sq ft), it's bi-level and there's lots of action on the dance floor. A popular spot with the college crowd – though it helps if they're on big allowances!

Passerby: 432 West 15th Street at Washington Street. Tel 212-206 7321. Subway A, C, E, 1, 2 3, 9 to 14th Street; L to 8th Avenue.
Hurry before everyone else discovers this place: plenty already have. Tiny but with an awesome disco floor.

PM: 50 Gansevoort Street. Tel 212-255 6676. Subway A, C to 14th Street; L to 8th Avenue.
Half a dozen doormen enforce the beautiful-person policy that's considered the most brutal in the area. But if you get in, you'll experience an island decor with big booths, big signs prohibiting dancing, and a big tab. The bottle service doesn't come cheap, but the attitude is laid back and the place gets really hot well past midnight.

NOHO

Pangaea: 417 Lafayette Street between Astor Place and 4th Street. Tel 212-353 2992. Subway 6 to Astor Place; N, R, W to 8th Street.
For anyone on the hunt for some star-spotting, this is celeb central. African safari decor with wooden masks make a perfect backdrop for stars such as Justin Timberlake, models, fashionistas and Wall Streeters.

Do make an effort to get dressed up if you are going clubbing. Don't wear trainers or jeans – you won't get in.

EAST VILLAGE

Bowery Ballroom: 6 Delancey Street between Bowery and Christie Street. Tel 212-633 2111. Subway F, V to 2nd Avenue.
If you've got one chance to visit the live music scene in Manhattan, this might be the place to go. A multi-level concert hall, the Bowery has lots of bars, good sight lines and an admission price that won't break your budget.

Lit: 93 2nd Avenue between 5th and 6th Streets. Tel 212-777 7987. Subway 6 to Astor Place; F, V to Lower East Side/2nd Avenue.
If you've always wanted to see a hot bartender in action, this art-meets-celebs joint is the place to come. A haven for indie filmsters, it has an art gallery – The Fuse – at the back along with a cellar-like dance room downstairs.

Plaid (formerly SPA): 76 East 13th Street between 4th Street and Broadway. Tel 212-388 1060. Subway L, N, Q, R, W, 4, 5, 6. Open Tues to Sat.

A plush hip-hop and house venue that has had a makeover since it was known as SPA and is still top of the clubbing tree. Rap superstar Busta Rhymes loves it.

Webster Hall: 125 East 11th Street between 3rd and 4th Avenues. Tel 212-353 1600. Subway L, N,Q, R, W, 4, 5, 6 to 14th Street/Union Square.
There are lots of different rooms with different sounds, so you're bound to find something you enjoy. The best area is the main dance floor in the huge, ornate ballroom. It attracts a fairly straight crowd from the suburbs, but is a fun night out.

CHELSEA

Bungalow 8: 515 West 27th Street between 10th and 11th Avenues. Tel 212-675 1567. Subway C, E to 122nd Street.
Here's where the hippest post-premiere parties are held and the gossip columnists get all their material. Cool decor and lots of attitude: it's an A-list kind of place.

Crobar: 530 West 28th Street between 10th and 11th Avenues. Tel 212-629 9000. Subway C, E to 23rd Street.
A New York import from Chicago and Miami, it's a paradox: a wild and crazy spot

ALL THAT JAZZ

A visit to New York City wouldn't be complete without an evening at one of the various jazz venues, but it can get very expensive, so it's good to know your way around. At all the main venues it'll cost you around $25 to hear one set which only lasts 1–1½ hours. It's worth it if you're happy with the music, but the idea of having to move on after only one set is a bit strange to us Brits, so it's good to be warned!

The most important new venue is **Jazz at Lincoln Center**'s new $128-million home at the AOL Time Warner Center at Columbus Circle, with three performance spaces, two large and one intimate. Visit **www.jalc.org** to find out about the dozens of events or call the JazzTix hotline, 212-258 9998.

THE MAIN CLUBS

One of the best jazz clubs is the **Iridium**, now at 1650 Broadway at 51st Street, tel 212-582 2121. It's not too touristy, is smaller than many clubs and has a nice intimate feel. The entrance fee varies but there's a $10 minimum. The **Village Vanguard** (178 7th Avenue South at Perry Street, tel 212-255 4037), probably the most famous club of all, always hosts great talent and sets last the full 1½ hours. Another famous Greenwich Village venue is the **Blue Note** (131 West 3rd Street between MacDougal and 6th Avenue, tel 212-475 8592), but this is a lot more touristy, very expensive and has a Las Vegas-style interior. **Swing 46 Jazz and Supper Club** (349 West 46th Street between 8th and 9th Avenues, tel 212-262 9554) offers big bands and small combos to suit hip downtown loungers and traditional uptown swingers – it's rapidly becoming an institution.

Other good venues include **Birdland** (315 West 44th Street between 8th and 9th Avenues, tel 212-581 3080) in Midtown West; the **Jazz Standard** (116 East 27th Street between Park and Lexington Avenues, tel 212-576 2232) near Madison Square; **Sweet Rhythm** (88 7th Avenue South between Bleecker and Grove Streets, tel 212-255-3626) in the Village; and **Bubble Lounge** (228 West Broadway at White Street, tel 212-431 3433) in TriBeCa, which has live music every Monday and Tuesday.

CHEAP AND CHEERFUL

One of the best off-the-beaten-track jazz venues is in the heart of Greenwich Village at the **Cornelia Street Café** (29 Cornelia Street, tel 212-989 9319), a haunt of the locals. Prix fixe dinner is $20 and is served from 5.30pm. The jazz starts at 8.30pm and costs from $5 to $15. They don't have big names, but they do have a lot of New York talent. **Zinc Bar** (90 West Houston Street between Thompson Street and La Guardia Place, tel 212-477 8337), is one of the most intimate places in town to enjoy live jazz, and it's only $5 to get in.

The cheapest jazz clubs tend to be in Harlem, Queens and Brooklyn, but because they can't afford to advertise you really don't hear about them. Furthermore, most don't even have names on the door. Good places to look for venues are the *New York Times* weekend edition and the *Village Voice*. The latter is a lot better and it's free, visit **www.villagevoice.com**.

that's very well run, and a new venue that evokes the huge clubs of the past.

UNION SQUARE

Underbar at the W Hotel Union Square: 201 Park Avenue South at 17th Street. Tel 212-358 1560. Subway 4, 5, 6, L, N, Q, R, W to 14th Street/Union Square.
The plush velvet couches, the insistent throb of the music and the curtained-off private nooks all help send a seductive message in a way that some find amusing, others find a touch unsubtle. Still, the crowds – especially Europeans – keep coming.

MADISON SQUARE

Cheetah: 12 West 21st Street between 5th and 6th Avenues. Tel 212-206 7770. Subway F, N, R to 23rd Street.
An intimate venue with attractive animal-print decor and snuggly booths. Attracts a great mix, ranging from ghetto fabulous to the supercool.

THEATER DISTRICT

Show: 135 West 41st Street between 6th Street and Broadway. Tel 212-278 0988. Subway N, Q, R, S, W, 1, 2, 3, 7, 9 to 42nd Street/Times Square.
A Moulin Rouge-inspired hot spot with scantily clad burlesque dancers, swinging trapeze artists, go-go girls aplenty and a gilded stage for dancing to the mainstream music. Edgier hip-hop is played in the small upstairs lounge.

Avoid the crowds at Manhattan jazz clubs by going for the late set during the week. Also remember that stormy weather puts New Yorkers off going out, so you could get a great seat if it's raining.

MIDTOWN EAST

Light: 125 East 54th Street between Park and Lexington Avenues. Tel 212-583 1333. Subway 6 to 51st Street; E, V to Lexington Avenue/53rd Street.
This has had a good run with young professionals and glamorous *Sex and the City* types. Sip a Cosmo and tuck into the Asian-inspired appetisers while DJs spin a wide range of lounge music from Wednesday to Saturday.

Vue: 151 East 59th Street between Lexington and 3rd Avenues. Tel 212-753 1144. Subway 6 to 51st Street; E, V to Lexington Avenue.
Is it the visuals projected on a planetarium-type dome or is it the great sound and big club feeling? Whatever… this is one of the most popular of the newest clubs.

MIDTOWN WEST

Copacabana: 617 West 57th Street between 11th and 12th Avenues. Tel 212-582 2672. Subway A, C, B, D, 1, 9 to Columbus Circle/59th Street.
A mostly Latin clientele who go for the live bands playing salsa and merengue. Everyone is fairly well dressed, not casual but not overdone. It's great but it does get packed.

Float: 240 West 52nd Street between 8th Avenue and Broadway. Tel 212-581 0055. Subway 1, 9, C, E to 50th Street; B, D, E to 7th Avenue.
Be warned, if you choose this paradise of stockbrokers and models, you will be parting with wads of cash for a good night out, but the environment is beautiful. There is a main dance floor plus loads of VIP areas for those who think they're important, and plenty of side rooms, small lounges and little cubbyholes to make everyone else feel at home. A fascinating nightspot for viewing the beautiful people.

UPPER EAST SIDE

DT UT: 1626 2nd Avenue between 84th and 85th Streets. Tel 212-327 1327. Subway 4, 5, 6 to 86th Street.
A coffee bar lounge that's been described as the closest thing to TV's *Friends'* hang-out, Central Perk.

UPPER WEST SIDE

Calle Ocho: 446 Columbus Avenue between 81st and 82nd Streets. Tel 212-873 5025. Subway 1, 9 to 79th Street; B, C to 81st Street.
Established Latino hot spot for a good-looking, tony (stylish) crowd of mixed ages. The atmosphere is sexy and the food is good.

Shalel Lounge: 65–1/2 West 70th Street between Central Park West and Columbus Avenues. Tel 212-799 9030. Subway B, C to 72nd Street.
Dark and dangerous – in the nicest kind of way. The exotic North African atmosphere transports aficionados directly to Morocco or a similar locale.

CHAPTER 10

Gay New York

The West Village was the original home of gays and lesbians in New York, but now that the city is so cosmopolitan and accepting, gay bars, clubs and restaurants have sprung up all over Manhattan. Chelsea, however, has become the new, popular locale.

If you'd like to get to know more about the gay and lesbian culture in New York, Big Onion's tour Before Stonewall – A Gay and Lesbian History Tour – gives a really good insight into the historical side, tracing the development of Greenwich Village as a community Mecca (see Big Onion Walking Tours, page 78). For a tour of the modern-day Gay New York, try Limotour's Gay Tour of New York, which can be arranged online **(www.limotours.com)** or visit **www.infohub.com**.

This chapter is dedicated to those who really do want to get to know the gay scene in the city, and has information on everything from accommodation to community centres, restaurants, bars and clubs. It should also be noted that many of the restaurants and bars are open to everyone, whatever their persuasion.

INFORMATION

LESBIAN AND GAY COMMUNITY SERVICES CENTER

✉ 208 West 13th Street between 7th and 8th Avenues

☎ 212-620 7310

www.gaycenter.org

By far the best organisation in New York for information, you'll find millions of leaflets and notices about gay life in the city. There are now around 400 groups that meet here and it also houses the National Museum and Archive of Lesbian and Gay History.

PUBLICATIONS

The main gay weeklies are *HX (Homo Xtra)* and *HX for Her*, which tend to be available in gay bars, clubs, hotels and cafés. They include listings of bars, dance clubs, sex clubs, restaurants and cultural events. Visit **www.hx.com** before you go. Good newspapers are the *LGNY* (Lesbian and Gay New York), though it's a lot more serious and covers political issues, and *The Blade*.

ACCOMMODATION

Turn to pages 203–4 for some Hotel Tips and booking info. Prices are per room.

CHELSEA PINES INN

Chelsea

✉ 317 West 14th Street between 8th and 9th Avenues

☎ 212-929 1023
cpiny@aol.com

🚗 Subway A, C East to 14th Street; L to 8th Avenue

$ Doubles and triples $99–149 including breakfast

In an excellent location in Chelsea on the border with the Village, this is just about the cheapest accommodation you could hope to get in New York, but you need to book at least six to eight weeks in advance. The hotel has recently been given a facelift, and now each room is named after a film star.

There are plenty of gay clubs in New York

Yes, there is a Judy Garland. In the morning, guests wake to the aroma of homemade bread and doughnuts. Open to both men and women.

CHELSEA SAVOY HOTEL

Chelsea

✉ 204 West 23rd Street
☎ 212-929 9353
www.chelseasavoynyc.com
🚗 Subway 1, 9, 3 to 23rd Street
$ Doubles $99–195

This hotel is in a superb location, being close to the Theater District, Financial District, great restaurants, museums and galleries, and SoHo just down the road. The rooms are a good size for NY with all essential amenities such as bathroom and television.

COLONIAL HOUSE INN

Chelsea

✉ 318 West 22nd Street between 8th and 9th Avenues
☎ 212-243 9669
www.colonialhouseinn.com
🚗 Subway C east to 23rd Street
$ Doubles $80–140

A beautiful place to stay and also spotlessly clean. The economy rooms are tiny, but all have cable TV, air con, phone and daily maid service, and smoking is allowed in rooms. The price includes breakfast, which is eaten in the Life Gallery where there are works by gay and lesbian artists. Book as early as you can because this place gets packed with groups coming into town for drag conventions and so on. It's especially popular in the summer months because of its roof deck with a clothing optional area. The hotel has a 24-hour doorman. Mostly for gay men.

EDISON HOTEL

Theater District

✉ 228 West 47th Street between Broadway and 8th Avenue
☎ 212-840 5000
🚗 Subway N, R to 49th Street
$ Doubles $160, suites from $200

One of New York's great hotel bargains. The Edison's 700 rooms have been totally refurbished, and it has a new coffee shop, the Café Edison, considered to be the best place to spot lunching theatre luminaries.

HOTEL WALCOTT

Midtown

✉ 4 West 31st Street between 5th Avenue and Broadway
☎ 212-268 2900
sales@wolcott.com
🚗 Subway N, R to 28th Street
$ Doubles $120–180

Well, darling, it's location, location, location, for this 300-room hotel. Just three blocks down from 5th Avenue and the Empire State Building, this is a favourite with the serious tourist and budget-minded business traveller. Call in advance to find out the bargain seasonal, weekend and holiday rates on offer.

INCENTRA VILLAGE HOUSE

West Village

✉ 32 8th Avenue between West 12th and Jane Streets
☎ 212-206 0007
🚗 Subway A, C east to 14th Street; L to 8th Avenue
$ Doubles $119–169

A moderately priced guesthouse in two red-brick townhouses from the 1840s (old by American standards!). The 12 suites all have kitchens, phones and private bathrooms and some can even accommodate groups of four or five. All the rooms are well decorated with different themes. The Bishop Room is a lovely split-level suite, the Garden Room has a private garden filled with flowers and the Maine Room has a four-poster bed. All rooms are smoker-friendly. A 1939 Steinway piano stands in the parlour and anyone who can is allowed to play.

THE INN AT IRVING PLACE

Gramercy Park

✉ 56 Irving Place between 17th and 18th Streets
☎ 212-533 4600
www.innatirving.com
🚗 Subway L, N, R, 4, 5, 6 to 14th Street/Union Square
$ Rooms $325–475

The building is filled with exquisite antique furniture and elegant decor. All 12 rooms have queen-size beds and come with private facilities, some even have study areas. There is a 24-hour concierge, plus laptops and fax on request, laundry and dry-cleaning, video rentals, gym within walking distance and 24-hour massage.

THE ROYALTON

Theater District

✉ 44 West 44th Street between 5th and 6th Avenues

☎ 212-869 4400

🚗 Subway 4, 5, 6 to 42nd Street; 7 to 5th Avenue

$ Rooms $235–475

Ian Schrager's beautiful hotel, designed by Philippe Starck, is now considered to be the best address for gays and lesbians into the power thing. A chic tone is set by the lively fashion and publishing crowd who frequent the lobby bar and restaurant. The modern rooms all have CD players, VCR, mini bar and two phone lines.

CLUBS AND LOUNGES FOR HIM

CHELSEA

Barracuda: 275 West 22nd Street between 7th and 8th Avenues. Tel 212-645 8613. Subway C, E, 1, 9 to 23rd Street.
Head to the rear lounge, which has a better atmosphere than the dingy front bar and a decent pool table. Monday night is the hilarious Star Search, where drag queens battle it out between each other to reign supreme. Open till 4am.

Centro-Fly: 45 West 21st Street between 5th and 6th Avenues. Tel 212-627 7770. Subway N, R, F to 23rd Street.
It costs $20–30 just to get in, but boy is it worth it. This is one of the best clubs in the city in terms of music, atmosphere and delicious clientele.

GBH on Friday nights is the big one, which has won numerous awards and has been running for four years. Guest DJs have included all the greats including LTJ Bukem and Armand Van Helden.

Discothèque: 17 West 19th Street between 5th and 6th Avenues. Tel 212-352 9999. Subway F, V, N, R, W to 23rd Street.
A great addition to the Chelsea scene, Friday is reserved for new dance party **Opening of Trade**.

Eagle: 554 West 28th Street between 10th and 11th Avenues. Subway C, E to 23rd Street. Tel 212-330 7043.
A spacious watering hole filled with congenial leather-clad New Yorkers.

El Flamingo: 547 West 21st Street between 10th and 11th Avenues. Tel 212-243 2121. Subway C east to 23rd Street.
If your thing is cross-dressing performers lip-synching along to disco numbers, then **The Donkey Show: A Midsummer Night's Disco** is for you. It runs from Wednesday to Saturday and costs $25–30 to get in, but you can also dance your ass off until the wee small hours after the show.

g: 225 West 19th Street between 7th and 8th Avenues. Tel 212-929 1085. Subway 1, 9 to 18th Street.
A super-popular nightly spot for hunks, open 4pm–4am. Its centrepiece is its oval bar, which the sexy clientele prop up when they're not shimmying to house music. It gets packed later on when the queues build up outside. Saturday nights are free.

Heaven: 579 6th Avenue between 16th and 17th Streets. Tel 212-539 3982. Subway F, V to 14th Street.
Decorated with wall-to-wall white paint and mirrors, this 3-storey club is a sparkling spectacle that simply must be seen and enjoyed during a trip to NY.

Kurfew: 208 West 23rd Street. Tel 212-533 1222. Subway C, E to 23rd Street.
America's youngest all-gay party, Friday night's college fest at Twirl is unmissable.

Rawhide: 212 8th Avenue at 20th Street. Tel 212-242 9332. Subway C, E to 23rd Street.
A darkly lit neighbourhood bar famous for its pool tables and beer specials.

Roxy: 515 West 18th Street between 10th and 11th Avenues. Tel 212-645 5156. Subway A, C east to 14th Street; L to 8th Avenue.
Saturday, $20 from 11pm for an evening of gorgeous guys, sexy drag queens and brilliant sounds. This is the award-winning big night out for gay New Yorkers. On Wednesday, put on your blades and have a blast at the roller disco.

SBNY: 50 West 17th Street between 5th and 6th Avenues. Tel 212-691 0073. Subway L, N, R, 4, 5, 6 to 14th Street/Union Square.
Formerly known as Splash, this a popular place to hang out on any night of the week, and not just because the handsome bartenders are shirtless. It's done out South Beach style, with a huge dance floor emporium and a downstairs bar for cruising. It's popular with preppy men and those who enjoy attention.

TRIBECA

Arc: 6 Hubert Street between Greenwich and Hudson Streets. Tel 212-343 1379. Subway 1, 9 to Franklin Street.
Be Yourself on Friday, $20, from 11pm with DJ/producer Danny Tenaglia playing the music. **Club Shelter**, Saturday from 11pm, $11, with DJ Timmy Regisford's spirit of the Paradise Garage. An alcohol-free night. **Body and Soul**, Sunday, $14, from 4pm. DJs Francois K, Danny Krivit and Joe Claussell spin the house classics.

GREENWICH VILLAGE

Crazy Nanny's: 21 7th Avenue at Leroy Street. Tel 212-366 6312. Subway 1, 9 to Houston Street
Great local place to hang out, with a pool table, good juke box and upstairs dance floor. There's a daily happy hour and karaoke on certain nights.

The Monster: 80 Grove Street at Sheridan Square. Tel 212-924 3558. **www.manhattan-monster.com**. Subway 1, 2, 3, 9 to Christopher Street/Sheridan Square.
Probably the most popular bar in Greenwich Village. Right on Sheridan Square across from the infamous Stonewall. Happy piano bar draws older crowd, downstairs dance floor draws younger hotties. There is a cover charge on weekends, probably the only club with cover in the Village. Opens at 4pm, party starts at 10pm.

WEST VILLAGE

Dugout: 185 Christopher Street between Washington and West Streets. Tel 212-242 9113. Subway L to 6th Avenue
A great neighbourhood bar and club especially popular for its Sunday afternoon beer busts.

The Starlight Room

Lips: 2 Bank Street at Greenwich Avenue. Tel 212-675 7710. Subway 1, 2, 3, 9 to 14th Street.
This buzzy place is the Hard Rock Café of drag, with supper and shows from 5.30pm–midnight weekdays and until 2am on Friday and Saturday. The **Bitchy Bingo Show** on Wednesdays, free, open from 8pm, sees Sherry Vine and Yvon Lame preside over the bitchiest bingo game in the world. On Tuesday you can enjoy drag karaoke.

EAST VILLAGE

B Bar & Grill: 40 East 4th Street between Lafayette Street and the Bowery. Tel 212-475 2220. Subway B, D, F, Q to Broadway/Lafayette Street; 6 to Bleecker Street.
Beige on Tuesdays, free, open from 9pm. This is a super-trendy lounge filled with models and gorgeous people. Madonna has been known to drop in.

The Cock: 188 Avenue A at East 12th Street. Tel 212-777 6254. Subway F to 2nd Avenue, 6 to Bleecker Street.
This gay bar is considered by many to have one of the wildest crowds in the city. For those tired of the lounge clubs lining the avenues of Chelsea, this continually lively spot provides a good alternative. The Cock attracts pretty boys, drag queens, gay celebrities and their friends, and then mixes it with lots of alcohol and some serious cruising. Drinks are cheap and there is usually no cover charge. Cash only.

Dick's Bar: 192 2nd Avenue at 12th Street. Tel 212-475 2071. Subway L to 3rd Avenue.
Dick's is primarily a gay bar, but it is also a place that some straight people may feel comfortable in. A friendly East Village dive, it features cheap drinks and a jukebox playing alternative rock and 1970s' music, as well as a disco ball and the occasional pornographic movie. Dick's is a homey place for aging gay men who fondly yearn for the latter days of disco. Cash only.

The Hole: 29 2nd Avenue at 2nd Street. Tel 212-743 9406.
Four nights a week Thursday to Sunday this infamous place holds some of the hottest cruising men around, according to the locals. It has a good-sized dance floor.

Wonderbar: 505 East 6th Street between Avenues A and B. Tel 212-777 9105. Subway F to 2nd Avenue.

A nightly lounge with a packed, mixed crowd enjoying soul and classic hits. Drinks are very reasonable, around $3.50 for a beer.

FLATIRON DISTRICT

Estate@Limelight: 660 6th Avenue at 20th Street. Tel 212-807 7780. Subway F to 23rd Street.
The club has recently undergone a major renovation and holds gay nights on Friday and Sunday.

MIDTOWN WEST

Chase: 255 West 55th Street between 7th and 8th Avenues. Tel 212-333 3400. Subway B, D, E to 7th Avenue; N, R, Q to 57th Street.
Chase is a sleek, chic gay bar in a neighbourhood with a growing gay population. Located 30 blocks north of Chelsea, it manages to avoid much of that area's attitude. Yet, it still provides everything one has come to expect from a gay bar, including attractive bartenders clearly not hired for their drink-making skills. Looking for love? The crowd is diverse enough for there to be someone for almost everyone.

Edelweiss: 137 7th Avenue (south) near 10th Street. Tel 212-929 5155. **www.clubedelweiss.com**. Subway C, E to 50th Street
A multi-level dance club for trannies, cross-dressers and their fans.

La Nueva Escuelita: 301 West 39th Street at 8th Avenue. Tel 212-631 0588. Subway A, C east to 42nd Street.
A fantastic Latino club famed for its fabulous shows and nights of salsa, merengue and Latin-style drag shows. No shows on Thursday nights, but 2.30am Fridays, 2am Saturdays and 9pm and 1.30am Sundays.

Xth Avenue Lounge: 642 10th Avenue at 45th Street. Tel 212-245 9088. Subway A, C east to 42nd Street.
Open daily with a Happy Hour 4–8pm. There is a light menu in the back room. Not exclusively for gays.

MIDTOWN EAST

Red: 305 East 53rd Street between 1st and 2nd Avenues. Tel 212-688 1294. Subway E, V to Lexington Avenue/53rd Street.
The best time to get dolled up and hit this NY hot spot is Thursday night, which is an anything-goes party that has the added bonus of being free. Inside, you'll be exposed to strippers, rub shoulders with porn stars and be dazzled by lap-dancing go-go boys.

UPPER EAST SIDE

Pegasus Bar: 119 East 60th Street between Park and Lexington Avenues. Tel 212-888 4702. Subway 4, 5, 6 to 59th Street; N, R to Lexington Avenue.
Gentlemen's piano bar featuring karaoke and cabaret shows on various rotating nights of the week. Friday and Saturday focus on entertainment for Asian gays. It's also the time of the week when the groovy back room opens up to reveal plastic-wrapped, leopard-print benches and intimate lighting.

HARLEM

Club Chaz: 454 West 128th Street, between Amsterdam Avenue and Convent Avenue. Tel 212-749 8055. Subway 1, 9 at 125th Street.
If you love Latin music, then pop in here on a Friday night to have yourself a sizzling time. If you're more of a hip-hop and house guy, drop in to **Industry** on a Tuesday. It's $3 before 12pm and $10 after. Open until 5am.

Club fliers

CLUBS AND LOUNGES FOR HER

CHELSEA

Heaven: 579 6th Avenue between 16th and 17th Streets. Tel 212-539 3982. Subway F, V to 14th Street.
Decorated with wall-to-wall white paint and mirrors, this three-storey club is a sparkling spectacle that simply must be seen and enjoyed during a trip to NY. **Julie's Salsa and Merengue Dance Party** is a long-running dance that comes here for its Wednesday night party, so Latin music lovers really will be in heaven! On Friday night it's the popular **Kaleidoscope Party**, a massive Girl Club Productions extravaganza with salsa and merengue on two floors. Wet T-shirt contests also feature. Happy Hour 5–7pm.

2i's: 248 West 14th Street between 7th and 8th Avenues. Tel: 212-807 1775. Subway A, C, E to 14th Street; L to 8th Avenue.
The ultra-cool Thursday evening party, **G Spot**, has weekly themes and music that includes hip-hop, R&B, reggae and house. From 7.30–9pm there are performances by comedians and spoken-word artists while it's Happy Hour behind the bar.

LOWER EAST SIDE

Bluestockings: 172 Allen Street between Rivington and Stanton Streets. Tel 212-777 6028. Subway F, V to Lower East Side/ 2nd Avenue.
A great neighbourhood joint that gives women the opportunity to showcase their talents at open-mike sessions.

Meow Mix: 269 Houston Street at Suffolk Avenue. Tel 212-254 0688. Subway F, V to Lower East Side/2nd Avenue.
A hip neighbourhood bar that welcomes both women and their male friends. Unpretentious but fun, it plays host to live bands, performances, raucous parties with go-go girls and even has karaoke. **Girlsalon** is held every Thursday 8–10pm when lesbians are invited to demonstrate their musical, acting, comic and writing abilities. **Gloss**, the big party, generally follows on Thursday 10pm–4am. There are go-go girls aplenty in a lively extravaganza that attracts a mixed crowd from the *über* glamorous to the butch!

WEST VILLAGE

Bar d'O: 29 Bedford Street and Downing Street. Tel: 212-627 1580. Subway A, C, E F, V to Grand Street; 1, 9 to Houston Street. **Pleasure** is a great party with a laid-back vibe with entry to men accompanied by a woman. What's more, the rap stars here genuinely like women!

Cubby Hole: 281 West 12th Street between West 4th and West 12th Streets. Tel 212-243 9041. Subway 1, 2, 3, 9 to 14th Street.
It looks as though the owners of this lesbian bar have raided a New Orleans thrift store a few days after Mardi Gras: hundreds of illuminated plastic blowfish, goldfish and Chinese lanterns dangle from the ceiling. Old-timers straggle in long before sunset for half-price drinks (until 7pm, Monday through Saturday); after 9pm, younger gals (and a fair number of guys) take centre stage. There's no karaoke here any more, but it almost doesn't matter. Like a pianoless piano bar, Cubby Hole is packed full of regulars who like to belt out tunes along with the jukebox.

Henrietta Hudson's: 438 Hudson Street at Morton Street. Tel 212-924 3347. Subway 1, 9 to Christopher Street/Sheridan Square.
A girl bar with great jukebox music. Even when there's no specific party, gals come from far and wide to hang out at this great watering hole. **Lush** on Sunday is a popular night with Latin sounds from DJ Culi, attracting an exotic crowd. **Mamacita** is a popular Thursday night dance with R&B, hip-hop and Latin music. If you're into go-go girls, the **Back Room Booty** Friday night extravaganza is the party for you – and hordes of other lesbians!

EAST VILLAGE

Starlight: 167 Avenue A and 11th Street. Tel 212-475 2172. Subway L to 1st Avenue.
A fabulous bar and lounge that is open Wednesday to Sunday until 3am. **Starlette** on Sunday evening is a popular party with a cool vibe that reflects its trendy East Village location.

MIDTOWN WEST

La Nueva Escuelita: 301 West 39th Street at 8th Avenue. Tel 212-631 0588. Subway A, C east to 42nd Street.
Fever on Friday night is a classic venue for a hot night out. Mostly filled with Latin women from the *über*-feminine to the ultra-butch, there are go-go dancers galore on which to feast the eyes, a drag show at 2am and a lap-dancing lounge.

THEATER DISTRICT

Cache: 221 West 46th Street between Broadway and 8th Avenue. Tel: 212-539 3982. Subway S, 1, 2, 3, 9, 7 to 42nd Street/Times Square; N, Q, R, W to 42nd Street.
Caché, a Girls Club Productions party for women who are 23 and over, on Saturday night is definitely a night to go glamorous and enjoy the classics, R&B and pop sounds in an elegant lounge.

RESTAURANTS

CHELSEA

Big Cup: 228 8th Avenue at 22nd Street. Tel 212-206 0059.
A truly gay coffee house that is a great place to hang out on a rainy day. It has a local vibe, and even has the movie times for the local cinema chalked on a blackboard so that you won't miss your film.

Eighteenth and 8th: 159 8th Avenue at 18th Street. Tel 212-242 5000.
The gay restaurant of the gay district of New York, it serves healthy American food. But be prepared for a long wait outside as it's tiny inside.

Empire Diner: 210 10th Avenue at 22nd Street. Tel 212-243 2736.
This humble diner has made appearances in countless commercials and movies. It's very low key and a great pit stop for a burger at the end of a heavy night. You'll be rubbing shoulders with all sorts of people, from drag queens to artists, in need of a late night snack (page 169).

Lola: 30 West 22nd Street between 5th and 6th Avenues. Tel 212-675 6700.
Famous for its American cuisine with Caribbean and Asian influences, it's packed on Sunday for gospel brunches.

Pad Thai: 114 8th Avenue at 16th Street. Tel 212-691 6226.
Elegant noodle lounge.

Restivo: 209 7th Avenue at 22nd Street. Tel 212-366 4133.
Great Italian cuisine at good prices.

SOHO, NOLITA and TRIBECA

Amici Miei: 475 West Broadway at Houston Street. Tel 212-533 1933.
A chic Italian restaurant open for lunch and dinner with outdoor seating.

Basset Café: 123 West Broadway at Duane Street. Tel 212-349 1662.
Tuck into a delicious salad or sandwich, or treat yourself to the homemade cakes at this light and airy haven.

El Teddy's: 219 West Broadway between Franklin and White Streets. Tel 212-941 7070.
A hip hangout with a great bar scene and excellent food.

La Cigale: 231 Mott Street between Prince and Spring Streets. Tel 212-334 4331.
Simple but imaginative continental food and a magical back garden.

WEST VILLAGE

Benny's Burritos: 113 Greenwich Avenue at Jane Street. Tel 212-727 3560.
The incredibly cheap and huge burritos attract a large student crowd who don't mind the poor service.

Caffe Dell'Artista: 46 Greenwich Avenue between 6th and 7th Avenues. Tel 212-645 4431.
A European-style café serving simple, light meals and desserts.

Cowgirl: 519 Hudson Street at West 10th Street. Tel 212-633 1133.
This isn't just great for men and women who feel at home surrounded by cowgirl memorabilia, but is also frequented by families. It serves cheap American food – fried onion loaf, huge spare ribs and chicken-fried steak – for $21–30 for a main course and is also known for its margaritas. The people-watching outside the restaurant in summer is a treat.

Florent: 69 Gansevoort Street between Greenwich and Washington Streets. Tel 212-989 5779.
Good French food served 24 hours a day at weekends and until 5am weekdays. Busy after the clubs close (page 161).

Garage Restaurant: 99 7th Avenue South between Barrow and Grove Streets. Tel 212-645 0600.
Serves American cuisine including steaks and a raw bar, with live jazz nightly and a friendly crowd (page 161).

Lips: 2 Bank Street at Greenwich Avenue. Tel 212-675 7710.
Italian menu with dishes named after popular queens, and waitresses in drag and plenty of entertainment (page 198).

Nadine's: 99 Bank Street at Greenwich Street. Tel 212-924 3165.
Eclectic and good-value food in a funky but glamorous setting.

Rubyfruit Bar and Grill: 531 Hudson Street at Charles Street. Tel 212-929 3343.
Not just for lesbians. Serves good eclectic food both downstairs and in the fun bar upstairs. Live music nightly.

Sacred Cow: 522 Hudson Street at West 10th Street. Tel 212-337 0863.
Healthy vegan food shop and café.

EAST VILLAGE

Astor Restaurant and Lounge: 316 Bowery at Bleecker Street. Tel 212-253 8644.
The Moroccan-style lounge plays host to a gay party on Wednesdays, as well as a French/Mediterranean restaurant.

B Bar: 40 East 4th Street between Lafayette Street and Bowery. Tel 212-475 2220.
Home to **Beige** on a Tuesday night, this gorgeous bistro serves excellent food.

Lucien: 14 1st Avenue at 1st Street. Tel 212-260 6481.
Always packed, this tiny French bistro serves delicious food and is particularly known for its Sunday brunch.

Pangea: 178 2nd Avenue between 11th and 12th Streets. Tel 212-995 0900.
Known for its wonderful homemade pastas and Mediterranean cuisine.

Stingy Lulu's: 129 St Mark's Place between Avenue A and 1st Avenue. Tel 212-674 3545.
A fabulous old-fashioned diner (page 163).

THEATER DISTRICT

Coffee Pot: 350 West 49th Street at 9th Avenue. Tel 212-265 3566.
Nice little coffee bar with live music and tarot card readings.

Mangia East Bevi: 800 9th Avenue at 53rd Street. Tel 212-956 3976.
An excellent, popular Italian in the middle of Midtown's gay district.

Revolution: 611 9th Avenue between 43rd and 44th Streets. Tel 212-489 8451.
A club-like restaurant with great food and music videos. It has a DJ every night, a youngish crowd and American menus.

Vintage: 753 9th Avenue at 51st Street. Tel 212-581 4655.
A hip bar/restaurant that serves dinner till midnight and cocktails till 4am.

MIDTOWN EAST

Comfort Diner: 214 East 45th Street between 2nd and 3rd Avenues. Tel 212-867 4555.
Authentic and delicious American cuisine served in a 1950s-style diner setting with a friendly atmosphere (page 169).

Regents: 317 East 53rd Street between 1st and 2nd Avenues. Tel 212-593 3091.
Attracts a fairly posh gay crowd for its eclectic cuisine. There is a rotating specials menu and a prix fixe menu at $17.95. Also has an upstairs back terrace and live cabaret nightly, including show tune theme nights and Sinatra specials.

Townhouse Restaurant: 206 East 58th Street between 2nd and 3rd Avenues. Tel 212-826 6241.
This is a real gay haunt – especially among the more mature crowd. It serves delicious food at reasonable prices.

Brooklyn Bridge

CHAPTER 11

Accommodation

As I explained in Chapter 1, the matter of choosing your hotel should be your last decision, so that you will have the chance first to work out what you want to do while you're in the Big Apple. That way you'll know where you'll be spending most of your time and can decide where best to locate yourself. It may be that if you intend to stay for a week it would work out best to stay at two hotels – one in Lower Manhattan and one in Midtown – so you can save on travelling time and expensive cab fares.

It is worth noting a few of the basic facts about New York hotels, too. For instance, space is a premium in Manhattan, so the average room size tends to be on the small side. The most upmarket hotels have always been clustered on the East Side from Midtown up to 96th Street. However in recent years this has changed with some first-class hotels now in SoHo, Greenwich Village and the Financial District. The best deals tend to be around Herald Square and on the Upper West Side, but if you go for these options check you won't be spending too much on transport. The average rate for a room that can accommodate two people is $200 a night – so if you get something for less (and there are plenty of ways to do this), you are doing well.

HOTEL TIPS

➡ There are now around 70,000 hotel rooms in New York, yet demand at certain times of the year is such that you will still have a hard time finding one. Your best bet for both ensuring a bed and getting the best price is to go in the off-peak times of January to March and July and August.

➡ Most hotels reduce their rates at weekends – including some of the poshest. If you're staying for more than a weekend, negotiate the best rate you can for the rest of your time or switch to a cheaper hotel.

If you are planning to take in the sights of Lower Manhattan, Chinatown, Lower East Side, SoHo and the Village, choose a downtown hotel. It'll save you loads of time on travel and money on cab fares.

➡ If noise is a particular problem for you, bear in mind that hotels downtown and uptown tend to be quieter than those in Midtown. Also, addresses on streets tend to

The Ritz-Carlton Liberty Suite

ALL WIRED UP!

Not only does America have a different style of plug, it also works on a different voltage. Ours is 230 volts, theirs is 115 volts, so you'll need a travel appliance that works on both voltages, or an adaptor plug.

be quieter than those on avenues, except those nearer the river.

➡ For longer stays, try to choose a hotel room with a kitchenette, then you won't have to eat out all the time.

➡ Smaller hotels tend not to book large groups, so they often have rooms available even during peak periods.

➡ When booking your room, check there isn't going to be a major convention on at the same time – if there is, ask to be put on a different floor.

➡ Ask for a corner room – they are usually bigger and have more windows and, therefore, more light than other rooms and don't always cost more.

➡ Renovation work is often going on in New York hotels, so when reserving a room, ask if any is being done at that particular hotel and, if so, ask for a room as far away as possible from the work.

BOOKING IT YOURSELF

Of course, you can use a travel agent to make room reservations, but you can also do it yourself through companies that specialise in offering excellent rates at off-peak and low-peak times or even just guarantee finding you a room during busy periods. They include:

Hotel America Ltd: Tel 01444 410555, **www.hotelanywhere.co.uk**
A British company providing hotel discounts anywhere in the world.

Hotel Conxions: Tel 212-840 8686, fax 212-221 8686, **www.hotelconxions.com**.
You can find out about availability and price, and book a room on their website.

When making a booking directly with a hotel, make sure they send you confirmation of your reservation (by fax is simplest).

Quikbook: Tel 212-779 ROOM, fax 212-779 6120, **www.quikbook.com.**
A service providing discounts on hotels all over America. They promise there are no hidden cancellation or change penalties, and pre-payment is not required.

A great internet discount reservation service can be found at **www.hotres.com** and **www.hoteldiscount.com** or look for cheaper rates through the hotel discount service on: **www.usacitylink.com/citylink/ny/new-york**.

When discussing room rates with any of these organisations, always check that the prices you are quoted include the New York City hotel tax of 13.25 per cent and the $2 per night occupancy tax or 4 per cent for a one-bedroom suite.

Below I've given a listing of hotels chosen for their location, service, price or the excellent value for money they offer. I have divided them up by price per room, starting with the most expensive, and then arranged them by location.

$	Less than $100
$$	$100–200
$$$	$200–300
$$$$	$300–400
$$$$$	$400 and over

TOTALLY DIVINE

BATTERY PARK CITY

RITZ-CARLTON NEW YORK $$$$$

✉ 2 West Street between Battery Place and West End
☎ 212-344 0800
Fax 212-344 3804
www.ritzcarlton.com
🚗 Subway 4, 5 to Bowling Green

A world-class hotel with Art Deco-inspired interiors, incredible views of the Hudson River and Statue of Liberty, state-of-the-art business support services and unparalleled service. A 39-storey glass-and-brick edifice in Lower Manhattan, it has 298 sumptuous guest rooms, 113 luxury residences, an outdoor waterfront deck and even the Skyscraper Museum (page 115).

The rooms come with the very finest Frette linens, feather beds and goose-down pillows, cotton bathrobe, Ritz-Carlton pyjamas, marble bathtubs and separate marble shower stalls, silk curtains, in-room safe, working desk with two chairs, dual-line cordless phones with voicemail and high-speed internet access. The extensive guest services include a fully equipped health club and spa, massage treatments, limo, complimentary shuttle service in Lower Manhattan and a bath butler! I can assure you, it really is to die for.

MIDTOWN

PLAZA $$$$-$$$$$

5th Avenue at 59th Street
212-759 3000
Fax 212-759 317
www.fairmont.com
Subway N, R to 5th Avenue

Built in the style of a French château, the Plaza overlooks Central Park. Inside is a treasure trove of antique furniture, dazzling chandeliers and elaborate ceilings and its famous Palm Court is the place to have afternoon tea in New York. Rooms are worn but charming and a good size. Celebrity guests include Marlene Dietrich and Catherine Zeta Jones and Michael Douglas, who held their wedding reception in the hotel's Grand Ballroom.

MIDTOWN EAST

FOUR SEASONS $$$$-$$$$$

57 East 57th Street between Madison and Park Avenues
212-758 5700
Fax 212-758 5711
Subway 4, 5, 6 to 59th Street

Put on your best power suits to rub shoulders with New York's movers and shakers. The Art Deco-style rooms come with electronically controlled curtains and marble-clad bathrooms.

NEW YORK PALACE $$$$-$$$$$

455 Madison Avenue between 50th and 51st Streets
212-888 7000
www.newyorkpalace.com
Subway 6 to 51st Street

The Palace rises 55 floors from its prime spot in Midtown Manhattan and is a favourite stopover for celebs visiting New York. The main hotel is in the Villard Houses, but the adjacent Towers are the more luxurious rooms to stay in. Although it was built in 1882, the furnishings are surprisingly modern, with high-back modern couches and quirky gold lamps in the lobby. It also houses the landmark Le Cirque 2000 restaurant (page 151) and the Villard Bar and Lounge (page 189).

If you're a smoker, make sure you ask for a smoking room as most hotels now predominantly provide non-smoking rooms.

DIAMOND DISCOUNTS

You can cut your room rates by taking advantage of the New York Travel Advisory Bureau's (NYTAB) tie-up with Express Reservations – call 303-218 7808 or visit **www.hotelsinmanhattan.com**. They offer major discounts on over 25 hotels across most price categories.

SHERRY-NETHERLAND $$$$-$$$$$

781 5th Avenue at East 59th Street
212-355 2800
Fax 212-319 4306
www.sherrynetherland.com
Subway 4, 5, 6 to 59th Street

A true New York secret, this is one of the grand hotels with real charm and is also the permanent home of many a celebrity.

WALDORF ASTORIA $$-$$$$$

301 Park Avenue at 50th Street
212-355 3000
Fax 212-872 7272
www.waldorfastoria.com
Subway 6 to 51st Street

A colossus of a hotel in more than one sense, it's an Art Deco marvel with a wonderful history that has been designated a New York City landmark since 1993. It all started in 1893 when millionaire William Waldorf Astor opened the 13-storey Waldorf Hotel at 33rd Street. It was the embodiment of Astor's vision of a grand hotel and came with two innovations – electricity throughout and private bathrooms in every guest chamber – and immediately became the place to go for the upper classes. Four years later the Waldorf was joined by the 17-storey Astoria Hotel, built next door by Waldorf's cousin, John Jacob Astor IV. The corridor between the two became an enduring symbol of the combined Waldorf and Astoria Hotels.

In 1929 it closed and on its original site now stands another icon of the New York skyline, the Empire State Building. In the meantime the Waldorf Astoria was rebuilt in Midtown Manhattan, opening its doors in 1931 and immediately being dubbed New York's first skyscraper hotel. It rose 42 storeys high, stretched from Park Avenue to Lexington Avenue and contained an astonishing 2,200 rooms. It was such an amazing event, opening as it did in the middle of the Depression, that President Herbert Hoover broadcast a message of congratulations. And ever since, the Waldorf Astoria has had a long association with presidents of countries and corporations.

The Art Deco aspects of the hotel were brought back into view during a restoration in the 1980s when architects found a huge cache of long-lost treasures, including a magnificent 148,000-piece mosaic, depicting the Wheel of Life, by French artist Louis Regal in the Park Avenue lobby, 13 allegorical murals by the same artist and ornate mouldings on the ceilings. The legendary Starlight Roof nightclub, which had epitomised glamour and sophistication in the 1930s and 1940s with its retractable roof, allowing views of the stars, was restored during the same period.

Another $60-million upgrade in 1998 saw the Park Avenue Cocktail Terrace and Sir Harry's Bar being restored to their full Art Deco glory. Oscar's, named after the Waldorf Astoria's famous style-setting maître d' Oscar Tschirky, was completely redesigned by Adam Tihany, the hottest restaurant designer in town.

Of course, if you plan to stay here, you'll want to know about the service – excellent – and the standard of the rooms – huge, beautifully decorated and with marble-encased ensuite bathrooms. What more could you ask for?

The Four Seasons

If you're not happy with the quality of your room, change it. Americans wouldn't tolerate anything but the best – so why should you?

WALDORF TOWERS $$$$$

✉ 301 Park Avenue at 50th Street
☎ 212-355 3100
Fax 212-872 7272
www.waldorf-towers.com
🚗 Subway 6 to 51st Street

A boutique hotel occupying the 28th to the 42nd floors of the Waldorf Astoria, this is one of the most exclusive addresses in New York, filled as it is with presidents of countries and global corporations. Thanks to the hotel's security arrangements (it has its own private car parking facilities underground), this is the place where treaties and mergers have been negotiated and signed, momentous peace initiatives have begun and unforgettable music has been made.

The hotel has its own dedicated entrance, lobby, concierge desk, reception and private lifts operated by 'white-gloved' attendants. Guests have included the Duke and Duchess of Windsor, who maintained their New York residence here, Jack and Jackie Kennedy, Frank Sinatra and Cole Porter, who wrote many of his most famous compositions here.

The rooms are not so much rooms or suites, but rather more like apartments in their own right. Many come with dining rooms, full kitchens and maids' quarters. Some even have televisions in their bathrooms!

UPPER EAST SIDE

HOTEL CARLYLE $$$$–$$$$$

✉ 35 East 76th Street between Madison and Park Avenues
☎ 212-744 1600
Fax 212-717 4682
www.rosewoodhotels.com
🚗 Subway 6 to 77th Street

Famous for its impeccable and discreet service, this is the place where the stars come. The apartment-style rooms are elegant and very plush – some even have grand pianos and all have whirlpools in the bathrooms. By the way, Woody Allen plays jazz here on Monday nights (page 190).

HOTEL PLAZA-ATHENE $$$$–$$$$$

✉ 37 East 64th Street between Madison and Park Avenues
☎ 212-734 9100
Fax 212 722 0958
🚗 Subway 6 to 68th Street

What its rooms lack in size they make up for in elegant French antique furnishings.

THE MARK $$$$–$$$$$

✉ 25 East 77th Street between 5th and Madison Avenues
☎ 212-744 4300
Fax 212-744 2749
www.mandarinoriental.com
🚗 Subway 6 to 77th Street

In terms of luxury, it vies with the Carlyle – only this hotel is infused with Italian neo-classicism compared with the Carlyle's English gentility. The city's first really beautiful upmarket boutique hotel, its discreet service is enjoyed by a long list of celebrity clients. Unfortunately, some of them have tended to get a bit out of hand and Johnny Depp and Kate Moss had their notorious lovers' tiff here, which took its toll on the furniture before Depp was finally arrested at 5am. Fellow celebrity guests George Michael and Ali McGraw were

The posh Mark hotel on the Upper East Side does such good weekend and summer rates that you could afford to stay there and enjoy all that fabulous luxury.

apparently deeply disturbed by Depp's tantrum. On a happier note, such an event is a rarity, which explains why many celebs make the hotel their home-from-home when they're in New York. There's a complimentary car service to Wall Street and the Theater District for all guests, a small health club, Molton Brown toiletries and a top-notch restaurant.

STANHOPE $$$$–$$$$$

✉ 995 5th Avenue at 81st Street
☎ 212-288 5800
Fax 212-517 0088
🚗 Subway 6 to 77th Street

Well located on Museum Mile, this security-conscious hotel is a hideaway for Hollywood stars and also caters to top business people. Anyone can enjoy its elegance and charm by taking afternoon tea here.

If you hire a car, bear in mind that most hotels charge a parking fee of around $25 a night.

UPPER WEST SIDE

MANDARIN ORIENTAL $$$$–$$$$$

✉ 80 Columbus Circle at 60th Street
☎ 212-805 8800
Fax 212-805 8888
www.mandarinoriental.com
🚗 Subway A, B, C, D, 9 to 59th Street/Columbus Circle

This is the city's much-anticipated new hotel, and it certainly lives up to the hype. Set in the top floors of the AOL Time Warner Center (page 52) on the north-west arc of the Columbus Circle, it sits steps away from Central Park and just a stroll from 5th Avenue. Inside, the luxurious rooms are simply breathtaking, with floor-to-ceiling windows offering spectacular views of the Manhattan skyline. Enjoy hanging out at the trendy Mobar, or flex your credit card and enjoy dinner in Asiate on the 35th floor which offers a fusion of French and Japanese cuisine. If you're tired after your journey, behave like a celeb and book yourself a massage at the hotel spa.

The Waldorf Towers

Hotels in the Financial District can be especially good value at weekends when many business people leave the city.

OUTSTANDING

TRIBECA

TRIBECA GRAND **$$$$–$$$$$**

✉ 2 Avenue of the Americas (6th Avenue) at Church Street
☎ 212-519 6600
UK freephone 0800-028 9874
Fax 212-519 6700
www.tribecagrand.com
🚗 Subway 1, 9 to Franklin Street

A new sister property to the extremely stylish SoHo Grand, this is the first major hotel to open in the TriBeCa area. It's popular with the film crowd, thanks to its 98-seat private screening room. In-room amenities include voicemail, data port, complimentary local phone calls and faxes, built-in TV and telephone, personal safes, high-speed internet access and free web access.

SOHO

MERCER **$$$$**

✉ 147 Mercer Street at Prince Street
☎ 212-966 6060
Fax 212-965 3820
🚗 Subway N, R to Prince Street

A bijou 72-room boutique hotel slap-bang in the middle of SoHo, it quickly gets packed with the fashionable and young corporate sets. Your room even comes with condoms in the bathroom and video games on the TV.

60 THOMPSON **$$$–$$$$$**

✉ 60 Thompson Street between Broome and Spring Streets
☎ 212-431 0400
Fax 212-431 0200
www.60thompson.com
🚗 Subway C, E to Spring Street

The latest boutique hotel to open in Manhattan is a real gem. It's a sleek, 14-storey, 100-bedroom hotel that is a great retreat from the bustling streets of SoHo. Rooms are designed for relaxing in, the best are on the top floor which have breathtaking panoramic views of landmarks including the Empire State Building. The front patio sheltered by black bamboo is a wonderful place to sit and people-watch. Outstanding!

SOHO GRAND **$$$$**

✉ 310 West Broadway between Grand and Canal Streets
☎ 212-965 3000
Fax 212-965 3244
www.sohogrand.com
🚗 Subway C east to Canal Street

Famous for its style, this was the first proper hotel to open in the SoHo area. Cocktails and light meals are served in the Grand Bar, an intimate, wood-panelled club room, as well as the fashionable Salon, a lively lounge that is excellent for people-watching (page 188).

GRAMERCY PARK

INN AT IRVING PLACE **$$$$–$$$$$**

✉ 56 Irving Place between East 17th and East 18th Streets
☎ 212-533 4600
Fax 212-533 4611
🚗 Subway L, N, R, 4, 5, 6 to 14th Street/ Union Square

Delightful, tiny Victorian boutique hotel. Each room has a romantic fireplace and four-poster bed.

MIDTOWN

BRYANT PARK **$$$$–$$$$$**

✉ 40 West 40th Street
☎ 212-869 0100
Fax 212-869 4446
www.bryantparkhotel.com
🚗 Subway D, B, V, F to 42nd Street

This hide-out for the fashion pack overlooks the park that gives the hotel its name. It's just off 5th Avenue, so ideal if you are on a shopping trip and convenient for visiting all of the major sights. Inside, the rooms resemble New York lofts, think white walls, sleek Italian furniture in warm orange and ochre and cool bathrooms with giant porcelain sinks and stainless steel shelves.

CHAMBERS **$$$-$$$$$**

✉ 15 West 56th Street between 5th and 6th Avenues

☎ 212-974 5656
Fax 212-974 5657
www.chambers-hotel.com

🚗 Subway B, Q to 57th Street

A new hotel that has certainly created a buzz. It's owned by the same team behind the Mercer Hotel in SoHo and has already attracted the likes of Jennifer Love Hewitt and Kid Rock to its gorgeous rooms. The ultra modern decor is comfortable and luxurious. The bath tubs are deep, cashmere throws adorn the beds and flat-screen TVs with DVD and CD players grace every room. Its restaurant, Town, is currently the in place to book for dinner.

LE PARKER MERIDIEN **$$$$-$$$$$**

✉ 118 West 57th Street between 6th and 7th Avenues

☎ 212-245 5000,
Fax 212-708 7477
www.parkermeridien.com

🚗 Subway B, D, E to 7th Avenue

A classic New York hotel in the design sense yet with a traditional French feel, this hotel is not only in an excellent location just minutes from Central Park and Carnegie Hall, but offers great service and amenities. The rooms, which have all recently been refurbished, have a Zen-like calmness to them thanks to the minimalist and cherry wood decor. Great touches include a revolving unit, which allows you to watch the massive TV screen either in the sitting area or in the bedroom. It also has a useful desk unit, CD and DVD players.

Make sure you look upwards when you enter the lifts of Le Parker Meridien – all three have a TV screen offering classic clips of *Abbott and Costello* or *Tom and Jerry*.

Even if you don't plan to use the pool, do visit its penthouse location to see the fab views of Central Park. Down in the basement is the massive Gravity gymnasium, which covers everything from Cybex training to aerobics, sauna, stretching, massage rooms, spa services and squash and racquetball courts.

Other facilities include the much-raved-about Norma's restaurant in the lobby, which serves creative breakfast dishes throughout the day (page 166). Their other restaurant is Seppi's (page 167).

PENINSULA NEW YORK **$$$$$**

✉ 700 5th Avenue at 55th Street

☎ 212-956 2888
Fax 212-903 3943
www.peninsula.com

🚗 Subway F to 53rd Street; 6 to 51st Street

A beautiful hotel which has undergone a massive $45-million renovation in the public areas, restaurants as well as all of the 241 guestrooms.

ROYALTON **$$$$-$$$$$**

✉ 44 West 44th Street between 5th and 6th Avenues

☎ 212-869 4400
Fax 212-869 8965
www.ianschragerhotels.com

🚗 Subway B, D, F, Q to 42nd Street

An 'in' place with the magazine and showbiz crowd, this hotel was designed by Philippe Starck. Each room has a futon, slate fireplace and round bathtub.

MIDTOWN EAST

BOX TREE **$$$-$$$$**

✉ 250 East 49th Street between 2nd and 3rd Avenues

☎ 212-758 8320
Fax 212-308 3899

🚗 Subway 6 to 51st Street

Despite the skyscrapers, New York still has a few traditional townhouses now turned into 'boutique' – i.e. small – hotels. The romantic Box Tree is one of the best.

ELYSEE **$$$$-$$$$$**

✉ 60 East 54th Street between Park and Madison Avenues

☎ 212-753 1066,
Fax 212-980 9278
www.elyseehotel.com

🚗 Subway 6 to 51st Street

Another boutique offering, dating from the 1930s. Its decor includes antique furnishings and Italian marble bathrooms. Guests have use of a nearby sports club.

Confusingly, American hotel lifts use the letter 'L' or the number '1' to indicate the ground floor. The L stands for lobby, by the way.

KITANO HOTEL $$$$–$$$$$

66 Park Avenue at East 38th Street
212-885 7000
Fax 212-885 7100
Subway S, 4, 5, 6, 7 to Grand Central/ 42nd Street

A first-class, Japanese-run hotel with top-notch service and a deliciously decadent, deep-soaking tub in each room.

MIDTOWN WEST

NEW YORK HILTON AND TOWERS $$$$$

1335 6th Avenue at 53rd Street
212-586 7000
Fax 212-315 1374
Subway B, D, F, Q to 47th–50th Streets/ Rockefeller Center

After a recent $100-million renovation, the city's largest hotel now has a beautiful new façade and entrance lobby, plus two new restaurants and lounges.

UPPER WEST SIDE

INN NEW YORK CITY $$$$–$$$$$

266 West 71st Street between Broadway and West End Avenue
212-580 1900
Fax 212-580 4437
Subway 1, 2, 3, 9 to 72nd Street

Taking the boutique notion to its limits, this well-positioned hotel has just four suites, each with a kitchen.

The Plaza

MEDIUM-PRICED GEMS

FINANCIAL DISTRICT

MILLENNIUM HILTON $$–$$$$$

5 Church Street between Fulton and Dey Streets
212-693 2001
Fax 212-571 2316
Subway 1, 9, N, R to Cortlandt Street

A black skyscraper geared to business, with fitness centre and a pool. For a stunning view of the harbour, ask for a high floor.

WALL STREET INN $$$

9 South William Street opposite 85 Broad Street
212-747 1500
Subway 2, 3 to Wall Street; J, M, Z to Broad Street

A boutique hotel in an old office building in the heart of the historic district. Original features include mahogany panels on the walls and granite floors.

MIDTOWN

CASABLANCA $$$–$$$$

147 West 43rd Street off Times Square
212-869 1212,
Fax 212-391 7585
www.casablancahotel.com
Subway 1, 2, 3, 7, 9, N, R, S to Times Square/42nd Street

Elegant Moroccan theme includes ceiling fans, palm trees and mosaic tiles. Service is good too.

CITY CLUB HOTEL $$$–$$$$

55 West 44th Street between 5th and 6th Avenues
212-921 5500
Fax 212-944 5544
Subway 7 to 5th Avenue; B, D, F, V to 42nd Street

The owner-manager Jeffrey Klein is one of the most socially visible hoteliers in the city and some of his very famous friends cocoon themselves in his hotel. Based in an old gentlemen's club building, it is one of the smartest but least showy boutique hotels in New York. There's no queuing in the lobby as check-in happens in your room, which has a big TV hidden in the wall, a day bed and possibly even the latest Jackie Kennedy Onassis biography. These rooms are designed to spend time in!

MANSFIELD $$$-$$$$$

✉ 12 West 44th Street between 5th and 6th Avenues
☎ 212-944 6050
Fax 212-764 4477
🚗 Subway B, D, F, Q to 47th–50th Street/ Rockefeller Center

A beautiful lobby with vaulted ceiling and white marble marks the Mansfield out as an elegant hotel for those also wanting the charm of a boutique hotel.

SHOREHAM $$$-$$$$$

✉ 33 West 55th Street at 5th Avenue
☎ 212-247 6700
Fax 212-765 9741
🚗 Subway F to 5th Avenue

This hotel has recently undergone a renovation and now has a new bar, restaurant, fitness centre and more good-sized rooms.

WARWICK $$$-$$$$

✉ 65 West 54th Street at 6th Avenue
☎ 212-247 2700
Fax 212-713 1751
www.warwickhotels.com
🚗 Subway B, D, F, Q to 47th–50th Streets/ Rockefeller Center

A medium-sized hotel built in 1927 with good quality rooms and excellent service in an excellent location. In its heyday many a Hollywood celeb stayed there, including Cary Grant. Randolph's Bar is a favoured meeting place and a great spot for lunch or a light dinner.

MIDTOWN EAST

70 PARK AVENUE HOTEL $$$-$$$$

✉ 70 Park Avenue at 38th Street
☎ 212-973 2400,
Fax 212-973 2497
🚗 Subway 4, 5, 6 to 42nd Street

A beautiful, four-star hotel with a bar, restaurant and excellent room facilities.

DYLAN $$$-$$$$

✉ 52 East 41st Street between Madison and Park Avenues
☎ 212-338 0500
Fax 212-338 0569
www.dylanhotel.com
🚗 Subway S, 4, 5, 6, 7 to Grand Central/ 42nd Street

Located in the former Chemist's Club building, this boutique hotel was developed to preserve the 1903 Beaux Arts structure. A mezzanine lounge and bar overlooks the dramatic, high-ceilinged restaurant, RX. In-room amenities include a state-of-the-art digital entertainment system with large cable TV, DVD and CD players that can access a library of thousands of video and CD titles, two-line telephones with voicemail and data port, large safes and complimentary newspaper.

FITZPATRICK $$$-$$$$

✉ 687 Lexington Avenue between East 56th and East 57th Streets
☎ 212-355 0100
Fax 212-355 1371
🚗 Subway 4, 5, 6 to 59th Street

The rooms are equipped with everything from trouser presses to towelling robes, useful after indulging in the whirlpool bath in many of them.

FITZPATRICK GRAND CENTRAL $$$

✉ 141 East 44th Street between Lexington and 3rd Avenues
☎ 212-351 6800
Fax 212-355 1371
🚗 Subway S, 4, 5, 6, 7 to Grand Central/ 42nd Street

The Fitzpatrick Family Group of hotels continues its Irish theme at this hotel just across from Grand Central Station. It includes an Irish pub and you can order a traditional Irish breakfast here.

The Grand Bar at the SoHo Grand

ROOSEVELT $$-$$$$

✉ East 45th Street at Madison Avenue
☎ 212-661 9600
Fax 212-885 6161
www.therooseveIthotel.com
🚗 Subway S, 4, 5, 6, 7 to Grand Central/42nd Street

Built in 1924, this classy hotel completed a $70-million renovation in 1998 in which the lobby was restored to its original grandeur with crystal chandeliers, columns and lots of marble.

WEST NEW YORK $$$-$$$$$

✉ 541 Lexington Avenue between 49th and 50th Streets
☎ 212-755 1200
Fax 212-644 0951
🚗 Subway 6 to 51st Street; E, F to Lexington/3rd Avenue

In 1998, Starwood Lodging joined forces with designer David Rockwell, celebrity restaurateur Drew Nieporent and nightlife impresario Randy Gerber to transform the former Doral Inn into an urban oasis for travellers looking for comfortable, sophisticated accommodation.

MIDTOWN WEST

HUDSON $$-$$$$$

✉ 356 West 58th Street between 8th and 9th Avenues
☎ 212-554 6000
Fax 212-554 6001
www.hudsonhotel.com
🚗 Subway A, B, C, D, 1, 9 to 59th Street/Columbus Circle

Built on the site of the former *Sesame Street* studios, this Ian Schrager and Philippe Starck collaboration is heaving with chic guests. It's loud and proud, so don't check in if you are looking for peace and quiet in the city. From the neon entrance escalator to the glowing glass floor of the Hudson Bar, you'll be in the limelight. The rooms are stylish but very small. In a great location for Central Park, the Lincoln Center and Theater District, but definitely on the west side of town so keep this in mind when considering your sightseeing plans.

MODERNE $$$-$$$$

✉ 243 West 55th Street between Broadway and 8th Avenue
☎ 212-397 6767
Fax 212-397 8787
🚗 Subway C, E, 1, 9 to 50th Street

Opened in 1998, this bijou hotel was converted from a five-storey dance studio. It's in a good location close to Carnegie Hall.

THEATER DISTRICT

NEW YORK MARRIOTT MARQUIS $$-$$$$

✉ 1535 Broadway at 45th Street
☎ 212-398 1900
Fax 212-704 8926
🚗 Subway N, R, S, 1, 2, 3, 7, 9 to Times Square/42nd Street

In 1998, the hotel completed a $25-million upgrade of all its rooms so each one now includes console desks, ergonomic chairs, two phone lines and voicemail. A sushi bar, Katen, is in the atrium lobby.

PARAMOUNT $$-$$$$$

✉ 235 West 46th Street between Broadway and 8th Avenue
☎ 212-764 5500
Fax 212-575 4892
www.ianschragerhotels.com
🚗 Subway C, E, 1, 9 to 50th Street

A hip hotel with a glorious, sweeping staircase in the lobby. Rooms are small but well-equipped. The mezzanine restaurant is good for people-watching.

PREMIER $$$-$$$$

✉ 45 West 44th Street between 6th Avenue and Broadway
☎ 212-768 4400
Fax 212-768 0847
🚗 Subway N, R, S, 1, 2, 3, 7, 9 to Times Square/42nd Street

The Millennium Broadway in Times Square built this 22-storey tower in 1999 to increase its total room count to 752. The Premier has its own private entrance on 44th Street and elegant, modern guestrooms with large bathrooms, two phone lines, voicemail and a separate modem and fax machine.

TIME HOTEL $$$

✉ 224 West 49th Street between 8th Avenue and Broadway
☎ 212-320 2900
Fax 212-245 2305
🚗 Subway C, E, 1, 9 to 50th Street

This boutique hotel in the heart of Times Square features colour-saturated rooms in red, yellow or blue, designed by Adam Tihany, and a restaurant run by celebrity chef Jean-Louis Palladin.

THE PERFECT APPLE

A major hotel chain, Apple Core, runs five hotels in excellent Midtown locations with extremely reasonable rates of $89–199 a night. They are: **Red Roof Inn Manhattan** on 32nd Street, west of 5th Avenue; **Comfort Inn Midtown** on 46th Street west of 6th Avenue; **Quality Hotel and Suites Rockefeller Center** on 46th Street off 6th Avenue (page 214); **Best Western Manhattan** on 32nd Street west of 5th Avenue and **Quality Hotel East Side** at 30th Street and Lexington Avenue.

All the hotels offer complimentary continental breakfast, well-equipped fitness centres and business centres. In-room facilities include cable television and pay-per-view movies, telephones with data port and voicemail, coffee makers, irons and ironing boards. The modern bathrooms all come with marble units and hairdryers.

Occupancy rates are above 90 per cent – so book early through Apple Core's central reservations: tel 212-790 2710, fax 212-790 2760, **www.applecorehotels.com**.

WESTIN NEW YORK TIMES SQUARE $$$$

✉ 270 West 43rd Street at 8th Avenue
☎ 212-201 2700
info@westinny.com
🚗 Subway A, C, E, N, R, S, 1, 2, 3, 7, 9 to 42nd Street/Times Square

A fab hotel for all types. Particularly family-friendly – families will love the Kids Club, which gives children a sports bottle, toys, colouring books and even a bedtime story! Toddlers get a Molton Brown designer amenities box with baby wash, nappy hamper, potty seat and step stool.

UPPER EAST SIDE

FRANKLIN $$$

✉ 164 East 87th Street between 3rd and Lexington Avenues
☎ 212-369 1000
Fax 212-369 8000
🚗 Subway 4, 5, 6 to 86th Street

Known for its good service, this pleasant hotel has lovely touches in its rooms that include canopies over the beds, fresh flowers and cedar closets.

EXCELLENT VALUE

FINANCIAL DISTRICT

HOLIDAY INN WALL STREET $$–$$$$

✉ 15 Gold Street at Platt Street
☎ 212-232 7700
Fax 212-425 0330
🚗 Subway J, M, Z, 2, 3, 4, 5 to Fulton Street

Opened in 1999, billing itself as the most high-tech hotel in New York, complete with T-1 speed internet connectivity.

CHINATOWN/LOWER EAST SIDE

HOLIDAY INN DOWNTOWN $$

✉ 138 Lafayette Street at Canal Street
☎ 212-966 8898
Fax 212-966 3933
🚗 Subway N, R to Canal Street

Well-equipped, spotless rooms at excellent prices.

GREENWICH VILLAGE

WASHINGTON SQUARE HOTEL $$

✉ 103 Waverly Place between 5th and 6th Avenues
☎ 212-777 9515,
Fax 212-979 8373
www.wshotel.com
🚗 Subway A, B, C, D, E, F, Q to West 4th Street/Washington Square

A family-run hotel with a bohemian air that overlooks Washington Square. The rooms are small but the rates very reasonable and include breakfast. Bob Dylan was known to stay there in the 1960s.

CHELSEA

CHELSEA HOTEL $$

✉ 222 West 23rd Street between 7th and 8th Avenues
☎ 212-243 3700
www.chelseahotel.com
🚗 Subway A, C, E, 1, 2, 3, 9 to 23rd Street

A true icon of New York City, this hotel has been associated with artistic and literary types since it opened in 1912. Residents have included Dylan Thomas, Jack Kerouac, Mark Twain and Thomas Wolfe and it still pulls in the celebs – Dee Dee Ramone of the Ramones is one of a handful of live-in artistes in the heart of New York's boho community. On the black side, Sex Pistols singer Sid Vicious is alleged to have killed his girlfriend Nancy Spungen here. Besides that, Andy Warhol filmed *Chelsea Girls* here, the stairwell has starred in Bon Jovi and Mariah Carey videos, and room 822 was used to shoot Madonna's book *Sex*. Downstairs in the basement is Serena's, a Moroccan den lounge, which has been attracting a new round of celebs, such as Leonardo DiCaprio and Brazilian supermodel Giselle, and is popular with the Brit-pack crowd.

FLATIRON DISTRICT

CARLTON $$–$$$

✉ 22 East 29th Street between 5th and Madison Avenues
☎ 212-532 4100
Fax 212-889 8683
🚗 Subway 4, 5, 6 to 28th Street

A tourist-class hotel with a view of the Empire State Building and in an excellent location for 5th Avenue and Garment District shopping. Restaurant, lounge and business services.

GIRAFFE $$–$$$

✉ 365 Park Avenue South between 26th and 27th Streets
☎ 212-685 7700
www.hotelgiraffe.com
🚗 Subway 6 to 23rd Street

Small boutique hotel, each floor has seven rooms, many with their own balconies. There's also an on-premises restaurant and access to a nearby health club for guests.

The Wellington Hotel

MIDTOWN

ALGONQUIN $$–$$$

✉ 59 West 44th Street between 5th and 6th Avenues
☎ 212-840 6800
Fax 212-944 1618
🚗 Subway B, D, F, Q to 47th–50th Streets/ Rockefeller Center

Famous for the literary meetings held here by Dorothy Parker and her cohorts, the Algonquin has recently undergone a $45 million refurbishment.

METRO $$–$$$

✉ 45 West 35th Street between 5th and 6th Avenues
☎ 212-947 2500
Fax 212-279 1310
www.hotelmetrony.com
🚗 Subway B, D, F, N, Q, R to 34th Street

Well located near the Empire State Building, which can be seen from its roof-top garden terrace, this hotel is great value for money, offering plenty of Art Deco style.

QUALITY HOTEL AND SUITES ROCKEFELLER CENTER $$

✉ 59 West 46th Street between 5th and 6th Avenues
☎ 212-719 2300
Fax 212-790 2760
🚗 Subway B, D, F, Q to 47th–50th Streets/ Rockefeller Center

A well-priced hotel with excellent amenities that include a fitness centre, coffee makers and irons in the rooms, free local phone calls and a continental breakfast. (See The Perfect Apple on page 213.)

WELLINGTON $$

✉ 871 7th Avenue at 55th Street
☎ 212-247 3900
Fax 212-581 1719
www.wellingtonhotel.com
🚗 Subway N, R to 57th Street

The best thing about this tourist-class hotel is its location – deep in the heart of Midtown within striking distance of Carnegie Hall, 5th Avenue, the Rockefeller Center and Times Square. If you can get a corner room with a view of 7th Avenue, you'll understand the big deal about the bright lights associated with the Theater District – they're absolutely stunning viewed from this position. Four adults can even stay in certain rooms that cost just $210–240 for the night and come with either two bathrooms or one bathroom and a kitchenette, while families can be accommodated in rooms with pull-out sofas. A true bargain.

MIDTOWN EAST

CLARION HOTEL 5TH AVENUE $$-$$$

✉ 3 East 40th Street just off 5th Avenue
☎ 212-447 1500
Fax 212-213 0972
🚗 Subway 7 to 5th Avenue; S, 4, 5, 6, 7 to Grand Central/42nd Street

In an excellent location near Grand Central Station. Rooms have all the latest business equipment.

MIDTOWN WEST

AMERITANIA $$

✉ Broadway at 54th Street
☎ 212-247 5000
Fax 212-247 3316
🚗 Subway 1, 9 to 50th Street; B, D east to 7th Avenue

Located just outside the Theater District and near Restaurant Row. Well-appointed with reasonable rooms.

WYNDHAM $$-$$$

✉ 42 West 58th Street between 5th and 6th Avenues
☎ 212-753 3500
Fax 212-754 5638
🚗 Subway B, Q to 57th Street; F to 5th Avenue

Large, basic rooms with walk-in closets. Great location – you're staying just across from the Plaza, but at half the price!

THEATER DISTRICT

COURTYARD BY MARRIOTT TIMES SQUARE SOUTH $$-$$$

✉ 114 West 40th Street between 6th Avenue and Broadway
☎ 212-391 0088
Fax 212-391 6023
🚗 Subway B, D, F, Q to 42nd Street

This new hotel, which opened in 1998, is part of the massive redevelopment of Times Square. The spacious rooms all have a sitting area, large work desk, two phones and in-room coffee.

HOLIDAY INN MARTINIQUE ON BROADWAY $$-$$$$$

✉ 49 West 32nd Street at Broadway
☎ 212-736 3800
Fax 212-277 2681
🚗 Subway B, D, F, N, Q, R to 34th Street

Opened in 1998 on the site of the former Hotel Martinique, this hotel is decorated in a French Renaissance style.

UPPER EAST SIDE

BENTLEY $$-$$$

✉ 500 East 62nd Street at York Avenue
☎ 212-644 6000
Fax 212-207 4800
🚗 Subway 4, 5, 6, N, R to Lexington Avenue/59th Street

A recently renovated hotel which is within walking distance of Bloomingdale's Rates include breakfast.

UPPER WEST SIDE

EMPIRE HOTEL $$-$$$

✉ 44 West 63rd Street between Broadway and Columbus Avenues
☎ 212-265 7400
Fax 212-315 0349
www.empirehotel.com
🚗 Subway A, B, C, D, 1, 9 to Columbus Circle/59th Street

In an excellent location just next door to the Lincoln Center, this can be great value for money, but ensure you get the standard of room you've booked – sadly that's not always the case. When the London Symphony Orchestra wanted to stay, they were shown recently refurbished rooms but were then put in tiny, ugly ones.

The Carlton Hotel

ACCOMMODATION REFERENCE GUIDE

Hotel	Area	Style	Price range	See page
60 Thompson	SoHo	Outstanding	$$$-$$$$$	208
70 Park Avenue Hotel	Midtown East	Medium-priced gem	$$$-$$$$$	211
Algonquin	Midtown	Excellent value	$$-$$$	214
Ameritania	Midtown West	Excellent value	$$	215
Bentley	Upper East Side	Excellent value	$$-$$$	215
Box Tree	Midtown East	Outstanding	$$$-$$$$$	209
Bryant Park	Midtown	Outstanding	$$$$-$$$$$	208
Carlton	Flatiron District	Excellent value	$$-$$$	214
Casablanca	Midtown	Medium-priced gem	$$$-$$$$	210
Chambers	Midtown	Outstanding	$$$-$$$$$	209
Chelsea Hotel	Chelsea	Excellent value	$$	213
City Club Hotel	Midtown	Medium-priced gem	$$$-$$$$	210
Clarion Hotel 5th Avenue	Midtown East	Excellent value	$$-$$$	215
Courtyard by Marriott	Theater District	Excellent value	$$-$$$	215
Dylan	Midtown East	Medium-priced gem	$$$-$$$$$	211
Elysee	Midtown East	Outstanding	$$$$-$$$$$	209
Empire Hotel	Upper West Side	Excellent value	$$-$$$	215
Fitzpatrick	Midtown East	Medium-priced gem	$$$-$$$$$	211
Fitzpatrick Grand Central	Midtown East	Medium-priced gem	$$$	211
Four Seasons	Midtown East	Totally divine	$$$$-$$$$$	205
Franklin	Upper East Side	Medium-priced gem	$$$	213
Gershwin Hotel	Flatiron District	Total bargain	$-$$	218
Giraffe	Flatiron District	Excellent value	$$-$$$	214
Herald Square Hotel	Flatiron District	Total bargain	$	218
Holiday Inn Downtown	Chinatown/Lower East Side	Excellent value	$$	213
Holiday Inn Martinique	Theater District	Excellent value	$$-$$$$$	215
Holiday Inn Wall Street	Financial District	Excellent value	$$$-$$$$	213
Hotel 17	Gramercy Park	Total bargain	$-$$	218
Hotel Beacon	Upper West Side	Excellent value	$$	217
Hotel Carlyle	Upper East Side	Totally divine	$$$$-$$$$$	206
Hotel Plaza-Athene	Upper East Side	Totally divine	$$$$-$$$$$	207
Howard Johnson Express Inn	Lower East Side	Total bargain	$-$$	217
Hudson	Midtown West	Medium-priced gem	$$-$$$$$	212
Inn at Irving Place	Gramercy Park	Outstanding	$$$$-$$$$$	208
Inn New York City	Upper West Side	Outstanding	$$$$-$$$$$	210
Kitano Hotel	Midtown East	Outstanding	$$$$-$$$$$	210
Larchmont	Greenwich Village	Total bargain	$-$$	218
Le Parker Meridien	Midtown	Outstanding	$$$$-$$$$$	209
Mandarin Oriental	Upper West Side	Totally divine	$$$$-$$$$$	207
Mansfield	Midtown	Medium-priced gem	$$$-$$$$$	211
Mark	Upper East Side	Totally divine	$$$$-$$$$$	207
Mayflower Hotel on the Park	Upper West Side	Excellent value	$$	217
Mercer	SoHo	Outstanding	$$$$	208
Metro	Midtown	Excellent value	$$-$$$	214
Millennium Hilton	Financial District	Medium-priced gem	$$-$$$$$	210
Moderne	Midtown West	Medium-priced gem	$$$-$$$$	212
New York Hilton & Towers	Midtown West	Outstanding	$$$$$	210
New York Marriott Brooklyn	Brooklyn	Excellent value	$$-$$$	217
New York Marriott Marquis	Theater District	Medium-priced gem	$$-$$$$	212
New York Palace	Midtown East	Totally divine	$$$$-$$$$$	205
Off SoHo Suites	Lower East Side	Total bargain	$-$$	217
Paramount	Theater District	Medium-priced gem	$$-$$$$$	212
Peninsula New York	Midtown	Outstanding	$$$$$	209
Pickwick Arms Hotel	Midtown East	Total bargain	$	218

Hotel	Area	Style	Price range	See page
Plaza	Midtown	Totally divine	$$$$-$$$$$	205
Portland Square Hotel	Midtown West	Total bargain	$	218
Premier	Theater District	Medium-priced gem	$$$-$$$$	212
Quality Hotel & Suites Rockefeller Center	Midtown	Excellent value	$$	214
Ritz-Carlton	Battery Park City	Totally divine	$$$$$	204
Roosevelt Hotel	Midtown East	Medium-priced gem	$$-$$$$	212
Royalton	Midtown	Outstanding	$$$$-$$$$$	209
Sherry-Netherland	Midtown East	Totally divine	$$$$-$$$$$	205
Shoreham	Midtown	Medium-priced gem	$$$-$$$$$	211
SoHo Grand	SoHo	Outstanding	$$$$	208
Stanhope	Upper East Side	Totally divine	$$$$-$$$$$	207
Thirty Thirty New York City	Flatiron District	Total bargain	$-$$	218
Time Hotel	Theater District	Medium-priced gem	$$$	212
TriBeCa Grand	TriBeCa	Outstanding	$$$$-$$$$$	208
Waldorf Astoria	Midtown East	Totally divine	$$$-$$$$$	205
Waldorf Towers	Midtown East	Totally divine	$$$$$	206
Wall Street Inn	Financial District	Medium-priced gem	$$$	210
Warwick	Midtown	Medium-priced gem	$$$-$$$$$	211
Washington Square Hotel	Greenwich Village	Excellent value	$$	213
Wellington	Midtown	Excellent value	$$	214
West New York	Midtown East	Medium-priced gem	$$$-$$$$$	212
Westin New York Times Square	Theater District	Medium-priced gem	$$$$	213
Wyndham	Midtown West	Excellent value	$$-$$$	215

HOTEL BEACON $$

✉ 2130 Broadway at 75th Street
☎ 212-787 1100
Fax 212-724 0839
www.beaconhotel.com
🚗 Subway 1, 2, 3, 9 to 72nd Street

Good-sized rooms with kitchenettes, plus the 25-storey hotel is well located for the American Museum of Natural History, the Lincoln Center and Central Park.

MAYFLOWER HOTEL ON THE PARK $$

✉ 15 Central Park West between 61st and 62nd Streets
☎ 212-265 0060
Fax 212-265 0227
🚗 Subway A, B, C, D, 1, 9 to Columbus Circle/59th Street

You'll get great views of Central Park here without paying through the nose.

BROOKLYN

NEW YORK MARRIOTT BROOKLYN $$-$$$

✉ 333 Adams Street at Tillary Street
☎ 718-246 7000
Fax 718-246 0563
🚗 Subway A, C, F to Jay Street/Borough Hall; N, R to Court Street; 2, 3, 4, 5 to Borough Hall just five minutes' walk away

Opened in 1998, this is Brooklyn's first new hotel in 68 years. Over the water from Manhattan, but you get excellent facilities at very good prices.

TOTAL BARGAINS

LOWER EAST SIDE

HOWARD JOHNSON EXPRESS INN $-$$

✉ 135 Houston Street between Forsyth and Eldridge Streets
☎ 212-358 8844
www.hojo.com

The Lower East Side can now celebrate the arrival of its first hotel – the modern, without frills but incredibly well-priced Howard Johnson. Right next door is the now renovated landmark Sunshine Cinema, which was once a showplace for Yiddish vaudeville and films and is now a multiplex for art films.

OFF SOHO SUITES $-$$

✉ 11 Rivington Street between Chrystie Street and The Bowery
☎ 212-979 9815
Fax 212-979 9801
www.offsoho.com
🚗 Subway F to Delancey Street

Good-sized, clean suites with fully equipped kitchens. Well-positioned.

GREENWICH VILLAGE

LARCHMONT $-$$

✉ 27 West 11th Street between 5th and 6th Avenues
☎ 212-989 9333
Fax 212-989 9496
www.larchmonthotel.com
🚗 Subway F to 14th Street

This is a clean, well-sought-after Village boutique hotel. No private baths in any of the rooms, however.

GRAMERCY PARK

HOTEL 17 $-$$

✉ 225 East 17th Street between 2nd and 3rd Avenues
☎ 212-475 2845
Fax 212-677 8178
🚗 Subway L, N, R, 4, 5, 6 to Union Square/ 14th Street

A very basic hotel with shared bathrooms.

FLATIRON DISTRICT

GERSHWIN $-$$

✉ 7 East 27th Street between 5th and Madison Avenues
☎ 212-545 8000
Fax 212-684 5546
🚗 Subway 6 to 28th Street

A character-crammed budget boutique with some of the best rates in the city. You can opt for plain doubles or dormitory-style rooms with 10 beds.

HERALD SQUARE HOTEL $

✉ 19 West 31st Street between 5th Avenue and Broadway
☎ 212-279 4017
Fax 212-643 9208
🚗 Subway N, R to 28th Street

Once the headquarters of *Life* magazine, now a small, extremely well-priced hotel near the Empire State Building and Macy's.

THIRTYTHIRTY NEW YORK CITY $-$$

✉ 30 East 30th Street between Park and Madison Avenues
☎ 212-689 1900
Fax 212-689 0023
www.3030nyc.com
🚗 Subway 6 to 29th Street

Formerly the Martha Washington Hotel, this was turned into a modern, sophisticated hotel in 1999.

MIDTOWN EAST

PICKWICK ARMS HOTEL $

✉ 230 East 51st Street between 2nd and 3rd Avenues
☎ 212-355 0300
Fax 212-755 5029
🚗 Subway 6 to 51st Street

A cheap place to stay in a pricey neighbourhood. The rooms are tiny but the hotel does have a roof garden and cocktail lounge.

MIDTOWN WEST

PORTLAND SQUARE HOTEL $

✉ 132 West 47th Street between 6th and 7th Avenues
☎ 212-382 0600
Fax 212-382 0684
🚗 Subway B, D, F, Q to 47th–50th Streets/Rockefeller Center

A family-run hotel (they also run the Herald Square Hotel, see left). The rooms are small but the hotel is very near the Theater District so convenient if that features on your itinerary.

OTHER OPTIONS

Abode Ltd: PO Box 20022, New York, NY 10021. Tel 212-472 2000, fax 212-472 8274, **www.abodenyc.com.** **$-$$$**
Unhosted, good-quality studios and apartments all over the city, but you have to book for a minimum of four days.

Bed and Breakfast (and Books): 35 West 92nd Street, Apt. 2C, New York, NY 10025. Fax 212-865 8740. **$-$$**
Hosted and unhosted apartments – and you may end up the guest of a writer.

Bed and Breakfast in Manhattan: PO Box 533, New York, NY 10150. Tel 212-472 2528, fax 212-988 9818. **$-$$$**
From comfortable to smart and both hosted and unhosted.

Jazz on the Park: 36 West 106th Street at Central Park West. Tel 212-932 1600, **www.jazzhotel.com.** **$**
Clean, comfortable rooms for the budget traveller. Double and 'dormitory' rooms, laundry room, roof-top terrace and garden. Price includes breakfast.

CHAPTER 12

Parks, Gardens and Sports

Visiting New York needn't be all action – you can chill out, too! Obviously Central Park is the main port of call and a beautiful one at that, but there are many other parks dotted throughout the city. The parks are very busy and remarkably safe, but one should be prudent about going into the less populated areas and especially cautious about visiting them at night when you are unfamiliar with the neighbourhood.

CENTRAL PARK

This is the New Yorkers' playground and meeting place and attracts 15 million visitors every year. Its 341 hectares (843 acres) stretch from Central Park South at 59th Street to Central Park North at 110th Street, with 5th Avenue and Central Park West forming its eastern and western boundaries. It was created over a 20-year period by architect Calvert Vaux and landscaper Frederick Law Olmsted and was completed in the 1860s.

To enter from the south, cross the street from **Grand Army Plaza** at 5th Avenue and 59th Street. Immediately in front of you is the **Pond**, and then the **Wollman Memorial Rink** (62nd Street), which hosts a Victorian amusement park in the summer and ice-skating in the winter. Close by is the **Visitor Information Center**, where you can pick up free maps and schedules of events, including the series of free concerts and dramas performed at the **SummerStage** (pages 128 and 225). Here also are the **Gotham Miniature Golf Course** (a gift from Donald Trump), the dairy and the antique carousel (65th Street). To the east is the **Central Park Wildlife Center** (63rd–66th Streets) and the **Children's Zoo and Wildlife Center** (page 127).

The **Sheep Meadow** (66th–69th Streets) to the north of the carousel is much used by New Yorkers for picnics and sunbathing. To its left is the **Tavern on the Green** restaurant (page 175) and to the right is the **Mall** (69th–72nd Streets), a tree-lined

Central Park

walkway. Follow the Mall to the top and you will find the **Central Park Bandshell** (70th Street), one of the park's concert venues. Further north is the **Loeb Boathouse** (74th and 75th Streets), which is home to the **Park View at the Boathouse** restaurant (page 174 and where you can hire bikes and boats (page 222).

Continuing north, you will find the **Ramble** (71st Street), a heavily wooded area which leads (if you can find the way through) to the Gothic revival **Belvedere Castle** (74th Street) housing another information centre. Also here are the **Delacorte Theater**, where summer productions are presented by the New York **Shakespeare Festival** (tel 212-861 7277 for tickets) and the **Great Lawn** (79th–86th Streets) where the **Philharmonic and Metropolitan Opera concerts** are held – the only time you can witness tens of thousands of New Yorkers all being quiet at the same time (page 225).

Further north again is the huge **Jacqueline Kennedy Onassis Reservoir** (86th–96th Streets). A well kept secret is the formal 2.4 hectare (6-acre), three-part **Conservatory Garden** (104th–106th

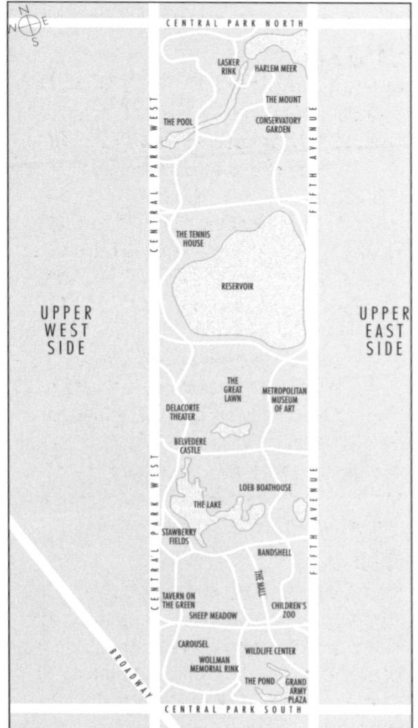

Central Park

The Philharmonic/Met Concerts are thrilling, surprisingly tranquil summer experiences. Join tens of thousands of New Yorkers in putting down your blanket on the Great Lawn and setting up your picnic two or three hours ahead of concert time. The first concert of the season ends with fireworks.

Streets), where dozens of wedding parties come for photographs on a summer weekend. It was bequeathed by the Vanderbilt family, and there are free tours and concerts in the summer.

Further details about great activities for children and the young at heart can be found in Chapter 7, Children's New York, starting on page 127).

THE MAIN PARKS

Battery Park: At the southern tip of Manhattan is a beautiful space with fabulous views of the Statue of Liberty and New York Harbor. In the nearby Hudson River Park, the Battery Park City Authority presents a Sounds at Sunset summer series of poetry readings, cabaret and classical music. Tel 212-416 5394 (page 32).

Brooklyn Botanic Garden: Across in the outer borough of Brooklyn, Cherry trees bloom mid-March to late May.

Bryant Park: Now cleared of ne'er-do-wells, this small park has a fancy restaurant and is a great spot for a picnic lunch. It even puts on free films and concerts (page 128) and offers a Beaux Arts-style carousel at $1.50 a ride.

Carl Schurz Park: In the family-friendly Upper East Side, this park sits right next to Gracie Mansion, the official residence of the mayor of New York, and has an esplanade along the river.

City Hall Park: Newly renovated space near the fabulous Woolworth Building and civic buildings (page 33).

Luna Park, Union Square: With an open-air restaurant, near a greenmarket – a farmers' market selling local produce and cheeses, locally raised meat and baked goods, plants etc – where regional purveyors sell their products at stalls in the middle of what is now one of the hippest new areas of New York. The Union Square market is one of the largest and operates year round on Monday, Wednesday, Friday and Saturday (page 45).

New York Botanical Garden: A must-see, these very extensive, wonderful gardens are in the Bronx (page 233), reachable by train from Grand Central Station.

Prospect Park: An incredible park laid out by the same designers as Central Park. It has a wealth of open spaces, activities, events and museums. Details are given in Chapter 7, Children's New York, on page 127 and Chapter 14, A Taste of the Outer Boroughs, on page 229.

Riverside Park: A narrow park running along the riverside from the West 70s to 158th Street, designed by Central Park's Frederick Olmstead, it has a marina at 79th Street where you can have a light meal and overlook the pleasure craft and houseboats.

Washington Square Park: Not so much a park as an area covered in tarmac and filled with a hotchpotch of individuals, many from New York University, it's still a great place to snack, though, while you watch the action (page 41).

SPECTATOR SPORTS

Ask any New Yorker and they'll tell you that they read their newspapers from back to front – that's just how important sports are to them. And they have plenty to choose between: two football teams and two baseball teams to support, plus basketball, hockey, tennis and racing. But it can be really tough to get in to watch some of the games, especially to see football's New York Giants and the Mets baseball team in action. Still, it's worth making the effort just to see another side of New York life. If you can't get tickets directly through the box offices listed below, then try TicketMaster on 212-307 7171 – they've got most games covered. An incredibly expensive alternative is to try one of the companies that specialises in selling tickets at exorbitant prices – anything from $100 for a football game to $1,000 for a baseball game. They include Prestige Entertainment on 1-800-2-GET-TIX and Ticket Window on 1-800-SOLD-OUT. A third alternative is to try a ticket tout – they're known as 'scalpers' in New York – outside Madison Square Garden. However, probably your best bet is to ask the concierge at your hotel – they have an amazing ability to come up with the goods.

MADISON SQUARE GARDEN

This venue on 7th Avenue at 32nd Street (subway A, C, E, 1, 2, 3, 9 to 34th Street/ Penn Street) is home to all the following teams, and all tickets must be ordered from TicketMaster on 212-307 7171.

NBA's New York Knicks basketball team: Season is from November to June.

NHL's New York Rangers ice-hockey team: Season is from October to April.

WNBA New York Liberty women's pro basketball team: From May to August.

Women's Tennis Association Tour Championships: November.

FOOTBALL

The two teams are the **New York Giants** and the **New York Jets**, who both play at the Giants Stadium at Meadowlands, New Jersey (get there on a bus from the Port Authority bus terminal at 42nd Street and 8th Avenue). The box office is 201-935 3900 and you'll have just as hard a time getting tickets for the Jets as for the Giants. The season runs from September to January.

BASEBALL

Try the Yankee Stadium (page 232) in the Bronx at 161st Street (subway C, D or 4 to 161st Street/Yankee Stadium) to see the **New York Yankees** at play. The box office is 718-293 6000.

The **New York Mets** play at Shea Stadium (page 235) in Flushing Meadows, Queens (subway 7 to Willetts Point/Shea Stadium). The box office is 718-507 8499. The season for both teams is from April to September. In October and November post-season games are played in which the best teams play each other for a gargantuan amount of money. It costs a fortune to get into one of these games, which is why the stands are usually filled with season ticket holders and celebs.

TENNIS

The US Open is held every year at the US Tennis Center in Flushing Meadows, Queens (subway 7 to Willetts Point/Shea Stadium), from late August to early September. Tele-Charge on 212-239 6250. Tickets for the finals are impossible to get, so go for the earlier rounds (page 235).

A really great way to find out more about Central Park's history and modern-day uses is by taking the Big Onion walking tour. See page 78 for details.

HORSE RACING

One of the four local tracks is Aqueduct Stadium in Queens (subway A to Aqueduct Racetrack) from mid-October to May every Wednesday to Saturday. Tel 718-641 4700. The Belmont Stakes, on a Saturday in early June, is the major event at the Belmont Racetrack (take the Long Island Rail Road's 'Belmont Special' from Penn Station at 7th Avenue and 34th Street) from May to July. Tel 516-488 6000.

GET STUCK IN

If you want to take part in some kind of sporting activity while in New York, your best bet is to go to Central Park. Probably the most popular sports here are boating, biking, skating and running.

BIKING

You can rent bikes from the Loeb Boathouse, Central Park, near 5th Avenue and East 74th Street (tel 212-517 2233) for $6–20 per hour including helmet plus credit card deposit; 10am–5.30pm. Try tackling the 11-km (7-mile) road loop that is closed to traffic at weekends. For other bike rental information, see Chapter 4, Seeing the Sights, Bike Tours (page 72).

BOATING

Also from the Loeb Boathouse (tel 212-517 2233), you can rent a rowing boat or even a chauffeured gondola for $10 per half hour with $30 deposit.

ICE-SKATING

The Wollman Memorial Rink, near East 64th Street (tel 212-4390-600, **www.wollmanskatingrink.com**) is open from November to March and rents skates for $4.75. It's $8.50 for adults ($11 at weekends), $4.25 and $4.50 for children, $4.25 and $7.50 seniors. The Lasker Rink at the northern end is a bit rougher but less crowded at $4.50 for adults and $2.25 seniors and students. Call 917-492 3856 for information on lessons.

RUNNING

Joggers go running in Central Park – generally around the reservoir – or Riverside Park on the west side of Manhattan. The Road Runners Club (tel 212-860 4455, **www.nyrrc.org**) can answer any questions you may have about running in New York.

The Yankee Stadium

CHAPTER 13

Festivals and Parades

All sorts of special events are going on in New York throughout the year, so once you have decided when to go, you'll want to know what's on while you're there so you don't miss out on any of the fun. Happily, New Yorkers like nothing better than a celebration – whether it be for the changing of the seasons, their roots or the arts. They clog up the streets for hours on end but they provide truly spectacular entertainment for the crowds every year. And what's more, apart from the cost of the food and drink you choose to imbibe, most of them are free!

EVENTS

JANUARY AND FEBRUARY

Winter Antiques Show: 7th Regiment Armory, Park Avenue at 67th Street. Tel 718-292 7392. Mid-January. If you're on a cheapie winter break to New York you'll be rewarded with one of the biggest and best antiques fairs in the world. Here you'll find everything from the very old to art nouveau plus vast collections from all over America. Admission charged.

Chinese New Year Parade: Chinatown at Mott Street. Tel 212-966 0100. Held on the first day of the full moon between January 21 and February 19. Although private fireworks have been banned, there are still plenty of firecrackers and dragons to dazzle onlookers in this stylish Chinese festival. Go to watch, eat, drink and be merry.

Black History Month: See the newspapers and guides for cultural events, concerts and lectures scheduled around the city during the month of February.

Grammy Awards: The Oscars of the world of TV now take place in Madison Square Garden. You won't get in but if you'd like a gawk at the stars as they arrive in their

Macy's Thanksgiving Day parade

AMERICAN HOLIDAYS

New Year's Day: January 1
Martin Luther King Jnr Day: Third Monday in January
President's Day: Third Monday in February
Memorial Day: Last Monday in May
Independence Day: July 4
Labor Day: First Monday in September
Columbus Day: Second Monday in October
Election Day: First Tuesday after the first Monday in November
Veterans' Day: November 11
Thanksgiving: Fourth Thursday in November
Christmas Day: December 25

limos, join the crowd. Late February. Call MSG on 212-465 6741 for information.

MARCH AND APRIL

Whitney Biennial: Whitney Museum of American Art (page 124), 945 Madison Avenue at 75th Street. Tel 212-570 3600. The Whitney's line-up of what it considers to be the most important art around is as controversial as our British equivalent of a sheep suspended in a glass cabinet. The next show is due to be held in late March to June of 2006. $12 adults, $9.50 students and seniors (under 12s free). However on Fridays 6–9 pm, it's pay what you wish – and the queues are LONG!

St Patrick's Day Parade: 5th Avenue between 44th and 86th Streets. Tel 212-484 1222. One of the bigger parades the city has to offer, taking place on March 17. If you're in town, you won't be able to miss the sea of green that goes with this annual Irish American day. Starting time is 11am for the parade up 5th Avenue and the festivities go on late into the night.

Greek Independence Day Parade: Along 5th Avenue to 49th Street usually on a Sunday around the end of March (it is sometimes in April and has even been held in May). Tel 718-204 6500. This one's a Zorba-style parade with plenty of Greek food, music and dancing.

Cirque du Soleil: Every other year in spring (more or less), this wonderful Canadian animal-free circus hitches up its tent in Battery Park to the delight of all. Call 800-678 5440 for more information. Admission charged.

Easter Parade: 5th Avenue between 44th and 59th Streets on Easter Sunday. Not an official parade, just a chance to watch strollers flaunting Easter bonnets from gorgeous to outrageous. The steps of St Patrick's Cathedral are an advantageous viewing spot. Kick-off is at 11am, so arrive early to bag a space.

New York City Ballet Spring Season: New York State Theater, 20 Lincoln Center Plaza, 65th Street at Columbus Avenue. Tel 212-870 5570 or TicketMaster 212-307 4100. Student rush tickets (available on day of performance) $10. Tel 212-870-7766. Late April to June. I have to admit I'm a ballet nut, and when away from London, I can think of nowhere better than the New York City Ballet to see some of the world's top dancers, who have made a name for themselves as masters of classics by Balanchine and Robbins.

The **American Ballet Theater** season at the Metropolitan Opera is May to July. Tel 212-362 6000.

A central number for New York events is 212-484 1222; and a website that reports many free events is www.newyorkled.com.

MAY AND JUNE

See also Cirque du Soleil, New York City Ballet and Whitney Biennial (above).

TriBeCa Film Festival: TriBeCa area, second week in May. Tel 212-866 FEST, **www.tribecafilm.com**. Founded by Robert De Niro and Jane Rosenthal, this film festival showcases independent movies, runs workshops and has a children's film programme. During the week, local restaurants offer cut-price meals.

9th Avenue International Food Festival: 9th Avenue between 37th and 57th Streets, mid-May. Tel 212-581 7217. Hungry? Then get on down to 9th Avenue where hundreds of stalls line the streets selling every type of food imaginable. Go for lunch and then walk it all off by strolling on down to Chelsea's fabulous art galleries nearby (pages 44–5).

Fleet Week: *Intrepid* Sea-Air-Space Museum (page 113), Pier 86, 46th Street at the Hudson River. Tel 212-245 0072. Unless you're a boat nut, it's normally not worth visiting the huge armada of US Navy and other ships that visit New York, but if you're here in the last week of May, they'll be hard to miss.

Washington Square Outdoor Art Exhibition: Tel 212-982 6255. An old and revered Greenwich Village event which happens on the last two weekends in late May (or early June) and the first two weekends in September. A huge, outdoor art show with easels and food trolleys set up in the streets all around the park.

Lower East Side Festival of Arts: Theater for the New City, 155 1st Avenue at 10th Street. Tel 212-254 1109. Last weekend in May. Deep in the heart of the neighbourhood that helped create the East Coast Beat movement, method acting and pop art, this is an annual arts festival and outdoor carnival.

Puerto Rican Day Parade: 5th Avenue between 44th and 86th Streets. Tel 718-401 0404. First or second Sunday in June from 11am. You'll get a real flavour of a big New York parade thanks to the floats, colour and noise of this display and the throngs lining the route.

Broadway Under The Stars: Bryant Park, 6th Avenue at 42nd Street. Tel 212-768 4242. Broadway moves outdoors to showcase its talents with a performance of major show songs. Usually the third Monday in June, heralding the start of many Bryant Park events.

Mermaid Parade: 8th Street between Steeplechase Park and Broadway, Coney Island, Brooklyn. Tel 718-372 5159. Catch the B, D or F trains to Stillwell Avenue on the Saturday following the first official day of summer (late June) to sample a wild and boisterous scene with floats and costumes.

New York Jazz Festival: Various clubs in mid to late June. Tel 212-501 1390. Even those of us who are not true aficionados of jazz can enjoy the festival atmosphere of the 300 acts that take part in this event.

Gay and Lesbian Pride Parade: From Columbus Circle along 5th Avenue to Christopher Street in Greenwich Village. Last Sunday in June. Call 212-807 7433 for information about a week of events commemorating the Stonewall Riots of 1969, when New York's gay community fought for public acceptance. The parade starts things off, and there is a packed club schedule and an open-air dance party on the West Side piers.

Thursday Night Concert Series: Main Stage, South Street Seaport, South Street at Fulton Street. Tel 212-732 7678. From the last Monday in May (Memorial Day) to the first Monday in September (Labor Day). Enjoy all types of music – free!

Museum Mile Festival: 5th Avenue between 82nd and 104th Streets. Tel 212-606 2296. Museum Mile is neither a museum nor a mile, but a series of museums stretching out along 5th Avenue and Central Park on the Upper East Side. All are worth a visit. During the Festival (either the first or second Tuesday in June), you can get into nine museums, including the fabulous Metropolitan, for free. An added perk is the fascinating street entertainment.

New York Restaurant Week: Tel 212-484 1200. More than 150 of the city's finest restaurants offer three-course fixed-price lunches and dinners at prices that reflect the year – in 2005 the cost of lunch is $20.05 (dinner $30.05) and in 2006 it will be $20.06. It lasts for one or two weeks, usually in late June.

Central Park SummerStage: Rumsey Playfield, Central Park at 72nd Street, June to August. Tel 212-360 2777, **www.summerstage.org**. You can experience many kinds of entertainment for free in New York and some of the best are the free weekend afternoon concerts put on by the SummerStage, featuring top international performers. On weeknights there are also dance and spoken-word events in the park.

New York Philharmonic/Metropolitan Opera Parks Concerts: Various sites in summer. Tel 212-875 5795 (Philharmonic), 212-362 6000 (Met) for information. These free, open-air events in parks are wildly popular so arrive early to stake out a site.

New York Shakespeare Festival: Delacorte Theater, Central Park at 81st Street. Tel 212-539 8750 or 212-861 7277. Late June to late August. See how top American actors do the Bard for free. There are two plays each year – one Shakespeare and one American with performances almost nightly.

Greenwich Village Halloween parade

Although free, you still have to get tickets, which are available from lpm on the day of the event – the queues are long.

Bryant Park Free Summer Season: 6th Avenue at 42nd Street. Tel 212-768 4242. Bryant Park is one of the few green spaces available in the Midtown area, and between June and August there is a series of free classical music, jazz, dance and film showings during the day and evening. The film hotline is 212-512 5700.

Check out the many street fairs from spring to autumn throughout the city with food, craft and other stalls. Visit www.nycstreetfairs.com and www.nyctourist.com.

Midsummer Night Swing: Lincoln Center for Performing Arts. Tel 212-875 5766. Considered the city's hottest outdoor dance party. Lots of dance instructors are on hand to give lessons in every type of dance from salsa to swing or you can just pop by to listen to the live music. From the end of June to the end of July.

Celebrate Brooklyn! Performing Arts Festival: Prospect Park Bandshell, 9th Street at Prospect Park West, Park Slope, Brooklyn. Tel 718-855 7882. Here's a very good reason to break out of Manhattan and visit one of the outer boroughs – a series of free music, dance, theatre and film events that lasts a full nine weeks.

JULY AND AUGUST

See also Thursday Night Concert Series, Central Park SummerStage, New York

A Central Park concert

St Patrick's Day parade

Philharmonic/Met Opera Concerts, New York Shakespeare Festival, Bryant Park Free Summer Season and Celebrate Brooklyn! Performing Arts Festival (all above).

Summergarden: Museum of Modern Art, 11 West 53rd Street between 5th and 6th Avenues. Tel 212-708 9400. An added bonus to visiting the little gem that is MoMA (reopened in autumn 2004 after major renovation, see page 111) is the series of free classical concerts that are presented in the museum's garden during July and August each year.

Lincoln Center Festival: For the whole of July and August, a veritable feast of dance, drama, ballet, children's shows and multimedia and performance art, involving both repertory companies and special guests at venues inside and outside at the Lincoln Center (page 183). For information, call 212-875 5766.

Fourth of July: The Americans still insist on celebrating achieving independence from their colonial masters, but at least they do it in style! Throughout New York there are various celebrations going on, but by far the biggest and most spectacular is Macy's Fireworks Display, which is held on the East River between 14th and 51st Streets. A good spot to see the $1-million, 30-minute firework extravaganza is from the FDR Drive (Franklin D Roosevelt Drive).

Harlem Week: Along 5th Avenue from West 125th to West 135th Streets. Tel 212-862 8477. Early to mid-August. The largest black and Hispanic festival in the world, its highlight is the street party with R&B, gospel and all that jazz. In addition to the music, there are films, dance, fashion, sports and exhibitions. What a great way to experience Harlem.

SEPTEMBER AND OCTOBER

See also Thursday Night Concert Series (above).

West Indian Day Carnival: Eastern Parkway from Utica Avenue to Grand Army Plaza, Brooklyn. Tel 718-625 1515. First weekend in September. Fabulous festival celebrating Caribbean culture. Brightly costumed marchers put on a special children's parade on Saturday, with an even bigger event on Labor Day (first Monday in September).

Feast of San Gennaro: Mulberry Street to Worth Street in Little Italy. Tel 212-768 9320. Eleven days in mid-September. Really the best time to see what is left of the once-bustling Little Italy that is now

Parades are great fun, but they also provide perfect opportunities for pickpockets, so keep your bags and wallets close to you at all times – and never put your wallet in your back pocket.

reduced to just Mulberry Street. There are lots of fairground booths, plenty of food and even more *vino.*

Columbus Day Parade: 5th Avenue between 44th and 86th Streets. Second Monday in October. The traditional celebration of the first recorded sighting of America by Europeans is now somewhat controversial in some quarters but, despite its lack of political correctness, Columbus Day still gets the big 5th Avenue parade treatment, which is well worth a view.

Broadway on Broadway: Times Square, mid-September. Free annual concert on a temporary stage featuring stars and production numbers from the season's top shows. Visit their website at **www.broadwayonbroadway.com**.

Halloween Parade: 6th Avenue between Union Square and Spring Street, Greenwich Village. Tel 212-475 3333 or visit **www.halloween-nyc.com**. October 31, 7pm. A uniquely Village event, with the outlandishly over-the-top costumes (or lack of them!) on (or off!) many of its participants. The organisers decree a different theme each year and a lot of work goes into the amazing outfits that range from the exotic to the nearly non-existent. It attracts between 60,000 and 100,000 ghouls, ghosts and onlookers.

New York City Marathon: Starts at the Staten Island side of the Verrazano Narrows Bridge as a mad pack of 35,000 men and women run 42km (26.2 miles) around all five boroughs, to finish at the Tavern on the Green in Central Park at West 67th Street. Last Sunday in October/first Sunday in November. If you want to enter the marathon you need to fill out an application form, pay a small fee, and then wait to see if you get picked. You can do this through **www.ingnycmarathon.org** or write to New York City Marathon, International Lottery, 9 East 89th Street, New York, NY 10128. Tel 212-860 4455.

NOVEMBER AND DECEMBER

See also New York City Marathon (above).

Macy's Thanksgiving Day Parade: From Central Park West at 79th Street to Macy's (page 86) on Broadway at 34th Street. Tel 212-494 5432. Thanksgiving Day at 9am. Definitely one for the family, this is the Big Mama of all New York's parades, with enormous inflated cartoon characters, fabulous floats and the gift-giving Santa Claus himself. New Yorkers in the know like to come by and watch it being set up the night before between 77th and 81st Streets off Central Park West. The parade is even televised for the rest of America. If you miss it, you can go to see Santa in Santaland in Macy's until Christmas.

Christmas Tree Lighting Ceremony: 5th Avenue between 49th and 50th Streets. Tel 212-484 3975. Early December. The Rockefeller Center (page 65) in front of the towering RCA building provides the magical setting for the switching on of nearly 8km (5 miles) of lights on the huge tree.

New Year's Eve Fireworks: 5th Avenue and 90th Street or Bethsheda Fountain (Central Park at 72nd Street) are the best viewing spots. The hot apple cider and spirit of camaraderie begin at 11.30pm.

New Year's Eve Ball Drop: Times Square (pages 49–51). This event is a real New York classic, though you may prefer to watch safely on TV rather than be packed in with the freezing masses. Remember, Times Square is a misnomer – it's a junction, so there isn't really that much room and all the side streets get packed too. If you do manage to get a good spot, though, you'll see the giant glitterball of 180 bulbs and 12,000 rhinestones being dropped to bring in the New Year.

CHAPTER 14

A Taste of the Outer Boroughs

For those with limited time in New York, you may not be able to get as far as the outer boroughs of the Bronx, Queens, Brooklyn and Staten Island. But they have a lot to offer in terms of museums, parks, restaurants, zoos, tours and atmosphere. If you do get a chance, this chapter will give you a few ideas.

A TASTE OF BROOKLYN

Brooklyn was once a city in its own right, until it became part of New York City in 1898. Some still refer to the event as its annexation and the borough certainly has its own unique style and language. Famous Brooklynites include Woody Allen, Barbra Streisand and Mel Brooks and there is still such a thing as Brooklynese, which is most obvious in the pronunciation of words such as absoid (absurd), doity (dirty), noive (nerve) and toin (turn).

Nowadays, many of the different parts of Brooklyn have their own unique cultures, but by far the two most important 'sightseeing' areas are Brooklyn Heights and Prospect Park (Maps 9 and 10).

BROOKLYN HEIGHTS

Whether you've had lunch or dinner, a walk across the stunning Brooklyn Bridge will certainly help the digestion. It's the most famous bridge in New York and was the world's largest suspension bridge when it was completed in 1883. The views are fantastic and strolling along the wooden walkway gives an insight into why it took 16 years to build. If you've walked to Brooklyn from Manhattan via the bridge, you'll find yourself in the heart of Brooklyn Heights. Down by the water's edge is the River Café (page 178), a refined and elegant setting to soak up fantastic views of the Manhattan skyline. Night-time is best – the twinkling lights in the skyscrapers look just like a picture postcard. Have a drink at the bar to enjoy the best views before tucking into a sumptuous supper. It is expensive and you will have to book in advance, but it's an experience you'll never forget. Jackets are essential after 5pm.

The Heights themselves are home to some of the most beautiful and sought-after brownstone townhouses in New York. These were built in the early 18th century when bankers and financiers chose to escape Manhattan, yet still be close enough to keep an eye on their money. Once again, Brooklyn Heights is much in demand as an area of tranquillity close to the madness and mayhem of Manhattan. If you walk along the Esplanade, you will see below you the former docks that were the setting for Marlon Brando's movie *On The Waterfront.*

NEW YORK CITY TRANSIT MUSEUM

✉ Schermerhorn Street at Boerum Place
☎ 718-243 3060
🚗 Subway M, N, R to Court Street; G to Hoyt/Schermerhorn Streets
🕘 Tues, Thurs, Fri 10am–4pm, Wed 10am–6pm, Sat and Sun noon–5pm
$ $4 adults, $2 children (under 12)

This is a great museum for children and transportation buffs of all ages and is located in an old subway station in Brooklyn Heights. There is a display of old subway cars that you can get on and you can even hang on to one of the original leather straps that created the nickname of 'straphangers' for people who use the subway. The straps have now been replaced by metal poles and bars. The museum has just undergone a major renovation and now has a new art gallery, a classroom for a children's workshop, a computer lab and a reference library. The main exhibit depicts the history of buses and trolleys in the city with interactive elements and a display of more than 200 trolley models. There is also a film about the building of the subway, old turnstiles, maps and a gift shop.

BROOKLYN MUSEUM OF ART

✉ 200 Eastern Parkway at Washington Avenue
☎ 718-638 5000
www.brooklynmuseum.org
🚗 Subway 1, 2 to Eastern Parkway/ Brooklyn Museum
🕘 Sun 11am–6pm, Wed to Fri 10am–5pm. First Sat of month 11am–11pm, all other Sats 11am–6pm
$ Suggested donation $6 adults, $3 students, seniors and children over 12, members and under 12s free

The spring of 2004 saw the opening of a manificent new glass entrance pavilion, complementing the beautiful 19th-century Beaux Arts building that has housed the museum since 1897. A new central lobby and public plaza have also been constructed making the building the most visitor-friendly museum in NYC. With one of the best collections of Egyptian art in the world and well known for its collection of African art, it was the first-ever museum to display what were once considered to be anthropological objects as fine art. It has a long tradition of collecting non-Western art and, since 1934, it has concentrated on fine art. The collections are divided into six different departments that comprise Egyptian, Classical and Ancient Middle Eastern Art; Painting and Sculpture; Arts of Africa, the Pacific and the Americas; Asian Art; Decorative Arts; and Prints, Drawings and Photography.

The Brooklyn Museum of Art is known for its ground-breaking exhibitions and has a cinema theatre in which it screens movies and documentaries that coincide with the exhibitions. It also has an Education Division that organises gallery talks, films, concerts, tours and performances for children and adults. On the first Saturday of each month is an event known as First Saturday, offering a free programme of events including a look at art, a film, activities for all the family and a live band to dance to.

A delicious cup of cappuccino or latte costs exactly the same as a cup of filter coffee at the Brooklyn Museum of Art, though the sarnies and rolls cost around $8.

It's useful to know that the museum, which has its own subway stop at Eastern Parkway, is just one stop down from Brooklyn's Grand Army Plaza. This stands in a complex of 19th-century parks and gardens that includes Prospect Park, the Brooklyn Botanic Garden and the Wildlife Center. It takes about 30 minutes to get to the museum from Midtown Manhattan.

BROOKLYN CHILDREN'S MUSEUM

See Chapter 7, Children's New York, page 149.

Brooklyn Botanic Gardens

Brooklyn Bridge

BROOKLYN BOTANIC GARDEN

✉ 900 Washington Avenue between Eastern Parkway and Empire Boulevard
☎ 718-623 7200
www.bbg.org
🚗 Subway 1, 2 to Eastern Parkway
🕘 Tues to Fri 8am–6pm, Sat and Sun 10am–6pm
$ $5 adults, $1.50 students and seniors, under 16s free

Right next door to Prospect Park and the Brooklyn Museum of Art, the Botanic Garden has a Rose Garden, Japanese Garden, a Shakespeare Garden and the Celebrity Path, which commemorates some of Brooklyn's more famous children. It is most famous, though, for its Japanese cherry trees and its huge collection of beautiful bonsai.

GRAND ARMY PLAZA AND PROSPECT PARK

✉ At the intersection of Flatbush Avenue, Eastern Parkway and Prospect Park West
☎ 718-287 3400
www.prospectpark.org
🚗 Subway 2, 3 to Grand Army Plaza; Q to 7th Avenue/Flatbush Avenue

This part of Brooklyn is one of its most beautiful areas. The enormous Prospect Park and Grand Army Plaza were laid out by Olmsted and Vaux after they'd completed Central Park, and many feel that these creations were even better. The park contains the following:

The Arch: New York's answer to the Arc de Triomphe, the elaborately carved, 24-m (80-ft) arch provides a grand gateway to Prospect Park, plus a majestic overview of both the park and Manhattan. It was built as a memorial to the defenders of the Union in the Civil War, and is now the base for a series of bronze sculptures that are grouped all around the Plaza, including one of John F Kennedy.

The Grand Army Plaza is home to the second largest open-air green market in New York. Held every Saturday 8am–4pm, it sells more than 600 varieties of farm-fresh fruits, vegetables, baked goods, dairy products and more.

Art in the Arch exhibitions are held in the spring and autumn, generally featuring artwork with a distinctly Brooklyn theme. The Arch is open to the public during spring and autumn when an exhibition is on. Weekends and holidays 1–5pm. For information about Arch exhibitions, call 718-965 8943.

Long Meadow: At nearly one mile in length, the Long Meadow stretches from the Park's northern end at Grand Army Plaza to its western end at Prospect Park Southwest. Once the home of grazing sheep and lawn tennis and croquet players, it is now frequented by strollers, kite-flyers and the Little League Baseball. At the Picnic House you'll find WCs and picnic tables, while the Metropolitan Opera and the New York Philharmonic Orchestra puts on summer events here (page 225).

The Long Meadow is accessible via the Grand Army Plaza and any entrance along Prospect Park West, such as 3rd Street or 9th Street. It is free to enter and is only closed 1–5am. For information on special events, call 718-965 8969.

The Big Onion does a walking tour of the landmark district of Park Slope, known as Brooklyn's Gold Coast because of its fine residential architecture and history. See page 78 for details.

The Bandshell: Close to the Long Meadow, this is one of the park's main attractions for live outdoor entertainment. With its three-storey high acoustic shell, raised stage and large circular plaza, the Bandshell features food and drinks, WCs and first-come, first-served seating in the 2,000-seat plaza or 5,000-seat lawn. In addition to musical performances, the Bandshell hosts film events on its 6.5-m (21-ft) high and 15-m (50-ft) wide movie screen. But it is best known for the **Celebrate Brooklyn!** Performing Arts Festival – a series of music, dance, film and spoken word performances each June to August, which attracts nearly 250,000 people per season (page 226). For further information about Bandshell events, call the Brooklyn Information and Culture events line on 718-855 7882 or visit **www.brooklynx.org**. The nearest subway is the F train to 15th Street/Prospect Park Station or the 2, 3 to Grand Army Plaza.

The Ravine: One of Prospect Park's most natural features, here you will find a steep narrow gorge lined with the trees and foliage of Brooklyn's only forest. Still recovering from decades of overuse that caused soil erosion, the Ravine and surrounding woodlands have been gradually restored by the Prospect Park Alliance since 1996. You can explore on your own or take one of the weekend guided nature tours. The Ravine is open from March to November on Saturday and Sunday 1pm–5pm with tours at 3pm from the Audubon Center at the Boathouse. For information on tours, call 718-287 3400. Best subways are the F to 15th Street/ Prospect Park or 7th Avenue; Q to 7th Avenue.

Children: Prospect Park has a wealth of activities and museums that are wonderful for children. They include the **Wollman Rink**, the **Audubon Center** and the **Boathouse**, the **Carousel, Prospect Park Zoo** and the **Lefferts Homestead Children's Museum**. Full details are given in Chapter 7, Children's New York, starting on page 127.

A TASTE OF THE BRONX

The Bronx has a scary reputation, but parts of it are very safe and have attractions that make a visit to the area well worthwhile. The Bronx history dates back to 1609 when Henry Hudson took refuge from a storm here. It is the northernmost borough of New York and the only one on the mainland. In 1639 Jonas Bronck, a Swedish captain from the Netherlands, settled here with his wife and servants. The story goes that when people left Manhattan to visit the family, they would say they were going to the Broncks' and the name stuck.

The horrible part is the south Bronx, but even here things are improving. In the north lies the beautiful Botanical Garden that includes a huge chunk of the original forests which once covered all of New York, and the Bronx Zoo, one of the world's leading wildlife conservation parks.

YANKEE STADIUM

✉ River Avenue at 161st Street
☎ 718-293 4300
🚗 Subway 4, C, D
🕐 Tours start at noon Mon to Sat. No reservations needed
$ Tickets from $8

Sporting aficionados will be delighted to see the tribute to past baseball players, the field, dugout, clubhouse, locker room and press box. Babe Ruth hit the first home run in the first game played here in 1923. For details on going to a game, see page 221.

Sports fans can take a break and enjoy a hot dog and a drink at the Sidewalk Café on the Plaza next to Gates 4 and 6.

NEW YORK BOTANICAL GARDEN

✉ 200th Street and Southern Boulevard
☎ 718-817 8700
🚗 Subway 2, 5 to Bronx Park East. If going there direct, take subway C, D or 4 to Bedford Park and then the BX36 bus
🕘 Tues to Sun and Mon holidays April to Oct 10am–6pm, Nov to March 10am–4pm
$ $3 adults, $1 under 12s, under 3s free; winter $1.50

Originally supported by magnates Cornelius Vanderbilt, Andrew Carnegie and JP Morgan, society folk still support it today. The iron and glass conservatory, which was modelled on the one at Kew Gardens, has been refurbished to perfection. In the grounds is the stunning Bronx River Gorge where the meandering waterway tumbles over a rocky outcrop formed by the retreat of the Wisconsin Ice Sheet. For thousands of years, New York was covered by a hemlock forest and a 16-hectare (40-acre) fragment remains in the gardens. Look for the rock carving of a turtle drawn by the Weckquasgeek Indians.

The Botanical Gardens are just a road away from the Bronx Zoo – sadly that is an eight-lane highway and the entrances are a mile apart. In the absence of a pedestrian link, take a short taxi ride. Call Miles Taxi Co on 718-884 8888.

LITTLE ITALY

Technically, this area is known as Belmont or simply Arthur Avenue, but it is tagged the Little Italy of the Bronx. Take the D train to Tremont Avenue and walk east to Arthur Avenue. Treat yourself to lunch at one of the many restaurants where you can eat fresh pasta, nibble pastries and sip cappuccino. The old-world Belmont District is a charming area filled with shops, selling every Italian delicacy you can think of, plus the Enrico Fermi Cultural Center in the Belmont Library (610 East 186th Street, tel 718-933 6410) and the old Belmont Italian American Theater (2385 Arthur Avenue, tel 718-364 4700), which still shows films. Afterwards, walk north on Arthur, then east on Fordham Road past Fordham University to the Bronx Park.

BRONX ZOO AND WILDLIFE CONSERVATION SOCIETY

✉ Bronx River Parkway and Fordham Road
☎ 718-367 1010 **www.wcs.org**
🚗 Subway 2, 5 to Bronx Park East
🕘 April to Oct Mon to Fri 10am–5pm, Sat to Sun 10am–5.30pm, daily 10–4.30pm for the rest of year
$ $11 adults, $7 seniors, $6 2–12s, under 2s free. Wednesdays suggested donation. Children under the age of 17 must be accompanied by an adult. Cheaper rates Jan to March. Congo Gorilla Forest and camel rides $3, skyfari, zoo shuttle, butterfly zone and Bengali express $2 each. Pay-One-Price ticket that includes admission and all rides, adult $19, children $14.

TAKE THE BUS

If the thought of heading off into the great unknown of the Bronx is daunting, take advantage of the bus tours conducted by New York Visions (page 74). The simple Bronx Tour, which starts at 9am and finishes at 1pm, takes in South Bronx, Yankee Stadium, the Art Deco architecture of the Grand Concourse, affluent Riverdale and Arthur Avenue. The day-long Triborough Tour (9am–6pm) includes all the highlights of the Bronx, Brooklyn and Manhattan's Lower East Side. A further tour of the outer boroughs, called Downtown & Brooklyn Tour, starts at 2pm and finishes at 6pm.

New York Visions: 690 8th Avenue between West 43rd and West 44th. Tel 212-391 0900. Subway A, C, E to 42nd Street. Area: Midtown.

The Bronx Zoo is respected worldwide for its tradition of conservation and ecological awareness alongside the naturalistic habitats it provides, such as the African Plains where antelope roam. It is the largest urban zoo in America and houses 4,000 animals and 560 species. The latest exhibit to open is the Congo Gorilla Forest, a $43-million, 2.5-hectare (6-acre) rainforest, inhabited by two troops of gorillas. Disney-style rides include a guided monorail tour through Wild Asia, an aerial safari, camel rides and a zoo shuttle. There is also a children's zoo. Some of the exhibits and rides are only open between April and October. For a tour by Friends of Wildlife Conservation, call 718-220 5141.

BRONX MUSEUM OF THE ARTS

✉ 1040 Grand Concourse
☎ 718-681 6000
$ $3 adults, under 12s free

Housed in an attractive glass building, the museum's collection consists of more than 700 contemporary works of art in all media by African, Asian and Latin American artists.

VAN CORTLANDT HOUSE MUSEUM

✉ Van Cortlandt Park, Broadway at West 246th Street, Bronx
☎ 718-543 3344
🚗 Subway 1, 9 to 242nd Street/Van Cortlandt Park
🕘 Tues to Fri 10am–3pm, Sat and Sun 11am–4pm
$ $2 adults, $1.50 students and seniors, under 12s free

Once an 18th-century, family-run plantation, Van Cortlandt House was turned into an historic house museum at the end of the 19th century by the National Society of Colonial Dames. Now you can see the family's public and private rooms, including a slave bed-chamber, along with decorative art collections from the colonial and federal periods.

A TASTE OF QUEENS

The largest of all the New York boroughs (Map 11), Queens has the highest percentage of first-generation immigrants. There are many distinct areas, although the most important in terms of attractions are Astoria, Jackson Heights, Jamaica, Flushing and Corona.

Given the borough's suburban look, it is hard to imagine it as the densely forested area it was four centuries ago. Then it was inhabited by the Algonquin Indian tribes, who fished in its freshwater streams and creeks, hunted game and gathered shellfish from its bays. It is also difficult to picture 17th-century Queens and its early Dutch and English farmers, along with Quakers, fighting for religious freedom.

Yet there remain places where such scenes can be easily reconstructed, such as at the **Jamaica Bay Wildlife Refuge** (tel 718-318 4340) on open marshlands, once the territory of Jameco Indians and now home to many species of birds, and the Queens County Farm Museum (page 237). This has the largest tract of farmland left in New York and its colonial farmhouse is thought to date back to 1772.

New York Botanical Garden

Today Queens is as much about the ethnic diversity of the borough, though, and in each of the places mentioned in this section, you will find many examples of the cultures of people from Asia, the West Indies, Latin America and Greece.

LITTLE INDIA

Take the International Express – subway 7 from Times Square to the 74th Street/ Broadway station and, at 74th Street between Roosevelt and 37th Avenues at Jamaica Heights, you will find this Indian haven. Stroll through the cumin-infused streets looking at the intricately embellished gold and silk on display. Two stops you should include are the **Menka Beauty Salon** (37 74th Street, tel 718-424 6851) where traditional henna designs are drawn on the skin, and the **Butala Emporium** (37 74th Street, tel 718-899 5590), which sells everything from Southern Asian art and children's books in Punjabi to Ayurvedic medicine and religious items.

Lunch: Travel one stop to 82nd Street in Elmhurst for an Argentinian lunch at La Fusta (80 Baxter Avenue, tel 718-429 8222) or two stops to the 90th Street station for Peruvian fare at Inti Raymi (86 37th Avenue, tel 718-424 1938).

QUEENS MUSEUM OF ART

✉ New York City Building, Flushing Meadows/Corona Park
☎ 718-592 9700
🚗 Subway 7 to Willets Point/Shea Stadium
$ $3

The most famous exhibit here is the miniature scale model of the entire city of New York, complete with miniature lights, which turn dark every 15 minutes, and aeroplanes flying into the airports. You can rent binoculars to check out where you're staying. The museum is on the site of the 1964 World Fair and has had a recent $15-million renovation.

SHEA STADIUM

☎ 718-507 6387

Stroll through Corona Park to the home of the Mets baseball team (page 221). On the way you will see huge remnants of both the 1939 and the 1964 World Fairs, plus a series of weird buildings such as the New York Hall of Science. The park also has barbecue pits and boating on the lake. This is where Flushing Meadows plays host to the US Open tennis championship.

Brooklyn Museum of Art

THE NEW YORK HALL OF SCIENCE

✉ 4701 111th Street, Flushing Meadows/ Corona Park at 48th Avenue
☎ 718-699 0005
www.nyscience.org
🚗 Subway 7 to 111th Street
🕘 Mon to Wed 9.30am–2pm, Thurs to Sun 9.30am–5pm
$ $7.50 adults, $5 seniors and children. Preschool $2.50. Sept to June Thurs 2pm–5pm, free

The bubble-shaped building features memorable daily science demonstrations and 175 interactive exhibits explaining the mysteries of digital technology, quantum theory, microbes and light and also offers seesaws, slides, whirligigs, space nets and a giant teeter-totter.

BOWNE HOUSE

✉ 37-01 Bowne Street, Flushing
☎ 718-359 0528
🕘 Tues, Sat and Sun 2.30pm–4.30pm
$ $2 adults, $1 children

You can walk to this NYC landmark from Corona Park. Built in 1661 by John Bowne, it is a rare example of Dutch-English architecture with an unusual collection of decorative arts, paintings and furniture, all of which belong to nine generations of the Bowne family. Bowne was a pivotal figure in the fight for religious freedom in the New World.

QUEENS BOTANICAL GARDEN

✉ 43 Main Street, Flushing
☎ 718-886 3800
$ Free

Walk back to the north-east corner of Corona Park to see the 16 hectares (39 acres) of plants, shrubs and trees that were created for the 1939 World Fair.

AMERICAN MUSEUM OF THE MOVING IMAGE

✉ 35th Avenue at 36th Street, Astoria
☎ 718-784 0077
www.ammi.org
🚗 Subway G, R to Steinway Street
🕘 Tues to Fri noon–5pm, Sat and Sun 11am–6pm
$ $8 adults, $5.50 seniors and students, $4.50 children (5–18)

If you're into the making of films, then you will want to take the 15-minute train ride out to Queens to see this museum. Set in the historic Astoria Studios, which are still used today, it is home to screening rooms, rebuilt sets, costumes, props, posters and other memorabilia.

The museum is full of interactive delights, such as the perennially popular diner set from *Seinfeld* and a life-sized dummy of Linda Blair from *The Exorcist*, complete with rotating head. Then there's the interactive Behind the Scenes exhibit, where you can see how it's all done and even make your own short film.

ALL THAT JAZZ

The **Queens Jazz Trail** shows you the homes of the jazz greats, their haunts and culture. It's a great tour even if you aren't a real jazz buff, as it gives an insight into the lifestyles of another era. The tour includes a visit to the newly opened home of Louis Armstrong, the Louis Armstrong archives at Queen's University (fantastic views of Manhattan's skyline) and the Addisleigh Park area, home to celebrated sports stars and top jazz and pop entertainers, including Ella Fitzgerald, Lena Horne, Count Basie, Billie Holiday, Milt Hinton and Thomas 'Fats' Waller. Other famous musicians who lived in different parts of Queens include Dizzy Gillespie, Bix Beiderbecke, Glenn Miller and Tony Bennett. The tour includes a delicious traditional soul food lunch or dinner and a jazz concert at the newly renovated concert hall at Flushing Town Hall.

If jazz really is your thing, then avoid the tourist-trap venues on Manhattan and head out to Queens for a cheap jazz night out. Underground clubs include **Carmichael's Diner**, 117 Guy Brewer Boulevard, Jamaica. Tel 718-224 1360. Entrance $10. Open 8–10.30pm on Wednesday nights. The action takes place in the basement. Be warned: there are no signs, but it definitely happens.

Contact **Flushing Town Hall** (137 Northern Boulevard, Flushing, tel 718-463 7700) for details of the Queens Jazz Trail, forthcoming jazz concerts and the **Cultural Collaborative Jamaica** (Jamaica Avenue and 153rd Street, Jamaica, tel 718-526 3217). Not only is it cheaper to get into venues in Queens, but you can also usually stay for both sets rather than being forced to leave after just one.

Astoria is the heart of New York's Greek community and filled with delis and restaurants. After you've been to the Museum of the Moving Image, head to 31st Street and Broadway for a spot of lunch.

MUSEUM OF MODERN ART

From June 2002, MOMA exhibitions were mounted in a temporary space at 45 33rd Street, near Queens Boulevard. This closed on September 23, 2004. The museum returns to its permanent home in West 53rd Street in Manhattan, reopening on November 20 (page 111).

ISAMU NOGUCHI GARDEN MUSEUM

✉ 36th Street and 43rd Avenue Sunnyside Queens
☎ 718-204 7088 or 718-721 2308
🚗 Subway 7 to 33rd Street
🕘 April to Oct only, Wed to Fri 10am–5pm, Sat and Sun 11am–6pm
$ Suggested donation $5 adults, $2.50 students and seniors

If you love your ballet and Balanchine in particular, you'll enjoy seeing some of the sets created by this Japanese artist, who strove to bring art and nature into the urban environment. These were Noguchi's studios where there are now more than 300 of his works on display. A fascinating spot for art and ballet buffs.

P.S. 1 CONTEMPORARY ART CENTER

✉ 22–25 Jackson Avenue at 46th Road, Long Island City
☎ 718-784 2084
🚗 Subway E, V to 23rd Street/Ely Avenue; G to 21st Street; 7 to 45th Road/Court House Square
🕘 Thurs to Mon noon–6pm
$ Suggested donation $5

All forms of artistic expression including paintings and videos of performance art, which depict elements of American culture and life in the 20th and 21st centuries.

SOCRATES SCULPTURE PARK

✉ Broadway at the East River, Long Island City
☎ 718-956 1819
🚗 Subway N to Broadway/Long Island City
🕘 Daily 10am–sunset
$ Free

A great place to take children as they can climb, romp and run around these massive sculptures laid out in the park.

QUEENS COUNTY FARM MUSEUM

✉ 73-50 Little Neck Parkway at Union Turnpike, Floral Park
☎ 718-347 FARM
www.queensfarm.org
🚗 Subway E, F to Kew Gardens/Union Turnpike, then take the Q46 bus to Little Neck Parkway
🕘 Mon to Fri 9am–5pm outdoor visiting only; tours of the farmhouse are available at weekends only from 10am–5pm Sat and Sun
$ Free, $2 hayrides

This 19-hectare (47-acre) site is the only working historical farm that still exists in New York and includes the 18th-century Adriance farmhouse, barns, outbuildings and a greenhouse.

LITTLE ASIA

✉ Roosevelt Avenue and Main Street

The nearby jumble of Chinese, Korean, Thai and Vietnamese markets and restaurants offers everything from soft-shell turtles, bentwood bows, kimchi and wire baskets. At 45 Bowne Street is the beautiful Hindu Temple Society of North America, which is adorned with carvings of Hindu gods.

The Queens Council on the Arts produces an annual Cultural Guide filled with information about the borough. Order from www.queenscouncilarts.org.

Dinner: Choopan Kabab House, 42 Main Street. Tel 718-539 3180. A great place to try out Afghan fare. Alternatively, you could sample Korean food at Kum Kang San, 138 Northern Boulevard. Tel 718-461 0909.

Nightclubs: Try Chibcha (79 Roosevelt Avenue, tel 718-429 9033, subway 7 to 82nd Street), a Colombian nightclub and restaurant. Or, if you prefer, Sunday night is Irish music night at Taylor Hall, 45 Queens Boulevard, subway 7 to 46th Street. For something more exotic, there are operettas,

Flushing Town Hall

flamenco and tango shows at the Thalia Spanish Theater, 41 Greenpoint Avenue. Tel 718-729 3880. Subway 7 to 40th Street. For more information, contact the Queens Council on the Arts on 718-647 3377 or visit **www.queenscouncilarts.org**.

A TASTE OF STATEN ISLAND

With its picturesque scenery, Staten Island deserves its Indian name 'Monacnong', which means 'enchanted woods'. This borough offers a relaxed contrast to the hustle and bustle of the city, and it's easy to reach by ferry or bus.

If you only have a few days in New York, you may not be able to squeeze in a visit, although you should try to fit in a trip on the Staten Island Ferry, which leaves Manhattan Island from Battery Park (page 66) and offers brilliant views of Downtown and the Statue of Liberty.

Historic Richmond Town

ALICE AUSTEN HOUSE

✉ 2 Hylan Boulevard, Staten Island
☎ 718-816 4506
www.aliceausten.8m.com
🚗 Bus S51 to Hylan Boulevard
🕐 March to Dec Thurs to Sun noon–5pm; closed major holidays
$ $2 adult, under 16s free

A unique museum in the restored Victorian house and garden of Alice Austen, one of America's first female documentary photographers. A great place to gain an insight into how life was in New York at the turn of the century.

AJAQUES MARCHAIS CENTER OF TIBETAN ART

✉ 338 Lighthouse Avenue
☎ 718-987 3478
www.fieldtrip.com
🚗 Bus S74 to Lighthouse Avenue
🕐 Daily dawn to dusk, closed Jan 1, Dec 25
$ Gallery $2, grounds free

One of New York's best-kept secrets, which the Dalai Lama visited in 1991. It has terraced gardens and a fishpond. Inside, there are Tibetan, Nepalese and Mongolian arts from the 17th to the 19th centuries.

ST MARK'S PLACE, ST GEORGE

Standing on the hill above the St George Ferry terminal, St Mark's Place is the only landmarked historical district on Staten Island. Here New York's fabulous skyline forms a dramatic backdrop to a wonderful collection of residential buildings in Queen Ann, Greek revival and Italianate styles. Visit **www.preserve.org/stgeorge** for a self-guided walking tour.

HISTORIC RICHMOND TOWN

✉ 441 Clarke Ave, Richmond Town
☎ 718-351 1611
🚗 S74 bus from the ferry to Richmond Road and St Patrick's Place

A magnificent 40.5-hectare (100-acre) village that features buildings from 300 years of life on the island including the oldest schoolhouse still standing, which was built in 1695 (that's really old by American standards!). In the summer season, costumed interpreters and craftspeople demonstrate the chores, gardening, crafts and trade of daily life in this rural hamlet.

CHAPTER 15 Niagara Falls and Woodbury Common

More and more Brits are combining a visit to New York City with one or two trips to other parts of New York State. Among the most popular are Niagara Falls and the bargain shopping Mecca of Woodbury Common in the Hudson Valley. The beauty of Woodbury Common is it can be done in a simple day trip or combined with a few nights' stay at a local B&B or the more upmarket Thayer Hotel, so that you can enjoy some of the beauties of the Hudson Valley.

NIAGARA FALLS

America is blessed with an abundance of natural wonders but the jewel in the crown of New York State is Niagara Falls. Just a 45-minute flight from New York, it's no wonder so many people like to combine a visit there with a trip to the city.

There are actually two falls: the American Falls – 58m (190ft) high and 320m (1,060ft) wide – and the Horseshoe, or Canadian, Falls – 56m (185ft) high and 675m (2,200ft) wide. The average waterflow over the Horseshoe Falls is an amazing 12,800–27,400m^3 (42,000–90,000ft^3) per second.

The Great Lakes were formed during the last Ice Age and the Falls were created 12,000 years ago as huge torrents of water, released by the melting ice, poured over the edge of the Niagara Escarpment at what is now the pretty village of Lewiston. Since then, the Falls have carved their way more than 11km (7 miles) upstream, creating the Niagara Gorge.

A bird's eye view of Niagara Falls

Such is the impact of the water on the region that Niagara has its own ecosystem. The moisture that evaporates from the lakes inhibits cloud formation in summer and moderates air temperature in winter, creating a temperate climate, warmer than the surrounding areas in winter, with more days of sunshine per year than many cities in what America calls the 'sun belt'.

Little is known of early inhabitants, but the Niagara River became an important link in the French water transport systems of the 17th century and, in 1679, they built a log fort at the mouth of the river where it joins Lake Ontario. Other more solid structures followed, culminating in a heavily fortified stone chateau, now known as the French Castle. During the 1750s, the French were so busy fighting the Native Americans that the British were able to gain control of the fort and Niagara region in 1759. It remained in British hands until 1796 when the US government took control.

Buy a Niagara Reservation Masterpass from any park attraction for discounts on the Viewmobile, Cave of the Winds, Festival Theater, *Maid of the Mist* boat tour, Observation Tower, Aquarium and other attractions; $23 adults, $16 for 6–12s.

In 1815, settlements sprang up, making the most of the fertile land and temperate climate. People soon began to see the potential of Niagara Falls as an attraction and when the Erie Canal opened in 1825, connecting the Hudson River from New York with Lake Erie, it quickly became part of a heavily travelled water route between the Atlantic and America's Midwest. In 1855, a suspension bridge was built for traffic and trains over the gorge, further linking the east coast with the growing cities of Detroit and Chicago.

British, German and Italian settlers established Niagara village in 1848 and by 1892, it had become a city. In 1885, New York State created the Niagara Reservation parks system to preserve the beauty of the Falls and guarantee that the public would always have free access to them. Ten years later, the Edward Dean Adams hydroelectric generating station opened, which for the first time enabled widespread use of electricity.

Today, the Niagara Reservation gets nearly 10 million visitors a year. The Visitor Center has exhibitions and a wide-screen cinema show, which gives a thrilling introduction to the Falls. In front of the centre are the Great Lakes Gardens, which include large-scale models of the Great Lakes system created from living plants.

GETTING TO NIAGARA

There is a range of internal flights from New York to Buffalo (flying time about 45 minutes), then it's a 30-minute drive to Niagara. The flat taxi fare is $40 (plus tip and toll), but there are regular scheduled buses from the airport to the Niagara hotels and some hotels have courtesy buses.

VIEWING THE FALLS

NIAGARA RESERVATION STATE PARK

✉ PO Box 1132, Niagara Falls, NY 14308-0132
☎ 716-278 1766
www.niagarafallsstatepark.com

The New York State Park surrounding the American Falls is the oldest state park in America. It includes the official information centre, Cave of the Winds, Prospect Point and Observation Tower.

Get your bearings at the Visitor Center, then use the State Park Viewmobile trams (716-278 1730) to get around the park. All-day tickets are $4.50 adults, $3.50 for 6–12s.

OBSERVATION TOWER AT PROSPECT POINT

Next to the Falls is the New York State Observation Tower (open March to December 9am–8pm), which stands 60m (200ft) above the base of the Niagara Gorge and has spectacular views. From here you can also get access to the Crow's Nest (50c) by a series of stairs to the edge of the American Falls, where you can feel the spray wash over you. From the observation deck, glass-walled lifts (50c) carry you down to the base for access to the *Maid of the Mist* boat tour.

NIAGARA FALLS STATE PARK VISITOR CENTER

✉ Prospect Park
☎ 716-278 1796
www.niagarafallsstatepark.com
🕘 Summer 8am–10pm, winter 8am–6pm, closed Christmas Day and New Year

An introduction to the Falls and surrounding parks with exhibits, tourist information, a café and WCs. The Festival Theater has a giant screen History Channel film called *Niagara, A History of the Falls,* plus there's a virtual-reality helicopter simulator ride. Entrance to the cinema show is $2 adults, $1 children (6–12). It's shown on the hour every hour 10am–8pm.

MAID OF THE MIST

✉ 151 Buffalo Avenue, Niagara Falls
☎ 716-284 5446
www.maidofthemist.com
🕘 April to Oct daily 10am–8pm
$ $11.50 adults, $6.75 children (6–12), under 6s free. Includes $1 for Observation Tower

Without doubt, this is the top-of-the-pile way to view the Falls – and one of the wettest, though the ticket includes a souvenir raincoat! You will be taken as close as is safely possible to the different falls and the spray – hence the name. The gorge has to be completely free of ice before boats can run, so check ahead if you're travelling in April, when the service starts; it continues until around the third week in October.

There are two boats on the American side and two on the Canadian side. Each holds 400 people and there are departures every 15–20 minutes so queues are rarely long.

CAVE OF THE WINDS TRIP

✉ Goat Island
☎ 716-278 1730
🕘 May to Oct daily 9am–11pm
$ $8 adults, $7 children (6–12). Free for under 5s. Children must be at least 106cm (3ft 6in) tall.

An incredible chance to soak up the Falls experience, this trip takes you closer to the waters than you thought possible. Clad in a yellow raincoat and wearing the special footwear provided, you ride in an elevator 53m (175ft) deep into Niagara Gorge, from where you follow a tour guide over wooden walkways to the Hurricane Deck, where the railing is a mere 6m (20ft) from the billowing torrents of Bridal Veil Falls. The rushing waters loom above you, dousing you with a generous spray, as you face the thundering falls head-on. Rainbows are usually visible day or night.

Admission is free for under 6s to all attractions in the Niagara Falls State Park, including the Observation Tower, Viewmobile, Cave of the Winds and Festival Theater.

THE GREAT BALLOON RIDE

✉ 310 Rainbow Boulevard South
☎ 716-278 0824
🕘 April, May and Oct daily 10am–10pm, June to Sept 8am–12pm
$ $18 adults, $9 children, under 3s free. Special rate for the Firework Spectacular evening on summer Friday nights is $25 adults, $13 children (under 12)

The newest attraction in Niagara, this is a soft adventure 15-minute ride to 120m (400ft) above Niagara in a stationary balloon giving unequalled views of the Falls. The weather is the major variable, although the balloon can withstand strong winds of up to 25 knots.

If you're taking a balloon ride, bear in mind that the wind tends to pick up late morning to mid-afternoon.

WHIRLPOOL JET

✉ At the Riverside Inn, Lewiston
☎ 1-905 468 4800
www.whirlpooljet.com
$ $43 adults, $37 children (under 14)

This is a white-water rapids ride from Lewiston up through the Devil's Hole Rapids to the Niagara Whirlpool. You can opt for the Wet Jet tour, which comes with a full-length splash suit, wet boots and lifejacket, or the Jet Dome tour, which gives you the white water excitement without having to get wet!

HELICOPTER RIDES

✉ Rainbow Air Inc, 454 Main Street
☎ 716-284 2800
www.rainbowairinc.com
🕘 Daily 9am–dusk

A fabulous 10-minute overview of the Niagara Falls and gorge.

BIKES AND HIKES

✉ 526 Niagara Street
☎ 716-278 0047
www.bikesandhikes.com
$ $15 an hour or $25 a day

Choice of bikes including mountain and comfort cruisers. The bike path starts across the road from this shop and it is less than half a mile to the Niagara Reservation State Park and the Falls.

THE SCHOELLKOPF GEOLOGICAL MUSEUM

✉ New York State Office of Parks, Recreation and Historic Preservation, off the Robert Moses Parkway near Main Street, Niagara Falls
☎ 716-278 1780
🕘 April to May 9am–5pm, May to Aug 9am–7pm, Aug to Nov 9am–5pm. Closed Nov to March.

Get an insider view of the history and geological background of the Falls at this museum, located within the park, just a few hundred metres north of the American Falls. Reach it by car, on foot or via the Viewmobile trams (page 240).

OTHER ATTRACTIONS

OLD FORT NIAGARA

✉ PO Box 169, Youngstown
☎ 716-745 7611
www.oldfortniagara.org
🕘 Daily 9am–dusk (4.30–7.30pm) year round
$ $8 adults, $5 children (6–12), under 6s free

One of the best non-Falls attractions is about 15 minutes from Niagara by car or bus. You can explore the Old Fort buildings, preserved as they were in the 1700s, see the old uniforms and watch musket demonstrations and other living-history displays. Then follow signs to the historic and picturesque village of Youngstown to browse around the shops and eateries at one of the first settlements to grow outside Fort Niagara in the late 1700s.

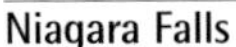
Niagara Falls

GRAND LADY CRUISES

✉ 100 Whitehaven Road, Grand Haven
☎ 716-744 8594
www.grandlady.com
🕘 May 1 to Oct 31
$ From $15 for cruise only to $44 for dinner cruise

Luxury lunch, brunch and dinner cruises on the Niagara River above the Falls. Tours last around two hours.

The Aquarium's first-floor observation deck has wonderful views of Niagara Gorge.

AQUARIUM OF NIAGARA

✉ 701 Whirlpool Street
☎ 716-285 3575
www.niagarafallsstatepark.com
🕘 Sept to May 9am–5pm and June to Aug 9am–7pm daily, except Thanksgiving and Christmas Day
$ $7.50 adults, $5.50 children (4–12), under 4s free

A great rainy day activity, the Aquarium is home to 1,500 aquatic animals including sharks, Californian sea lions, eels and even a colony of endangered Peruvian penguins. Sea-lion feeding times every 90 minutes, plus regular penguin and shark feeding.

NIAGARA AEROSPACE MUSEUM

✉ 345 Third Street
☎ 716-297 4148
www.niagaramuseum.org
🕘 Tues to Sat 10am–3pm
$ $2 seniors, $3 adults, $5 family

One for buffs of anything that is metal and flies, this museum has an extensive range of artefacts and displays on the local contribution to the Apollo Lunar Landing and Agena Rocket Engines, classic aircraft engines, aircraft restoration facilities and the Aviation Hall of Fame.

NIAGARA'S WAX MUSEUM OF HISTORY

✉ 302 Prospect Street opposite New York State Parking Lot
☎ 716-285 127
🕘 Summer 9am–10pm otherwise 10am–5pm
$ $4.95 general admission

Life-size wax figures of explorers, statesmen and others prominent in the history of the Frontier, plus a replica Native American village, old-time street and store scenes and the barrels used for going over the Falls and through the rapids.

ARTPARK

✉ 450 South 4th Street, Lewiston
☎ 716-754 4375
www.artpark.net
🕘 April to Dec for matinee and evening performances every day except Mon

The *Maid of the Mist* at Niagara Falls

This is an 81-hectare (200-acre) park that has its own musical theatre season, as well as presenting live theatre shows, concerts and musicals. It also has art workshops for children and adults. It is in the pretty and historic village of Lewiston, which has retained much of its character (unlike Niagara city) and is well worth a visit. Just 10 minutes from the Falls, it is also home to the **Lewiston Historic Museum** (469 Plain Street, tel 716-754 4214). Further details from the Visitor Information Center at the Gateway to Greater Lewiston, 732 Center Street, Lewiston. Tel 716-754 9500, **www.niagara-lewiston.org**.

WHERE TO STAY IN NIAGARA

ELIZABETH HOUSE BED & BREAKFAST

✉ 327 Buffalo Avenue
☎ 716-285 1109
A Georgian-style house within walking distance from the Falls and with an outdoor swimming pool.

HOLIDAY INN SELECT

✉ 300 Third Street
☎ 716-278 2622
Fax 716-285 3900
www.holiday-inn.com
The biggest hotel in town is convenient for all attractions and the convention centre. The rooms are comfortable and spacious and the hotel has a sky-lit indoor swimming pool, whirlpool, saunas and exercise equipment, plus a wedding chapel service.

RAMADA INN AT THE FALLS

✉ 240 Rainbow Boulevard
☎ 716-282 1212
Fax 716-282 0051
www.ramada.com
A full-service hotel conveniently located near all the major attractions.

RED COACH INN

✉ 2 Buffalo Avenue
☎ 716-282 1459
Fax 716-282 2650
www.redcoach.com
Essentially just an inn, this has a lot of appeal because of its quaintness and the fact it overlooks the rapids as they approach the Falls. It has only 14 suites/apartments so book well in advance.

WHERE TO EAT IN NIAGARA

COMO RESTAURANT

✉ 2220 Pine Avenue
☎ 716-285 9341
Classic American family dining, serving delicious Italian and American food at reasonable prices.

GOOSE'S ROOST

✉ 343 4th Street at the corner of Niagara Street
☎ 716-282 6255
An unpretentious American diner serving breakfast, lunch and dinner. You can also order take-aways.

HARD ROCK CAFE

✉ 333 Prospect Street
☎ 716-282 0007
🕒 Daily from 11am
1950s-style outdoor/indoor diner owned by local Tommy Ryan, so the boast is it's better than the chain.

LA HACIENDA

✉ 3019 Pine Avenue
☎ 716-285 2536
In the heart of Niagara's Italian district, this classic Italian restaurant has been run by the Aldo Evangelista family for decades. Delicious food, well-priced and busy, so book in advance if you plan to give it a try.

RED COACH INN RESTAURANT

✉ 2 Buffalo Avenue
☎ 716-282 1459
www.redcoach.com
This is as posh as it gets at Niagara Falls and at lunchtime it's usually filled with local business people as well as tourists. A quaint building, good service and delicious gourmet American cuisine. However, booking is advisable.

TOP OF THE FALLS RESTAURANT

✉ Falls end of Goat Island
☎ 716-285 3311
www.niagarafallsstatepark.com
A fabulous spot, open seasonally, overlooking the Horseshoe Falls.

WHERE TO SHOP IN NIAGARA

PRIME OUTLETS

✉ 1900 Military Road, Niagara Falls
☎ 716-297 0933
www.primeoutlets.com
🕒 Daily 9am–9pm
Little do we Brits know, but Niagara is popular for something other than the falls:

its factory outlet shopping mall, with more than 150 shops. A free, regular trolley service provides transport between the mall and Niagara hotels. Shops include Liz Claiborne, Off 5th, Reebok, Guess, Gap, Van Heuson, Brooks Brothers, Tommy Hilfiger, Burberry's, Levis, Donna Karan plus toys and shoes. Nearby is the Red Lobster restaurant, famous for its steaks and seafood.

It's worth looking at the Prime Outlets website before your visit to Niagara to check out any offers.

GETTING MARRIED AT THE FALLS

Niagara is the undisputed honeymoon capital of America with an estimated 50,000 couples starting their lives together here. Locals put it down to the negative ions generated by the falling water, said to be an aphrodisiac, but it may just be its affordability! Many couples are now also getting married here.

All you need do is get a marriage licence from Niagara Falls City Hall, 745 Main Street, tel 716-286 4396. There is a 24-hour waiting period after the application has been filed and divorcees will need certified copies of their most recent divorce. No blood test needed; current fee is $100 (Canadian dollars).

NIAGARA WEDDING CHAPEL

✉ Inside the Holiday Inn Select, 300 3rd Street
☎ 716-278 2622
www.traveltoniagara.com

Chris Shiah has been running his own wedding chapel service for more than a decade and conducts up to 1,500 ceremonies a year. You can wed in the chapel or at other spots including Goat Island, Terrapin Point and Luna Island, next to Bridleview Falls. Most people marry between May and October, though October is the busiest month owing to people coming to see the autumn colours. Chris gets a lot of Brits contacting him and can organise just about everything via email. He has his own romantic two-roomed Chapel Inn with fireplace and maid service for honeymooners, which costs $99–399 a night depending on the time of year.

WOODBURY COMMON

For shopaholics this American colonial-style village with more than 220 discount shops is the equivalent of paradise. For ordinary folk, it's still a wonderful place to make useful and fun purchases. And at just 1½ hours' bus ride away from central Manhattan, it can easily be incorporated into a trip to New York.

WOODBURY COMMON SHOPPING

✉ 498 Red Apple Court, Central Valley
☎ 1-845 928 4000
www.premiumoutlets.com
🕘 Mon to Sat 10am–9pm, Sun 10am–8pm

Upon arrival by Gray Line (tel 800 669 0051) you'll be dropped off close to the tower entrance where you'll also find the information office, two-way radio rental (yes, really!), pushchairs (essential with a young child on a hot day), lockers, telephones, cashpoints and WCs.

During busy times queues can really mount up at Woodbury Common – the quietest days to visit are midweek.

Pick up a copy of the full-colour *Shopping Guide* and in the centre you'll find a map with the five different sections in different colours. The colour coding is carried throughout the village, so as you walk around you can work out which area you are in by the colour of the apple above each shop sign.

The information tower is in the main red section, called Red Apple Court, which is largely dedicated to designer boutiques; to its south is Evergreen Court, home to many lifestyle stores; to the north of Red Apple Court is the Food Court and then the blue Bluebird Court. To the left from the main entrance is the purple Grapevine Court.

Filled with the most upscale designer shops, **Grapevine Court** is serious Droolsville territory and the first port of call for Japanese shoppers, who tend to be known as Goochers thanks to their love of

Take the weight off your slingbacks and make the most of the free trolley that tours Woodbury. Trolley stops are shown in the main *Shopping Guide.*

Gucci. Here you'll find Betsey Johnson, Chanel, Christian Dior, Fendi, Giorgio Armani General Store, Hugo Boss, Nieman Marcus Last Call, Off 5th – Saks Fifth Avenue, La Perla and the Thyme To Eat Restaurant.

Big names in **Red Apple Court** include A/X Armani Exchange, Burberry, Brooks Brothers, Carolina Herrera, DKNY Jeans, Escada, Giorgio Armani General Store II, Gucci, Liz Claiborne, Polo Ralph Lauren, Salvatore Ferragamo and Versace.

SALES TIMES

You can save even more money on your favourite labels by heading to Woodbury at sales times. Before you go, visit **www.premiumoutlets.com** to check out the next sales date – there's usually one a month. However, the big sales times coincide with all the American holidays including July 4, Memorial Day, President's Day, Labor Day Weekend, Columbus Day and the day after Thanksgiving.

Best time of all, though, is around Christmas when some of the biggest savings are to be had – along with the biggest crowds, so arrive early!

Good shops to head for in the **Bluebird Court** are Claire's Accessories, Bombay Outlet, OshKosh B'Gosh, Perfumania, Le Sportsac, Bebe and Nike Factory Store. In the **Evergreen Court** the Cosmetics Company Store has great deals on brands including Clinique, Estée Lauder, Bobbi Brown, MAC, Prescriptives and Origins. Other great stores include the Lancôme Company Outlet, Timberland, the Zegna Outlet Store, Benetton, Banana Republic, Club Monaco, Reebok and Claiborne Menswear.

STAYING NEAR WOODBURY COMMON

The Orange County Bed & Breakfast Association offers shop-and-stay packages and can be contacted on 800-210 5565.

THE THAYER HOTEL

✉ 674 Thayer Road, West Point, New York
☎ 845-446 4731 or freephone 800-247 5047
Fax 845-446 0338
www.TheThayerHotel.com

A three-star hotel at West Point – the scene of a decisive battle in the War of Independence and now home to one of the most famous officer training camps in America – with fabulous views of the Hudson River. It has comfortable en suite rooms, which have recently been refurbished, and a restaurant that's open for breakfast, lunch and dinner. The lounge overlooks the river, and drinks and light meals are served 11.30am–11.30pm Sunday to Thursday and 11.30am–1am Friday and Saturday. Shop-and-stay packages are available.

Shopping at Woodbury Common

CHAPTER 16

Safety First

Finding your way around Manhattan

TRAVEL INSURANCE

The one thing you should not forget when travelling to America is insurance – medical cover is very expensive and if you are involved in an accident you could be sued, which would be very costly indeed. If you do want to make savings in this area, don't avoid getting insurance cover, but don't buy it from tour operators as they are notoriously expensive. I took a random selection of premiums offered by tour operators specialising in North America and found that two weeks' worth of cover for one person varied in price from £42 to a staggering £90. If you're travelling for up to four weeks, the premiums go up to nearly £110 per person.

The alternative, particularly if you plan to make more than one trip in any given year, is to go for an annual worldwide policy direct from the insurers. These can start at around £60 and go up to £120, and will normally cover all trips taken throughout the year up to a maximum of 31 days per trip. These worldwide annual policies make even more sense if you're travelling as a family. For instance, cover for four people bought from your tour operator could easily cost you £160 for a two-week trip, which is little different from an annual worldwide family policy premium.

Companies offering annual worldwide insurance policies include the **AA** (0191-235 6513, **www.theaa.com**), **Barclays** (0345 573114, **www.bbg.co.uk**), **Bradford & Bingley** (0800 435642, **www.personal.barclays.co.uk**), **Columbus** (020 7375 0011, **www.columbus-insurance.com**), **Direct Travel** (01903 812345, **www.direct-travel.co.uk**), **General Accident Direct** (0800 121007), **Our Way** (020 8313 3900), **Post Office** (0800 169 9999, **www.postoffice.co.uk**), **Premier Direct** (0990 133218, **www.premierdirect.co.uk**) and **Travel Insurance Direct** (0990 168113, **www.oinc.com**). Many of these companies also offer straightforward holiday cover for a given period, such as two weeks or three weeks, which again will be cheaper than insurance offered by tour operators.

CHECK YOUR COVER

Policies vary not only in price, but in the cover they provide. In all cases, you need to ensure that the one you choose gives you the following:

➡ Medical cover of at least £2 million in America.

➡ Personal liability cover of at least £2 million in America.

Central Park

➡ Cancellation and curtailment cover of around £3,000 in case you are forced to call off your holiday.
➡ Cover for lost baggage and belongings of around £1,500. Most premiums only offer cover for individual items worth up to around £250, so you will need additional cover for expensive cameras or camcorders.
➡ Cover for cash (usually around £200) and documents, including your air tickets, passport and currency.
➡ A 24-hour helpline to make it easy for you to get advice and instructions on what to do, if necessary.

THINGS TO WATCH OUT FOR

Sharp practices: In some cases your tour operator may imply that you must buy their travel insurance policy. This is never the case: you can always arrange your own. Alternatively, they may send you an invoice for your tickets that includes travel insurance unless you tick a certain box – so watch out.

Read the policy: Always ask for a copy of the policy document before you go and if you are not happy with the cover offered, cancel and demand your premium back – in some cases you will only have seven days in which to do this, so look sharp!

Don't double up on cover: If you have an 'all risks' house insurance policy on your home contents, this will cover your belongings outside the home and may even cover lost money and credit cards. Check if this covers you abroad – and includes your belongings when in transit – before buying insurance for personal possessions.

MORE THINGS TO CHECK

Gold card cover: Some bank gold cards automatically provide you with travel insurance cover if you buy your air ticket with the gold card but, in fact, only the Nat West Gold MasterCard provides sufficient cover for travel in America.

Dangerous sports cover: In almost all cases, mountaineering, racing and hazardous pursuits such as bungee jumping, skydiving, horse riding, windsurfing, trekking and even cycling are not included in normal policies. There are so many opportunities to do all of these activities and more – and they are so popular as holiday extras – that you really should ensure you are covered before you go.

Make sure you qualify for full cover: If you have been treated in hospital during the six months prior to travelling or are waiting for hospital treatment, you may need medical evidence that you are fit to travel. If your doctor gives you the all-clear (the report may cost £25) and the insurance company still says your condition is not eligible for the insurance you want, shop around to find the right cover.

Always carry plenty of water even in the depths of winter. Air con and heating are incredibly dehydrating and you'll find yourself wanting to keel over very quickly without lots of liquid. It is also best to avoid drinking alcohol during the day.

HEALTH HINTS

Don't allow your dream trip to New York to be spoilt by not taking the right kind of precautions – be they for personal safety or of a medical nature.

MEDICATION

If you are on regular medication, make sure you take sufficient for the duration of your trip. Always carry it in your hand baggage, in case your luggage goes astray, and make sure it is clearly labelled. If you should need more for any reason, remember that many drugs have a different name in the US, so check with your GP before you go.

It cannot be stressed enough that you should only ever walk about with as little cash as possible and never, ever count your money in public.

IN THE SUN

Although the biggest season for New York is winter, many Brits still travel to America at the hottest time of the year – the summer – and most are unprepared for the sheer intensity of the sun. Before you even think about going out for the day, apply a high-factor sun block, as it is very easy to get

EMERGENCIES

For the police, fire department or ambulance, dial **911** (9-911 from a hotel room).
If it's a medical emergency, call the front desk of your hotel as many have arrangements with doctors for house calls. If they don't, they may tell you to go to the nearest casualty (emergency) department, but that's really not a good idea (I mean, have you seen *ER*?). Instead, you have three choices: contact **New York Hotel Urgent Medical Services** on 212-737 1212, **Dial-a-Doctor** on 212-737 2333, or walk in or make an appointment at a **DOCS Medical Center.** There are three in Manhattan: 55 East 34th Street (tel 212-252 6001), 1555 3rd Avenue (tel 212-828 2300) and 202 West 23rd Street (tel 212-352 2600). There are several 24-hour pharmacies, mostly run by the **Duane Reade** chain. The most centrally located 24-hour pharmacy is at Broadway and 57th Street (tel 212-541 9208), near Columbus Circle.

For a dentist, you can call 212-679 3966 or 212-371 0500. If you need help after hours, try the 24-hour **Emergency Dental Associates** on 1-800 439 9299.

sunburnt when you are walking around sightseeing or shopping. It is also a good idea to wear a hat or scarf to protect your head from the sun, especially at the hottest times 11am–3pm, to prevent you from getting sunstroke. If it is windy, you may be lulled into thinking that it's not so hot.

SECURITY

AT YOUR HOTEL

In America, your hotel room number is your main source of security. It is often your passport to eating and collecting messages so keep the number safe and secure. When checking in, make sure none of the hotel staff mentions your room number out loud. If they do, give them back the key and ask them to give you a new room and to write down the new room number instead of announcing it (most hotels follow this practice in any case). When you need to give someone your room number – for instance when charging a dinner or any other bill to your room – write it down or show them your room card rather than calling it out.

When in your hotel room, always put on the deadlocks and security chains and use the door peephole before opening the door to strangers. If someone knocks on the door and you don't know who it is, or they don't have any identification, phone down to the hotel reception desk. When you go out, make sure you lock the windows and door properly, even if you just leave your room to go to the ice machine.

CASH AND VALUABLES

Most hotels have safe deposit boxes so use these to store important documents such as airline tickets and passports. Keep a separate record of your travellers' cheque numbers. When you go out, do not take all your cash and credit cards with you – always leave at least one credit card in the safe as an emergency back-up and only take enough cash with you for the day.

Using a money belt is a good idea and if your room does not come with its own safe, leave your valuables in the main hotel safe. Also, be warned: American banknotes are all exactly the same green colour and size so familiarise yourself with the different bills in the safety of your hotel room before you go out. Keep large denominations separate from small ones.

SAFETY IN CARS

Unless you have a driver, a car in New York is not a good idea. If you do hire a car, however, be sensible. Never leave your car unlocked nor leave any valuable items on the car seats or anywhere else where they can be seen. Always put maps and brochures in the glove compartment as these will be obvious signs that your car belongs to a tourist.

NEW YORK STREET SAVVY

The city is nowhere near as dangerous as it used to be, but it is still a large city and there are always people on the lookout for an easy opportunity. To reduce your chances of becoming a victim of street crime, follow these simple guidelines:

➡ Always be aware of what is going on around you and keep one arm free – criminals tend to target people who are preoccupied or have both arms laden down with packages or briefcases.

➡ Stick to well-populated, well-lit areas and, if possible, don't go out alone.

NYPD cop

➡ Don't engage any suspicious people, such as street beggars, in conversation, though you can tip buskers if you wish.

➡ Visible jewellery can attract the wrong kind of attention. If you are a woman wearing rings, turn them round so that the stone or setting side is palm-in.

➡ If you're wearing a coat, put it on over the strap of your shoulder bag.

➡ Men should keep wallets in their front trouser or inside coat pockets or in a shoulder strap.

➡ Pickpockets work in teams, often involving children, who create a diversion.

➡ Watch out for pickpockets and scam artists especially in busy areas, as you would in any big city.

➡ Do not carry your wallet or valuables in a bumbag. Thieves can easily cut the belt and disappear into the crowds before you've worked out what has happened.

➡ A useful trick is to have two wallets – one a cheap one carried in your hip pocket or bag containing about $20 in cash and some out-of-date credit cards and another hidden somewhere on your body, or in a money belt containing the bulk of your cash and credit cards. If you are approached by someone who demands money from you, your best bet is to get away as quickly as possible. Do this by throwing your fake wallet or purse in one direction, while you run, shouting for help, in the other. The chances are that the mugger will just collect the wallet rather than chasing after you.

If you hand over your wallet and just stand still, the mugger is more likely to demand your watch and jewellery, too. This advice is even more important for women who could be vulnerable to personal attack or rape if they hang around.

Having given you some essential safety advice, however, it is important to remember that this is very much common sense and applies if you are travelling almost anywhere in the world, especially in a major city. New York is a busy, feisty city but it is a great holiday destination and I have no doubt you'll have a briliant time and want to come back for more!

Quilty's

Index

Page numbers in **bold** refer to major references

INDEX

PHOTOGRAPH ACKNOWLEDGEMENTS

21 Club 155; Peter Aaron/Esto for the Jewish Museum 119; S Berger/NYC & Company Inc. 183; Blue Note Jazz Club 75; Bull and Bear 167; Carlton Hotel 215; Circle Line Cruises 79; G Davies/NYC & Comapny Inc. 227; Firebird 171; Four Seasons Hotel 206; Frick Collection 114; Giocello/NYC & Company Inc. 226; Jeff Greenberg/NYC & Company Inc. 2, 23, 26, 35, 46, 59, 67, 70, 83, 86, 90, 98, 99, 102, 106, 115, 118, 126, 150, 159, 163, 166, 174, 202; Group Photos, Inc./NYC & Company Inc. 223; Markku Immonen 91, 195, 199; Le Cirque 151; Le Parker Meridien 178; Le Zinc 158; Leonardo.com 219; Leonland 39; Lower East Side Tenement Museum 111; Kevin McCormick/NYC & Company Inc. 62; Darren McGee/NYC & Company Inc. 110; MAC boutique 95; Marriot Marquis 190; Miscellaneous 34, 94, 247; Michael Mundy 170; Nasdaq 63; New York Hall of Science 123; Niagara Falls Convention and Visitors' Bureau 239, 242, 243; NYC & Company Inc. 11, 18, 19, 22, 38, 47, 50, 54, 55, 66, 74, 103, 107, 122, 146, 147, 178, 179, 182, 191, 222, 226, 231, 234, 235, 238, 239; Jon Ortner/NYC & Company Inc. 14, 15; Ritz-Carlton 58, 186, 203; Joseph de Sciose for the Brooklyn Botanic Gardens 230; SoHo Grand 187, 211; Starlight Room 198; Amanda Statham 7, 10, 30, 31, 34, 43, 71, 87, 154, 207, 210, 247, 250; Tavern on the Green 175; Mark Thomas 42, 78, 250; Waldorf Astoria 51; Wellington Hotel 214; Lane Wilser/NYC & Company Inc. 127; Woodbury Common 246; Zoe in SoHo 162.

PICTURE ACKNOWLEDGEMENTS